Transnational solidarity

Manchester University Press

Racism, Resistance and Social Change

FORTHCOMING BOOKS IN THIS SERIES

Citizenship and belonging   Ben Gidley
Spaces of Black solidarity: Anti-black racism and urban activism in Paris   Vanessa Eileen Thompson

PREVIOUSLY PUBLISHED IN THIS SERIES

Revolutionary lives of the Red and Black Atlantic since 1917   David Featherstone, Christian Høgsbjerg and Alan Rice (eds)
A savage song: Racist violence and armed resistance in the early twentieth-century U.S.–Mexico Borderlands   Margarita Aragon
Race talk: Languages of racism and resistance in Neapolitan street markets   Antonia Lucia Dawes
Black resistance to British policing   Adam Elliott-Cooper
The Red and the Black: The Russian Revolution and the Black Atlantic   David Featherstone and Christian Høgsbjerg (eds)
Global white nationalism: From apartheid to Trump   Daniel Geary, Camilla Schofield and Jennifer Sutton (eds)
In the shadow of Enoch Powell   Shirin Hirsch
Black middle-class Britannia: Identities, repertoires, cultural consumption   Ali Meghji
Race and riots in Thatcher's Britain   Simon Peplow

Series editors' foreword

*John Solomos, Satnam Virdee
and Aaron Winter*

The study of race, racism and ethnicity has expanded greatly since the end of the twentieth century. This expansion has coincided with a growing awareness of the continuing role that these issues play in contemporary societies all over the globe. *Racism, Resistance and Social Change* is a new series of books that seeks to make a substantial contribution to this flourishing field of scholarship and research. We are committed to providing a forum for the publication of the highest quality scholarship on race, racism, anti-racism and ethnic relations. As editors of this series we would like to publish both theoretically driven books and texts with an empirical frame that seeks to further develop our understanding of the origins, development and contemporary forms of racisms, racial inequalities and racial and ethnic relations. We welcome work from a range of theoretical and political perspectives, and as the series develops we ideally want to encourage a conversation that goes beyond specific national or geopolitical environments. While we are aware that there are important differences between national and regional research traditions, we hope that scholars from a variety of disciplines and multidisciplinary frames will take the opportunity to include their research work in the series.

As the title of the series highlights, we also welcome texts that can address issues about resistance and anti-racism as well as the role of political and policy interventions in this rapidly evolving discipline. The changing forms of racist mobilisation and expression that have come to the fore in recent years have highlighted the need for more reflection and research on the role of political and civil society mobilisations in this field.

We are committed to building on theoretical advances by providing an arena for new and challenging theoretical and empirical studies on the changing morphology of race and racism in contemporary societies.

Transnational solidarity

Anticolonialism in the global sixties

Edited by

Zeina Maasri, Cathy Bergin
and Francesca Burke

MANCHESTER UNIVERSITY PRESS

Copyright © Manchester University Press 2022

While copyright in the volume as a whole is vested in Manchester University Press, copyright in individual chapters belongs to their respective authors, and no chapter may be reproduced wholly or in part without the express permission in writing of both author and publisher.

Published by Manchester University Press
Oxford Road, Manchester M13 9PL

www.manchesteruniversitypress.co.uk

British Library Cataloguing-in-Publication Data
A catalogue record for this book is available from the British Library

ISBN 978 1 5261 6156 7 hardback
ISBN 978 1 5261 9159 5 paperback

First published 2022
Paperback published 2025

The publisher has no responsibility for the persistence or accuracy of URLs for any external or third-party internet websites referred to in this book, and does not guarantee that any content on such websites is, or will remain, accurate or appropriate.

EU authorised representative for GPSR:
Easy Access System Europe – Mustamäe tee 50,
10621 Tallinn, Estonia
gpsr.requests@easproject.com

Typeset by Newgen Publishing UK

Contents

List of figures	ix
List of contributors	xii
Foreword: imperialism will inevitably be defeated – Vijay Prashad	xviii
Acknowledgements	xxiv
Introduction: transnational solidarity in the long sixties – Zeina Maasri, Cathy Bergin and Francesca Burke	1
1 'We took the notion' – Bernadette Devlin McAliskey	28
2 The voice of the immigrant worker and the rise and fall of France's long 1968 – Matt Myers	37
3 Comités Palestine (1970–72): on the origins of solidarity with the Palestinian cause in France – Abdellali Hajjat	55
4 Cultural guerrilla: Tricontinental genealogies of '68 – Paula Barreiro López	78
5 New Left encounters in Latin America: transnational revolutionaries, exiles and the formation of the Tupamaros in early 1960s Montevideo – Marina Cardozo	109
6 Connected struggles: networks of anticolonial solidarity and the liberation movements of the Portuguese colonies in Africa – Víctor Barros	131
7 'Action needed': the American Committee on Africa and solidarity with Angola – Aurora Almada e Santos	154
8 On transnational feminist solidarity: the case of Angela Davis in Egypt – Sara Salem	180

9 'Don't play with apartheid': anti-racist solidarity in Britain with South African sports – Christian Høgsbjerg	202
10 The Gulf Committee: interview with Helen Lackner, September 2020	225
11 'The brilliant sun of revolt' rising in the East: solidarity in Britain with the uprising in Pakistan of 1968–69 – Talat Ahmed	232
12 Palestine through the prism of Pakistani cinema: imagining sameness and solidarity through *Zerqa* (1969) – Sabah Haider	255
13 The long sixties and Islamist activism: radical transregional solidarities – Claudia Derichs	280
14 *A Witness of Our Time* (1972): drawings by Dia al-Azzawi	300
15 Greece in the Third World: solidarity through metonymy in a refugee magazine from the GDR – Mary Ikoniadou	309
16 Solidarity as an absence: the productive limits of Adorno's thought – Patricia McManus	334
Index	355

Figures

Every effort has been made to obtain permission to reproduce copyright material, and the publisher will be pleased to be informed of any errors and omissions for correction in future editions.

I.1	Poster, 'The struggle continues in Palestine and in El Salvador, and the revolution will be victorious', Jihad Mansour, Popular Front for the Liberation of Palestine, c.1981. Reproduced courtesy of The Palestine Poster Project Archive (www.palestineposterproject.org).	5
2.1	Poster, 'French immigrant workers all united. Equal labour, equal pay', Atelier Populaire ex-Ecole des Beaux-Arts, May 1968, France. Source: gallica.bnf.fr/Bibliothèque nationale de France.	50
4.1	The exhibition *Painters and Guerrillas* at the Galería Latinoamericana of the Casa de las Américas, Cuba, opened 18 July 1967. Reproduced Courtesy of Archivo Casa de las Américas.	86
4.2	Mural, *Cuba Colectiva*, Havana 1967.	87
4.3	Poster, Roberto Jacoby, 'A guerrilla fighter does not die to be hung on the wall', 1969. Reproduced courtesy of the artist.	95
4.4a	Pamphlet cover, 'Three continents, one common enemy, a unified struggle, a new world!!!' Tricontinentale Sorbonne, Comité des Trois Continents, 1968. Reproduced courtesy of The Freedom Archives (https://freedomarchives.org/).	103

4.4b	Table of contents, 'Three continents' pamphlet, 1968.	104
4.5	Manifesto, 'For the cultural congress of Havana', published in *Opus International* 3 (1967). From the collection of Paula Barreiro López.	106
7.1a and 7.1b	Booklet cover and inside flap *Sun of Our Freedom: The Independence of Guinea Bissau*. Publisher: Chicago Committee for the Liberation of Angola, Mozambique and Guinea (CCLAMG), 1/1974. Reproduced courtesy of The Freedom Archives (https://freedomarchives.org/).	177
7.1c	From *Sun of Our Freedom* (pp. 30–31), featuring a statement on solidarity by Amílcar Cabral.	179
10.1	'Britain and U.S. out of the Gulf – Down with all Shahs and Sultans – Victory to the PFLOAG [Popular Front for the Liberation of Oman and the Arab Gulf]', the Gulf Committee, *c*.1972. The poster features a film still from *The Hour of Liberation has Arrived* by the Lebanese director Heiny Srour. Courtesy of Helen Lackner.	228
12.1a and 12.1b	Double pages from the pressbook of the film *Zerqa* featuring the lyrics of its songs. From the collection of Sarfaraz Nihash.	260
12.2	Official poster for the film *Zerqa* (1969), by Riaz Shahed. From the collection of Sarfaraz Nihash.	262
12.3	'Rights for Film *Zerqa* Given to Al-Fatah: Director Riaz Shahid calls for all recreation tax collected from *Zerqa* film ticket sales to be given to Al-Fatah', *Daily Jang Newspaper*, Karachi, 25 October 1969. Courtesy of the Jang Newspaper Archives.	264
12.4	A recoloured photo of the crowds upon the film's cinematic release at Lahore's now iconic Gulistan Cinema on 16 October 1969. From the collection of Sarfaraz Nihash.	268

14.1a–14k	Artist's book by Dia al-Azzawi: *Shahid min hatha al'asr: yawmiyyat shaheed qutila fi majzarat al-urdun aylul 1970* (Baghdad: Iraqi Ministry of Information, 1972). Photographic documentation by Agop Kanledjian. Courtesy of the collection of Abboudi Bou Jawde, Beirut. Reproduced with permission from the artist.	300
15.1	*Pyrsos* magazine, front covers 1961–68. All images are reproduced from the author's personal collection. Copies of *Pyrsos* magazine are also held at the Contemporary Social History Archives (ASKI) in Athens.	310
15.2	Cover compositions by artist and *Pyrsos*' art director Nikos Manoussis.	321
15.3	Vietnam, The 'Humanists' Chemical War, *Pyrsos* #3, 1965, pp. 6–7. Captions (anti-clockwise from the left): 'Two worlds in the same country. The People's Army of Vietnam helping a villager to transport his hut'; 'Resting before the struggle for the freedom of the country'; 'The foreign invader inspects his lethal weapons'; 'The 'humanist' interrogates'.	324
15.4	Din and her guerrillas, from the column 'For you Women', *Pyrsos* #1, 1966, pp. 36–37.	325

Contributors

Talat Ahmed is Senior Lecturer in South Asian History at the University of Edinburgh. She is the author of *Mohandas Gandhi: Experiments in Civil Disobedience* (Pluto Press and University of Chicago Press, 2019) and of *Literature and Politics in the Age of Nationalism: The Progressive Episode in South Asia, 1932–56* (New Delhi: Routledge, 2009). She is Co-Director of the Centre for South Asian Studies at the University of Edinburgh and a Fellow of the Royal Asiatic Society.

Dia al-Azzawi began his artistic career in 1964, after completing a degree in archaeology at Baghdad University in 1962 and graduating from the Institute of Fine Arts in Baghdad in 1964. Alongside his prolific debut as an artist, Azzawi worked in museums across Iraq and became an insightful writer on Arab modern art. He organised several important events in Iraq and the UK, such as al-Wasiti Festival (1972), the Baghdad International Poster Exhibition (1979) and the Third World Biennale of Graphic Art (1980). Since 1976, Azzawi has lived and worked in London and his artwork has been exhibited worldwide and collected by numerous prestigious museums and institutions.

Aurora Almada e Santos is Researcher at the Institute of Contemporary History at NOVA University of Lisbon. She is the author of *A Organização das Nações Unidas e a Questão Colonial Portuguesa, 1960–1974* (Instituto de Defesa Nacional, 2017) and co-editor of *The United Nations and Decolonization* (Routledge, 2020).

Paula Barreiro López is Full Professor of the Université Grenoble Alpes/LARHRA and Head Researcher of the international platform MoDe(s) (Decentralised Modernities). Her research focuses on cultural networks and politics in Spain, Western Europe and Latin America during the Cold War as well as the diverse and divergent developments of modernities within an increasingly globalised world. Her latest publications are *Atlántico Frío: Historias transnacionales del arte y la política en los tiempos del telón de acero* (Brumaria, 2019), *Avant-garde Art and Criticism in Francoist Spain* (Liverpool University Press, 2017), *Modernidad y vanguardia: rutas de intercambio entre España y Latinoamérica* (Museo Reina Sofia, 2015, edited with Fabiola Martínez).

Víctor Barros is a researcher at the *Instituto de História Contemporânea*, NOVA University of Lisbon where he worked on a project on Amílcar Cabral. Barros was a Calouste Gulbenkian Foundation Research Fellow and received grants to support his research in Angola, Cabo Verde, Guinea-Bissau, France, Mozambique and Portugal. He is the author of *Campos de Concentração em Cabo Verde: As Ilhas Como Espaços de Deportação e Prisão no Estado Novo* (Coimbra University Press, 2009) – about the colonial concentration camps in Cabo Verde – as well as of several articles on Portuguese colonialism, anticolonialism, the politics of memory and history writing.

Cathy Bergin is Principal Lecturer on the Humanities Programme at the University of Brighton. She works on forms of transnational class solidarity in the context of African American and Afro-Caribbean cultural history. Her books include *Bitter with the Past, But Sweet with the Dream* (Brill, 2015) and *American Anti-Colonial Thought: 1917–1937* (Edinburgh University Press, 2016). She has recently written on African American anti-fascism in *Anti-Fascism in a Global Perspective* edited by K. Braskén et al. (Routledge, 2020). She also works collaboratively with Anita Rupprecht, they co-edited a special issue of *Race and Class* on the theme of Reparative Histories in January 2016.

Francesca Burke is Senior Lecturer in Politics at the University of Brighton. She led the British Academy funded research project

'Higher Education and Political Change in the Arab World' and her publications include work on activism through museums (*Critical Military Studies*, 2020), by universities as institutions (Routledge, 2017), and within student movements (Cambridge Scholars Publishing, 2013).

Marina Cardozo Prieto is Associate Professor in Contemporary History at the University of the Republic (Uruguay) and a PhD candidate in Social Sciences at the Institute of Economic and Social Development and the National University of General Sarmiento (Argentina). Her research explores the Left in Latin America and Europe between the 1960s and 1980s, with a particular focus on Uruguay, and Latin American political exiles in Europe during the dictatorships of the twentieth century.

Claudia Derichs is Professor of Transregional Southeast Asian Studies at Humboldt Universität zu Berlin, Germany. She has studied Japanese and Arabic in Bonn, Tokyo and Cairo, and holds a PhD in Japanology (1994, University of Bonn). She was awarded a Heisenberg scholarship by the German Science Foundation in 2007, and received a fellowship from the University of Tokyo, Japan, in 2020. Her research covers transregional political-religious movements in Southeast Asia and the Middle East. Her work promotes new orientations in Area Studies. In 2017, she published the monograph *Knowledge Production, Area Studies and Global Cooperation* (Routledge, 2017).

Bernadette Devlin McAliskey is an Irish civil rights leader and former politician. She served as Member of Parliament for Mid Ulster (1969–74) and was the youngest woman ever elected to the British Parliament. McAliskey helped establish People's Democracy, a socialist student movement focused on civil rights. In 1969, having been given the keys to New York by the city's mayor, McAliskey handed them to the Black Panthers in solidarity. McAliskey is Chief Executive of the South Tyrone Empowerment Programme (STEP). STEP provides services and advocacy in community development, training, support and advice for migrants, policy work and community enterprise.

Sabah Haider is a filmmaker and PhD candidate at the Centre for Interdisciplinary Studies in Society and Culture at Concordia University in Montreal, Canada in cotutelle with the Department of Social Anthropology at the EHESS in Paris, France. Her doctoral project explores the participation of Pakistanis as volunteer fighters in the Palestinian armed struggle in Lebanon between 1971 and 1982. Her research interests are in the areas of digital, visual and material cultures of the Global South. She works for Google as a cultural and behavioural anthropologist. Some of her work can be found at www.sabahhaider.com

Abdellali Hajjat is Associate Professor of Sociology at the Université libre de Bruxelles. He has been EURIAS Junior Fellow at the Institute for Advanced Studies in the Humanities (University of Edinburgh). His research interests focus on various issues: citizenship and race in French law; urban uprisings and political mobilisations by postcolonial immigrants; Islamophobia; hate crime and criminal justice system; postcolonial controversies in Belgium. He recently published *Islamophobia. How the French elites forged the "Muslim problem"* (University of Georgia Press, 2022, with Marwan Mohammed), *The Wretched of France: History of the 1983 March for Equality and Against Racism* (Indiana University Press, 2022).

Christian Høgsbjerg is Lecturer in Critical History and Politics in the School of Humanities and Social Science at the University of Brighton. He is the author of *C.L.R. James in Imperial Britain* (Duke University Press, 2014) and has also edited and co-edited several volumes for the C. L. R. James Archives series with Duke University Press, including *Marxism, Colonialism and Cricket: C.L.R. James's Beyond a Boundary* (2018). He is also the co-author with Geoff Brown of *Apartheid is Not a Game: Remembering the Stop the Seventy Tour Campaign* (Redwords, 2020).

Mary Ikoniadou lectures in Photography at University of Central Lancashire and is a member of the Research Centre for Migration, Diaspora and Exile (MIDEX). Her research is situated at the intersection of visuality and politics with a focus on the role of print cultures during the Cold War. Her research on the juxtaposition of image and text, and the ways that the entanglement of visual and material objects can encourage aesthetic and political shifts and intervene in the socio-political sphere, has been published in the *Humanities* journal, 2020; Centrum Modernes Griechenland/ CeMoG at Freie Universitat Berlin, 2017; and Routledge 2017.

Helen Lackner studied at SOAS (1968–71), worked in rural development in more than thirty countries, and lived in Yemen for fifteen years in the past half century. She now writes mostly about Yemen. Her latest books are *Yemen in Crisis: The Road to War* (2nd ed.) (Saqi, 2022) and *Yemen: Poverty and Conflict* (Routledge, 2022).

Zeina Maasri is Senior Lecturer and Degree Leader of the interdisciplinary BA in War and Conflict at the University of Brighton (UK) and a former faculty member at the American University of Beirut (Lebanon). Her recent monograph *Cosmopolitan Radicalism: The Visual Politics of Beirut's Global Sixties* (Cambridge University Press, 2020) is the co-winner of the 2021 British-Kuwait Friendship Society Book Prize. She is the author *Off the Wall: Political Posters of the Lebanese Civil War* (IB Tauris, 2009) and curator of related travelling exhibitions and online archival resources (www.signsofconflic.org). Maasri is also the co-editor (with K. Bassil, W. Raad and A. Zaatari) of *Mapping Sitting: On Portraiture and Photography* (Arab Image Foundation, 2002).

Patricia McManus works in the School of Humanities and Social Science at the University of Brighton. Her research takes an interdisciplinary approach to literary history, in particular to the political work made possible or impossible by forms of fiction. This research asks questions about the type of cultural practice solidarity needs, in particular if solidarity can be a reading practice or if the very idea of the reading public is an evasion of solidarity. She is working on a book on Theodor Adorno and Dystopia.

Matt Myers is Lecturer in Modern History at St John's College, University of Oxford. He wrote his doctoral thesis on the crisis of the British, French, and Italian left at the end of the long seventies.

Vijay Prashad is Director of Tricontinental: Institute for Social Research, Chief Editor of LeftWord Books and Chief Correspondent for Globetrotter. His books include *The Darker Nations: A People's History of the Third World* (New Press, 2007) and *The Poorer Nations: A Possible History of the Global South* (Verso, 2012), and *Washington Bullets* (Monthly Review Press, 2020). He co-hosts a weekly news show called *Give the People What They Want*.

Sara Salem is Associate Professor in Sociology at the London School of Economics. Her research interests include political sociology, postcolonial studies, Marxist theory and global histories of empire and anticolonialism. Her recently published book with Cambridge University Press is entitled *Anticolonial Afterlives in Egypt: The Politics of Hegemony* (2020). A selection of published journal articles include: on Angela Davis in Egypt in the journal *Signs*; on Frantz Fanon and Egypt's postcolonial state in *Interventions: A Journal of Postcolonial Studies*; on Gramsci and anticolonialism in the postcolony in *Theory, Culture and Society*; and on Nasserism in Egypt through the lens of haunting in *Middle East Critique*.

Foreword: imperialism will inevitably be defeated

Vijay Prashad

When Fidel Castro, the Prime Minister of Cuba, took the stage on the last day of the First Solidarity Conference of the Peoples of Africa, Asia and Latin America (January 1966), he was only thirty-nine years old. The Cuban Revolution, which he had led to victory in 1959, had just celebrated its seventh anniversary, which meant that he was only thirty-two when the dictator Fulgencio Batista was run out of power. His comrades who drove into Havana after two years in the Sierra Maestra were as young as Fidel, ranging from Camilo Cienfuegos (only twenty-six) to Juan Almeida Bosque (only thirty-one) to Celia Sánchez (only thirty-eight). By 1966, Castro already had a gravity, the depth of his voice and the composure of his frame. Five years previously, the Cuban Revolution had defeated the United States and its Central Intelligence Agency at the beaches of Playa Girón, and by 1966 Castro had personally foiled several assassination attempts. 'Imperialism will inevitably be defeated', he told the over five hundred delegates that came from Chile to Vietnam. No-one in the room doubted him.

Cuba is under 150 kilometres from the shores of the United States. It had been the playground of US elites since it was seized in 1898 from Spain. Wretched had been its situation for the six decades that it lay under the thumb of New York financiers and Las Vegas gangsters. The Revolution of 1959 had been welcomed by the vast majority of the Cuban people. They were not going to allow their gains to be revoked by the overthrow of this revolutionary government. Whatever privations the United States would place upon Cuba, its people would be resolute. This was what gave

Fidel the confidence that Cuba's adversary – imperialism – would suffer a total defeat.

Fidel stood at the podium in his military fatigues. He would wear this till the end of his life. In Frantz Fanon's *The Wretched of the Earth* (1961), he mused about Fidel's clothing. Castro 'attending the UN in military uniform does not scandalise the underdeveloped countries', Fanon wrote. 'What Castro is demonstrating is how aware he is of the continuing regime of violence. What is surprising is that he did not enter the UN with his sub-machine gun; but perhaps they wouldn't have allowed that.' Fidel and the Cubans were ever prepared for the hybrid war that was ongoing, the blockade – which was economic warfare – and the attacks – which continue to this day.

'Who taught us this lesson' that imperialism would inevitably be defeated, Fidel asked on the last day of this conference that became known as the Tricontinental? 'The peoples have taught it to us. Who amongst the peoples have in our times taught us the most extraordinary lesson? The people of Vietnam.' Despite using their full arsenal – including aerial bombardment and chemical weapons – 'Yankee imperialists have not been able to crush the people of Vietnam.' In the years before the Tricontinental Conference, Vietnamese revolutionaries had taken the fight to US military camps inside southern Vietnam, such as attacking a US airbase in Bien Hoa (1964) and a Special Forces camp in Pleiku (1965). The US government intensified aerial bombardment of the northern part of Vietnam, including the capital of Hanoi. By the end of 1965, there were 200,000 US troops in Vietnam. The pressure on the Vietnamese revolution was immense, which was why Che Guevara, then in Tanzania contacting revolutionaries from the Congo, left behind his 'Message to the Tricontinental' to be read at the meeting in January 1966. In this text, Che Guevara called for revolutionaries to create 'two, three, more Vietnams' as he hoped to do in Congo and later in Bolivia. Pressure had to be lifted from the Vietnamese people, as the hydra of revolution had to draw the US away from their focus on that edge of Asia.

No doubt that the upsurge of protest in 1968 across the North Atlantic states took place as a consequence of – and inspired by – the anticolonial struggles in places such as Vietnam and Algeria and of the civil rights struggles inside their own borders. The slogans of the student unrest were defined by anti-war sentiment and by an anti-racist platform (this was brought together in France by the great antipathy to the Paris massacre of as many as two hundred Algerians in 1961 who had been demonstrating against the colonial war in North Africa). In the United States, anti-war students – organised into the Students for a Democratic Society – galvanised popular sentiment against the war into a set of campaigns from 1965 onward (shaped by the 1966 National Mobilization Committee to End the War in Vietnam, which produced the 1967 March on the Pentagon and the 1968 protest at the Democratic National Convention in Chicago). Across Europe, the tenor in 1968 was against the involvement of their governments in colonial wars, especially the war on Vietnam. France's 1968 begins not at the Sorbonne, but at Nanterre, where the members of the National Vietnam Committee were arrested as they protested in front of an American Express office. This was on 22 March, giving birth to the Mouvement du 22 mars, which went from criticism of the war on Vietnam to a denunciation of the capitalist university and the capitalist system in general.

In its general political declaration, the Tricontinental affirmed 'the inalienable right of all peoples to full political independence and to resort to all forms of struggle that may be necessary, including armed struggle, to conquer their right'. Six years previously, the United Nations General Assembly had passed a resolution on colonialism, which noted 'that the process of liberation is irresistible and irreversible and that, in order to avoid serious crises, an end must be put to colonialism and all practices of segregation and discrimination therewith'. That resolution from 14 December 1960 noted that 'all armed actions or repressive measures of all kinds directed against dependent peoples shall cease in order to enable them to exercise peacefully and freely their right to complete independence, and the integrity of their national territory shall be respected'. The UN did not say, as the Tricontinental would, that armed action was permissible, but it did not criticise such means either; the criticism of arms was directed at the imperialists, whose harshness imposed the armed struggle on the colonised. This was the experience of the African Party for the Independence of Guinea and Cabo Verde (PAIGC), whose leader Amílcar Cabral was in Havana for the conference, and whose experience was based on harsh Portuguese repression against their civil struggle that forced them to take up the gun. From the podium Cabral told his fellow revolutionaries,

> The past and present experiences of various peoples, the present situation of national liberation struggles in the world (especially in Vietnam, the Congo and Zimbabwe) as well as the situation of permanent violence, or at least of contradictions and upheavals, in certain countries which have gained their independence by the so-called peaceful way, show us not only that compromises with imperialism do not work, but also that the normal way of national liberation, imposed on peoples by imperialist repression, is *armed struggle.*

The key word here is *imposed*. The armed struggle is not a choice. This is what Fanon argued in *The Wretched of the Earth*. It is what Patrice Lumumba experienced at his assassination on 17 January 1961, just a month after the UN resolution, when his attempt at a civil struggle was stopped by the imposition of violence upon a people fighting for freedom.

Vietnam, Palestine, Guatemala, Congo, Zimbabwe – these, and many others, were the contours of the radical 1960s. That decade opens with the Cuban Revolution in the morning of the new year of 1959 and is partly defined over the next two decades by a range of revolutionary victories: Ethiopia (1974), Vietnam (1975), Laos (1975), Guinea-Bissau and Cabo Verde (1975), Mozambique (1975), São Tome (1975), Angola (1975), Afghanistan (1978), Grenada (1979), Nicaragua (1979), and Zimbabwe (1980). Communist revolutionaries and national liberation forces fought protracted battles – such as in Vietnam or Nicaragua – or else found themselves in a position of strength when the state system collapsed after a political crisis and opened the door to their victory – such as in Ethiopia and Grenada. What united these forces was – as the 1960 UN resolution put it – desire for complete independence and sovereignty, with the depth of commitment to the social revolution at different levels in each of the contexts. In other places, such as Palestine, South Africa and Western Sahara, the process of liberation was blocked in this period. The energy of these national liberation movements gathered force in the halls of the United Nations to pass the 1974 resolution on a New International Economic Order (NIEO), a vision for a more humane present.

Most of these revolutionary breakthroughs would not be allowed to breathe. The US began Operation Cyclone (1979) to fund the worst of Afghan society who became the Mujahideen and would paralyse the communist government; the US would mine Managua harbour and make every attempt to suffocate the Nicaraguan left government by funding Nicaragua's variant of the Mujahideen, namely the Contras. Fidel and his comrades at the Tricontinental meeting in 1966 were well aware of the policy of asphyxiation pursued by the imperialist powers. At the meeting, they discussed the archipelago of military bases held on to by the old colonial powers – from Britain's base in Diego Garcia to France's base in Dakar – and by the new imperialist power – the United States, which would eventually create at least eight hundred military bases in almost all the countries of the world. Imperialist threats against Cuba had not succeeded, however imperialist coups in a range of countries had hampered the growth of humanity's advance; the coups in Brazil (1964) and Indonesia (1965) destroyed the Left in these two large countries in South America and Asia for at least a generation, creating the example for the coups against national liberation in the Third World. By 1977, a US government report noted, 'The United States faces a politically multipolar and economically interdependent world which, except for Southern Africa, has been remarkably stabilized.' What they meant is that apart from the continued insurgencies of Southern Africa, the rest of the world had been managed by military coups in South America, by dirty wars in Central America, and by military coups in Southern Asia (notably in Pakistan in 1977). The Iranian revolution in 1979 would disturb this stability for decades to come, but otherwise, the US felt that it had been able to manage effectively the radical 1960s.

The great Indian communist poet Makhdoom Mohiuddin took the measure of the granite block that exerted itself from the imperialist core, that granite that fell upon Palestine in 1967 and that fell on Martin Luther King, Jr. in 1968. This is the dusk of the dispossessed, he sang, *hai sham sham-e-ghareebaan*. Those hands that pushed someone to the gallows, *voh haath jisne chadhaaya kisi ko sooli par*, those hands are still at work in the valley of the Sinai, in Vietnam, *voh haath vaadi-e Sina mein, Vietnam mein hai*.

The measure of the radical 1960s has not vanished into the fluff of collaboration and despair but remains alive in the struggles imposed on us by the atrocity of imperialism. Certainly, the mood is different, the military fatigues have faded, and victories do not come as swiftly as they did in those epochal decades before the Third World debt crisis. But when 250 million Indian workers and peasants conduct a general strike, as they did during the pandemic in 2020, and when the people of Bolivia overturn a military coup as forcefully as the people of Venezuela and Cuba defend their revolutionary processes from regime change, then it is hard to sniff into the wind and say that the 1960s is merely fodder for nostalgia. Our struggles for socialism – linked directly to the Tricontinental and its era – emerge not as an ideal to be established in the world, but out of the real movement which seeks to abolish the present state of things. The previous sentence paraphrases Marx and Engels from *The German Ideology*, written in 1845–46; if that sentence remains as true today as it did when it was written, the mood captured within it which resonated with Cabral and Castro in the 1960s remains true for us today. Our movement is not born out of a choice. It is a necessity.

Acknowledgements

This book has been a collective project. It emerged from a conference, 'The Radical Sixties: Aesthetic, Politics and Histories of Solidarity', we held in Brighton in the summer of 2019, where energetic discussions gave the initial ideas a real momentum. A subsequent workshop (moved online in the midst of the COVID-19 pandemic) brought together a smaller group of contributors who offered engaged feedback on each other's work. This volume has benefitted immeasurably from the lively spirit of interdisciplinary collaboration and commitment shared by the project's participants to de-centre the West in conceptions of the era.

At the University of Brighton, the Centre for Applied Philosophy, Politics and Ethics, the Centre for Design History, the Centre for Memory, Narrative and Histories, and Radical Futures provided the funding that has enabled this book to emerge. Colleagues at Brighton also supported this project in a myriad of intellectual and practical ways, as well as through their continued enthusiasm for the project. Bob Brecher has been especially supportive of our work. We are also particularly grateful to Struan Gray, Ian Sinclair, Megha Rajguru, Andrea García González and Jeremy Aynsley.

The book is enriched by the images it contains and we are especially honoured to be able to reproduce artwork by Dia al-Azzawi, made available courtesy of the collection of Abboudi Bou Jawde and skillfully photographed by Agop Kanledjian. Likewise, we are grateful to The Freedom Archives for making an extraordinary wealth of digitised materials free to use.

Acknowledgements

At Manchester University Press, Tom Dark and Lucy Burns have been keen supporters of this book and we are grateful for their grace and efficiency throughout the publication process.

Last but not least, the powerful image on the cover is a detail from the poster 'The struggle continues in Palestine and in El Salvador, and the revolution will be victorious' (Figure I.1) designed by Marc Rudin (signed as Jihad Mansour) held by the Palestine Poster Project Archive. We would like to especially thank Dan Walsh of the Palestine Poster Project Archive who, in the spirit of solidarity, made the image available 'as a way of honouring Marc and Palestine'.

Introduction: transnational solidarity in the long sixties

Zeina Maasri, Cathy Bergin and Francesca Burke

In May and June of 2020 hundreds of thousands of people around the world took to the streets in solidarity with protests in the United States against homicidal police brutality and the systemic racism that underpins it. People chanted 'George Floyd! Say his name! Say his name!' in anger and in condemnation of the brutal murder of an unarmed African American man, George Floyd, by a white police officer. The familiarity of this phone-captured image of black death did not diminish its capacity to horrify. Elsewhere, Floyd's portrait was drawn on derelict walls in war-torn Idlib, Syria and on Israel's apartheid wall in the Palestinian town of Bethlehem. In Derry, graffiti quoting Martin Luther King Jr. that 'Injustice anywhere is a threat to justice everywhere' appeared in solidarity with the protesters in the US. Lebanese activists sent a 'quick guide' of protest tactics via Twitter signed 'From #Lebanon to #Minneapolis, solidarity everywhere'. In Chile, an illustration of Floyd alongside Camilo Catrillanca, a 24-year-old indigenous Mapuche man killed by Chilean police in 2018, was circulating on social media platforms.[1] Palestinians also saw in Floyd's lethal stranglehold at the hands of the police, the violent techniques that the Israeli state enacts against them.[2]

Public expressions of transnational solidarity erupted across a range of contexts in which protest movements had been mobilising. The widespread political and affective identifications with Floyd were articulated with local demands for social justice and struggles against racism. Demonstrators in the UK, for example, carried placards insisting that the 'UK is not innocent' and challenged the ways in which historical figures were remembered and commemorated in public spaces which valorised and lionised British imperial history. Most obviously this was manifested in the toppling of the statue of the Atlantic slaver Edward Colston in Bristol. Rallies opened up the many silences around British imperial history and developed into increasingly pressing calls to 'decolonise' cultural institutions, knowledge frameworks and curricula.

These contemporary instances of border crossing anti-racist solidarity attest to the historical erasures and unfinished decolonisation projects that belie our supposedly postcolonial time. Indeed, some of the symbolic moments of solidarity in transnational circulation today bear an uncanny resemblance to – and often explicitly reclaim – the political contestations animating the long sixties. Transnational solidarity then was central to the radical imagination that connected New Left and civil rights movements with anticolonial and anti-imperialist struggles across what has since been identified as the Global South. Yet despite its centrality to activists then and now, transnational solidarity as a powerful mobilising force, together with its associated set of aesthetic, political and cultural practices remain relatively understudied. In its focus on the unfinished decolonisation struggles of the 'long sixties', this book is concerned with precisely that lacuna.

Decentring 'the sixties'

The 1960s continues to engage scholars from many disciplines in debates over what exactly changed and, indeed, whether the various protest movements were in fact radical at all in their political demands. Both nostalgically celebrated as a revolutionary heyday and lamented as a failed political project, the decade continues to haunt veterans and preoccupy scholars over fifty years on. However, long-held evaluations of this tumultuous decade have too often remained parochially centred on European and North American experiences in a handful of cities. 'The sixties' have conventionally been universalised on the basis of myopically Western speculations about what makes radical politics possible.[3] Speculations that limit our understandings of what transnational solidarity might look like and the kinds of political imaginaries and radical aesthetic practices it created. For this is a period which in fact challenged 'the legitimacy and power of the global colour line and its oppressive political economies of inequality'.[4] Crucially, the Global South, despite its centrality for activists in the 1960s, is conspicuously marginalised in the scholarship. It has been argued – and demonstrated – that anticolonial liberation struggles and anti-imperialist resistance spanning the three continents of the South, from Cuba to Algeria to Vietnam, both politically informed a new generation of contestation and offered a new radical horizon for leftist internationalism.[5] Thus, Samantha Christiansen and Zachary Scarlett contend in their edited collection, *The Third World in the Global 1960s*: 'The Third World became the vehicle for the social, cultural, and political transformation in the West.'[6] It is precisely the erasures of Third Worldist radical politics from memories of May '68 in France, as Kristin Ross has argued, that have reduced this event to a mere lifestyle youth revolt and quests for individual autonomy. It is, she notes, 'the price that must be paid for "saving" May as a happy month of liberated "free expression"'.[7]

In addition to recent calls to decentre the Western loci of the sixties, there have been sustained efforts to look beyond the 'moment' of '68, with accounts starting in the mid-1950s and following the radical trajectory well into the 1970s.[8] While a number of studies expand the time under analysis without widening the conventional geographic purview, Christiansen and Scarlett utilise the idea of the 'long sixties' as part of their project to centre the Third World as a site of radical political movement throughout this period.[9] Approaching activism in these chronologically elongated terms not only encourages reflection on either side of '68 but also calls attention to a different set of political milestones that informed transnational imaginaries in this period, including: the Cuban Revolution (1953–59); the Bandung Conference of 1955 that inaugurated Afro-Asian Solidarity and the Non-Aligned Movement; the Algerian War of Independence (1954–62); the Tricontinental Conference in Cuba (1966) that broadened the remit of Afro-Asian solidarity to include Latin America; the Arab-Israeli June War (1967) and the subsequent rise of Palestinian guerrilla organisations; the US massacre of Vietnamese civilians at Mỹ Lai (1968); and the fall of Saigon (1975).

Our volume builds on recent efforts to expand and complicate the spatiality and temporality of the global sixties and offers new analyses of this critical historical conjuncture through the lens of solidarity, with and across anticolonial liberation struggles. It is primarily concerned with the emergence of transnational solidarity as a nodal theme for the Left, which is more often cited than actively explored in traditional studies of the period. Solidarity often provided tangible networks and practical, organisational resources that activists could draw on as well as contribute to. It also emerged as a means of framing political discourse and thereby positioning specific situations within a broader anti-imperialist struggle aligned with other liberation movements. The very term 'transnational solidarity' is one that needs to be theorised and explicated in relation to this radical conjuncture. The chapters that follow explore how solidarity was conceived, imagined and radically enacted in the border crossings, both spatial and ideological, of activists, freedom fighters, artists, students, intellectuals, sports fans, medics and filmmakers in the long sixties. Crucially, this volume is concerned with solidarity's transnational politics, associated itineraries and cultures of circulation.

Our 'global' approach here does not seek simply to carve out spaces for neglected stories of radical interconnections. The point is not merely to 'add' to the story of the radical 1960s and expand its geographical map. Rather, these neglected stories offer us a different, if not always competing, narrative of what was 'radical' about the long sixties, centring anticolonial struggles and the concept of what anticolonialism meant for liberation politics. These writings illuminate the ambitious and uneven attempts to make a series of connections based on a set of assumptions not only about what liberation might mean, but who was the subject of liberation, and who was the agent for revolutionary politics. It is on that basis that our volume contributes to decentring the sixties from long-held Western epistemological moorings. It is a project of political restitution and historical redress that foregrounds anticolonial solidarity at the heart of the period's radical political movements. In so doing, this book speaks directly to recent work on solidarity as a neglected paradigm for understanding anticolonial history and makes a twofold contribution to an emerging scholarship that seeks to emphasise the agency of the colonised: first, in writing transnational histories of decolonisation away from Western-centric teleology;[10] and second, in centring this history in the making of a New Left radicalism in the global sixties.

Figure I.1 Poster, 'The struggle continues in Palestine and in El Salvador, and the revolution will be victorious', Jihad Mansour, Popular Front for the Liberation of Palestine, *c.*1981. Marc Rudin, *aka* Jihad Mansour, is a Swiss-born and trained artist who joined the PFLP in the late 1970s as graphic designer. He lived in Palestinian refugee camps in Lebanon (until 1982) and Syria until the early 1990s, during which he designed some of the PFLP's most remarkable posters.
Reproduced courtesy of The Palestine Poster Project Archive (www.palestineposterproject.org).

Anticolonial solidarity in the global sixties

> 'My people' – the people who knew about oppression, discrimination, prejudice, poverty and the frustration and despair that they produce – were not Irish Americans. They were black, Puerto Rican, Chicano.[11]

With these provocative words, Bernadette Devlin McAliskey, the Irish civil rights activist reflected upon the relationship between civil rights in Ireland and the US in 1969. Not long after this, she was given a key to New York City which she then presented to the Black Panthers, 'to whom this city and country belong'.[12] Her sense of peoplehood did not fit into fixed ideological constructs of nation, ethnicity, or race. She crossed these borders to identify with those who shared similar conditions of oppression and discrimination. This is what Devlin McAliskey understood solidarity to be; this is how she linked her local struggle in Northern Ireland to that of others elsewhere in the world. Nearly fifty years later, Devlin McAliskey reconfirmed the anticolonial politics of this transnational solidarity by noting: 'Where we came to in 1968, where Palestine came to, where South Africa came to, where Quebec came to, where the Afro-Americans came to in the sixties was written in the sands of the birth of the British Empire, and European empires.'[13] Devlin McAliskey's outlook is one example – though a particularly notable one – of many forgotten militant voices, networks and cultures of transnational solidarity that this book is concerned with and aims to unravel.

In his pioneering book, *The Darker Nations: A People's History of the Third World*, Vijay Prashad rewrites the history of the 'Third World' as a project of anticolonial solidarity that carried the hopes for dignity and dreams of self-determination of the peoples of Africa, Asia and Latin America. His analysis centres transnational meetings – in Bandung (1955), Cairo (1961), Havana (1966) among many others – and the ensuing institutional platforms whereby newly independent states and their leaders carried their Third Worldist project forward. However, while interstate diplomacy has had an important role in shaping this project, we know very little about grassroots transnational solidarity beyond these official channels. How did non-state actors imagine themselves as part of a Third Worldist anticolonial project? How did militants act in solidarity with and within such a project? How did grassroots activists connect anticolonial struggles to anti-capitalist struggles and to what extent was transnational solidarity centred on the new forms of self-determination that were forged in the battles against Empire?

Commenting on the limited knowledge available on such Afro-Asian networks, Reem Abou-El-Fadl et al. have eloquently stated in a recent manifesto:

> If the Third World was a project to which millions contributed, then historians have yet to unravel the many threads by which they did so and to approach its history with the spirit with which it was originally imagined: one that sought communication and solidarity across difference.[14]

Likewise, David Featherstone notes that subaltern histories of solidarity have been largely silenced and marginalised. Examining solidarities from early twentieth-century maritime labour struggles to contemporary anti-climate change activists, he urges instead a reframing of internationalism to examine its creation 'from below', arguing that 'solidarities can be a powerful force for reshaping the world in more socially equitable and just ways'.[15] Our volume echoes these calls to foreground subaltern histories of transnational solidarity and extends this optic to meet the contingencies of the long and radical struggles for decolonisation. Our focus is specifically on the long sixties as a site of political optimism and sustained struggle, what Jacques Rancière calls 'a time of historical faith', that illuminates histories and politics which were determinately revolutionary and self-consciously internationalist.[16] Beyond its articulation within the Global South, the anticolonial project conjured up a broader framework of solidarity that intersected with African American civil rights movements and revolutionary anti-imperialism in the North and, not least, mobilised diasporic and immigrant communities in the metropoles. These threads of solidarity weave together a more complex transnational political imagination than the horizontal and vertical axes of South-South and North-South geographic connections would allow us to consider.

Anticolonial revolts, in both ideological framework and praxis, inspired and informed anti-imperial dissent in the metropoles. The impact of anticolonial struggles on global forms of resistance has a history as long as empire itself – and one that has been systematically overlooked. As Priyamvada Gopal recently argued in the case of the British Empire, connections between the colonies and the imperial centre were dialogical.[17] Her argument joins with others to undo the many silences in imperial history about the agency of the colonised. She reveals how concepts such as 'freedom', 'liberation' and 'self-determination' were understood by anticolonial insurgents and interpreted in the diaspora, thus shaping their understanding in the metropole.[18] In doing so, she challenges long-held views on the Eurocentric provenance of such emancipatory claims and their supposed unidirectional transmission to the colonies. Crucially, Gopal prioritises the politics of solidarity over those of paternalist humanitarianism in enabling this dialogical intellectual exchange: 'Far from neutralizing the other within a safe mode of "difference", resistance brought home the fact of a commonality that could not be contained by the familiar disposition of benevolence. What was required was solidarity.'[19]

Gopal's argument can be productively extended to the long sixties' radical history of decolonisation when such dialogical exchange was amplified by the intensity of global flows that marked the period. Fredric Jameson's seminal periodisation of the sixties traces its radicalism historically back to 'Third World beginnings',[20] as does Kristin Ross in her pioneering historical redress of May '68 and its afterlives in French history. She foregrounds dialogical relations between anticolonial struggle, in Algeria and Vietnam, and political dissent in France, noting that:

> French third-worldism was in one sense nothing more than the recognition, beginning in the late 1950s, that the colonized, through their wars of liberation, had emerged as a new figuration of the people in the political sense ('the wretched of the earth'), eclipsing any manifestation of a European working class by universalizing or giving a name to a political wrong that in turn mobilized students and others in the West.[21]

Beyond earlier colonial timeframes that Gopal investigates, ideas of 'liberation' saw an even more significant reverse flow from colonies to metropoles in the long sixties. It was not only the figure of the freedom fighter – the colonial militant – that inspired agency and solidarity as the new revolutionary subject. It was, crucially, also revolutionary thought and praxis from the Global South – Fanon, Cabral, Césaire, Guevara and Mao among others – that dislocated left politics from their Communist Party moorings and decentred both Soviet Marxism and Europe in the radical imagination of May '68 militancy.[22]

The trajectories and local translations of anticolonial and antiimperialist liberation struggles from South to North is also powerfully visible in black liberation movements of the period. The black transnational imagination had long transgressed the boundaries of the nation across the African diaspora.[23] Cynthia Young notes that in the sixties the black radical struggle in the US was 'informed by the global' where 'an imagined black nation was produced in and through Third World identification and solidarity'.[24] She demonstrates how a Third World Left emerged among leftists of colour in the US who were inspired by events in the decolonising world in Africa, the Caribbean and Asia. This 'US Third World Left' enabled internal contestations of economic, racial and cultural arrangements and 'emphasized solidarity based on material circumstance rather than racial, ethnic, or geographic kinship'.[25] Its formation, adds Young, rested on the cultures of circulation that characterised the global sixties, from travelling texts, mobile print cultures and moving images to literally travelling bodies.[26] African American activists identified with the continent of Africa and the African diaspora, but pan-Africanism was inflected in a way which encompassed all those who suffered colonial oppression. As Black Panther Kathleen Cleaver simply stated it: 'in a world of racist polarization we sought solidarity'.[27] In addition to Cuba, Jamaica, Algeria and Congo, the black liberation movement in the US also articulated its solidarity with the Palestinian struggle. Moreover, that solidarity – which has seen significant 'renewal' since 2014 with the rise of the Black Lives Matter movement – is understood 'not only as a principled response to a specific historical injustice, but also as the signpost of an analytical understanding of imperialism, colonialism, and white supremacy as global phenomena that subsume the Black American condition'.[28]

Situated historically at the threshold of contemporary globalisation, the sixties bear witness to the acceleration of capitalist modernisation and the concurrent expansion of consumer societies, the commercialisation of the jet plane and the advent of television, all of which lend the era its global significance in giving time-space compression an everyday – often bitter – reality.[29] Nonetheless, this period's intense political movements, etching their way independently from, and against, the circuits of capital and state patronage – yet in conjunction with new technologies of circulation and synchronous replication – map a globally complex and decentred web of interconnected relations of solidarity. This is what makes the long sixties, in both the northern metropoles and in the decolonising south, radically cosmopolitan in worldview and radically imaginative in outlook; a 'cosmopolitan radicalism'[30] shaped 'from below' by the politicoscapes of anti-imperialism and anticolonial solidarity.[31]

Indeed, the politics of transnational solidarity will vary, depending both on the activist's subject position, gender, race and class identifications, and on their location in the network of political relations. Consider, for instance, the following set of interconnected relations of solidarity and the complex politicoscapes these would entail. French students mobilising in solidarity with Arab colonial immigrant workers in the neighbouring factories of Nanterre. These workers' relations to exiled Palestinian intellectuals in Paris who act as conduits to bring the Palestinian cause to the attention of militant French intellectuals and artists. French intellectuals and artists who travel to convene with fellow militants at congresses in Algeria and Cuba, and to meet freedom fighters in Bolivia and *fida'iyeen* in Lebanon and Jordan. Peasants turned freedom fighters who in turn have answered a call to arms as dispossessed subjects of the world, identifying with and joining their comrades in North Vietnam. Though they may never have travelled to meet them, they have read enough manuals and seen enough films and images about guerrilla tactics and a 'people's war' to know that they are fighting the same battle on different fronts, and that in strategic terms they are encircling the cities from the countryside to spark a world revolution. A Third World internationalism that in turn reverberates in the voices of striking workers in Turin as they proclaim 'Vietnam is in our factories'[32] and is echoed across the Atlantic by defiant African American protesters shouting in the streets of Chicago 'bring the war home'.[33]

Transnational solidarity is by no means an equal dialogical exchange and seamless border-crossing that does not get lost in circulation and translation. It is historically contingent and replete with differentials of power, missed encounters, silences, disappointments and misrecognition that seep right through the political relations that bind networks of transnational actors into solidarity. Indeed, the forms of solidarity that make up this volume are as informed by the mistranslations that arise as well as by determined efforts to forge connections across barriers of race and nation. Sometimes these connections were imaginative acts of will, where the solidarity expressed with far-away struggles was based on the identification of a shared form of oppression. Sometimes they were actively made by militants who met, argued, struggled and fought side by side. Nodal cities such as Havana, Beirut, Algiers, Cairo, Paris, London, East Berlin and Montevideo were not only temporary meeting places for state officials at Third Worldist summits, nor simply urban theatres of New Left dissent that became visible in the emblematic year of 1968. These cities provided alternative spaces of cultural encounter, intellectual exchange and political organisation that stretched throughout the *longue durée* of the sixties. Colonial immigrants, students and workers, exiled intellectuals and artists, refugees and itinerant militants, all met and exchanged radical ideas and revolutionary hopes and tactics.

Among cities of the South, Algiers, for instance, acted as a nodal city on the global terrain of revolutionary anti-imperialism. Named 'the Mecca of revolution' by Amílcar Cabral – Africa's iconic anticolonial leader – early in the 1960s, the North African city had attracted 'insurgents that travelled the globe but also insurgents with respect to a global order'.[34] In the aftermath of the 1967 Arab-Israeli war, Beirut took on a similar nodal role.[35] Dubbed the 'Arab Hanoi' – a base and springboard for the liberation of Palestine[36] – the city attracted intellectuals, militants and artists from the Arab world and further afield to join their Palestinian comrades in lending visibility to their liberation struggle. Solidarity materialised on the battlefield and through the arts, as poetry, literature, films, song, radical print cultures and art exhibitions gave 'Arab Hanoi' a resonance both in Beirut and far outside it.[37]

Likewise, in Montevideo, the Uruguayan radical left that formed the nucleus of the Tupamaros – a guerrilla organisation that acquired mythical status – was in close contact with revolutionary exiles from Argentina and Brazil, as well as with itinerant militant intellectuals such as Régis Debray and a network of Latin American guerrilla groups and peasant movements inspired by the success of the Cuban insurrection (see Cardozo in this volume). In turn, the revolutionary figure of the freedom fighter was a quintessential translocal trope that crossed borders, traversed imaginations and inspired agency as it became aestheticised in films, on posters and in periodicals.[38] It is translocal in the way that it articulates identification in two interlocking imagined spatialities: a situated national liberation struggle and a globally interconnected Third World internationalism.[39] Film and print cultures of the radical sixties foreshadowed the electronic mediascapes that Arjun Appadurai has argued are essential to the collective imagination – itself a constitutive feature of modern subjectivity and central to forms of agency in the global order.[40] Transnational imagination, notes Jeremy Presthold, was at the core of a meaningful solidarity: it 'is a mode of perception that frames local circumstances within a global historical trajectory and shapes collective desires and actions as a result'.[41] The symbolic appeal of Che Guevara, for instance, as the guerrilla archetype of the long sixties 'helped to build and sustain a radical imagined community'.[42]

Key to our understanding of solidarity is not just the causal connections that were made between decolonising nations, decolonising peoples, anti-imperialist and revolutionary politics and practices, but the political and cultural imaginings upon which solidarities could be envisioned and explicated. What connected people was not what they shared in terms of their given identities, but how their differences could be re-inscribed in relation to specific power structures which enabled a way of seeing the world outside the lens of the immediately experiential. It is here that the question of radical cultural forms as a key space for imaginative identification and transformation is central to this volume, not least in the shaping of the 'new sensibility'[43] and 'structures of feeling'[44] that prefigured the era's radical horizons of possibility.[45]

Transnational networks of artistic solidarity were central to this period's radicalism.[46] These too have been long forgotten by the art history canon.[47] Artists met at different international cultural congresses and biennials in the Global South and organised to protest global causes and local issues. For example, the Black Panther

Party artist, Emory Douglas accompanied his revolutionary artwork to the Pan-African Festival in Algiers in 1969,[48] and his illustrations appeared on the legendary posters of the Cuban-based Organization of Solidarity with the People of Africa, Asia and Latin America (OSPAAAL).[49] The latter's bulletin, *The Tricontinental* (1966–88; 1995–2019), was particularly active in reporting on anticolonial and anti-imperialist struggles and propagating revolutionary discourse along with corresponding visual rhetoric and aesthetics.[50] OSPAAAL's posters and periodicals were published in at least three languages (Spanish, English, French and sometimes Arabic) and distributed through subsidiary networks in Cuba, India, Panama, Mexico and Lebanon.[51] The visual malleability and portability of such printscapes extended the revolutionary imagination across national borders and language barriers and helped define conceptions as well as aesthetic sensibilities of transnational solidarity among readers and viewers. Furthermore, artists donated artworks and formed part of broader solidarity networks that organised travelling exhibitions and museums-in-exile, of which the International Art Exhibition for Palestine, the Museo de la Resistencia Salvador Allende (MIRSA) and Art Against Apartheid are key examples.[52] Far from being reduced to mere propaganda, this was a period of artistic fecundity and experimentation. New modes of artistic practice and of public exhibition were sought as tactical alternatives to the market system and entry into public culture and politics. Strategies of guerrilla warfare inspired artists to devise a 'cultural guerrilla' approach to artistic practice. As for instance Paula Barreiro López shows in this volume, the manifesto of 'cultural guerrilla' announced at the Cultural Congress in 1968 Havana in the presence of a host of international artists, had no small role in the militant artistic practices that took central stage in May 1968 in Paris.

The border crossing of transnational solidarity

Barbara Smith, a founder member of the Combahee River Collective, recently reflected upon how, as an African American socialist and feminist, she positioned herself in the 1970s:

> We were third world women. We considered ourselves to be third world women. We saw ourselves in solidarity and in struggle with all

third world people around the globe. And we also saw ourselves as being internally colonized. We were internally colonized within the United States. We identified as third world people. And that kind of solidarity was not just true of the very new Black feminism that we were building.[53]

Smith's understanding of the subject position of African American women during the long sixties is one that foregrounds solidarity as a means of understanding not only the struggles of others but her own struggle. The idea of the Third World here was not a geographically experiential one but a matter of history and of politics. Solidarity was transformative in terms of how it positioned the African American woman; in this case, not just as the multiply oppressed minority within a minority in a racialised state, but as an oppressed majority within an anticolonial global movement of resistance. Significantly this was during a time of 'a global assault on empire'.[54] Smith's self-positioning underlines that the question of solidarity was a dialectical one, one in which identity was potentially enriched rather than diminished when imagined outside of experiential paradigms. Furthermore, the African American woman had a stake in global liberation struggles and these struggles were themselves interdependent. This idea of the revolutionary subject as a subject in transition, being remade not only by the direct struggles of which she was a part, but also by the struggles of others which created hitherto unseen connections between who she thought she was and who she might become, is key to the politics expressed throughout this volume.[55] This is, of course, a dynamic process where identifying Smith's relocation of political subjecthood to that of the Third World woman, like Devlin McAliskey's border crossing identification with radical anti-racism, are expressions of a politics which insists not only on tracing transnational radical links but on refusing the limits of proscribed identities which would literally and metaphorically keep them 'in their place'.

The commitment to revolutionary change through shared oppression and investment in the liberation of others is not a mere anachronism of the long sixties – a politics that is irrelevant to the present. As Jacques Rancière notes in his powerful reflection on the French Left and the Algerian War, *The Cause of the Other*: 'Politics does not exist because of some faith in the triumphant future of emancipation. Politics exists because the cause of the other exists.'[56] Rancière does not use the word 'solidarity'; rather, his essay is erected on the concept of identification and, crucially, of disidentification; a disidentification with the French state 'that had done this in our name and removed it from our view'.[57] Though seemingly far removed from the remaking of the self as described by Barbara Smith, Rancière's refusal to identify with a certain self underlines the multidirectional flows of political solidarity insisted upon by Smith. The relationship here between 'I' and 'other' is not one which is based on a 'respect' for difference, or a refusal to speak to the struggles of others. Nor is it a co-option of those struggles. What is necessary here is a transformational shift in order to see the 'other' *outside* the violent inscriptions of the state which renders the other, and indeed the actions of the state, as invisible. This is not a politics of acting *on behalf* of another but of the recognition of collective liberation in which the cause of the other produces changes in 'us'. As James Baldwin put it in a different context 'as long as you think you're white, there's no hope for you'.[58]

Like Gopal, Rancière repudiates the classic liberal position which busies itself with the '"cause" of the "other"' and thus 'retreats from politics to ethics'.[59] Expressed as 'duties towards the suffering', such a liberal position reinscribes the power dynamic that structures colonial power relations. Rancière does not present this work on identification as a definition of political solidarity but it is a compelling theorisation of the dialectical transformation that solidarity can engender.[60] The retreat to 'ethics' is precisely the refusal of a politics which demands transformative change in the colony *and the metropole*, of those in the oppressor nation as well as the oppressed territory. The ethics of solidarity in a liberal humanitarian sense – which are demystified in very different ways by Gopal and Rancière – are not what motivates many of the activists who appear in this volume, or indeed the editors of this collection. Rather it is the politics of solidarity in all their necessarily messy and inspiring dimensions which are so startling; a model of solidarity that eschews any notion that political interconnections are formed through either the erasure of or the reification of difference. The point is that solidarity, as Chandra Talpade Mohanty argues, 'is always an achievement, the result of active struggle to construct the universal on the basis of particulars/differences'.[61] Moreover, and particularly important for the work in this volume, she insists that 'rather than assuming an enforced commonality of oppression, the practice of solidarity foregrounds communities of people who have chosen to work and fight together'.[62] It is the myriad nature of these 'chosen' solidarities that the chapters in this volume reveal. They are forms of solidarity where political identities are reimagined through interconnected translocal struggles. The grassroots focus of the volume is itself a decentring process where the practices of these activists complicate any neat divisions between 'here' and 'there', and when spatially determined models of belonging and unbelonging became blurred and contested. What is rooted in the local is not reducible to the local. As Doreen Massey argues in a different context: 'the global is locally produced; and global forces are just as material, and real, as is the local embeddedness'.[63] The site of struggle was also to be defined in terms of the relationship between particular groups of oppressed people and those whose liberation politics were invested in the overthrow of that oppression. The motto of Aboriginal activists in 1970s Australia captures precisely this: 'If you have come here to help me, you are wasting your time. But if you have come because your liberation is bound up with mine, then let us work together.'[64]

Solidarity is not of course a concept which is available only to the Left. As our own era attests, the concept of solidarity can be tethered to whiteness, to nation and to the most sinister of political imaginaries in what Paul Gilroy has called a 'dismal dance of absolutism'.[65] The transnational solidarities forged in the long sixties were ones untethered from the naturalised, mythologised and racialised roots of blood and soil. It was a solidarity that was invested in a transformed future where identities could be made and remade. To note this, however, is not to invest in a misty-eyed romanticism: the hot wars of the period were bloody and lethal. Moreover, transnational solidarities could pose risks to activists with these forms of identification and organisation being targeted by government authorities. The term 'solidarity' also has a history of marginalising particular types of differences, not least in relation to forms of Western feminism which mobilised a 'colour blind' solidarity of gender, a form of 'sisterhood' dependent upon the erasing of gender oppression as experienced by working-class women and women racialised as other than white. Indeed, it is in this period that vivid alternative forms of feminism emerge, and where the authority of who defines the terms of solidarity was challenged. Examining the case of Angela Davis' meeting with Egyptian feminists in the early 1970s, Sara Salem demonstrates in this volume that it is the work of contextualising identity within material structures that affect both Egyptian women and African American women, which enables a transnational feminist solidarity to emerge. It is one that neither erases difference nor prevents identification.

To study the long sixties with particular emphasis on the Global South is to engage with a politics of solidarity which insists on the connectedness of the globally oppressed. The connectedness is forged on a commitment to anticolonialism and the concurrent mobilisations around migrancy and 'race'. As Laleh Khalili notes:

> These Third World movements ... seismically shifted the language of power, rights, and freedom and provided a parallel channel in which narratives of might and duty spun by imperial centers could be disputed, defied, and displaced. They made spaces to celebrate decolonizing struggles; the end of (formal) empires; and the possibility of dignity, equality, and freedom.[66]

This commitment is palpable in the writings of activists of the period and in the memoirs of those activists in following decades. The reality of these interconnections were, of course, more complex than their often beautiful articulations; the expression of solidarity is the beginning and not the end of the political project of transforming the world. What is startling about these solidarities is the transnational imagination they inaugurated. The shape and nature of transnational solidarities do not exist prior to the political connections which they establish, but nor are they independent of local histories and geographies. In order to best understand these solidarities as transnational, we need to locate them in the context of their local articulations as much as their international significance. Nikhil Pal Singh thus observes that the 'revolutionary intercommunalism' of black political imagination of the 1960s was the 'combination of its grassroots insurgency and global dreams'.[67] The global dreaming which forged these connections between Derry and Selma, Paris and Bissau, Montevideo and Algiers, was a reimagining of the forces of revolutionary transformation. As the chapters in this volume attest, such reimagining was also an investment in the agency of other anticolonial activists, sometimes through practical assistance, sometimes through a recognition of a shared oppressor and a polyglot revolutionary language of resistance.

Crossing disciplinary borders

This volume is interdisciplinary in its exploration of transnational solidarity of the global sixties, bringing together for that purpose essays from a variety of, and often intersecting, disciplinary perspectives and methodological tools: history, politics and international relations; ethnographic and cultural studies; art and design history; and critical theory. We firmly believe that in order to understand the manifold ways in which a concept such as solidarity is thought, imagined and enacted, and to enquire into the very conditions which enable it to emerge historically, it is crucial to cross the artificially imposed boundaries of academic knowledge structures. Activism – and life *tout court* – is not organised like this and neither should be our attempts to understand it. Furthermore, decentring the sixties and examining the transnational dimension of solidarity that shaped its global impetus requires following the trajectories being mapped and being attentive to the translocality of revolutionary texts and cultural forms in circulation. This requires knowledge of the particularity of local contexts and access to archives and sources in various locations and languages. This cannot be achieved by a single person, let alone a single disciplinary formation: it needs to mobilise scholarship beyond the confines of nation-centric and area studies interpretive frameworks. The chapters in this volume illuminate neglected locations of struggle, such as Indonesia, Pakistan and Uruguay, and shed light on forgotten – if not outright erased – histories of solidarity with anticolonial struggles in Portuguese colonies, Palestine and elsewhere. The importance of migration emerges as a central theme throughout the volume, as does the figure of the anticolonial freedom fighter as the new revolutionary subject. The border crossings of transnational solidarity which these chapters uncover, reconfigure the map of the global sixties and reveal new perspectives on commonly known sites.

Both Matt Myers and Abdellali Hajjat centre, respectively, the figure and active role of immigrant workers in their redress of the French long sixties. Myers argues that the immigrant worker was foundational to a political imaginary of the French New Left that allowed to simultaneously imagine a new political order born from global anticolonial revolt, working-class rebellion and generational change. Hajjat's chapter supplements Myers' by providing insight into the largely erased activist role of Arab immigrant workers and students. Focusing particularly on the Committees in Support of the Palestinian Revolution, known as 'les comités Palestine', Hajjat uncovers how these short-lived solidarity movements that formed part of the French long sixties were foundational to the Arab Workers' Movement in France, established in 1972.

Likewise, Paula Barreiro López recovers Cuban-based international cultural encounters and experiments with revolutionary art to trace Tricontinental genealogies of artistic militancy and collectivism that took central stage in May '68 France. The Latin American history of revolutionary anti-imperialism is further explored by Marina Cardozo who shifts the discussion away from Cuba to provide in-depth insight on the formation of the Tupamaros in Uruguay, foregrounding the transnational networks of Latin American revolutionaries and exiles meeting in Montevideo.

These 'forgotten' histories are unearthed in relation to the anticolonial struggle in Angola, Mozambique and Guinea-Bissau in the work of Víctor Barros. He traces extraordinary moments of transnational solidarity organised through conferences in Khartoum, Driebergen and Rome dedicated to smashing Portuguese colonialism. Radical border crossings are addressed in a very different way in Sara Salem's illuminating work on Angela Davis' feminist journeys in Egypt in the early 1980s. Solidarity is an active process of recognising and dismantling hierarchies but this is neither blithe nor uncomplicated as Salem demonstrates through her engagement with Davis' deeply reflective anti-racist feminism. The complexities of transnational solidarity are further explored by Aurora Almada e Santos in her study of the American Committee of Africa in relation to anticolonial struggles in Angola. She investigates how this solidarity was 'performed' in the context of competing and tension-filled contexts on the ground in Africa in relation to politicised humanitarian campaigning.

The day-to-day processes of building solidarity are investigated by Christian Høgsbjerg in his work on how South African anti-Apartheid exiles in the UK worked with British campaigners to build the sporting boycott movement. This was a process that enacted solidarities which blurred the imperial distinctions between racism at home and abroad, unsettling Britain's unspoken *and* loudly enunciated whiteness in relation to its past and present. Breaking down the boundaries and the legacies of British imperialism is also reflected on by Bernadette Devlin McAliskey. The transnational inauguration of her politics in the Northern Ireland civil rights movement disrupt the parochial lens through which the Northern Irish 'Troubles' have been understood. This place *of* and yet *other* to Britain's national imaginary erupted in the late 1960s as part of the global struggle against targeted oppression. Delineating an anti-imperialist voice which eschews the narrowly national, she draws attention to the violence of the British colonial state and its insistent grip on the present.

The transformation of global horizons in the period is also reflected upon by Helen Lackner. In her interview for this volume, she relates how at the University of London School of Oriental and African Studies (SOAS), Arab Marxists encouraged UK students to develop an interest in the anti-imperialist struggles in the Gulf. Britain's intrenched imperial amnesia was consistently challenged by new generations of post-colonial immigrants where transnational circuits of activism created a space in which colonial apathy was challenged. In Talat Ahmed's chapter on the tumultuous events in Pakistan in 1968 she highlights London as a key site for those wishing to challenge General Ayub Khan's regime. She charts the transnational solidarity of the anti-Ayub movement by Pakistani students, other South Asian communities and labour activists in the UK, recovering the oft-occluded story of Pakistan's political revolts of 1968–69.

Linking Pakistan to South Lebanon by way of the Palestinian liberation struggle, Sabah Haider excavates a deeply buried history of South-South solidarity in her chapter on the popular film *Zerqa* (1969). She analyses how this film functioned as an ideological call to solidarity with the Palestinian cause in Pakistan, revealing the translocal forms of imaginative identification that centred a shared Muslim identity in the struggle against colonialism and Israeli occupation. Transregional Muslim connections are echoed in Claudia Derichs' chapter which focuses on Indonesia to retrace a longer history of Islamist resurgence movements. While important to

Afro-Asian anticolonial solidarity, Indonesia's Islamist activism has been neglected in the literature on post-Bandung social movements.

At a moment when Pakistani volunteers were travelling to join the Palestine Liberation Organisation (PLO) in South Lebanon, and while Arab activists were actively forming the Comités Palestine in Paris, Iraqi artists and intellectuals on the Left were engaged in a similar passage from Baghdad. In particular, Dia al-Azzawi's book *A Witness of Our Time* (1972), from which selected drawings are reproduced in this volume, pays tribute to the revolutionary promise of the Palestinian *fida'i* (guerrilla combatant). The translocal figure of the anticolonial freedom fighter that inspired revolutionary art practice from Cuba emerges yet again as the quintessential revolutionary subject that rallied Arab artists and intellectuals on the Left in solidarity with the Palestinian cause.

The important role of political exiles, that Cardozo foregrounds in the formation of the Tupamaros, is central once again to Mary Ikoniadou's chapter which unravels the complex layers of transnational solidarity in East Germany by Greek political refugees. Ikoniadou examines aesthetic manifestations of solidarity in the illustrated magazine *Pyrsos* (1961–68) where solidarity with 1960s anticolonial and liberation struggles was not merely a discourse dictated by the Greek Left or by state socialism. Rather, it was intellectually, aesthetically and hence affectively entangled with notions of identification and metonymy. Aesthetics and its role in the formation of solidarities is also the subject of Patricia McManus' critical engagement with the possibility of repurposing Adorno's work on solidarity outside of its conceptual origins. Like Ikoniadou she looks at the potentially debilitating effect of Cold War mobilisations of state 'socialism' on conceptualising solidarity. Her engagement with the possibilities and limitations of Western Marxism of the period is undertaken in order to 'refigure what a radical imagination of solidarity can do'.

The advantage of an edited collection of essays lies precisely in the possibility to bring together a variety of articulations into a single volume. It allows us to include the narratives and experiences of veteran activists, as we do here with the testimonies of Bernadette Devlin McAliskey and Helen Lackner, as well as shed light on forgotten voices in the archives, as with the manifesto of artists at the Salón de Mayo in Cuba in 1967; and to reproduce artistic expressions of transnational solidarity, such as the work of Dia al-Azzawi. In doing so, we attempt to trouble the supposed gap between academics and activists, historical document and artwork. Research on activism is not only enriched by the testimonies of activists but often comes from an experience of activism or *is* a site of activism, not least in the will to expose epistemological violence and produce knowledge that undoes the silences in history. We are not claiming to have a complete overview of the period's transnational networks of solidarity: there is much we have not covered and more of which we remain unaware. This volume is an invitation for more work on solidarity and in solidarity.

Notes

1 Jorge Poblete and Patrick J. McDonnell, 'For Many Chileans, U.S. Demonstrations Spark Reminders of Impassioned Chile Protests', *Los Angeles Times*, 15 June 2020.
2 Ahmed Masoud, 'Let's Measure the Exact Angle: A Palestinian Perspective on the Maxine Peake controversy', *Ceasefire*, online magazine, posted on 30 June 2020, https://ceasefiremagazine.co.uk/lets-measure-exact-angle/.
3 See for instance, Gerd-Rainer Horn, *The Spirit of '68: Rebellion in Western Europe and North America, 1956–1976* (Oxford: Oxford University Press, 2007); Ernesto Laclau and Chantal Mouffe, *Hegemony and Socialist Strategy: Towards a Radical Democratic Politics* (London: Verso 2001 [1985]), pp. 161–73; Arthur Marwick, *The Sixties: Cultural Revolution in Britain, France, Italy, and the United States, c.1958–c.1974* (Oxford: Oxford University Press, 1998).
4 Manning Marable, *Transnational Blackness: Navigating the Global Colour Line* (New York: Palgrave Macmillan, 2008), p. 7.
5 Foundational literature includes: Samantha Christiansen and Zachari Scarlett (eds) *The Third World in the Global 1960s* (Oxford: Berghahn Books, 2013); Fredric Jameson, 'Periodizing the 60s', in S. Sayres, A. Stephanson, S. Aronowitz and F. Jameson *The 60s Without Apology* (Minneapolis: University of Minnesota Press in cooperation with *Social Text*, 1984), pp. 178–209; George Katsiaficas, *The Imagination of the New Left: A Global Analysis of 1968* (Cambridge, MA: South End Press, 1987); Kristen Ross, *May '68 and its Afterlives* (Chicago: University of Chicago Press 2002); Jeremy Varon, *Bringing the War Home: the Weather Underground, the Red Army Faction, and Revolutionary Violence in the Sixties and Seventies* (Berkeley: University of California

Press, 2004); Cynthia Ann Young, *Soul Power: Culture, Radicalism, and the Making of a U.S. Third World Left* (Durham, NC: Duke University Press, 2006).
6 Christiansen and Scarlett, *The Third World in the Global 1960s*, p. 1.
7 Ross, *May '68 and its Afterlives*, p. 9.
8 See Jameson, 'Periodizing the 60s'; Ross, *May '68 and its Afterlives*, p. 26.
9 Christiansen and Scarlett, *The Third World in the Global Sixties*, pp. 3–5. For related work, see also Chen Jian, Martin Klimke, Masha Kirasirova, Mary Nolan, Marilyn. Young and Joanna Waley-Cohen (eds), *The Routledge Handbook of the Global Sixties: Between Protest and Nation-Building* (London: Routledge, 2018); and Tamara Chaplin and Jadwiga E. Pieper Mooney (eds), *The Global 1960s: Convention, Contest and Counterculture* (London: Routledge, 2017).
10 This scholarship has a wide historical and geographical scope – we name just a few of the important works that have placed the agency of the colonised at the centre of their studies. The work on transnational solidarity in the Atlantic world of Marcus Rediker and Peter Linebaugh's *Many Headed Hydra* (Boston: Beacon Press, 2000); recent work on African American anticolonial politics by Minkah Makalani, *In the Cause of Freedom* (Chapel Hill: University of North Carolina Press, 2011) and Benjamin Balthaser *Anti-Imperialist Modernism* (Ann Arbor: University of Michigan Press, 2016); Priyamvada Gopal's seminal *Insurgent Empire: Anticolonial Resistance and British Dissent* (London & New York: Verso, 2019); John Chalcraft, *Popular Politics in the Making of the Modern Middle East* (Cambridge: Cambridge University Press, 2016); see the Roundtable 'Why Decolonization', convened by Cyrus Schayegh and Yoav Di-Capua, in the *International Journal of Middle East Studies*, 52 (2020), 137–145; Ruth Craggs and Claire Wintle (eds) *Cultures of Decolonization: Transnational Productions and Practices, 1945–1970* (Manchester: Manchester University Press, 2016).
11 Bernadette (Devlin) McAliskey, 'A Peasant in the Halls of the Great', in M. Farrell (ed.) *Twenty Years On* (Dingle, Ireland: Brandon Book Publishers, 1988), p. 87.
12 Gregory M. Maney 'Transnational Mobilization and Civil Rights in Northern Ireland', *Social Problems*, 47:2 (2000), 169–70.
13 Devlin McAliskey's keynote delivered during the conference 'The Radical Sixties: Aesthetics, Politics and Histories of Solidarity', at the University of Brighton, 27–29 June 2019, transcribed in this volume.
14 Reem Abou-El-Fadl, Leslie James, Rachel Leow, Su Lin Lewis, Gerard McCann and Carolien Stolte, 'Manifesto: Networks of Decolonization in Asia and Africa', *Radical History Review*, 131 (2018), 176.
15 David Featherstone, *Solidarity: Hidden Histories and Geographies of Internationalism* (London: Zed Books 2012), p. 12.

16 Jacques Rancière, 'The Cause of the Other', *Parallax*, 4:2 (1998), 31.
17 Gopal, *Insurgent Empire*, pp. 6–7.
18 Ibid., p. 7.
19 Ibid., p. 18.
20 Jameson, 'Periodizing the 60s'.
21 Ross, *May '68 and its Afterlives*, pp. 10–11.
22 Ibid., pp. 82–4.
23 Robin Kelley, *Freedom Dreams: The Black Radical Imagination* (Boston: Freedom Press, 2002); Hakim Adi, *Pan-Africanism and Communism: the Communist International, Africa and the Diaspora 1919–1939* (Trenton: Africa World Press, 2013); Cedric J. Robinson, *Black Marxism* (London: Zed, 1983); Jonathan Derrick, *Africa's Agitators: Militant Anti-Colonialism in Africa and the West, 1918–1939* (New York: Columbia University Press, 2008); Brent Edwards, *The Practice of Diaspora: Literature, Translation, and the Rise of Black Internationalism* (Cambridge, MA: Harvard University Press, 2003).
24 Cynthia Young, *Soul Power: Culture, Radicalism, and the Making of a U.S. Third World Left* (Durham, NC: Duke University Press, 2006), p. 52.
25 Ibid., p. 5.
26 Ibid., pp. 9–10.
27 Kathleen Cleaver and George Katsiaficas (eds) *Liberation, Imagination and the Black Panther Party* (London & New York: Routledge, 2001), p. 125.
28 Noura Erakat and Marc Lamont Hill 'Black-Palestinian Transnational Solidarity: Renewals, Returns, and Practice', *Journal of Palestine Studies* 48:4 (2019), 8.
29 Jeremy Varon, Michael S. Foley and John McMillian. 'Time is an Ocean: The Past and Future of the Sixties', *The Sixties*, 1:1 (2008), 1–7.
30 Zeina Maasri, *Cosmopolitan Radicalism: The Visual Politics of Beirut's Global Sixties* (Cambridge: Cambridge University Press 2020), p. 13.
31 We borrow the suffix 'scapes' from Arjun Appadurai in describing the political landscapes imagined and shaped by transnational networks of solidarity to stress that these are perspectival constructs: Appadurai, *Modernity at Large: The Cultural Dimensions of Globalization* (Minneapolis: University of Minnesota Press, 1996), p. 33.
32 Ross, *May '68 and its Afterlives*, p. 81.
33 Varon, *Bringing the War Home*. p. 124.
34 Jeffrey James Byrne, *Mecca of Revolution: Algeria, Decolonization, and the Third World Order* (Oxford: Oxford University Press, 2016), p. 8.
35 Maasri, *Cosmopolitan Radicalism*, pp. 8–11.

36 See Yezid Sayigh, *Armed Struggle and the Search for State: The Palestinian National Movement, 1949–1993* (Oxford: Oxford University Press, 1999), p. 200 and Fawwaz Traboulsi, 'De la Suisse orientale au Hanoi arabe: une ville en quête de rôles', in Jad Tabit (ed.), *Beyrouth* (Paris: Institut français d'architecture, 2001), pp. 28–41.

37 See Omar Jabary Salamanca, 'The Palestinian 1968: struggles for dignity and solidarity', *Rekto: Verso* published online 31 May 2018; for solidarity with Palestine in print cultures see Maasri, *Cosmopolitan Radicalism*; in art exhibitions see Kristine Khuri and Rasha Salti (eds) *Past Disquiet: Artists, International Solidarity, and Museums-in-Exile* (Warsaw: Museum of Modern Art in Warsaw, 2018); in theatre and literature, particularly in the Moroccan-based magazine *Souffle*, see Olivia Harrison, *Transcolonial Maghreb: Imagining Palestine in the Era of Decolonization* (Stanford: Stanford University Press, 2016); in film see Nadia G. Yaqub, *Palestinian Cinema in the Days of Revolution* (Texas: University of Texas Press, 2018) and Olivia Harrison, 'Consuming Palestine: Anticapitalism and Anticolonialism in Jean-Luc Godard's Ici Et Ailleurs', *Studies in French Cinema*, 18:3 (2018), 178–91.

38 Maasri, *Cosmopolitan Radicalism*, pp. 216–20.

39 Ibid., p. 222.

40 Appadurai, *Modernity at Large*, p. 31.

41 Jeremy Prestholdt, 'Resurrecting Che: Radicalism, the Transnational Imagination, and the Politics of Heroes', *Journal of Global History*, 7:3 (2012), 509.

42 Ibid., 507.

43 Herbert Marcuse, *An Essay on Liberation* (Boston: Beacon Press, 1969).

44 Raymond Williams, *The Long Revolution* (London: Chatto & Windus, 1961).

45 Studies of social movements have increasingly focused on the role of emotion in political mobilization, see for example: Jeff Goodwin, James M. Jasper and Francesca Poletta (eds), *Passionate Politics: Emotions and Social Movements* (Chicago: University of Chicago Press, 2001) ; Helena Flam and Debra King (eds), *Emotions and Social Movements* (London: Routledge, 2005) ; 'Emotions and Contentious Politics [Special Issue]', *Mobilization: An International Quarterly* 7:2 (2002), 107–229; Joachim C. Häberlen and Russell A. Spinney (eds) 'Emotions in Protest Movements in Europe since 1917 [Special Issue]', *Contemporary European History*, 23:4 (2014), 489–655.

46 Over the last few years, there has been several exhibitions, conferences and volumes dedicated to international networks of artistic solidarity, including: Jessica Stites Mor and Maria del Carmenr Suescun Pozas (eds) *The Art of Solidarity: Visual and Performative Politics in Cold*

War Latin America (Texas: University of Texas Press, 2018); Khuri and Salti's edited volume *Past Disquiet* and related touring exhibition, on show at the Museu d'Art Contemporani de Barcelona (2015), the Haus der Kultur en der Welt in Berlin (2016) and Sursock Museum in Beirut (2018); the conference 'Axis of Solidarity: Landmarks, Platforms, Futures' organised by Tate Modern in London (2019); Mary Ikoniadou's and Zeina Maasri's session 'Visual Solidarities: Crossing borders in Aesthetic Practices' at the Association for Art History (2019); the exhibition 'Notes on Solidarity: Tricontinentalism in Print' curated by Debra Lennard and hosted by The Center for the Humanities James Gallery in New York (2019); the exhibition 'Designed in Cuba: Cold War Graphics' at the House of Illustration in London (2019).
47 Khuri and Salti, introduction to *Past Disquiet*.
48 Emory Douglas, *Black Panther: The Revolutionary Art of Emory Douglas* (New York: Rizzoli, 2007), p. 62.
49 Ibid., pp. 100–1.
50 See Anne Garland Mahler, *From the Tricontinental to the Global South: Race, Radicalism, and Transnational Solidarity* (Durham, NC: Duke University Press, 2018).
51 For further insight on OSPAAAL's posters see: Lincoln Cushing, *Revolución! Cuban Poster Art* (San Francisco: Chronicle Books, 2003) and Richard Frick (ed.) *The Tricontinental Solidarity Poster* (Bern: Comedia-Verlag, 2003).
52 Khuri and Salti, *Past Disquiet*, p. 45.
53 Keeanga-Yamahtta Taylor, *How We Get Free* (Chicago: Haymarket, 2017), pp. 44–5.
54 Robin Kelley, *Freedom Dreams: The Black Radical Imagination* (Boston: Beacon Press, 2003), p. 63.
55 This transformative element of political solidarity is touched upon in Featherstone's enriching work on solidarity which he defines as 'a relation forged through political struggle which seeks to challenge forms of oppression', Featherstone *Solidarity*, p. 5.
56 Jacques Rancière 'The Cause of the Other', *Parallax*, 4:2 (1998), 31.
57 Ibid., 29.
58 James Baldwin, cited in Bill V. Mullen *James Baldwin: Living in Fire* (London: Pluto Press, 2019), p.115.
59 Rancière, 'The Cause of the Other', 31.
60 Ibid., 31.
61 Chandra Talpade Mohanty, *Feminism Without Borders: Decolonizing Theory, Practicing Solidarity* (Durham, NC: Duke University Press, 2003), p. 7
62 Ibid.,

63 Doreen Massey, *World City* (Cambridge: Cambridge Polity: 2007), p. 21.
64 Cited in Quỳnh N. Phạm and Robbie Shilliam (eds), *Meanings of Bandung* (London & New York: Rowman & Littlefield, 2016), p. 101.
65 Paul Gilroy, *Between Camps: Nation, Culture and the Allure of Race* (London: Penguin, 2000), p. 218.
66 Laleh Khalili, *Time in the Shadows: Confinement in Counterinsurgencies* (Stanford: Stanford University Press, 2013), p. 227.
67 Nikhil Pal Singh, *Black is a Country: Race and the Unfinished Struggle for Democracy* (Cambridge, MA: Harvard University Press, 2005), p. 161.

1

'We took the notion'[1]

Bernadette Devlin McAliskey

If you look at that period of the mid-sixties, in an international sense, you could ask what possessed a small group of people on the island of Ireland to get so obstreperous and annoyed, when there were bigger things happening in the world. The sixties saw the beginnings of the second wave of feminism, which came to fruition in the early seventies. We saw the beginning of the youth movement, where young people, a sufficient distance from Second World War poverty and the memory of war, were themselves becoming obstreperous. For example, I grew up in a generation which astounds my granddaughter. She's now twenty-two, and she just cannot believe the things her poor grandmother had to put up with, like not being able to drink beer out of a pint glass. Young women, certainly where I lived, weren't allowed unaccompanied into public houses (pubs) in the sixties. If we went in a group with at least one male to get us through the door, there was a certain area in public houses where females, not 'tamed by any real human being', would be allowed to sit, usually where nobody else could see them. Now that, to my granddaughter's generation, is probably a greater sin than the fact that we didn't have the vote; and that, by 1968, we'd had emergency legislation in place for almost fifty years.

The Northern Ireland in which I came to be a young teenager was the product of history, and the reality of life for us was that we knew our place. And our place was not to question the things that were reality in our daily lives. Not to question the fact that this small 'country', which isn't a country, it isn't an anything, it's not really a region, it's not a province, because all the bits of borders divide the region, the province, the country – but it's a place, and it's home. In that place, if the nationalist population – a population that is, and considers itself first and foremost to be, Irish – and if the population that is, and considers itself first and foremost to be, British, were delineated by skin colour you could have visibly identified segregation and separatism that might have been equalled only in South Africa. And to this day, at the end of a long peace process that's still the reality. The legacy is that we still have separate education; we still have effectively separate housing; and when it comes to electoral areas, in 86 per cent of our electoral districts, the population of one side or the other still exceeds 70 per cent.[2]

So, we still have a political system, as we did at that time, that is based on that dichotomy. It's been that way since the country was partitioned in 1921–24. And ever since then we have lived in a divided and conflicted place.

When we came to 1968 something happened, something was happening, that created another reality – the pretence of normality could no longer hold; that tension could no longer hold. And we have to look and see what caused that. Part of it was what was happening outside. If I look to myself, what was it that influenced me? What was it somehow that made me look at what was happening and get on the 'civil rights bus'? And I got on it, it just stopped, it stopped near me, and I got on it. But what brought me to that point? And what brought other people to the point where we felt that bus had stopped where we were; that we were destined to get on it, that it was our bus?

There were a number of things. The single biggest thing that people will point to, outside of Ireland, was the black civil rights movement in America. Now that didn't mean that we were all studying it or understood it but that it was the single biggest thing to which we related; and what created that was the availability of television from the mid-fifties. We could see what was happening on the screens. We could see people in America, whose skin was a different colour to ours, but I don't remember noticing that as a matter of distinction. What I saw was a matter of commonality. People marching to say that they had no votes. And we're looking at them saying 'Neither have we! Neither have we, we're the same as them'. People who are marching to say that because of who they were they couldn't get work. That they had to live in certain areas, and essentially weren't able and weren't allowed to spread out to somewhere else and couldn't afford to. Simplistically: they were us, and we were them!

In that sense our first understanding, and quite a lot of people my age would say that, our first understanding of who we were, came from looking at others who were in the same boat as us, and yet, if you were coming from a different perspective, they were very different from us. So we made our first solidarity with our own pain. There was no great moral solidarity with other people's plight. It was people who were much the same as us.

From '64 to '68 there had been a movement that was mirroring, copying, learning, in a broad sense, from the various parts of the American movement. That's really what was happening. People were, before we had the internet or before we had today's technology, cutting and pasting, that's what we were doing. There was no real analysis, there was no depth of understanding, we were 'cutting and pasting', from '64 to '68. There was a broad social justice reform movement that was doing all the things people ought to do – lobbying politicians. And it actually built a strong Irish reform movement in the British Labour Party.

But no matter what they did, nothing was moving in Northern Ireland. So in 1968 the leaders of that reform movement had slogans that were very simple: 'One man, one vote; One family, one house' – because housing and votes were tied. Now, it wasn't that we didn't have a vote at a Westminster election, we did, but because of the segregation of housing, and where people were allowed to live, who could get elected to Westminster was the same all the time.[3] At local government level the voting system was based on the rates system. If you were a slum landlord, and had a hundred slum housing units, in which people lived, you got a hundred votes. And the hundred people who lived in your slum tenancies got none. This was nineteen hundred and sixty-eight in the 'mother of all parliaments': in the United Kingdom. You hear that phrase very often, as if it was 'the birthplace of democracy'. Well, we got no votes. So the impact of the voting system was overcrowding, and you see the South African parallels, you see the Palestinian parallels. Overcrowding and poor conditions and slum dwellings were intricately tied to not having a vote and to the gerrymandering of the Westminster and the Stormont elections.

The other slogan was 'One person, one job'. It also was actually 'One man, one job', but none of us noticed. We assumed that if women had a vote, and were allowed out of the house, they should have equality of employment too. And again in 1968, because we're talking about the things that caused an uprising, the economic boom across the UK created work and opportunities. This meant that in the 'mainstream' or unionist population, unemployment fell in many areas below 4 and 5 per cent. But when you looked in Derry, in Strabane, in the Catholic ghetto areas, unemployment remained as high as thirty per cent. And not because people were 'lazy', or all the other things we hear about the unemployed. There was simply no work in these areas.

There was something else very crucial that happened at that point. I was born in 1947 – that's not really the significant thing that happened – 1947 was also when the Westminster authority pushed the Education Act into effect in Northern Ireland over the heads of the Stormont parliament in Belfast who voted against it. The Act effectively allowed the poor to be educated; it equalised education. John Hume and the Social Democrats, the reformers, were the first generation of Catholics to benefit from the Education Act. They were the people who got to university, got professions, and then were aware of the ceiling they couldn't get through. It didn't matter what they had, they couldn't get 'in' to the society in which they lived.

People like me were the second generation. And two things happened at that point. The second generation of beneficiaries get to be ungrateful. We saw education as our right. Our mothers' and fathers' generation saw education as a hard-won concession. Something happens then in folk memory, that you remember something that you thought you didn't know in the first place, but somewhere within your DNA, you always knew it. There was a saying that was said down generations of our people: 'Lie down, lie down, you Fenian hound, don't bite the hand that feeds you.' And my generation was a generation of young people who decided we'd bite the arm off them if we took the notion. And that was part of that whole international impact of seeing things were happening; seeing what was happening in the student movement; the whole youth rock rebellion of elbow room for kids. We were in this revolution, if that's what it was, we were in this maelstrom, we were riding this tsunami, before we even knew we were in it. And it was controlling us before we learned to surf the wave. And by the time we'd stopped cutting and pasting and were beginning to understand and analyse deeper – because the more active you were, the deeper you had to think – we were already halfway to military conflict.

What took us there was a number of things: the inability of the British government to behave in any way other than it had always done to defend its imperialist colonial interest, which was to repress, to oppress, and then, finally, to shoot everything that moved; and our inability to clearly understand that, historically having always responded in armed resistance, to understand that's why we always 'got beat'. And we went straight back into it again. But what historically took us to that point went further back than those bits and pieces of what was happening in the world and what was happening in the lifetime of the state. Where we came to in 1968, where Palestine came to, where South Africa came to, where Quebec came to, where the Afro-Americans came to in the sixties was written in the sands of the birth of the British Empire, and European empires. And as my father taught me – I was well reared – my father taught me as a child, of the rape and plunder of Africa and the Southern Hemisphere, to fatten the British Crown.

And notable here is that space between what is individual, let us say, what's highly personal, and what is the collective experience. They feed into each other, but they're very different, and they are quite often in significant tension. Part of the thing that I remember over the whole period of struggle, was that we didn't cry at funerals. If you ever, ever look at them you can see that we, in Ireland, through the whole conflict, do not cry at funerals. And that was because there was a collective determination not to – because we had to fight our way to funerals – if you've ever seen some of the videos of funerals in Northern Ireland, looking back at them, they're traumatic. You'd have the military and the police trying to prevent a public burial, from their point of view – being used as a demonstration. For everybody this was a public mobilisation, including for the people who were burying primarily their fathers, their sons, their brothers, their loved ones. And nobody cried, nobody was 'allowed' to cry, nobody allowed themselves to cry. So that leads to not talking either, about what happened.

One of the biggest things for me was that I was on the platform on Bloody Sunday.[4] I'm the only person who's looking in the opposite direction to the crowd with the exception of a few other people on the platform, but I had been just about to speak, when the army opened fire. The bulk of people couldn't see what was happening, because they had their backs to the army. There were people down at the back who were directly in the firing line, but I could see. It took thirty years to get a public inquiry, and then we were all called to give testimony, and it was at that point that many of us, including myself, realised that after that day, after the funerals, after I'd hit Reggie Maudling – and I didn't hit him hard enough – we never actually spoke of Bloody Sunday again.[5] We marched about it, but amongst ourselves, we never spoke about it, until we all had to give these statements and individually remember it. The conversation about Bloody Sunday started thirty years later. One of the things I said: 'Do you know what I remember most, you all left me there. I was on the platform and you all scattered, and left me.' It never came up for thirty years. And then at that moment I remembered the small things of it rather than the politics. I remembered somebody came back for me, but the person who came back for me didn't come from Derry, he was a person from my own town. He wasn't even from the city. That knowledge/memory lay undiscovered in my mind for thirty years.

There's a bit about carrying the narrative of the struggle that – dangerously I think, when you reflect on it – removes pain. You have to erase a lot of truth to erase pain but you also erase a lot of learning, so that when it comes, as we say in Ireland (because we've had 700 years of it) when it comes to the next time round, you don't know where you are. You don't know where you are because you can't envisage what you don't know, and the knowledge has been buried or erased. There is something frightening about that erasure that almost predestines you to make the same mistake again, and to think it doesn't and won't hurt to be mistaken.

I think when we say 'we're not allowed' we collectively and individually do not allow ourselves because we have battles to fight, we have wars to win, we have lines to hold. It's a choice. But it's a choice that you almost aren't totally conscious that you're making, until you're out the other side of it; and then there's no collective language for it.

There was a peace and there's a whole separate narrative about what the peace process did. But the lived reality is worse than the story because of world changes – we're not in the booming economics of the sixties. We're sitting on the verge of world fascism. We're living in a time of austerity. The word has been stood on its head. Thatcher created decades of really crass, vulgar, inhumane neoliberalism, which I just call capitalism.

And in that context, we almost have less than we had when we started, but we're supposed to be grateful that we have peace. But if we had got what we were entitled to before we started, we never would have had war, to be grateful for peace. But there are whole layers of people who, buying into the narrative, then didn't get the peace dividend. So you begin to see where not truly understanding, not taking time to reflect, leads. These young people say, 'Well, we fought our way to the negotiating table, and didn't get enough, so we need to start and fight our way to another table'. But that's not actually what happened. We got to a negotiating table because it finally dawned on everybody that you could fight ad-infinitum and it wasn't going to solve anything. But that knowledge and truth is lost.

And when you get to the other side of the equation, and the dreaded British public, which fascinates me, how could a population on an island be so ignorant of who they are? How can the population of this island (Great Britain), never mind the one I live on, be so ignorant of who they are? Of their own history? Because it's an imperialist country, history was only taught in a certain way, and when the history didn't hold, how would you go into the poor areas of London and tell them how Britain was great? Because they'd be saying, 'Well, where's my share? How come I got none of it?' So in all of that pain, and having no language, it feeds populism, and blindly following people who *do* have words is the way to go. Those for whom *Rule Britannia* no longer cuts it, they don't have anything real, because they're not ruling.[6] The marginal benefit of being on the same side as the king, or going home on the winners' bus, is the only cultural benefit. But this no longer exists for those in poverty who are loyalists, for the poor who believe in Rule Britannia. There is nothing real, and they have no words, no new direction and to my mind, we forget those people at our peril because they're also our people. They are also ours. And they're stuck in that mindset. So I think there's something very important around that which needs to be done.

If we are in the serious business of recognising that the Empire is done, then we are no longer in a position of fighting the Empire. We have to be in the discussion of what kind of island are we going to build. That is the discussion. And we cannot build an island, we cannot build a nation, we can't build a state, we can't build a new republic, that has at its core a new disadvantaged, marginalised, isolated community, which is the Northern Protestant. We can't do that.

Part of the legacy of our past is the denial of pain. When we come to the legacy of the past, if we are honest and truthful with ourselves, we will never go to war again. And if we can't hold the British government to account, we will see them in the Hague before we're finished, for war crimes against the people of the North of Ireland. And I do not say that lightly, because whether we wanted to be or not, we were their citizens, and it would appear from the evidence we now see that they armed both sides of their own population through MI5 and MI6 and sustained a war; that they 'ran the war', controlled, funded and sustained it, themselves, for thirty years. Their soldiers and their agents in Republican and Loyalist organisations; their death squads, with the knowledge of the state and with impunity, just killed all around them. That takes us back to another question: where did they learn that? They learned that in Palestine, they learned that in Aden, they learned that in Africa. Why would they not do it when it is that which made them great? And when the British people understand that they have a different history to the one they imagine – their learned history is a lie or the perspective only of their imperial lords – then we might actually have a federal socialist republic of these two islands.

The inevitable demise for Empire and Kingdom comes when somebody who didn't buy into the programme tells the truth, that the emperor has no clothes, and everybody else realises it: 'Oh my god, this is true'. That day is coming.

Notes

1 The following text is abridged from a speech given at the opening roundtable of 'The Radical Sixties: Aesthetics, Politics and Histories of Solidarity' Conference held at the University of Brighton, UK, from 27 to 29 June 2019. Contextual annotations have been added by Cathy Bergin.
2 The Good Friday Agreement signed in 1998 is generally seen as ending the 'Troubles' in Northern Ireland which were a period of state and counter-state violence of over thirty years. The peace process has for many seen the entrenchment of the sectarian divide between Protestants and Catholics.
3 As a region of the United Kingdom, Northern Ireland's parliamentary system includes representation in the UK seat of Government at Westminster in London and representation in the Northern Irish legislative assembly at Stormont in Northern Ireland.
4 On Bloody Sunday, 30 January 1972, the British Parachute Regiment opened fire on a civil rights demonstration in Derry killing fourteen unarmed protesters.
5 The day after the massacre of Bloody Sunday, Reginald Maudling, the Conservative Home Secretary, defended the actions of the soldiers in the Westminster Parliament. Bernadette, MP for Mid Ulster and witness to the events of the day before, was refused the floor and slapped Reginald Maudling for his lies and refusal to let her speak.
6 *Rule Britannia* is a jingoistic British song which extols the glory of empire and colonialism.

2

The voice of the immigrant worker and the rise and fall of France's long 1968

Matt Myers

Michel de Certeau, writing in the aftermath of May 1968, argued that 'Last May, speech was taken [*on a pris la parole*] the way, in 1789, the Bastille was taken.'[1] Echoing de Certeau, Kristen Ross has described May as a 'flight from social determinations, with displacements that took people outside of their location in society, with a disjunction, that is, between political subjectivity and the social group'.[2] Yet if one follows de Certeau's phrase to the next line, one finds the subject and space which this speech has been reclaimed by and within. What had been stormed by the '*travailleurs étudiants* [student-workers]' and '*ouvriers* [manual workers]' was command over the means of communication which had previously imprisoned them within their old subaltern roles.[3] 'Emerging from who knows where, suddenly filling the streets and the factories, circulating among us, becoming ours but no longer as the muffled noise of our solitude, voices that had never been heard began to change us.'[4] In the following decade, those on the left most imprinted by their 1968 experience sought to find, nurture and to channel this insurgent collective voice into a project of total social transformation. The immigrant worker and their unskilled and semi-skilled workmates would become the subjects *par excellence* of this imagined rupture. By attempting to relate to this multinational, gendered, racialised and culturally diverse sector of the working class, the proliferating revolutionary organisations which grew out of the libertarian and anti-hierarchical culture of May's student and intellectual milieu attempted to create spaces where they could capture this group's right to speak.[5] Disruptive new understandings of class solidarity broke from the confines of the nation-state and its working-class citizenry. By focusing on the importance of the immigrant worker's imagined voice for the French New Left, this chapter shows the fundamental importance of new conceptions of solidarity in sustaining a moment of revolutionary hope.

This chapter argues that this insurgent worker's voice described by de Certeau had an important, though overlooked, articulation. The defining collective subject of the 'long 1968s' revolutionary *prise de parole* was not an abstract *ouvrier* but a worker of a certain type: the 'O.S.' (*Ouvrier Specialisé*). With resonances with the concept of the *operaio massa* (mass worker) in Italy, the O.S. were confined to the most monotonous, alienating, segmented and dangerous tasks on the factory production line. These 'semi-skilled' workers were recruited by industrialists predominantly from former French colonies, Europe's Mediterranean hinterlands and France's own rural or peripheral population.[6] An inclusive category of class rather than 'race' provided the French New Left with a language to imagine the amalgam of culturally diverse national groups as a collective subject. Xavier Vigna has noted that 'the O.S. symbolised another industrial working class: combative of course, but above all composed of young people, women, and immigrants'.[7] Laure Pitti has shown the convergence of experiences between the conditions of young workers and the immigrant O.S., even as their representation in historical memory since 1968 has radically diverged.[8] Indeed three of the main subjects of the 'new social movements', which Alain Touraine defined outside the world of work, were over-represented amongst the O.S. Though immigrant workers have been central to the development of 'Fordism' in the twentieth century and the spread of the production line (*la chaîne*) in the global car industry, they have appeared less prominently in narratives of labour and working-class protest during the long seventies.[9]

The scholarly turn away from labour history after the mid-1970s and framing of May 1968 as a primarily cultural and intellectual revolt has underplayed the central role of immigrant workers. This chapter argues that the immigrant worker is neither secondary to the 'long 1968', nor were immigrants confined 'to the margins' in its aftermath.[10] For those to the left of the PCF (the French Communist Party) during 1968, the immigrant O.S. replaced the skilled metal worker as the archetype working-class political subject.[11] Without legal, social or cultural ties to the nation-state, immigrant workers were seen as autonomous of the corporatist, reformist or 'revisionist' positions seen to hold back the native working class from its revolutionary potential. The French New Left sought to offer solidarity to these workers not only due to their marginalisation and experience of racism, but because their structural position within the labour process and the global division of labour was perceived to be industrial capitalism's weak link. The alienation of the O.S. from their work on the production line and their inability to upskill generated expectations on the French far-left that they could overturn the whole capitalist factory-labour system without the need for electoral victories or trade union mediation. A rebellion in French factories was hoped to undermine 'imperialism' and the conditions that had produced the poverty, unemployment and underdevelopment propelling migrants from their countries of origin. Such workplace struggles over categorisation, conditions, speed-ups and dignity in the early 1970s would in turn generate wider political, intellectual and journalistic interest outside the radical left.[12]

French leftist activists relating to immigrant workers and their struggles was not new. Solidarity actions by thousands of French sympathisers of the FLN (Front de libération nationale) and the Algerian cause had earned them the title of '*les Porteurs de valises*'.[13] The kinds of actions and imaginaries of the post-1968 generation were, however, distinct, even if there were clear overlaps in personnel, imaginaries and repertoires. Nor was the French left the only one to centre immigrant workers. At a pan-European conference in Zurich, the Italian group Potere Operaio argued that the 'mass worker' – the Italian equivalent of the O.S. – had become almost totally synonymous with the immigrant worker.[14] The effort to relate to the immigrant workers in their respective countries allowed such groups across the industrialised core in Western Europe to think globally while acting locally.

The Union des jeunesses communistes marxistes-léninistes (UJCml) (later Gauche Prolétarienne (GP)), Vive la Révolution, Révolution!, Ligue Communiste, and other far-left groups through the 'long 1968' understood the O.S. immigrant worker to be an exemplary revolutionary subject. Making up a multinational workforce without formal citizenship rights (such as right to vote in French national elections – or even until the early 1970s – in trade union elections), they were portrayed as emblematic both of an 'epoch of imperialism' as well as the increasing globalisation and centralisation of capital. As one Moroccan immigrant worker and GP activist called Mokhtar put it: 'if there is no participation of the immigrant industrial workers (*ouvriers immigrés*) in the revolution in France, there will be something but there will never be a revolution ... never the workers in power'.[15] The *ouvrièrisme* (workerism) of groups like the GP was founded not on the 'traditional' working class composed of older, qualified French worker-citizens but of the newly gendered, racialised and young sections of the 'new' working class. Though never counting more than a few thousand activists and with a highly amorphous membership structure, the GP became prominent in French national life during the early 1970s for its adept use of well-publicised actions and super star intellectual supporters. Amongst its members, sympathisers or close collaborators stood many of those who would define French intellectual and cultural life over the following decades: Benny Lévy, Alain Geismar, Serge July, Olivier Rolin, Gérard Miller, Jean-Claude Milner, Marin Karmitz, André Glucksmann, Robert Linhart, Christain Jambet, Michel Le Bris as well as Jean-Paul Sartre, Simone de Beauvoir, Gilles Deleuze, Michel Foucault, Jacques Rancière and Jean-Luc Godard. Despite its prominence and the lasting impact its sympathisers had on French society, the GP has elicited very little serious archival or historical work.

Immigrants into workers

Given the political focus by the 1968 left on the industrial working class, the weight of O.S. within French industry was of political as well as an economic or sociological significance. Immigrant workers made up 6.3 per cent of the French workforce in 1968 (1.25 million) and around 20 per cent of all industrial workers.[16] This increased through the 1960s until the mid-1970s. Between 1962 and 1974 foreign workers made up around 80 per cent of the total increase in male workers in France.[17] In 1954 the O.S. made up 28 per cent of the industrial workforce; this rose to 37 per cent in 1975 to equal the number of qualified workers for the first time.[18] Moreover, the vast majority of immigrant workers in France were concentrated in manual industry: 68.5 per cent in semi-skilled (O.S.) or unskilled posts (36.6 per cent for the former and 31.6 per cent for the latter).[19] Certain national groups were invariably over-represented as O.S. and unskilled workers: Portuguese, 70 per cent; Tunisians, 70.3 per cent; Moroccans, 81.4 per cent Algerians, 87.2 per cent. Previous waves of European populations like Spaniards, Italians and Poles were less likely to be unskilled and semi-skilled, having progressed up the skill hierarchy as new arrivals replaced them at the bottom. In the Lyon metal industry, the division between French and immigrant workers was matched onto division of skill and status: 17 per cent of French employees were managers or technicians, 6 per cent were other non-manual, 59 per cent were skilled manual workers, while only 18 per cent were unskilled or semi-skilled (O.S.). Meanwhile North African workers made up 0.15 per cent of the non-manual, 5.7 per cent of the skilled and 94 per cent of the O.S. or unskilled while Italian migrants made 1 per cent of the non-manual, 33 per cent of the skilled workers and 66 per cent of the O.S. or unskilled.[20] The vast majority of immigrant workers in France worked either as O.S. or as unskilled labourers, while only a tiny proportion rose into higher grades.

Even though immigrant workers made up a sizeable part of the industrial working class during the largest general strike in European history, their image in 1968 and in subsequent years has often been expunged or downplayed (even if elements of the Left at the time had foregrounded their actions). At Renault Billancourt in 1971 – the factory that was said to 'give France a cold every time it sneezed' – 69.1 per cent of the workers were O.S. while 40.1 per cent of these were North African (95 per cent of Algerian workers at the most symbolic factory in France were O.S.).[21] At the gates of the Renault-Flins factory which saw fierce battles between workers, students, and the police in June 1968, the role of student activists was overemphasised in news reports at the expense of immigrant workers who were (misleadingly) described as playing little role in the strikes and fleeing from the disorders (sometimes back to their country of origin).[22] Given that the demands won by the general strike of May–June 1968 did not foreground specific demands of the O.S. (with the Confédération générale du travail (CGT) union taking specific interest in the early 1970s), the revolutionary potential of this worker-category would only be drawn to popular attention from 1971 with the strikes by 'these new unskilled workers' at Renault Le Mans and then at Penarroya in Lyon in February–March 1972, and then in Renault Billancourt in March–April 1973.[23] The *gauchiste* left had, however, been long predicting these forms of 'worker insubordination' which was still largely conceived within the bounds of the factory.[24] A document by the *gauchiste*-linked Renault Billancourt 'Immigrant Group' for an international conference on the auto-industry activists involving participants from Italy, Britain, Germany, Switzerland and France in April 1973 reported that the O.S. was 'the driving force behind the wage-struggle movement for greater social wealth … it is in the large car factories that most of the advanced objectives and forms of struggle have been developed, to be then generalized by the whole working class'.[25]

The struggles of the O.S. attracted many leading Hexagon-based left intellectuals like Jean-Paul Sartre, Michel Foucault, André Gorz and Manuel Castells to take an active interest in their conditions.[26] A mimeographed document by Michel Bosquet (the alias for André Gorz) was circulated by militants and other sympathisers of the group Vive la Revolution! in the state-of-the-art Renault car-factory in Flins. In his piece – originally written in *Le Nouvel Observateur* – Gorz describes how Fordist productive relations had created a segment of the working class totally alienated from the work process.[27] Gorz argued for the absolute centrality of the O.S. in the unmaking of the classical working-class subject, and decentred the 'new working class' of technical and white collar workers theorised during the 1960s.[28] Unlike the traditional skilled craft worker which was historically better organised, provided the PCF with its most solid base in the factories, and could more easily barter its *savoir-faire*, the O.S. appeared a spectre heralding the emancipation *from* capitalist labour rather than an emancipation *within* it.

If the new system of scientific production of the Fordist era, replete with the infinite fragmentation of tasks is to function, Gorz argued, then it is not the skilled and secure (and often French-national) 'true workers' which allows it to function.[29] The latter still held on to their '*culture ouvrière*', their class consciousness, their command over skill and even autonomy over their bodily movements. The policing of tasks had been invented consciously to reduce the worker of any space for initiative, invention or ruse like reclaiming a handful of seconds to smoke a cigarette or stretch their muscles.[30] Capital has done this, Gorz argues, 'not because the workers are idiots, but because they are clever. As far as the workers are given a margin of control, they will use it against those that exploit them'. Having been alienated from the production process by capital restructuring, demands of the traditional labour movement and political parties for *autogestion* rang hollow.[31] Such national and electoral demands was argued to matter little to those with no previous experience of the disciplining of industrial society and what E.P. Thompson termed 'factory time' – many had been peasants and farmers before making the trip to Europe and hoping to return.[32] To make the O.S., Gorz continues, capital goes to find their workers in the countryside, in the colonies and semi-colonies, as well as those rejected and labelled 'un-adapted' by the national school system. In other words, from those people who have the least experience of 'scientific production' – the '*non-ouvriers*' – and least roots in any strong workers' culture and from those whose lives until that point least resemble the rhythms and disciplines of the factory.

Workers' voice

This was a worker-subjectivity that was readily apparent to Gauche Prolétarienne activist Robert Linhart in the Citroën Choisy plant in Paris. As a former ENS Ulm student of Louis Althusser, leading militant in the UJCml (and later GP), and born clandestinely in Nice in 1944 to Polish Jewish parents who had emigrated in the 1930s, Linhart was one of the two to three thousand young French intellectuals and students who left their studies to work in the factories as part of a movement called établissement.[33] Working at Citroën's Choisy plant in the 15th Arrondissement from autumn 1968 (given a marginally higher category than O.S. on account of his French nationality), he found his co-workers were unlike the working class he had imagined.

A recurring theme of Linhart's memoir *L'Établi* is the workers' voice. The exploitation of the factory and the prison-like '*foyers*' in which immigrants lived (often supervised by former colonial officials, CRS, or army veterans) provided barriers to their *prise de parole* on the model of de Certeau. Conversing on the production line was almost impossible due to the noise and prying foremen, company interpreters or the *syndicat jaune*, and was compounded for many by lack of confidence in speaking the French language. As Linhart notes:

> In the outside world '*établissement*' appears spectacular, the papers make it into quite a legend. Seen from the factory, it's not very important in the long run. Everyone who works here has a complex individual story, often more fascinating and more embroiled than that of the student who has temporarily turned worker. The bourgeoisie always imagine they have a monopoly on personal histories. How ridiculous! They have a monopoly on speaking in public, that's all … The others live their stories with intensity, but in silence.[34]

De Certeau's *prise de parole* meant more than slogans scrawled on the walls of the Sorbonne. It meant creating space (through political organisation) where these workers could speak. As fellow GP militant (and future founder-editor of *Libération*) Serge July wrote in *Le Monde*, 'we want to destroy the dividing machine between those who "work" and those who "think" '.[35] Wrenching the monopoly of the bourgeoisie over speaking in public and giving it to immigrant workers was a prerequisite for Linhart and the GP. A somewhat antinomical political formation, the GP combined both a Maoism of the Cultural Revolution and spontaneist and libertarian elements common to the radicalised student and intellectual milieu of France's 1968.[36] Though less doctrinaire than more orthodox Maoist currents, the GP shared their Third Worldism and overwhelming emphasis on the industrial working class. Jean-Paul Sartre would go on to be the nominal editor of the group's newspaper *La Cause du peuple* during a government crackdown. The paper was conceived explicitly as a publication of a new type where 'the masses would inform the masses'.[37] What appealed to Sartre – as well as other sympathisers (or members) like Simon de Beauvoir, Michel Foucault, Jacques Rancière, Gilles Deleuze, Jean-Luc Godard and Maurice Clavel – was the group's 'anti-authoritarian revolutionary praxis' and call to relate in new and direct ways with the insurgent outsider-subjects like immigrant workers.

The voice that the GP sought to foreground was seen by Sartre to be unmediated by existing arty or organisation, expressed spontaneously through what he labelled in *Critique of Dialectical Reason* the 'fused-group'. Sartre praised *La Cause du peuple* in the introduction to the 1972 book *Les Maos en France* because

> For the most part the articles came from workers and country people, who described in their own writing or to interviewers their strikes, their acts of sabotage, their occupation of the lands of absentee landlords. They spoke not in the language of one party but in the language of the people, and the violence that came to light came from the people ... Its articles – brutal, unrefined, simplistic, but true – resounded with the voice of the people, and that is just what its bourgeois readers could not tolerate. They learned that the masses violently rejected slavery, in other words, the exploitative society in general. The bourgeois could not listen to this voice. They could put up with the revisionists [i.e. the PCF] talking to *them about* the masses, but not the masses talking *among themselves* without caring whether or not the bourgeois were listening.[38]

The insurgent voices of immigrant workers were often foregrounded in GP publications – invariably with invective against the system and traditional institutions of the Left and the labour movement (an issue some have criticised in subsequent years).[39] In one issue of the Renault-Flins Marxist-Leninist newspaper *L'Unité Ouvrière* from 1969, 'A maoist from the body-section [*tolerie*]' spoke from the first person:

> I am an immigrant worker and I sweat like you for Renault. When I came to France, I was told: 'Freedom, equality, fraternity'. What in fact I was given here: 'racism, informers [*petit chefs mouchards*], hellish production line speeds'. Already, I am doing the work of two workers and what's more I have the bosses [*chefs*] on my back all day. When an immigrant worker revolts, the 'Cocq' [the name of a supervisor] tells him: 'If you are not happy, go back to your country'. There's no right to revolt if you are a worker and moreover an immigrant.

> Lecocq we are not your slaves, and if you continue, the immigrant workers will wait for you at your door! We'll make the snitches [*mouchards*] tremble (Bernard, the team leader, for example), those who give us warnings when we go to eat too early, those who shout at us when we want to take a short break to catch our breath. We don't accept having to work ourselves to death for nothing. Last Saturday

when you gave us crumbs of a pay-slip we stopped working. The next time, bosses [*patrons*], it will be worse for you than in May 68![40]

For 1968-era *gauchistes* of many tendencies this 'brutal, unrefined, simplistic, but true' voice was not being represented by parties like the PCF or Parti Socialiste (PS) or even the trade unions. 'We don't hide the fact that we are resolutely opposed to the trade unions' began a 1972 supplement to *La Cause du peuple*.[41] As Donald Reid has noted, '*Gauchistes* touted immigrant workers combatively as an alternative to the apparent conservatism of French workers and their PCF and CGT representatives.'[42] Sartre, like the GP, saw in the spontaneous rebellions outside the unions (realised through *comités de lutte*), the sabotage of production and direct confrontation with factory supervisors and police, as bringing the predictions of Fanon home to France. No traditional political organisation was understood to be able to recuperate such actions.

A multinational workforce meant a high diversity of spoken languages within even a single work-group. Such diversity was a boon for management seeking to avoid workplace disruption. The process of translation and the communication across linguistic barriers was a prerequisite to any political activity. For worker militants like the *établis* there was a need to co-ordinate struggles, write leaflets and spread news from within and outside the factory to their workmates to break their mutual isolation. This required the translation of one language to the other, finding common ground that could sustain collective activity. Robert Linhart helped organise a strike with his workmates against the small lengthening of the work-day in late 1969 in an effort of Citroën to win back some of the workers' gains of 1968.[43] Linhart describes in intimate detail the tensions about whether the machines would stop at the time agreed for the unofficial stoppage (outside the framework of the unions), and how the silence of the machines opened up a brief dream of an alternative production model. Flyers deposited in the Gauche Prolétarienne archives show their reproduction in Spanish, Portuguese, Arabic and Serbo-Croat for the occasion. One was titled '*On n'est pas des esclaves*'.[44]

Like Linhart, the *établis* had followed Mao's suggestion to uproot from the universities, schools and small jobs and 'establish' themselves amongst the people.[45] As a number of their memoirs make clear, to 'organise the working class' meant creating spaces where the voice of the working class could be heard. The relationship of individual *établis* with their co-workers, however, was restricted to geographically and temporally restricted spaces defined by the organisation of the factory itself. Nicolas Dubost – *établi* with the Revolution! group (a split from the Trotskyist Ligue communiste) and the CFDT trade union – describes in his memoir *Flins Sans Fin* how militants would only have an hour each day to politically agitate with the workers at the Renault-Flins factory where he worked. This would be confined to the changing of shifts on the forecourt outside the factory's central gate through which all workers passed in intervals at 1:30 pm and 2:05–2:30 pm. Dubost describes the workers' initial incomprehension of the agitation outside the gates by the *Base ouvrière* between 1969 and 1971 (which had only brought a sound-system, some posters and some sketches). The GP, however, then started a 'more effective agitation' which was both '"spectacle" and direct democracy':

> A sound-system, that's it; a militant from outside the factory starts with a few words, information from the outside or from the inside the factory, then he gives it over to a worker militant or sympathiser of the *comité de lutte*, who speaks of his workshop, and each take their turn to speak 'into the mike'. Finally, 'each', I exaggerate, but they are many who are generous enough to call to their co-workers. Group discussions, hustle and bustle, *prise de parole*, above all in the evenings where something has happened inside the factory.[46]

This practice was copied by Dubost with his CFDT union section.[47] Meetings were addressed by a *maghrébin* colleague in Arabic, another in Portuguese, another in *sarakolé* for the West Africans. Creating this kind of space for a radical *prise de parole* – especially for immigrant workers – held more importance than political propaganda for Dubost. It implied a politics of release, an overcoming of fear, and a rebellion against the strictures of the assembly line endured inside the plant. As Dubost argued:

> The power-knowledge of speech is far more fascinating than the pen which writes leaflets or posters; a microphone is quite terrifying. When one works in a factory where the right to speak is systematically suppressed, lacking in use for the work itself, then there is a panic behind the microphone. *Encore plus*. However, there is a really

strong *need* to speak, but it rests jammed, like a ball that capital places in the throat.[48]

Dubost found that this was a problem for *établis* like himself. Particularly at ease behind the microphone and able to write leaflets and pamphlets swiftly, whenever he finished speaking and attempted to pass the microphone to a colleague, 'direct democracy finished. No-one wanted to take it.' Those who knew how to speak refused: ' "it will only be repeating things" or "you do it so well" '. 'Too well', Dubost adds. A theme of Dubost's memoir is the crumbling of the idealistic *Image d'Épinal* of the working class as he feels his colleagues are increasingly relying on him as a figure of meditation. Dubost had broken with his studies and future career of university teaching for the factory in order to watch the workers liberate themselves and not, in his eyes, to have their liberation done for them.

The importance of the wager on the voice of the oppressed in the imaginaries of the 1968 left is affirmed by the silence that followed. Having been one of the leading figures of May '68 – the charismatic leader of the UJC (ml) – Robert Linhart was one of the most marked. In a personal and collective memoir of both her father and the children of the '68 revolutionaries, Virginie Linhart – Robert's daughter – sought to explain her father's silence after the spring of 1981. Just before the election of Francois Mitterrand's government, her father had attempted suicide by drug overdose when she was just fourteen, after which he became mute, unable to talk either of the past or the future. Virginie asked him to speak of his past. 'It's me ... the king of silence,' he replies.

> Yes, it's you the king of silence, the prince of obscurity. But you aren't dead, and for twenty years now I have seen only your silence, so I want to understand. Because it is a part of my life as well ...
>
> It's our secret, *ma petite fille* ...
>
> What's our secret?
>
> That you know everything, and that I speak no-more.[49]

Yet far from explaining her father's silence as a medical condition, Virginie Linhart sees it as a conscious political choice. The year of his silence is critical. The year 1981 marked three years since

Linhart had given up on active politics, three months after his close friend and former teacher Louis Althusser had been confined to a mental asylum after murdering his wife Hélène, a month before many of his former comrades would ride the electoral wave into the Mitterand government, and the critical year in the ongoing restructuring of the French working class. Linhart became mute at the moment where he felt the collective voice he had searched for had been extinguished, opening up a brave and unrecognisable new world:

> That's why my father killed himself. There was no confrontation possible with those who continue to speak, to live in the present, to expose themselves politically in the media or through literature. They don't exist in the same problematic. They followed their route. My father had to turn off so as not to divide his life between being behind the scene and the psychiatric hospital. In his condition, he has shown a profound wisdom. In his personal isolation, he has been the perfect master of his own destiny ... Now, I understand why my father has chosen to stay silent.[50]

The story of Robert Linhart is also the story of 1968 and the unmaking of its revolutionary imaginaries. The *prise de parole* which de Certeau saw as the defining element of May was, in Linhart's case, reduced to silence as the constituent elements which nourished commitment to – and expectation of – a new world unravelled. This vision, shared by a number of revolutionary currents across Western Europe and the world, re-born in 1968, was indelibly linked to the insurgent voice of the young, semi-skilled, immigrant worker at the heart of the era's industrial production. Their alienation from the productive process and their dehumanisation was hoped to open the way for a politics which would seek to abolish rather than valorise the worker as the motor of capitalist production. Without the perceived conservatism and corporatism of the legitimised status allotted to the skilled citizen-worker or the same ties to the ideological strictures of the national polity, the immigrant O.S. was imagined to have the most to win and least to lose in radical and total transformation. The O.S. were seen to have little stake in piecemeal electoral reform and sectional demands. With a 'double absence' – in the words of Abdelmalek Sayad – from both France as well as their countries of birth, the 1968 Left hoped this multinational and socially displaced working class would remind French workers of their own, temporarily forgotten, revolutionary traditions.⁵¹

The struggles of a multi-national working class made up of immigrants, women, and the young had allowed left activists in France to briefly conceive the prospects of global revolution starting

Figure 2.1 Poster, 'French immigrant workers all united. Equal labour, equal pay', Atelier Populaire ex-École des Beaux-Arts, May 1968, France.

from the confines of the factory walls. Yet this imaginary was not to last, nor did it result in the hoped-for revolutionary rupture. As the machines fell silent in the factories in which the O.S. worked and industrial restructuring erased the jobs the immigrant workers were brought to France to serve, Linhart's wager on their collective voice ended with his own. That silence has had an indelible effect on France's political imaginaries since. Nonetheless, during the 1980s publications like *Sans frontière* (1979–86) and movements like the 1983 March for Equality and Against Racism show that the eclipse of the French left's concern for the worker's voice also marked the opening of new era of immigrant activism.

Notes

1 M. de Certeau, *The Capture of Speech and Other Political Writings* (Minneapolis: University of Minnesota Press, 1997), p. 11.
2 K. Ross, *May '68 and It's Afterlives* (Chicago: Chicago University Press, 2003), pp. 2–3.
3 The 1997 English language version of this piece translates this wrongly as 'wage-earners' instead of the industrial-manual worker term *ouvrier* implied by the French. See M. de Certeau, *La prise de parole: et autres écrits politiques* (Paris: Éditions du Seuil, 1994), p. 40.
4 De Certeau, *The Capture of Speech*, p. 11.
5 For one of the few engagements with the role of immigrant workers in 1968 and after see D. Gordon, *Immigrants & Intellectuals – May '68 & The Rise of Anti-Racism in France* (Pontypool: Merlin Press, 2012).
6 For important articulation of the radical potential of the O.S. see the account by B. Coriat, *L'Atelier et le Chronomètre* (Paris: Christian Bourgeois, 1979).
7 X. Vigna, *L'espoir et l'effroi. Luttes d'écriture et luttes de classes en France au XXe siècle* (Paris: La Découverte, 2016), p. 142.
8 This was not helped by the Gaullist attempt to paint the May events as being driven by immigrant workers. For further discussion of this dynamic see L. Pitti, ' "Travailleurs de France, voilà notre nom": les mobilisations des ouvriers étrangers dans les usines et les foyers durant les années 1970', in Ahmed Boubeker and Abdellali Hajjat (eds), *Histoire politique des immigrations (post)coloniales: France, 1920–2008* (Paris, Editions Amsterdam, 2008), pp. 95–111.
9 B. J. Silver, *Forces of Labor: Workers' Movements and Globalization since 1870* (Cambridge: Cambridge University Press, 2003), p. 46.

10 R. Wolin, *Wind from the East* (Princeton: Princeton University Press, 2010), p. 87; M. Seidman, *The Imaginary Revolution* (Oxford: Berghan Books), p. 174; Y. Gastaut. *L'immigration et la opinion publique sous la Ve Republique* (Paris: Éditions du Seuil, 2000), pp. 37–51. For overlooking or downplaying the role of immigrant workers in the long 1968 during the fiftieth anniversary see N. Ramdani, 'A French Revolution that Pushed Immigrants to the Margins', *Guardian* (28 April 2018) www.theguardian.com/commentisfree/2018/may/08/france-may-1968-racial-legacy-empire-50-anniversary; D. Palumbo-Liu, 'France Must Move Beyond May 1968 and Tackle the Racial Legacy of Empire', *Guardian* (8 May 2018) www.theguardian.com/commentisfree/2018/may/08/france-may-1968-racial-legacy-empire-50-anniversary.

11 P. Saunier, *L'ouvriérisme universitaire: du sublime à l'ouvrier-masse* (Paris: L'Harmattan, 1993).

12 For two studies *Le Monde* and *L'Humanité* journalists see J-P. Dumont, *La Fin des OS?* (Paris: Mercure de France, 1973) and M-R. Pineau, *Les OS* (Paris: Éditions sociales, 1973). For a searing description of this process in action, see Robert Linhart's description of a skilled worker colleague in Citroën's Javal factory in 1969 seeing his work process 'rationalised' by a factory technician. R. Linhart, *L'Établi* (Paris: Les Éditions de Minuit, 1981), pp. 161–78.

13 For background to this period see D. Reid, 'The Politics of Immigrant Workers in Twentieth-Century France', in C. Guerin-Gonzales and C. Strikwerda, *The Politics of Immigrant Workers: Labor Activism and Migration in the World Economy since 1830* (New York: Holmes & Meier, 1998).

14 Potere Operaio, *Per una internazionale delle avanguardie rivoluzionarie [Convegno internazionale a cura di Potere operaio]: Zurigo, novembre 1970* (Florence: Clusf, 1971).

15 *Les Nouveau Partisans: Histoire de la Gauche Prolétarienne par des militants de base* (Paris: Al Dante, 2015).

16 S. Castles and G. Kosack, *Immigrant Workers and Class Structure in Western Europe* (London: Oxford University Press, 1973), pp. 61, 115.

17 F. Briot and G. Verbunt, *Immigrés dans la crise* (Paris: Éditions ouvrières, 1981), p. 20.

18 L. Thévenot, 'Les catégories sociales en 1975: l'extension du salariat', *Économie et statistiques* no. 91, July–August 1977, 3–31.

19 Castles and Kosack, *Immigrant Workers*, p. 80.

20 Ibid., p. 81.

21 L. Pitti, 'Les luttes centrales des O.S. immigrés', *Plein droit*, 63:4 (2004), 43–7. See also J. Fremontier, *La Forteresse ouvrière: Renault* (Paris: Fayard, 1971).

22 Gastaut, 'Le rôle des immigrés'.
23 'A l'origine du conflit Renault: l'"O.S. ", nouveau manœuvre', *Le Monde* (25 May 1971).
24 X. Vigna, *L'insubordination ouvrière dans les années 68. Essai d'histoire politique des usines* (Rennes: Presses Universitaires de Rennes, 2007).
25 La contemporaine, Paris, F delta res 0576/5/2/2/4.
26 J-P. Sartre, *Sartre in the Seventies: Interviews and Essays* (London: André Deutsch, 1978); Gordon, *Immigrants and Intellectuals*, pp. 120–8; A. Gorz and P. Gavi, 'La bataille d'Ivry', *Les Temps modernes*, 26 (March 1970), 1398–414; M. Castells, 'Immigrant Workers and Class Struggles in Advanced Capitalism: The Western European Experience', *Politics and Society*, 5 (1975), 33–66.
27 A. Gorz, 'L'usine-bagne', *Le Nouvel Observateur*, 384 (20 March 1972). An abridged English translation of this piece was published in the *New Left Review*. See A. Gorz, 'The "Prison Factory"', *New Left Review*, 73 (May–June 1972). The mimeograph document can be found in La contemporaine, Paris, F delta res 0612/1/3.
28 The most classic example being S. Mallet's *La Nouvelle classe ouvrière* (Paris: Éditions du Seuil, 1973).
29 La contemporaine, Paris, F delta res 0612/1/3.
30 James Scott would later call this form of resistance the 'weapons of the weak'. See J. Scott, *Weapons of the Weak: Everyday Forms of Peasant Resistance* (New Haven: Yale University Press, 1985).
31 A new approach to socialist strategy was needed, which Gorz developed in his work particularly from the mid-1970s.
32 See J. Berger and J. Mohr, *A Seventh Man* (London: Verso, 2010) for discussion of the affective experience of the migrant from agriculture to the industrial city of northern Europe.
33 The best general overviews can be seen in *Les Temps Modernes: Ouvriers volontaires, les années 68: l'établissement en usine*, 684 (2016); M. Dressen, *De l'amphi à l'établi: les étudiants maoïstes à l'usine, 1967–1989* (Paris: Belin, 2000), p. 11; V. Linhart, *Volontaires pour l'usine vies d'établis (1967–1977)* (Paris: Éditions du Seuil, 2010); D. Reid, 'Etablissement: Working in the Factory to Make Revolution in France', *Radical History* Review, 88 (2004).
34 Linhart, *The Assembly Line*, p. 76.
35 S. July, 'Pour la cause du peuple', *Le Monde* (11 April 1970).
36 For background see F. Hourmant, *Les Années Mao en France. Avant, pendant et après Mai 68* (Paris: Odile Jacob, 2018); C. Bourseiller, *Les maoïstes: la folle histoire des gardes rouges français* (Paris: Edité par Plon, 1996). For the GP's precursors see P. Buton, 'Inventing a Memory on the Extreme Left: The Example of the Maoists after 1968',

in J. Jackson, A-L. Milne and J. S. Williams (eds), *May 68: Rethinking France's Last Revolution* (Basingstoke: Palgrave Macmillan, 2011); A. Belden Fields, *Trotskyism and Maoism: Theory and Practice in France and the United States* (New York: Autonomedia, 1988).
37 J-P. Sartre, *Sartre in the Seventies – Interviews and Essays* (London: André Deutsch, 1978), p. 165.
38 Ibid., pp. 165–6.
39 The *gauchiste* stress on the radical and autonomous power of immigrant workers, unable to be controlled or recuperated by traditional labour movement institutions like the PCF and CGT, has been criticised as paving the way for political isolation of immigrants. See O. Brachet, 'Pourquoi Lyon fait-il parter de ses immigrés', *Les Temps modernes*, 40 (1984), 1687–88.
40 'Renault-Flins: L'Unité ouvrière', journal des marxistes léninistes prolétariens de Renault-Flins', 1 and 4 (June and October 1969). La contemporaine, Paris, F delta res 0612/1/1.
41 *La Cause du peuple/J'Accuse*, 20 (15 January 1972).
42 D. Reid, 'The Politics of Immigrant Workers in Twentieth-Century France'.
43 Linhart, *The Assembly Line*, pp. 85–106.
44 'Groupe Communiste Maoïste de Citroën', La contemporaine, Paris, F delta res 0576/5/2/1.
45 Dressen, *De l'amphi à l'établi*, p. 11.
46 N. Dubost, *Flins san fin* (Paris: La Découverte, 1979), pp. 112–13. See also N. Dubost, 'Neuf ans et demi d'usine: aucun regret?', *Les Temps Modernes*, 684–5 (2015), 246–53.
47 For further discussion on the changes within the CFDT during the 1970s see F. Georgi, ' "Le monde change, changeons notre syndicalisme" La crise vue par la CFDT (1973–1988)', *Vingtième Siècle. Revue d'histoire*, 4:84 (2004), 93–105.
48 Dubost, *Flins san fin*, pp. 112–13.
49 V. Linhart, *Le jour où mon père s'est tu* (Paris: Points, 2010), p. 12. [Author's translation].
50 Ibid., p. 166.
51 A. Sayad, *La double absence: des illusions de l'émigré aux souffrances de l'immigré* (Paris: Points, 2014).

3

Comités Palestine (1970–72): on the origins of solidarity with the Palestinian cause in France[1]

Abdellali Hajjat
(Translated from French by Rayya Badran)

This chapter sheds light on a forgotten chapter of the long sixties: the origins of solidarity with the Palestinian cause in France. In the historiography of May '68 in France, solidarity with Palestine and the activist role of Arab immigrant workers and students have been largely sidelined. While conventional accounts (in French and English) might suggest that the radical sixties focused on the Vietnam War and was led by white students and workers, this chapter argues that the Israel-Palestine conflict and Arab postcolonial immigrants held an important role in French radical politics, both in factories and in universities.[2] Scholarship about the history of French movements in solidarity with the Palestinian cause is practically non-existent in English and still in its infancy even in the French language.[3] This study thus contributes to undoing the silence on the topic in English-language historiography of the long '68 in France in particular and in the literature on the global sixties more broadly. The aim here is not to present an exhaustive history of the movements in solidarity with the Palestinian cause,[4] but rather to shed light on the involvement of Arab immigrants in France, particularly les Comités de Soutien à la Révolution Palestinienne (committees in support of the Palestinian revolution or CSRP), also known as the 'Comités Palestine' (Committees for Palestine). Created in reaction to Black September (1970) and dissolved in 1972, the Comités Palestine were mostly composed of Arab workers and students. They were part of the first organisations to stand in solidarity with the Palestine people in France, and the creators of the Mouvement des travailleurs arabes (Movement of Arab Workers or MTA) in June 1972.[5] Aligned with the Maoists of the Gauche Prolétarienne (GP), the Arab activists of the Comités Palestine had close links with the Palestinian organisations in the Middle East (in Lebanon and Palestine) and in France, in terms of the latter namely with the first unofficial representatives of the Palestine Liberation Organisation (PLO), Mahmoud Hamchari and Azzedine Kalak. This chapter explores three key aspects underpinning the actions of the Comités Palestine: the politicisation of Arab activists in a broader Arab revolutionary context and in the ideological framework of Marxist Arab nationalism; the organisation and actions of these committees; and finally, the factors explaining their dissolution and the transition to the MTA.

The political space of Arab activists in Paris in the late 1960s

The Comités Palestine were composed of Maoist Arab and French activists. The first were students who had recently arrived to Paris and were not politically active in their countries of origin, as well as workers who were politically engaged in the Palestinian struggle and/or the French far left. They arrived from Tunisia, Morocco, Algeria, Lebanon and Syria, convinced that the Arab postcolonial revolution was underway and that it was able to transcend narrow national affiliations. The reconstitution of the Arab workers' political and migratory trajectories[6] shows that they broke with several social orders (patriarchal, national, and related to immigration), which attuned them to social justice and predisposed them for political action. Social characteristics that pertained to their marital status, level of education, student status, experience of illegal work, and the heritage of anticolonial struggles, facilitated their political engagement. The last of these was rather unlikely because the overwhelming majority of immigrant workers were not politically active: it's the exception that proves the rule. Solidarity with the Palestinian people thus played a catalyst role in the political awakening of Arab militants in and through the Comités Palestine.

However, the activists who mobilised for the Palestinian cause were not only Arab. The term 'Comité Palestine' – like the 'Comité Vietnam' – was already widespread in the 1960s. The activists of the CSRP were distinct because they were more sensitive to the conditions of immigrant workers in France. The Comités Palestine were not exclusively dedicated to the Palestinian cause but formed a true political laboratory in which solidarity with the Palestinian people, the fight against racist crimes, and the struggle to improve immigrant workers' living conditions merged.

The political engagement of immigrants in French society was not commonplace. On the contrary, one of the major characteristics of most immigrants' political engagement was that it exclusively involved their country of origin. For instance, opposition to the regime of Hassan II in Morocco or Habib Bourguiba in Tunisia was prioritised over efforts to improve the lives of North African immigrants in France. However, the members of the Comités Palestine were the first 'political immigrants' (i.e. they had a political awareness and engaged in political activities) who considered France as a terrain of struggle for the 'immigrant cause' and not only for a national cause (an example of the latter would be the French Federation of the Front de Libération Nationale (FLN) which had mobilised the Algerian community in France in the service of Algeria's independence). Contrary to most Arab militants in Paris, the political immigrants in the Comités Palestine developed a greater sensitivity to the problems faced by North African immigrants in France.

The militants of the Comités Palestine were immersed in a political space of immigrant mobilisations which centred on the following issues: the acute attention to events in Arab countries, which in turn prevented consciousness-raising about the living and working conditions of immigrant workers and thus hindered collective mobilisation to improve these; the political weight of the Amicales, which consisted of consular organisations of North African states that aimed to politically control their nationals in France; their disillusionment regarding the waves of independence, which led to the immigrants' increasing disengagement with the representative institutions of their countries of origin; the absence of an organisation that communicated the needs and concerns of immigrant workers, especially those for whom the prospect of returning to their countries had begun to dissipate. All these factors had contributed to the discouragement and political disengagement of Arab immigrants, thus giving rise to two new major political movements: solidarity with the Palestinian people and immigration struggles, concerning their work in factories, their housing and work permits.

If the militants of the MTA were the first to have taken up the concerns of the immigrant workers in France, it was because their political trajectories within the political space of Arab militants predisposed them to disengage with the struggles of their home countries and to begin a more precocious involvement in the French political arena. The last to arrive in France after the *Circulaires Marcellin-Fontanet*,[7] which applied harsh restrictions on migration in 1972, they became aware of the impossibility of returning. Without necessarily cutting ties with their countries of origins, according to the MTA's leaflets, they believed that the struggles of Arab workers in France were part of the Arab Revolution. But the conversion to the idea that one must fight for the condition of workers in French factories occurred solely through the experience of the Comités Palestine.

The political activity of this group in France can be explained by the existence of a greater proximity to the Maoist groups, particularly the Gauche Prolétarienne (proletarian Left). Within the latter, political action pushed some of them to fight for Palestine and immigration issues. Based on their vision of the French political terrain or their affective adherence to Maoist theories, most of them found in the GP an organisation that Arab militants could belong to, as opposed to the French Communist Party and the Confédération générale du travail (CGT or the General Confederation of Labour). If this evaluation of the organisation is indeed pertinent, what remains to be understood are the sociological and historical impulses behind their membership to the GP.

The appeal of the Gauche Prolétarienne for Arab militants

Writing the history of the Comités Palestine and the MTA as a footnote of the GP's history would completely impair the object of research. While the influence of the Maoist organisation in the political formation of several MTA militants cannot be denied, it would be reductive to view them as an Arab clientele that merely obeyed the orders of the GP's political bureau. The lines that separated the two organisations were certainly porous, but the Comités Palestine benefitted from a real autonomy of action and often found themselves in radical opposition with the GP. Rather, what is at stake in the GP's relationship with the CSRP (and later with MTA) is the question of autonomy regarding struggles of the Arab workers. While the assertion of this autonomy was fundamental for them, the few existing archival documents do not make for a conclusive reading on the matter.

Despite this uncertain political situation, we may be able to shed light on three major issues. The first being cultural autonomy. While the dominant vision on immigration in France was predicated on the concept of assimilation and integration – a directive that called for immigrants to blend in the 'French melting pot'[8] – the cultural demands of the Comités Palestine militants (from learning Arabic, to the recognition of religious holidays, etc.) deviated from it without succumbing to cultural and religious 'separatism'. The second issue was political and organisational autonomy. Whether in factories or in workers' housing units, the immigrant workers' rights to speech and decision-making were denied, which explains why they wanted to self-organise and emancipate themselves from both the union and corporate tutelage. The third issue pertained to the double isolation of the workers who, in order to be efficient and gain political authority, sought to avoid being cut off from French society and from North African immigration in France. But the necessity of this autonomy was not readily apparent and the engagement of several MTA militants, students and workers alike, considered their participation in the GP as a 'natural' outcome.

Some of the militants became involved in the GP before founding the Comités Palestine. The first contacts took place during meetings and in cafés, and the GP's Arab Maoists did not know each other when they became members of the organisation. Several of these members formed links on the subject of the Palestinian cause through such encounters. Others made connections in factories, as was recommended by Maoist practice at the time. The social profiles of French students and young Arab intellectuals were similar, which led to a more likely political proximity: Arab students in Paris, who were 'francized', exiled, Marxist-Leninists and committed to the Palestinian cause, and so on. In fact, these connections were made with the students in the streets – several Arab militants indicated that the Maoists were the only ones working 'on the ground' in the markets and cafés of Barbès and Belleville – during the actions of solidarity with the Palestinian revolution.

While traditional union bodies balked at the idea of incorporating specificities related to immigrant struggles (such as residency permits, work permits, etc.), the tracts and discussions held with the Maoists seemed to be more respectful of the history of immigrant workers. Contrary to an older generation of workers from North Africa, whether they were members of CGT and the Confédération française démocratique du travail (the French Democratic Confederation of Labour or CFDT), the young North African workers constituted the largest 'recruitment reservoir' of the GP in factories. Since the Maoist strategies consisted of entering the factories to 'sow the seeds of the revolution' – despite the great difficulty to act from within because of the hostility of central unions and management repression – the young North African workers represented a privileged 'target' for them because they were not yet 'supervised' by the unions or fellowships.

Their personal trajectories and emigration paths predisposed them for political action, which came to be expressed in one of the most interesting organisations of solidarity with the Palestinian cause. The Trotskyist discourse for a 'socialist Palestine' did not resonate with those for whom the Palestinian cause was a nationalist and anticolonial struggle. Unlike the Ligue Communiste Révolutionnaire (LCR), who advocated 'critical support', the GP accepted Palestinians 'as they were' and supported the national character of their struggle for independence. The Union des jeunes communistes marxistes-léninistes (UJC[ml]), which preceded the GP, had been the first to support the PLO in France during the 1967 war by marching in Paris from the Gobelins to the Rue Moufftetard. With the help of China, who was in support of the Palestinians, the UJC displayed a radical anti-Zionism.

On 10 February 1969, the Palestinian left initiated the creation of the Comités Palestine. However, as will be discussed in the section below, their actions only began to seriously materialise after September 1970. The political platform of the GP's Comités Palestine had a fixed objective 'of supporting the revolutionary struggle of the Palestinian people against Zionism and imperialism, as spearheaded by the United States, and to actively support the Palestinian liberation movement'.[9] By faithfully adopting the political positions of the PLO, these committees gave their solidarity to the national demands of Palestinians to reclaim the entire historic territory of Palestine. They also adopted a radical anti-Zionist position: 'The C.P. support the Palestinian liberation movement in its will to destroy the State of Israel as a state with on theocratic, racist, colonialist, capitalist and fascist structures, and to build a secular, democratic and socialist Palestine.'[10] The platform also established links with anti-Zionist Jews and condemned 'Zionist and antisemitic racism, which are at the origins of the creation of the state of Israel'. The party members of the GP were made aware of the stakes of the conflict by Adel Rifaat (an older member of the Arab-Jewish family of Tony and Benny Lévy), and Bahgat El-Nadi, who were known by their pen names as 'Mahmoud Hussein'.[11] Adel Rifaat, who was living in Paris, had connections with the first official representative of the PLO, Mahmoud Hamchari.

In January 1969, the GP organised a meeting in solidarity with the Palestinian people with slogans such as: 'Fateh will conquer!' or 'Zionism shall not pass!' Hamchari proposed they visit the Palestinian camps and the GP accepted the invitation in August 1969.[12] The representatives of the GP, Alain Geismar and Léo Lévy (Benny's spouse) travelled to the Karameh camp in Jordan where the general staff of the PLO and the military branch of Fateh (Yasser Arafat's party), called Al-Assifa,[13] were located. Recognised by the members of Fateh, Geismar was even invited as a guest on Palestinian radio. His conversations with Palestinians centred on two main points: why did Jean-Paul Sartre, who had given his unwavering support to the Algerian Revolution, turn towards Zionism during the 1967 June War? And how does one approach the Israeli opposition, who could be a potential ally on the road to peace in Palestine? Geismar volunteered to facilitate such contacts through his Parisian networks. In the fall of 1969, Olivier Rolin, an expert in military operations at the GP was contacted by an emissary of the Popular Front for the Liberation of Palestine (PFLP), led by George Habash, who proposed giving free military training in the Palestinian camps. However, the GP refused because it wished to 'safeguard its autonomy'.[14]

Solidarity with the Palestinian cause was more symbolic than military, especially when spectacular actions were concerned. On the night of 25 September, Maoists wrote on the walls of the residence belonging to the Rothschilds, who were considered as being 'at once the oppressors of the Palestinian people, the treasurers of Israel, and the oppressors of the French people',[15] slogans in red paint such as 'Fateh will win', 'Rothschild, the French and Palestinian peoples will win', as well as 'Ben-Gurion is a fascist'. On the following day, 300 Arab and French protesters met at the metro station of Notre-Dame-de-Lorette and set fire to the headquarters of the Rothschild bank. Later that day, protesters threw stones at the offices of *L'aurore* newspaper, on Rue Richelieu, from which they also hung a Palestinian flag.

The year 1970 was a pivotal one for the Gauche Prolétarienne (GP) because it illustrated the transition from the organisation's peak (in the media) to the beginning of its split. It turned to clandestine activism after its dissolution by the government on 27 May 1970. Confronted with state repression (arrests and confiscations), the strategy of the GP's political bureau can be summarised as such: 'To open up the organisation, without dispersing to all the winds'.[16] It was a strategy through which immigrant workers found a more important role. At the beginning of the summer in 1970, the GP focused on three objectives: to dedicate more time to the working-class milieu, specifically its immigrant constituency, by reinforcing committees of struggle in the factories; to create a 'democratic front' through the Secours rouge[17] to 'protect' itself by forming an alliance with known 'democratic' intellectuals; and to assert the autonomy of the military wing, led by Rolin, which took on the name of the Nouvelle résistance populaire (New Popular Resistance) or the Milice ouvrière multinationale (Multinational Workers' Militia).

A 'natural' and implicit agreement was established between the Arab militants who wanted to organise the solidarity with Palestinian people and the Maoists who sought new recruits. For both the GP and the Arab militants, what was at stake was how the explosive potential of the Arab world could be channelled to fuel and unify, from a revolutionary perspective, the growing revolts of immigrant workers in French factories. The connection between the struggle of the Palestinian people and that of immigrant workers in France was established in view of mobilising all the affection, anger and hope that the *fida'iyeen* (Palestinian guerrilla fighters) could conjure, in order to reorient them to the class struggle in France. Without denying the sincerity of their engagement and their 'use' of the Palestinian cause, Palestine proved to be an effective means of political mobilisation in which the figure of the *fida'i* came to constitute a powerful symbol of identification.

The shock of Black September

The month of September 1970 was a critical turning point in the history of the Arab world and delivered a major blow to the hopes of revolutionary Arabs: the Egyptian President Gamal Abdel Nasser (a key supporter of Third World liberation movements) died on 28 September, and the Palestinian camps in Jordan were decimated by King Hussein's offensive on 16 September. Besides the fact that Palestinian combatants were militarily outweighed by the Royal Jordanian Forces, thousands of refugees, among them women and children, were brutally killed. This bloodbath made a considerable impact on people in France, and in particular on Arab militants. The political milieu of Arab students was shaken by the news and the Arab Maoists militants felt the urge to meet and organise an action in solidarity with Palestinians. While the Comités Palestine had existed formally within the GP since February of 1969, they had not engaged in any activity. It was indeed the 'Arab Maoists' who initiated the Comités Palestine, as some of them had met during their study groups of Mao's *Little Red Book*.

Black September was the event that triggered the creation of the Comités Palestine, which were formed after an emergency meeting at the Maison du Maroc (a student residence) shortly after the events. Among those who attended were Lebanese, Moroccans, Syrians, Tunisians and Palestinians from the General Union of Palestinian Students (GUPS), including Kalak,[18] and the militants of the future MTA: Gilles aka 'Fathi', Said, Hamza, Farid, Ali aka 'Ali Clichy', 'Mokhtar', Thérèse and Fawzia. The 'French of May '68'[19] were also in attendance and provided necessary material for the mobilisation (such as a mimeograph, ink, cars, etc.). The Comité was conceived in the same way as the Comité Vietnam (CVB).[20] For the Maoists, the purpose of the Comités was to popularise an anti-imperialist struggle and to draw links between the living and working conditions of the workers (or the 'masses') in France. One of the CVB and the Comités Palestine's specificities was their total alignment with the political inclinations of the combatants.

However, the Comités Palestine, which were nonhierarchical, were not limited to Maoists alone. The only criterion for participation was adherence to the ideas of the Comités Palestine as articulated in the GP platform in February 1969. Faced with the urgency of the situation, the Comités Palestine echoed Yasser Arafat's message: 'O Arab masses, rise!' They published *Fedaï* on 15 October 1970, a newspaper dedicated to supporting the Palestinian revolution,[21] whose editorial staff also worked in a former newspaper, *Feda'iyeen*,[22] initiated by Hamchari.

At the end of September 1970, GUPS organised a large meeting in solidarity with the Palestinian cause at the Mutualité, where they called for blood donations. For Fawzia, who had just arrived from Tunis, it was her first form of activism in France. The priorities of the Comités Palestine responded to the immediate needs of the Palestinian combatants by sending them material aid (funds), medical aid (blood donations) and political support (conferences, newspapers, etc.). After 20 September, the organisation of this urgent relief focused on the Cité Universitaire and high schools, while remaining attentive to the neighbourhoods of North African workers in the Parisian regions of Gennevilliers, la Goutte d'Or, Belleville, Choisy, Aubervilliers, and Saint-Denis. Militants of the CSRP used the Palestinian cause to mobilise North African workers: 'The support of the Palestinian resistance was a form of struggle that enables the constitution of an autonomous political force for the North African workers in the neighbourhoods, ghettos, and factories.'[23]

In November 1970, the CSRP in the Parisian region made a positive report of their campaign concerning Black September. The enthusiasm of Arab workers was measured by the sales numbers for the *Fedaï* newspaper and by the large audiences who attended the public meetings in cinemas or markets during October 1970. In certain areas where there was no local Comité, the mere distribution of leaflets and poster campaigns helped draw hundreds of workers to a meeting. In Nanterre, six hundred workers, and a hundred French and foreign workers, organised an informative meeting of solidarity. North African workers from another town organised a network of material support that succeeded in collecting 2,000 Francs, which the local Comité Palestine transferred to an Arab embassy. Several workers even approached militants to go to war alongside the Palestinian *fida'iyeen*. The factories were the political terrains of choice through which the Comités were able to distribute tracts and sell their newspaper at the gates. The campaign brought together several North African workers, who later became activists in the factory workshops, by spreading information about Palestine. However, the repression by the police or their inability to host meetings (at the Mutualité and the Cité Universitaire) greatly diminished the Comités Palestine's capacity to mobilise. In Gennevilliers, for example, a meeting held in the street was interrupted and led to fifty-one arrests.

The Palestinian cause, especially in the aftermath of Black September, aroused the enthusiasm of North African immigrants. All of the interviewed militants claimed that if a dozen militants assembled and marched with a Palestinian flag in Barbès, hundreds of residents of the neighbourhoods would follow them; and as one militant observed, the 'Palestinian flag sprouts like wheat!'.[24] But it is difficult to determine the meaning behind the mobilisation of the 'Arab masses'. To say that they mobilised because they were Arab would reduce their solidarity to a culturalist approach: that is, Arabs manifested their solidarity with Arabs only because they were Arabs. The militants of the Comités Palestine willingly adopted this line of thinking but underscored the fact that 'the Palestinian revolution is the living example of suffering and hatred; it is the force of the Arab masses against imperialism. It [the Palestinian revolution] crystallises the hope of vanquishing imperialism for all the Arab masses, including those in France.'[25] For them, there was a similarity between the North African workers facing French capitalism and the Palestinians facing the Zionist and American capitalism: 'the ghettos perceive the *feda'iyeen* as those who transformed the refugee camps into resistance camps'.[26]

The student committees, who mobilised in universities, ran out of steam during October 1970. The Comités Palestine saw this situation as the result of the rupture with the North African immigrants: 'Cut off from the masses, the committees crumbled or degenerated. In fact, without the support of the Arab masses, any support would have been limited and was likely to be crushed.' In order to create this 'mass movement', the Arab students took on a central role:

> They have a role to play on the level of trust. They were the bridge that connected the French militants with the Arab workers in terms

of the language, the psychological weight of the Arab students, their knowledge of the problems that Arab workers encountered in their own countries, of the Palestinian cause, and so on.[27]

They went to cafés and markets frequented by North African workers to 'cause some agitation and propaganda' in order to create Comités. The major concern in terms of organising was that they needed to be led by activist workers and not students:

> If we want to be deeply rooted, we must help immigrant workers to take over organisational and leadership tasks [in the Comités Palestine]. Only proletarianisation [of the Comités Palestine] can allow their development and turn them into a real political force.

According to this logic, the proletarianisation of the leadership was indispensable because the workers' choices were informed by their experience and condition. Workerism was in the spirit of the times: the global revolution was tangible and realisable for radical left militants and the Comités Palestine did not break with these principles.

The Palestinian cause and the immigrants' cause

While its solidarity campaigns were increasing, the Comités Palestine encountered other problems including racist crimes. In February 1971, the Algerian President Houari Boumediene nationalised the country's oil production, provoking an anti-Arab hate campaign in France.[28] The North African immigrant community was subject to frequent attacks that both legitimised and trivialised anti-Arab racism. From February until March 1971, the CSRP mobilised in solidarity with the Palestinian revolution, and campaigned for the freedom of speech of immigrant workers and against racist attacks. However, the repression of pro-Palestinian militants intensified. Law enforcement attempted to deport a number of them: Abd al-Massih in Lille, 'Vasco' in Paris, and Nabil in Lyon. Hamza, a young high school student, was arrested on 29 December 1970 while distributing a tract in support of Palestine in front of the Citroën factory in Nanterre and was convicted to six months in prison for carrying and transporting firearms (three of which were suspended). On 14 January 1971, Hamza began a hunger strike at the Fleury-Mérogis prison.[29] Upon his release from prison, the police headquarters summoned him to a deportation hearing on 30 June but a solidarity campaign in his support led by high school students, as well as threats of strikes, led to its suspension. Nonetheless, Vasco was deported before a special hearing ruled on his case. The threat of deportation weighed heavily on Arab militants who had to renew their papers every fifteen days and who were under constant surveillance (with frequent 'visits' to their homes to verify their papers). Furthermore, these 'attacks' targeted two militants from Suresnes, and the committees in Marseille were intimidated by police officers, who thought they were clandestine cells of the PFLP in France.

On 23 July 1971, King Hussein of Jordan was invited by French President Georges Pompidou to the Elysée Palace. The Comités Palestine were adamant that his visit to France would not go uncontested and proceeded to denounce Hussein's annihilation of the Palestinian resistance. On the day of the visit, a small circle of Maoist militants[30] secretly organised a coordination meeting in the amphitheatre of Dauphine University, where hundreds of people in attendance, some of whom where Comités Palestine members, were made aware of the objective and plan of action. Protesters left the venue in small groups and crossed the Bois de Boulogne public park in the direction of the Jordanian embassy, which was located on the Maurice-Barrès boulevard in Neuilly. At 6.30 pm, they kicked in the entrance gate and threw several Molotov cocktails into the building housing the diplomatic representatives and the office of ambassador Ali About Naouar (who was accused by the militants of participating in the massacres of Black September). Just as the fire began to blacken the facade, the protesters retreated, leaving behind a Palestinian flag, which they hung on a fence. Immediately after the fire, Christian Riss, a former student at the *École Normale Supérieure* and co-founder of the UJC(Marxist-Leninist) was apprehended at the Porte Maillot (an access point into Paris). Riss was shot by the police and left lying on the ground with a bullet in his lung for half an hour before he was transported to hospital. On 29 July, a committee in his defence was created by prominent French intellectuals, such as Michel Foucault, Maurice Clavel and Jean-Marie Domenach.

The attack was supposed to be followed by a meeting at the Mutualité to explain the meaning behind the action. But due to the CSRP militants' poor preparation, the meeting was cancelled. The absence of an explanatory public meeting was considered to be a grave political mistake because the action could have been perceived by the public as an act of personal vendetta against King Hussein and not as a political act. In fact, it was the type of action that was not democratically agreed upon within the Comités, and not everyone was informed. It seemed as though the action was the personal initiative of a few militants. In any case, it provoked a debate within the Comités:

> The divisions became apparent after the attack on the embassy. Some people preferred to spend their time arguing in meetings rather than go back and explain to the masses. Others wanted to form organisational Comités of eighty people who were capable of executing military actions, instead of organising a large group of Arabs in the fight against Zionism.[31]

The summer report in 1971 explained this shift as a consequence of the isolation of workers and 'bad working habits' that had led to a rupture with the North African workers. The militants of the Comités Palestine learned the following political lesson: 'If we wanted to expand the Arab revolution and support the Palestinian revolution, it was not enough to perform actions but to mobilise a maximum of people, with propaganda and clear and precise targets.'[32]

After the attack on the Jordanian embassy, 'it became very difficult' for the 'grassroot' militants in the committees.[33] Mohammed was questioned by the Parisian police. The interrogation focused on his acquaintances, his possible participation in certain events as well as his supposed trips to the Middle East. He responded that they merely had to ask his factory about his absences, and he maintained that it was not illegal for him to support the Palestinian cause, as many others did. According to Mohammed, the militants of the *banlieue* (the Parisian suburbs) who were working 'on the ground' were 'disturbed' by the commando military action: 'They were a bit scared.' This concerned the new North African workers who were wary of the hardline political direction of the Comités and police repression: 'It was at that moment that we started to lose militants.' From a political perspective, 'it was a bit too hasty'.

Even if circumstances precipitated things, the Comités were unable to 'consolidate large numbers' of people to politically support the attack. For Mohammed: 'We must be honest, we made a mistake ... unfortunately we never made a report, it was our fault too.' This was an important fact because the attack on the embassy did the mobilisation a disservice: 'It contributed to the demobilisation of the population, but not the militants.'

In the summer of 1971, the internal divisions of the CSRP were considerable. The archives do not indicate precisely what the arguments advanced by the defenders of the proposition were but certain militants apparently suggested the dissolution of the Comités. In fact, this idea was only expressed to be refuted in the report presented by the Comité of Gennevilliers:

> It was in the CSRP that the Arab workers learned to find their dignity as Arab workers and where they developed a resistance *en masse*. It was in the CSRP that the autonomy of the Arab worker movement developed. ... The disbanding of the CSRP would be a grave error. On the one hand, it [the Palestinian revolution] is a weapon used to continue uniting the large Arab masses. On the other, the Palestinian needs the support of Arab people more than ever: we will not betray their revolution.[34]

However, the internal divisions led the majority of the Comités to 'rehabilitate':[35] 'During the summer, we fought the Right within our ranks. The Right expressed itself as such: not to wage a war against the racists and the police; to break with the factories; to do routine work in the cafés.' It seems that the targets of 'rehabilitation', which concluded with an increase of defections, were activists who opposed the increasingly 'militarist' direction of the committees.

The dissolution of the Comités Palestine

In the aftermath of the Marrakech campaign[36] and the Djilali Ben Ali case,[37] the attention shifted towards the Comités Palestine. The Djilali case revealed an undeniable fact: the Algerian Amicale had been weakened by successive compromises. For the Arab militants of the Comités, 'there is an empty ... space in the 18th [arrondissement], it's the space that the FLN occupied during the revolution. In Barbès, it is time to create an underground organisation of the masses.'[38] Moreover, militants recognised that the agitation techniques of the Maoists did not succeed in raising awareness and increasing political engagement among North African workers: 'As long as the masses don't start organising themselves into networks, we will not be able to call for meetings, we will not be able to meet with the immigrant workers.' The rally that was organised for Djilali pushed the Comités to recognise the existence of a breeding ground for militants in the Barbès neighbourhood and that North African workers were ready to organise to continue to fight anti-racism. The Comités explicitly referenced the methods of the Algerian FLN such as organising through a clandestine cell system. The objective was to create an organisation whose grassroot cells were the café and the housing units of the immigrant workers. They worked towards a radical transformation of the Comités in both their organisational and activist practices: 'We think that the Comités Palestine should transform into an organisation consisting of large Arab masses, and to do that we must abandon the working style of the group of agitators.' Relinquishing the agitation techniques aimed to ensure the activists' respectability and to create relations of trust for the serious men and women who had a sense of duty and responsibility:

> It must be a serious organisation: we can't work haphazardly, without a locale, without finances, without material organisation (mimeograph, etc.). If we are not serious, the masses will no longer trust us and they are right not to. That is why these material issues (the library, locale, membership cards) are very important.

It was through the creation of another organisation that the Comités Palestine decided to dissolve.[39] By 1972, they could no longer adapt to the changing times in the way that they had when they formed in 1970. Since the Arab militants set themselves the goal of 'liberating the initiative of the masses', they had to reckon their political analysis of the situation with several missing foundational elements. For the activists involved, this meant either 'following the mass movement', or adapting to the reality of the terrain, in order to amplify its momentum and to give it forms of organisation. To be sure, North African workers or families waged a number of struggles in France beyond those focused on Palestine. These struggles emerged at the end of 1971 and into 1972 and signalled the overarching themes of the political mobilisations to come: such as struggles of people living in poor housing (working-class families and single-person households), struggles of undocumented immigrants and struggles in factories by immigrant workers.

Facing a shortage of accommodation in Paris and the poor quality of buildings inhabited by low-income families since 1969, an important movement of squatting in empty buildings began happening. North African and French families occupied empty buildings in the 14th, 18th, 19th and 20th arrondissements of Paris. In the spring of 1972, the most emblematic occupation took place on boulevard de la Chapelle, which led to the creation of a Comité to work for improvements in their accommodation. The militants of the Comités Palestine helped the residents in their fight for better housing.

Furthermore, the number of strikes led by immigrant workers increased. The first large-scale strike occurred in Girosteel, a small company in Bourguet that employed 120 immigrant workers. The immigrant workers organised a strike group and occupied the factory for two months, from the beginning of February until 14 April 1971. A section of the CFDT supported the strike but it was denounced by the CGT. On 20 January 1971, a strike began at the Pennaroya factory (a nonferrous metal smelting company) in Saint-Denis by 120 Moroccans, Algerians, Tunisians, Malians and Senegalese immigrant workers and lasted seventeen days. The strikers demanded health benefits because of the lead poisoning they were exposed to. The majority of the workers were hired without a medical check-up upon their arrival in France and were deported to their countries of origin once they fell ill. Thanks to their coordination, the immigrant workers at the Pennaroya factories in Saint-Denis, Lyon, and Escaudoeuvres handed in three files of demands on the 27 December 1971, which the administration rejected. The workers occupied two of the factories in February 1972, for two days in Saint-Denis, and thirty-two in Lyon. The strikers did not receive the support of the unions because the CGT did not follow up with their demands. They organised themselves autonomously by creating a group within the CFDT. They also succeeded in creating support links with the farmers of the Lyon region and the strikers of Girosteel for whom they raised funds and organised a gala in solidarity.

Moreover, the immigrant workers also mobilised in the Chausson enterprises, as well as in the sugar factory Lebaudy. In the latter, located in the 19th arrondissement in Paris, the mobilisation was triggered by the death of Said Bouchariou, an Algerian worker. The engineer in charge of the sugar factory asked Bouchariou to clean a tank, but as soon as he climbed down a mobile ladder, a machine started and killed him on the spot. The workers denounced the working conditions and negligence of the administration, who had not checked the equipment in seventeen years.

Before the Circulaires Marcellin-Fontanet of 1972 which, a few months later, restricted access to residence permits and triggered the undocumented worker movement, the members of the Comités Palestine received news about the first case of hunger strike of an undocumented worker. In October 1971, in Amiens, French authorities decided to deport Sadok Djerdi a Tunisian worker who had arrived in France with his family two years earlier, because they claimed he was no longer able to work (despite the numerous medical visits and second examinations proving the opposite). Maoist militants created an anti-racist group and organised a demonstration for Sadok who obtained his permit as a result. In the same period, Comités Palestine activists began to respond to cultural and religious needs, which constituted the first ruptures with the immigrant worker myth of returning to their home countries and confirmed the permanent settlement of North African families in France. At the end of January 1972, they had organised the Eid al-Fitr holiday in the streets of Belleville, despite the heavy deployment of law enforcement. The previous year, they raised funds in *zakat* (charity) for the Palestinian Red Crescent.

From the perspective of the Comités Palestine members, the emergence of the movement of the mal-logés (the inadequately housed), the increase of anti-racist struggles, the strikes organised by North African workers and the new cultural needs of North African families necessitated the dissolution of the Comités and their restructuring into an autonomous organisation of Arab workers. On the whole, the decision to dissolve the Comités, as well as the apparent renunciation of the agitation tactics of the Maoists took place during this period. Arab militants in the Comités Palestine found themselves at a political impasse. For them, the needs of the 'Arab masses' demonstrated the necessity to survive politically. From their point of view, not responding to the expectations of the North African workers would have amounted to an historical aberration and political suicide. A number of these militants noted: 'You talk to us about Palestine, but we are in deep shit. Who is going to defend us?'[40] They recognised that the spirit of the workers had changed and to have continued in the same militant direction no longer corresponded to their lived experience. Hence, Mohammed's state of mind at the moment of the Comités Palestine's dissolution: 'We have to do something otherwise we are going to lose ground ... for us not to lose ground, we decided to create the MTA.'

The creation of the MTA in June 1972 did not diminish from the importance of solidarity with the Palestinian cause, on the contrary. The Comités Palestine served as an organisational base for the MTA across France. In Paris, Marseille, Aix, Lyon, Grenoble, Lille, Roubaix and Toulouse, militants of the former Comités Palestine mobilised their political experience and knowledge of the Palestinian cause to create associations or collectives in support of the Palestinian cause. Even today, the former militants of the MTA, who became 'independent' or members of local collectives, still participate in this movement, which reveals a continuous attachment to the Palestinian liberation struggle.

Political platform of the Palestine Committee[41]

Monday, 10 February 1969

1 The Comités Palestine are created with the purpose of supporting the revolutionary struggle of the Palestinian people against Zionism and imperialism, as spearheaded by the United States, and to actively support the Palestinian liberation movement.
2 The C.P. reject any negotiated solution that does not take into account the national rights of the Palestinian people in all of Palestine. As a result, the C.P. reject the Security Council resolution of 22 November 1967.
3 The C.P. support a people's war, which is the only way for the Palestinian people to reclaim their historic and legitimate

rights. This struggle is inscribed in the context of a global struggle against imperialism and its objective allies, the internal oligarchies.

4   The C.P. support any struggle linked to the movement of liberation of Palestine against any regime, Arab or not, reactionary or pseudo progressive, that seeks to either eliminate it, or co-opt the struggle of the Palestinian liberation movement.

5   The C.P. support the Palestinian liberation movement in its will to destroy the State of Israel as a state with theocratic, racist, colonialist, capitalist and fascist structures, and to build a secular democratic and socialist Palestine. Just like the Palestinian liberation movement, the C.P. thus supports all of the political organisations and militants, including Jewish militants, who fight, either inside or outside Israel, for the same objectives as the Palestinian Arabs.

6   The C.P. fights against Zionism and antisemitic racism, which are at the origins of the creation of Israel and against the racist exploitation (anti-Jewish or anti-Arab) of the Palestinian cause by groups of fascists and neo-fascists.

7   The C.P. consider that the revolutionary struggle of the Palestinian people is an integral part of the global revolution, that it plays an important role in the anti-imperial consciousness-raising in Europe and France and that it finds itself at the vanguard of the revolutionary struggle in Arab countries and the Middle East.

8   The C.P. form a coordination. This coordination is composed of two delegates from each Palestine committee. Militants are mandated by assembly for specific tasks, they are revocable at any moment.

Long live the revolutionary struggle of the Palestinian people!
Comité Palestine

Notes

1   This chapter is an abridged English version of an article which first appeared in French as 'Les comités Palestine (1970–1972): Aux origines du soutien de la cause palestinienne en France', *Revue d'études palestiniennes*, Les éditions de Minuit (2006), pp. 74–92.

2 See also X. Vigna, 'Une émancipation des invisibles? Les ouvriers immigrés dans les grèves de mai-juin 68', in A. Boubeker and A. Hajjat (eds), *Histoire Politique Des Immigrations (Post)Coloniales, France, 1920–2008* (Paris: Editions Amsterdam, 2008), pp. 85–94; D. Gordon, ' "Il est recommandé aux étrangers de ne pas participer": les étrangers expulsés en mai-juin 1968', *Migrations Société*, 15:87–88 (2003), 45–65

3 With the exception of Alexandre Mamarbachi's recent doctoral thesis (*Émergence, construction et transformations d'une ' cause': sociologie historique des dévouements en faveur de la ' cause' des Palestiniens 1960–2010: recherche historique et enquête ethnographique* [PhD dissertation. Université Paris Nanterre, 2020]), the Palestinian cause's history of struggle within France has hitherto not garnered scholarly interest in the social sciences. The first accounts on the subject were written by journalists: S. Kassir and F. Mardam-Bey, *Itinéraires de Paris à Jérusalem: la France et le conflit israélo-arabe. Tome 2* (Paris: Minuit, 1993); D. Sieffert, *Israël-Palestine, une passion française: la France dans le miroir du conflit israélo-palestinien* (Paris: La Découverte, 2004).

4 Mamarbachi, *Émergence, construction et transformations d'une 'cause'*.

5 A. Hajjat, 'The Arab Workers' Movement (1970–1976). Sociology of a New Political Generation', in J. Jackson A-L. Milne and J. S. Williams (eds), *May 68. Rethinking France's Last Revolution* (London: Palgrave MacMillan, 2011), pp. 109–21.

6 Ibid.

7 In January and February 1972, the Interior Minister Raymond Marcellin and the Labour Minister Joseph Fontanet signed two government decrees that intended to combat French workers' unemployment by making more difficult the coming and the staying of foreign workers, especially those from North Africa and Portugal.

8 A. Hajjat, *Les Frontières de l"identité Nationale': L'injonction à l'assimilation En France Métropolitaine et Coloniale* (Paris: La Découverte, 2012).

9 See the platform in the appendix.

10 Ibid.

11 M. Hussein, *La Lutte de classes en Egypte de 1945 à 1968* (Paris: Maspero, 1969).

12 The delegation was composed of militants from the GP, Ligue Communiste (Pierre Rousset), and the Association de Solidarité Franco-Arabe, but also individuals who were not affiliated to any organisation.

13 It was the city in which the first guerrilla action was led by the PLO in Palestine, on the eve of 1 January 1965. It became the title of a version

of the MTA newspaper and the name of a theatre troupe affiliated with the MTA.
14 H. Hamon and P. Rotman, *Génération. Tome 2: Les années de poudre* (Paris: Seuil, 1987), p. 94.
15 'Freedom, Freedom, you will all the enemies of Fateh! We are all feda'iyeen!', *La Cause du Peuple*, number 13, 13 October 1969.
16 Hamon and Rotman, *Génération*, p. 187.
17 The Secours rouge (Red Aid) was created by the GP to widen the organisation's audience by encompassing non-Maoists who were engaged in several struggles (against racism, solidarity with immigrant workers, etc.) in light of its increasing isolation and strong repression by the state.
18 Kalak becomes the unofficial representative of the PLO in France after the assassination of Hamchari, who was killed on 9 January 1973, after an attack by the Israeli secret service on 8 December 1972. Kalak himself became a target of a lethal attack on 3 August 1978 in Paris.
19 Interview with Fawzia, Paris, 25 January 2005.
20 Created in 1967, the CVB represented the typical form of French Maoist organisations. By wanting to break with traditional organisations, the CVB gave its members maximum autonomy 'at the grassroots' level who practised fieldwork, closer to the grassroots, particularly in working-class neighbourhoods (Ross, pp. 97–9).
21 The idea of a charter and statuses of the CSRP is not mentioned until September 1971.
22 Their articles are not exclusively dedicated to Palestine. We can also find information on the struggles of the working class in Morocco and Tunisia. Kalashnikovs adorn the logo.
23 Cf. 'Comités Soutien à la Révolution Palestinienne. Éléments de travail proposés par le comité d'initiative. Bilan politique de deux semaines de travail', Bibliothèque de documentation internationale contemporaine (BDIC), Mfc 215/6.
24 Interview with Mohammed, Paris suburb, 9 April 2005.
25 'Comités Soutien à la Révolution Palestinienne. Éléments de travail proposés par le comité d'initiative'.
26 Ibid.
27 Ibid.
28 R. Brahim, *La race tue deux fois: Une histoire des crimes racistes en France (1970–2000)* (Paris: Syllepse, 2021).
29 See the letter sent from prison by Hamza Bouziri in 'Un détenu politique arabe explique pourquoi il fait la grève de la faim', BDIC F delta rés. 576/5/9/1, in which he writes: 'I was judged and convicted to 6 months in prison because I am an Arab and because I support the

Palestinian Revolution. I stand in solidarity with the struggle of all the other political prisoners in France who fight against the penitentiary system to obtain their political rights. But also, the hunger strike that I started, following the glorious example of our FLN comrades during the Algerian war, is the only way for me actively support the Palestinian Revolution.'

30 Organised by the group 'Karameh' by the Milice Ouvrière Multinationale (MOM).
31 'Bilan des Comités de Soutien à la Révolution Palestinienne', not dated (Summer 1971), BDIC F delta rés. 576/5/9/1.
32 Ibid.
33 Interview with Mohammed.
34 'Supplément au bilan des Comités de Soutien à la Révolution Palestinienne'.
35 CSRP, 'Bilan Septembre 1971', Mfc 215/6, written by the tenants of the rehabilitation.
36 On 17 September 1971, the regional tribunal of Marrakesh made public its judgement of militants and members of the Union nationale des forces populaires (UNFP) who were accused of public disturbance, possession of arms, and a coup attempt. The Comités Palestine launch a campaign in solidarity with the accused.
37 Djilali Ben Ali is a young Algerian teenager aged seventeen who was assassinated on 27 October 1971 in the neighbourhood of la Goutte D'Or in Paris by the boyfriend of his building's concierge. It triggered a large anti-racist movement that culminated in a protest of 3,000 people unprecedented since 17 October 1961 in Paris. See A. Hajjat, 'Alliances inattendues à la Goutte d'Or', in P. Artières and M. Zancarini-Fournel (eds), *68, Une Histoire Collective* (Paris: La Découverte, 2008), pp. 521–7.
38 'Where are the Comités Palestine since the antiracist campaign of Djelali?', note dated (end of 1971, beginning of 1972), BDIC Mfc 215/6.
39 Cf. the declaration of the dissolution of the Comités de Soutien à la Révolution Palestinienne, BDIC Mfc 215/6, not dated (March–April 1972).
40 Interview with Mohammed.
41 Source: BDIC, F delta 576/3/3/1.

4

Cultural guerrilla: Tricontinental genealogies of '68

Paula Barreiro López

From 4 to 12 January 1968, in Havana, the Cuban government held an event of international magnitude: *Congreso Cultural de La Habana. Reunión de intelectuales de todo el mundo sobre problemas de Asia, África y América Latina* (the Cultural Congress Meeting of intellectuals from around the world about issues of Asia, Africa and Latin America), which intended to gather (and somehow centralise at the core of the Caribbean) an active movement of Third Worldist solidarity within the Cold War arena. This international meeting followed from the Tricontinental spirit founded in Havana two years prior – the first Afro-Asian-Latin American Peoples Solidarity Conference – foregrounding, in this instance, culture as its key agenda. Taking place just two months after the assassination of the global *guerrillero* Che Guevara, the Cultural Congress gathered over 470 delegates (artists, writers, art critics, scientists and philosophers) from sixty-five nations from across the world. Throughout ten days, delegates from various backgrounds and provenances discussed ways of supporting anticolonial and anti-imperialist liberation movements that had been engaged in revolutionary armed struggle and guerrilla methods across the Global South.[1] Third World problems were approached from economic, cultural, technological and scientific angles, conferring a primary role to the figure of the intellectual. Of particular note during the congress was an appeal for direct political action through the arts, referred to as 'cultural guerrilla', introduced by the Chilean painter Roberto Matta.[2] The Argentinean kinetic artist Julio Le Parc mirrored this call to action in February 1968 by publishing a radical manifesto in the Parisian journal *Robho* examining the possibility of a cultural guerrilla warfare.[3] Two months later, the anti-imperialist imperative and the Third World agenda that the Cuban Congress had exemplified reverberated in the visual politics of the artists of 1968, such as Le Parc and Matta among others, who put forward actions of cultural guerrilla.

Even though guerrilla warfare can be traced back to the nineteenth century, its key strategies became widely adopted in anticolonial and anti-imperialist liberation struggles from War World II onwards.[4] Successful examples of the Indochina wars, as well as the Cuban Revolution and the Algerian war of liberation, had shown that guerrilla tactics could have a decisive impact on fighting traditionally organised, larger and militarily superior troops – and that they were quite effective for confronting US hegemony and destabilising the balance of power during the Cold War.[5] Inspired by the anti-imperialist guerrilla of colonised peoples and new political subjects (e.g., students, workers, migrants, women), the intention to challenge the established bipolar system of the Cold War underpinned the aims of the cultural guerrilla.

Identifying with the 'wretched of the earth' in their struggle against the (seemingly) all-mighty forces of (neo)imperialism, artists felt compelled to adopt and re-interpret those guerrilla tactics in the heady political moment of 1968 activism. In this chapter, I explore the Tricontinental genealogies of '68, by analysing the transnational experiences and identification of several artists and intellectuals with the revolutionary movements of the Global South during the years of Third Worldist solidarity.[6] While scholars have been attentive to the Third Worldist underpinnings of '68 in connection with Maoism (firmly rooted in French intelligentsia),[7] the alternative Latin American impulses and connections are often overlooked. Just a few months before their political activism in the event of May '68 in France, key artists had direct experiences of the connection between artistic avant-garde and political avant-garde on site in Havana, Cuba. My argument will focus on two critical events that constitute a Latin American genealogy to '68: the Salón de Mayo 1967 and the Cultural Congress of 1968.

This chapter will present experiments in the configuration of a belligerent conception of artistic practice via the concept of a cultural guerrilla. By locating these strategies within their respective socio-cultural contexts or transnational itineraries from Havana to Paris and Buenos Aires, I will explain how the cultural guerrilla of '68 was seen as part of a global revolutionary process against imperialism.

Tricontinental echoes in the cultural world

Bringing artistic practices to the fore of social and political battles of '68 echoed the progressive solidarity of artists and intellectuals with Third World anticolonial struggles. Matta's and Le Parc's call to action and participation respectively in Havana and in Paris in 1968 was directly connected to their growing identification with the revolutionary anti-imperialism underway in Latin America.[8] In fact, as a socialist state, and in defiance to the politics of so-called 'peaceful coexistence' established by the two superpowers (the US and the Soviet Union), Cuba had been backing (morally, politically and economically) African and Latin American national liberation movements.[9] With the First Tricontinental Conference in Havana (1966), the efforts of the revolutionary government were ratified with the configuration of a transnational movement of resistance and solidarity in the Global South (Latin America, Africa and Asia). This transnational network of solidarity was founded with a two-fold aim: first, explicitly defending armed struggle and guerrilla action as a means to achieve national liberation, independence and sovereignty (with Cuba at the centre as the capitalising force of the global guerrilla); and second, uniting the revolutionary forces, bringing together political movements, revolutionary organisations, trade unions, student movements, intellectuals and artists positioned against imperialism, apartheid and racial segregation in all contexts, and who found in these structures a network of solidarity, support and inspiration.[10]

At the time, the bipolar opposition of the Cold War was increasingly being spurned in the West by left-wing intellectuals and artists who sought to disalign themselves from either side of the US-USSR ideological divide. For this purpose, the Tricontinental solidarity movement in its endorsement and support of revolutionary guerrilla methods presented an appealing alternative. It extended beyond the battlefield to become a useful tactic in artistic spheres in Europe, the United States and Latin America. Indeed, since the advances of Augusto César Sandino in Nicaragua, guerrilla warfare had been rooted in a programme of national independence and liberation, opposing the forces of capitalist and colonial oppression. The victory of Fidel Castro and Che Guevara over Fulgencio Batista in January 1959 reinforced this idea.[11] Thus, for the revolutionary Left, armed struggle was becoming a legitimate means of violence, synonymous to the revolution itself. Fanon and Guevara understood anticolonial violence as a morally legitimate 'defence with attack' against the endemic violence of imperial subjugation and oppression of colonised populations in the Global South: 'the wretched of the earth'.[12] For Guevara, the *guerrillero* was not only a military strategist but also a 'social reformer'[13] involved in the radical implementation of a new egalitarian system of economic, political, social and cultural organisation. Within this context, artists, art critics, writers, and 'intellectual' workers in general – as Castro named them during the Cultural Congress of Havana[14] – were called upon to participate in a *cultural guerrilla movement*: an internationalist movement combating imperialism through culture.

Connecting artists and intellectuals from the North and South on both sides of the Atlantic, this congress brought together many practitioners at the centre of a counter-offensive against the capitalist, imperialist and colonial social system of the West, where many of them lived and felt they were, in the words of the writer and art critic Alain Jouffroy, 'exiles in [their] own society'.[15] The notion of guerrilla to which the participants at the Cultural Congress were exposed was at that time much broader than a military tactic. The idea was to fight from within the very practices of everyday life, to wage guerrilla warfare in every field of human experience in order to eradicate the infrastructures sustaining imperialism. The demand was to create a 'cultural guerrilla' or a 'Vietnam in the field of culture', adapting from Che Guevara's famous incentive to 'build one, two, many Vietnams'.[16] This demand was supported with enthusiasm by the intellectuals and artists who were present and circulated globally almost immediately through networks of friendship and solidarity (for example in the Moroccan journal *Souffles*, the Spanish *Cuadernos Ruedo Ibérico* or the French *Opus International*). As Gilman explains, the transition from the committed intellectual in Sartrean terms – bearing witness to socio-political realities – to the revolutionary intellectual who takes part in anti-imperialist movements as cultural agents at the service of the revolution, even joining guerrilla action groups, was now made official.[17] This process would complicate (and even stifle) the creative practices of many of them, due to the exigencies of submitting their creative work to the political struggle.

Matta and Le Parc, as well as a significant number of artists, intellectuals and students who later took part in the events of 1968 around the world, were inspired by the resistance movement(s) that had developed throughout the Southern hemisphere earlier in the sixties. They rejected the political, social and cultural models represented by the United States and the Soviet Union and identified instead with Third Worldist struggles for national liberation. The latter provided them with an arsenal of causes for which to fight, as well as ideas for the renewal and regeneration of their own cultural and artistic practices.

The Cultural Congress of Havana was a clear manifestation of the massive transnational solidarity networks developing across the Global South. It was also, crucially, a platform to configure the role of modern art in the anti-imperialist struggle. Nonetheless, to better understand the debate that took place in Havana in January 1968 – particularly concerning the visual arts – we need to consider its relation to a previous international gathering, that took place only a few months prior, during the exhibition Salón de Mayo in July 1967. This earlier event greatly contributed to shaping a new relation between art and revolution for some of the most committed artists of the Parisian '68.

The Latin American summer of art and revolution

During the summer of 1967 over one hundred artists and intellectuals visited Havana on invitation from the revolutionary Cuban government. This delegation, a Europe-based leftist elite, was invited to stay several weeks, in order to paint, write, travel and collaborate with the local population, 'with workers and students who were transforming Cuban society'.[18] Even though they were monitored by the government, these festive encounters between artists, intellectuals and their Cuban counterparts, revolutionaries, *guerrilleros*, Tropicana dancers and ordinary citizens were perceived as fundamental experience by all sides.

Around two hundred artworks were presented at the Salón de Mayo in Cuba, the majority of which belonged to modern artists of the generation of the Cuban artist Wifredo Lam,[19] who was responsible for organising the event, along with Carlos Franqui (the cultural attaché of the Cuban Embassy in Paris). Artists included Picasso, Léger, Calder and Magritte. There was also a group of postwar émigré artists living in Paris, who came from all over the world (such as Spain, Switzerland, Argelia, Canada, China, Argentine, Turkey, Cuba), thus comprising several Cuban artists integrated in the Parisian and Caribbean avant-garde (such as Loló Soldevilla). The exhibition also included an important section devoted to the artists of the Salon de la Jeune Peinture, who became strongly involved a few months later in the Parisian May '68.

Created in 1950, the Salon de la Jeune Peinture was by the mid-1960s an 'intense centre of political and artistic experimentation', supporting radical politics, anti-imperialism and collective art. Eduardo Arroyo and Gilles Aillaud were part of the board, under the presidency of Henri Cueco and were to a great extent responsible for its political radicalism during the 1960s. The Salon federated multiple artists based in Paris who had migrated from different countries of Europe and Latin America. It was openly engaged with Third Worldist solidarity movements, looking for a 'third way' against both Western bourgeois capitalism and Soviet communism. If an important part of the Jeune Peinture's artists travelled to 1967 to Cuba (such as Adami, Arroyo, Aillaud, Erró, Monory, Rancillac and Rebeyrolle), ten years later with new artists joining its ranks, the Salon was actively involved with other revolutionary causes, such as the Palestinian liberation movement.[20]

Those invited to Cuba in 1967 constituted a heterogeneous compendium of modern art languages (from various forms of abstraction to figuration). This ensemble worked well with the Cuban government's ambivalence regarding aesthetic languages (encapsulated in 1961 Fidel's cryptic statement 'with the revolution all, against the revolution, nothing').[21] By that time, Cuba had not yet renounced integrating the experimental potential of the avant-garde into its revolutionary programme, seeking to underline the independent path that Cuba was seemingly ready to take in relation to Soviet and Chinese guidelines.[22]

The confluences between modern art's ambitions and the revolutionary agenda of the Cuban state were emphasised strongly by officials during the event. For example, the Cuban Minister of Foreign Affairs, Raúl Roa, stressed in the catalogue: 'If the Salón de Mayo is the universal expression of the revolution in painting ... Cuba today embodies ... the dream and the reality of the Revolution across the Atlantic and a path full of audacities and surprises of the revolution within the Revolution.'[23] Artists such as Eduardo Arroyo and Gilles Aillaud (both members of the Salon de la Jeune Peinture in Paris) reaffirmed this connection by seizing the opportunity to support the Cuban revolutionary cause and bringing their work to an anti-imperialist use. This was in line with an artistic vision they had developed in Paris (where they worked) years before. In that sense, they were the perfect guests for the Cuban experiment of 1967.[24] Wifredo Lam, the central figure organising the exhibition, presented an artistic model of what he called 'Un acto de descolonización' (decolonisation action).[25] Confronting and combining modernist aesthetics with Afro-Cuban subaltern imagery, he expressed in a poetical and violent way the essence of the Third World, in his 1966 painting *El tercer mundo* (which was offered as a gift to the revolutionary government).[26] Besides Lam, the aims of connecting modern art with processes of decolonisation were evident in other artists' works, especially those created during their stay on the island. The guest artists expressed their commitment to revolutionary processes, somehow emulating Lam's ambitions to become 'a public prosecutor and represent the Third World'.[27]

The Cuban Salon, which opened on the 29 July, and lasted 22 days, received 150,000 visits at the Pabellón Cuba in Havana (a selection would go to Santiago de Cuba weeks later).[28] The show took place at the same time as the Festival of the *Canción Protesta* (Protest Song), at La Casa de las Américas, and the First Conference of the Latin American Solidarity Organization (OLAS), at the Cine Chaplin. The latter was an aftermath of the Tricontinental Conference that was trying to unify the revolutionary forces in Latin America and support the collective action of guerrilla warfare. Therefore, Havana in July 1967 was an eventful nodal city, bringing together militants of the OLAS, intellectuals and artists of the Salón as well as Protest Song musicians. This galvanised solidarity across social sectors and nations, putting in motion the unification of revolutionary guerrilla action and opening up its reach to intellectual and artistic means. While this chapter is mainly concerned with the role of visual artists, the argument could, nonetheless, be extended to a much larger community including musicians, film directors, writers and poets.

The coinciding dates of these events revealed a clear objective: to join forces from all fronts, at a time when guerrilla warfare in Latin America was at its peak, with Che Guevara fighting in Bolivia.[29] The exhibition was as much a cultural transatlantic encounter as an international demonstration of solidarity with guerrilla resistance. This was at the core of the Salón's history, as it had been founded in 1943 during the Second World War by the French Resistance movement against fascism; an internationalist struggle that, within different sectors of French society, shifted towards an anticolonial stance in the 1960s that was very much involved in the Tricontinental anti-imperialist cause.[30] The artists who were invited to Cuba displayed clear sympathies for the revolution. They were asked to forsake their ivory tower without giving up their specific means of action, and to take a part in the cultural army of a Third World guerrilla war against imperialism. Indeed, one of the leitmotifs of the exhibition was the words of the head of the South Vietnamese delegation (who was invited to visit the exhibition): 'a painting of protest is worth a grenade or a rifle'.[31] This motto actually quoted Picasso, whose statement, made during World War II opened the catalogue of the Salón in Cuba: a painting was much more than a decoration, it was to be understood as 'an instrument of war, attack and defence against the enemy'.[32]

The search for a new status for artworks as bearers of a value equivalent to actual material guerrilla weapons was one of the most fascinating tropes among left-wing artists from that moment on, especially during '68.[33] And it was extolled by the Mayo Salón painters. However, in Havana, the anti-capitalist, Third Worldist matrix of the Tricontinental, the equivalence between the artistic avant-garde and the political avant-garde was as literal as it was metaphorical. Although the goals were clear, the means of joining the revolution were not as evident and had to be negotiated between the invited artists and the revolutionary establishment: such as the creation of in-situ paintings reproducing guerrilla iconography and building a collection of modern art for the revolution (at the initiative of the invited artists).[34]

But on Fidel Castro's initiative, artworks cohabited with the revolutionary arsenal which the island had used for the revolution, such as anti-aircraft guns.[35] The exhibition space opened up onto a tropical garden and an animal show featuring Canadian cattle that had recently been brought to Havana in order to improve the quality of Cuban milk reserves.[36] This peculiar showcase put modern art on the same level as symbolic artefacts of the political, social and economic realities in Cuba; de-identifying and dislodging the artistic objects from their bourgeois space and charging them with a completely new value and purpose.

The communion between artworks and everyday objects of the guerrilla was expanded by further events which were organised simultaneously, such as the exhibition *Painters and Guerrillas* (Figure 4.1).[37] Under the slogan 'the duty of every revolutionary is to stage the revolution', artworks by Cuban painters (such as the celebrated revolutionary pop artist Raul Martínez) were displayed in a jungle-like atmosphere alongside photographs of the guerrilla

Figure 4.1 The exhibition *Painters and Guerrillas* at the Galería Latinoamericana of the Casa de las Américas, Cuba, opened 18 July 1967.

front and protest movements, images of Che, paintings, posters of the recently inaugurated Tricontinental Organization and actual Kalashnikovs aesthetically placed on the walls and floor.

The event physically brought together within the exhibition space the ongoing ambitions of the Tricontinental as well as the artists. We can only imagine how such an orgy of paintings and Kalashnikovs fascinated the international audiences. Havana was crowded with painters, writers, intellectuals, *guerrilleros* and political delegates attending the various events, such as the Black Panther Party leader Stokely Carmichael.

Transgressing their traditional status, weapons and paintings bore witness to the direct collaborations between artists and *guerrilleros* during the formers' stay on the island, exemplified by the collective creation of the mural *Cuba Colectiva* (Collective Cuba) (Figure 4.2). During the night of the 17–18 July, approximately ninety people from different backgrounds, including the artists of the Salón de Mayo, Cuban artists and *guerrilleros*, accompanied by Tropicana dancers and a live orchestra, manifested the communitarian spirit of the revolution through a festive celebration of art, rum and revolution; a guerrilla-happening of total spectacle, broadcast live on national television![38] The collective painting, the artistic climax of the Latin American summer of art and revolution, depicted a spiral consisting of individually painted areas, created by artists, critics, intellectuals, and *guerrilleros*, which evoked the

Figure 4.2 Mural, *Cuba Colectiva*, Havana 1967.

centrifuge and expanding energy of the revolution. Departing from Lam's syncretic and telluric hybrid figuration of a version of his painting *Threshold*, full of pantheistic references, the spiral displayed a combination of visual and textual references to the revolution. In this collective painting, Che, Fidel and José Martí were just part of a heterogenous collective effort which, for the participants, was embodied by the regime of the 26th of July. The painting merged multiple styles, languages and qualities (pop art strategies, revival of surrealist forms, new figuration, abstraction and even poetic and political slogans) developed in a spiral maze. Some of the artists involved (such as Erro, Antonio Recalcati and Lam) had previously engaged in collective work to protest against the French military in the Algerian War. The work was entitled *Grand tableau antifasciste collectif* (Milan, 1961).[39] However, in the Cuban case, the combination of individual expressions through the collective collaboration of artists, students, militants and intellectuals, transformed *Cuba Colectiva* into something else: a conscious challenge to the Western values of the (bourgeois) conception of art, introducing a hybrid and performative – as well as mediated – dimension into the entire creative process (increased by the press and TV coverage). Painted in a public space, outside the Pabellón Cuba, and in dialogue with the visual arsenal of Cuban posters, this collective creation became an act of destabilisation of Western artistic conventions, seeking to re-establish the avant-garde as a transforming agent.

Against the 'anachronistic domination of the privileged class'

The contact with the Cuban government and the experiences in Havana reaffirmed to *in-situ* participants the necessity of revolutionary action, the importance of visual culture in this process and the remarkable capacity that collectivisation and participation could have in this respect. At the end of their stay, they wrote a collective manifesto confirming: 'how close – in Cuba – the relationship between culture and revolution is'[40] (see the complete manifesto following this chapter, Figure 4.5). Artists and intellectuals, it read, faced with the 'anachronistic domination of a privileged class' that violently enforced its power upon Asia, Latin America and Africa's population, had the moral imperative to support (and join) the guerrilla struggle.

This manifesto was written in support of Havana's Cultural Congress to be held some months later, in January 1968 with the attendance of Lam, Franqui and other former guests of the Salón de Mayo: the painters Antonio Saura, Asger Jorn and Roberto Matta, as well as the writers Alain Jouffroy and Michel Leiris.[41] Discussing the role and problems of the 'Third World', the congress stressed an anti-imperialist agenda autonomous from Soviet and Chinese directions. Such aims confirmed the claims of the Salón de Mayo's manifesto, making it an 'imperative duty of intellectuals' to resist and support the 'fight of national liberation and social emancipation of the people of Asia, Africa and Latin America and the struggle against imperialism'.[42] The commitment of intellectuals 'must be reflected in taking position against US politics of cultural colonisation'.[43] Regarding the arts, the place of the avant-garde was clarified following the Salón de Mayo experiences. So, although the congress declared that 'the action of the avant-garde should always be informed by a clear political perspective',[44] it also underlined that its experimentation and creative freedom were untouchable.

Specific examples of such political, free and avant-gardist expressions had been provided, as previously mentioned, during the Salón. These were expanded during the congress with Jorn and Saura's abstract and gestural works which, stimulated by the empathic rhythms of the revolution – full of colour and lively shapes – covered the walls of the Revolution Archives. The power of art and design in the expanded understanding of the cultural guerrilla was already visible, in fact since the creation of the OSPAAAL in 1966. The Tricontinental had built an effective visual apparatus via cinema, photography, as well as poster production that integrated the struggles of the three continents, creating an imagined community connecting revolutions around the world (from Vietnam to Central America and Nicaragua). Through a sophisticated graphic design nourished by pop strategies, the posters were a necessary tool of the Tricontinental. They built a visual continuum – via iconographic iterations (of which the repetition of the Kalashnikov motif is a clear example) and visual models of *guerrilleros* (men, women and even children) – transferred from the photo reportages of anticolonial wars to painting and graphic design through the work of Cuban artists (such as Alfredo J. González Rostgaard, Raul Martínez, René Mederos Pazos), as well as by invited international artists (Linda Norling and Emory Douglas from the US, and Roberto Matta from Chile).[45]

However for the delegates of the Havana Congress, a much more experimental project was issued from the Cuban avant-garde, which offered more potentialities for embodying the revolutionary claims of the Third World than previous experiences had been able to do. Along with lengthy debate sessions and specific resolutions, 'The Problems of the Third World' were specifically dealt with *visually* in a collateral exhibition, entitled *The Third World* (El tercer mundo), held during the Cultural Congress and displayed at the Pabellón Cuba (like the Salón de Mayo six months earlier). The exhibition was organised by a team of young Cuban artists (including a filmmaker – Rebeca Chávez, an architect – Fernando Pérez O'Reilly, and a designer – José Gómez Fresquet-Frémez) and was strongly supported by the Cuban state (over 100 hundred people worked to develop the project). It brought different media together: photography, painting, comics, cinema, music, along with environmental sounds and even specimens of the island's flora and wildlife.[46] Using montage and contrapositions, the exhibition staged six episodes of a fragmented and militant history of the Third World, from colonisation to liberation, aiming to encourage the viewers' participation. The exhibition thus unfolded into a multisensorial agitprop experience which directly denounced US imperialist policies. With a direct and unequivocal contraposition of images, sounds and political messages, the organisers reinforced the destabilising role that visuality and collective action could play in the struggle against imperialism. The exhibition raised the question of the place that the 'wretched of the earth' held in global politics.[47]

The conclusions of the Salón de Mayo and the Havana Congress, as well as the personal experience of the close relationship between artistic objects and revolutionary life, could not be more appealing to the 1968 international artistic community. It was through these experiences in revolutionary Cuba, that European and Latin American artists and intellectuals would shape their participation in the struggle against corporate and capitalist power just a few months later in various parts of the world.

In Paris, like in Cuba, the integration of artists into the realm of revolution took place by renouncing their integration into (bourgeois) institutionalised arts spaces, as well as their aesthetic value to join street battles with other militants using their own means of action. On account of their multiple, inexpensive and easily distributed nature, posters and silkscreen prints became the means for visual experimentation and revolutionary participation for artists. The call for a Tricontinental solidarity in and through revolutionary armed struggle was visible on prints revealing the transnational framing of the uprising in Paris. One such poster created by the *Comité des Trois Continents* at the Sorbonne University clearly exemplifies this broader Tricontinental remit (see Figure 4.4).

Sharing the symbolic motifs of the Tricontinental logo designed by the Cuban artist Alfredo Rostgaard (in charge of the OSPAAAL design office), the poster depicted three flat, racialised masculine silhouettes representing solidarity across the three continents of the South (Asia, Africa and Latin America), holding together a single rifle. In contrasting black and white, the image was accompanied by the slogan: '*Trois continents, un même ennemi, un seul combat, un monde nouveau!!!*' (Three continents, one common enemy, a unified struggle, a new world!!!). Adapting from the Tricontinental, ideological and iconographic repertoires, the Sorbonne poster did not just entrench the Parisian '68 within an internationalist decolonising horizon, it also rehabilitated the role of visuality within political struggle.

Debates on the militant role of images were part of the discussion within the activist circles of May '68. The members of the *Atelier Populaire of Paris' École Nationale Supérieure des Beaux-Arts* were clear concerning the necessity of not defining their productions in terms of artistic character and aesthetic value, but, instead by their function and political effectiveness, considering them as: 'weapons in the service of the struggle [whose] rightful place [was] in the centre of conflict, that is to say, in the streets and on the walls of the factories'.[48] Their posters and paintings, created collectively and anonymously, left the gallery to take part in the struggle alongside other objects of revolt – among Molotov cocktails and the famous cobblestones of the Rue Saint Michel. Posters became necessary alternative information channels – away from the government's domination of the media – and foregrounded collective action and solidarity during the strike between different social groups (students, artists and workers) and nationalities.

However, some of the former visitors to Cuba were also involved in other actions, such as the occupation of the state-owned Argentinean house at the Cité Internationale Universitaire de Paris. It was taken from the director's hands (a civil servant of the Argentinean Onganía dictatorship, in power since the coup d'état of 1966) by the students and workers who organised an occupation committee which garnered support from multiple committed intellectuals of the time (e.g. Jean-Paul Sartre, Gaëtan Picon, Julio Cortázar, Michel Ragon, Michel Leiris, Carlos Fuentes). Changing its name, from Maison de l'Argentine to Pavilion Che Guevara, it was transformed for two months into a utopian antibourgeois space for experimentation, radical culture, expanding the struggles of the Quartier Latin to the whole Latin American community. This included a significant number of Latin American artists, who participated in the occupation with their own artistic means.[49] Roberto Matta and Antonio Seguí, for instance, painted a mural depicting the dictator Onganía ridiculously falling off a horse due to the intervention of a personification of liberty (quoting the famous personification of Liberty by Delacroix in *La Liberté guidant le peuple*). Using the direct graphic language of the May posters, the irreverent scene mocked and contested the Argentinian dictatorship, stressing a new sovereignty of the people being built by interconnected struggles of '68 around the world.[50]

The urgency of reaffirming the Tricontinental internationalism that fuelled the brush strokes and actions of Parisian artists (in the Quartier Latin, as well as at the Argentinean house) became a necessity for many artists of the late sixties. In the case of the Argentinian experimental movements, this decision cannot be dissociated from the Cuban expansion of guerrilla actions and the revolts and protests on the boulevards of Paris (as stated by the artists themselves). Thus, at the same time as the artists occupied the Argentinean house in Paris, in Buenos Aires the artists of the Cycle of Experimental Art were consciously forging direct links with their colleagues abroad. During the summer of 1968, they affirmed that 'the life of Che Guevara and the action of French students are works of art greater than most of the silly things hung in a thousand museums of the world'.[51] A form of artistic-political intervention was inaugurated within the Argentinian avant-garde of the sixties, understood in terms of artistic *foquismo*, adapted from Régis Debray's *foco* theory building from Guevara's revolutionary guerrilla method and Cuban experience. Artistic *foquism* went from symbolic gestures to direct militancy: for instance, dying the fountains of the City of Buenos Aires red on the anniversary of Che's death in on 8 October 1968; or supporting the workers' demands in the Tucumán region, through a counter-information action called *Tucuman Arde* that denounced the precarious situation of the workers after the closure of the sugar mills in order to hand them over to North American private corporations.[52] Presented as a participatory exhibition in various trade unions, artists used posters, books, video and sound for generating an anti-bourgeois exhibition space that shared a similar aesthetic to the multisensorial spaces of the *Third World* exhibition at the Congreso Cultural de la Havana in January 1968. These actions, as Ana Longoni explains, 'implied an operation of translation: the "militant" practices, resources and procedures (the leaflet, the graffiti, the act of lightning, sabotage, kidnapping, clandestine action, etc.) [were] appropriated as artistic matter'.[53]

Conclusion: revolution, radical chic and the trouble(s) of memorialisation

These acts of translation and the integration of art into the arsenal of revolution was short-lived and fraught with much tension. Just as artists integrated processes of revolt and transformed their actions and productions into revolutionary objects, their participation seemed, for the political avant-garde, insufficient or became unbearable.

On the one hand, the demands of political effectiveness ended up suffocating the creative practices of many artists, who, after an initial flirtation with the revolutionary world, returned to their studios.[54] On the other hand, even though multiple artists were willing to submit to the rigours of direct action and militancy in the streets, they found that this could hardly be equated to artistic militancy. The ethics of sacrifice that defined the revolutionary guerrilla movement could barely be carried out through artistic action. Hence, the militancy of artists involved in collective protests and the belief in direct action led some of them to leave their artistic past behind and join the guerrilla fighters. For example, in Argentina, Eduardo Favario left his artistic practice, after his participation in *Tucumán Arde*, in order to join the Partido de los Trabajadores Revolucionarios.[55]

Furthermore, while the symbolic power of guerrilla movement contributed to their ubiquity within the artistic practices of the sixties and seventies, that movement also participated in its own reification within the capitalist and media system of that era. Thus, the artists quickly perceived that actions, gestures and objects produced by the guerrilla artists were at risk of becoming empty symbols, co-opted by consumer society. The rapid transmutation of Che Guevara into a counterculture celebrity and youth idol, who shared the walls of teenagers with rock stars, was an example of what Raoul Vaneigem considered to be 'radical chic', produced in parallel with the politicisation of artistic circles.[56]

Just two years after the assassination of Che Guevara, the Argentinian artist and sociologist Roberto Jacoby pointed to the dangers of the fetishisation of guerrilla warfare[57] (Figure 4.3). On the subject of the appropriation of the famous and mediatic portrait of the *comandante* made by Korda in 1960, he warned that '*Un guerrillero no muere para que se lo cuelgue en la pared*' (A guerrilla fighter does not die to be hung on the wall). For the first issue of the semi-clandestine magazine *SOBRE* (the culture of liberation), published in Buenos Aires, Jacoby took 1968's revolutionary object *par excellence* (a poster), and proposed the opposite, an anti-poster. *SOBRE* consisted of a folio-sized envelope containing documents without any apparent organisation (such as pamphlets, reports, graphic material of different formats). Also understood as an anti-magazine, *SOBRE* was presented to clandestine militant networks and designed to circulate as an instrument of struggle in order to stimulate action and as an instrument of thought to be used and to be destroyed: 'to be thrown away like a grenade, THIS IS A WEAPON'. Jacoby's disturbing anti-poster, which was included in the collection, was a contradictory artefact – as its name itself indicates – which denounced the banalisation of 'radical chic', while seeking to encourage action within leftist artistic circles in the Argentinean context. The presence of this work in the inaugural issue of *SOBRE* could not but demonstrate that the yearnings for struggle had to face not only a repressive state, but also a capitalist media system in which the art institution participated and which was as dangerous as the former.

Figure 4.3 Poster, Roberto Jacoby, 'A guerrilla fighter does not die to be hung on the wall', 1969.

Jacoby was rather presciently weary of the future memorialisation processes of '68, which Kristin Ross later described in 2002, in reference to the French case, as a de-politicisation of the revolts by turning them into a cultural movement (in the best-case scenario): 'an individualistic and spiritual quest announcing the watchword of the 1980s, "freedom" '.[58] However, back in the days when '68 still had momentum, Jacoby, along with other artists and intellectuals, learned first-hand that within an oppressive capitalist and colonial system it was through the actions of guerrilla warfare that the 'wretched of the earth' could actually have a chance of being heard.

Tricontinental networks, with their demands for justice and solidarity, became an appealing horizon for leftist intellectuals and artists who wanted to join the battle against imperialism. This is what I call the Tricontinental *effect*, the reverberation of an ideological stance within the artistic practices which eventually spanned multiple continents and practitioners. The identification with revolutionary processes (re-)configured the political imaginary of artists, intellectuals and students, as well as the Cold War geography of the long sixties. It contributed to a shift in their political perception, leading the revolutionary imaginary to (ideologically) replace the Soviet Union with the Third World.[59] The roles of the Latin American Tricontinental imagery, the 'cultural guerrilla' programme, and the Cuban experience were key for this shift in the minds of multiple artists who held prominent roles in the Parisian '68 revolts, as well as within the contestation processes that the Argentinian avant-garde developed in the itineraries of '68.

Driven by the winds of revolutionary movements in the South, the '68 'moment' was firmly rooted in Tricontinental anti-imperial and anticolonial solidarity. The social disorder that the revolt motivated and encouraged brought artists not just to reproduce guerrilla warfare in their work, but to participate in it by collaborating in its visual configuration and even in its violent methods of attack, albeit in most cases only for a brief period of time. Advocating for the guerrilla meant to be in solidarity with the revolutionary cause of the Third World, but also making it one's own, that is, developing a political position aligned with the radical left, but with all its consequences: attacking the bourgeois artistic institution, the structures of the art market, fighting for social justice in one's own country and even exiting the art world in favour of political or armed struggle. Despite the tensions of bringing side by side artistic and political avant-gardes, the association did offer models of collective and anonymous production, striking against social, institutional and artistic structures; thus demonstrating the permeability between representation and action, between solidarity and struggle.

Acknowledgements

Research for this chapter was done in the framework of the projects MoDe(s)2: Modernidad(es) Descentralizada(s): Arte, política y contracultura en el eje transaltántico durante la Guerra Fría, 2 (HAR2017–82755-P) funded by the Spanish Government and Résistance(s) Partisane(s): Culture visuelle, imaginaires collectifs et mémoire révolutionnaire (ANR-15-IDEX-02), IDEX, Université Grenoble Alpes.

Notes

1 R. Acosta de Arriba, 'El Congreso olvidado', *La Gaceta de Cuba*, 1 (2013), 19–23. R. Gordon-Nesbitt, *To Defend the Revolution is to Defend Culture: The Cultural Policy of Cuban Revolution* (Oakland: PM Press, 2015).
2 The 'Cultural Guerrilla' was introduced in the context of the debate of the sub-commission 5 (responsible for discussing the role of avant-garde art) during the Congress. Roberto Matta (Santiago de Chile 1911–Rome 2002) was a Chilean painter of international reputation. A member of the French Surrealist group since the 1930s, he was a seminal figure for the configuration of the Abstract Expressionist movement in the USA. Politically active within the circles of the Tricontinental, he became part of the leading artists supporting the Allende government and one of the detractors of the Pinochet dictatorship (for more information see C. Poullain (curator), *Matta, du Surréalisme à l'histoire* (Marseille: Musée Cantini, 2013).
3 J. Le Parc, 'Cultural Guerrilla Warfare?', in Yves Aupetitallot, *GRAV: strategies de participation: 1960–1968*, cat. exh. Grenoble, Centro de Arte Contemporáneo, 7 junio–6 septiembre, 1998, pp. 229–32. Julio Le Parc (Mendoza, 1928) is an Argentinean artist based in Paris, a founding member of the kinetic art Groupe de Recherche d'Art Visuel in Paris (1960–1968). After being awarded the painting prize for foreign artists at the Venice Biennial in 1966, he became very active during May 1968. He was part of the Ateliers Populaires of the École Nationale des Beaux-Arts in Paris. From that date onwards, he reinforced his collaboration with Tricontinental networks, which coincided with the development of a figurative body of work and his participation in anti-imperialist artistic groups, such as the Collectif des peintres antifascistes, the Grupo Denuncia (denouncing torture

practices in Latin America), etc. (I Plante, *Argentinos de Paris* (Buenos Aires: Edhasa, 2013)).
4 W. Laqueur, *Guerrilla Warfare: A Historical and Critical Study* (Routledge, 2017); Smichtt, *The Theory of the Partisan: A Commentary/Remark on the Concept of the Political* (Berlin: Duncker & Humblot, 1963).
5 J. Bryne, *Mecca of Revolution: Algeria, Decolonisation & the Third World Order* (Oxford: Oxford University Press, 2016); A. Marchesi, *Latin America's Radical Left. Rebellion and Cold War in the Global Sixties* (Cambridge: Cambridge University Press, 2018); C. Kalter, *The Discovery of the Third World: Decolonisation and the Rise of the New Left in France, c.1950–1976* (Cambridge: Cambridge University Press, 2019).
6 V. Prashad, *The Darker Nations: A People's History of the Third World* (London & New York: The New Press, 2007).
7 J. Galimberti, N. De Haro and V. Scott, *Global Maoism: Art, Aesthetics and the Cultural Revolution* (Manchester: Manchester University Press, 2019).
8 From Cuba, Matta called for a cultural guerrilla 'in all fields of subversive thinking and imagination', which Le Parc echoed from Paris in his manifesto calling for 'organizing a sort of cultural guerrilla warfare against the current status quo, highlighting contradictions, creating situations in which people recover their ability to bring about change, fighting against every tendency towards the stable, the durable, and the definitive, fighting everything that increases a state of dependency, apathy, and myths – and other mental patterns born of a conditioning that colludes with the structures of power'. (See Matta quoted in Alain Jouffroy, 'La guérilla individuelle', *Opus International*, 5, Paris, February, 1968, 86 and Le Parc, 'Cultural Guerrilla Warfare?', 231.)
9 O. A. Westad, *The Global Cold War: Third World Interventions and the Making of Our Times* (Cambridge: Cambridge University Press, 2005).
10 Prashad, *The Darker Nations*, pp. 105–15; A. Garland Mahler, *From the Tricontinental to the Global South. Race, Radicalism and Transnational Solidarity* (Durham, NC: Duke University Press, 2018).
11 D. Craven, *Art and Revolution in Latin America, 1910–1990* (New Haven Yale University Press, 2006), p. 9.
12 E. Guevara, *El socialismo y el hombre en Cuba* (Mexico City: Editorial Grijalbo, 1971), p. 64.
F. Fanon, *Les damnés de la terre* (Paris: Éditions Maspero, 1961).
13 Guevara, *El socialismo y el hombre en Cuba*, p. 64.
14 F. Castro, 'Discurso de clausura del Congreso Cultural de La Habana', *Pensamiento crítico*, 12 (1968).

15 A. Jouffroy, 'Che si', *Opus International*, 3 (1967), 21–31.
16 E. Guevara, 'Crear dos, tres ... muchos Vietnam [sic], es la consigna', in Ulises Estrada and Luis Suárez (eds), *Rebelión tricontinental: Las voces de los condenandos de la tierra de Africa, Asia y América Latina* (New York: Ocean Press, 2006), p. 36.
17 C. Gilman, 'El intelectual como problema. La eclosión del antiintelectualismo latinoamericano de los sesenta y los setenta', *Prismas. Revista de historia intelectual*, 3 (1999), 73–93.
18 L. Stokes Sims, *Wifredo Lam and the International Avant-garde, 1932–1982* (Austin: University of Texas Press, 2002), p. 155.
19 Wifredo Lam (Sagua 1902–Paris 1982) was a Cuban painter based in Paris and Italy. As Stokes Sims explains, by merging Cubism and Surrealism with Afro-Cuban motifs, Lam's work held a singular position within the history of modern art. He was deeply committed to the Cuban revolution, with which he collaborated even though he developed his career mostly in Paris and Italy (see Stokes Sims, *Wifredo Lam*).
20 In 1976 a whole Salon was devoted to Palestine and in 1978 it was involved in the organisation of the 1978 *International Exhibition of Solidarity with Palestine*, which took place in Beirut. Claude Lazar a Parisian painter member of the Jeune Peinture, and close friend of the writer Ezzeddine Qalaq (the PLO representative in France since 1973), was a major player in the organisation from Paris of the Beirut Exhibition and one of the most active figures to galvanise solidarity among the artists in favour of the Palestinian cause in the French capital. Regarding the Salon and its activities see C. Dossin, 'Jeune Peinture. The Parisian Third Way of the 1960s', in G. Schöllhammer and R. Arevshatyan, *Sweet Sixties: Specters and Spirits of a Parallel Avant-garde* (Berlin: Stenberg Press, 2014) pp. 276–88. And for the 1978 Beirut Exhibition see K. Khouri and R. Salti (eds), *Past Disquiet: Artists International Solidarity and Museums in Exile* (Warsaw: Museum of Modern Art in Warsaw).
21 Castro, 'Palabras a los intelectuales'.
22 The relations between the avant-garde and the Cuban revolutionary government were complex and unequal, changing along the years. While during the 1960s the avant-garde was given room to develop, from 1971 onwards, with the Soviet turn in Cuban politics, avant-garde projects became suspicious. There were various censorship cases and many international artists and intellectuals withheld their support, see J. Fornet, *El 71. Anatomía de una crisis* (La Habana: Letras Cubana, 2013); and Craven, *Art and Revolution*.

23 R. Roa, 'Palabras de apertura del Salón de Mayo', in: *Salón de Mayo* (exh. cat.) (La Havane, Pabellón Cuba, 30 July, 1967), p. 2.
24 The Spanish Paris-based painter Eduardo Arroyo (Madrid 1937–2018) and the French painter Gilles Aillaud (Paris 1928–2005) were both committed leftist artists, part of the Figuration Narrative movement and board members of the Salon de la Jeune Peinture. They collaborated in organising the Salón de Mayo, providing Lam with a preliminary list of possible guests (P. Barreiro López, 'Algarabía tropical en la vanguardia: Wifredo Lam, la izquierda cultural española y la Cuba revolucionaria', in C. David (ed.) *Wifredo Lam*. Catálogo de exposición (Madrid: Museo Reina Sofía, 2016).
25 G. Mosquera, 'Mi pintura es un acto de descolonización', *Bohemia*, 25 (1980), 10–13.
26 Stokes Sims, *Wilfredo Lam*.
27 Mosquera, 'Mi pintura es un acto de descolonización'.
28 D. López Campristuos (curator), *La gran espiral. Cincuenta años del Salón de Mayo de 1967* (Museo de Bellas Artes de la Habana, 2017).
29 Marchesi, *Latin America's Radical Left*.
30 This was the case of the journal *Partisans* edited by François Maspero that directly connected the antifascist cause of the partisans with the 'new partisans' and guerrilleros of the Tricontinental. In its pages Fidel Castro, Ernesto Guevara, Amílcar Cabral found a place to circulate within French radical Left. Maspero was also the editor of the Spanish version of the journal *Tricontinental* of the OSPAAAL. Those connections are being studied within the international project *Partisan Resistance(s): Visual culture, collective imagination and revolutionary memory*, based at the Université Grenoble Alpes, France.
31 G. Gassiot-Talabot, 'La Havane: peinture et révolution', *Opus International*, 3 (1967), 16.
32 *Salón de Mayo*, exh. cat., La Havane, Pabellón Cuba, 30 July, 1967.
33 P. Barreiro López, 'Un Vietnam en el campo de la cultura: objetos promiscuos en el arsenal de la guerrilla', in P. Barreiro López (ed.), *Atlántico frío: historias transnacionales del arte y la política en los tiempos del telón de acero* (Madrid: Brumaria, 2019), pp. 117–54.
34 The invited painters produced multiple canvases in Cuba during their stay, which were donated to the State in order to create a museum of Modern Art. The collection is now held at the Museo de Bellas Artes of Havana.
35 C. Franqui, *Cuba la revolución: ¿mito o realidad? Memorias de un fantasma socialista* (Barcelona: Península, 2006).
36 L. Llanes, *Salón de Mayo de París en la Habana, julio 1967* (La Habana: Artecubanoediciones, 2012), p. 51

37 The exhibition took place at the Galería Latinoamericana of the Casa de las Américas from 18 July 1967.
38 J. P. Ameline, *Figuration Narrative: Paris 1960–1972* (Paris: Galeries nationales du Grand Palais, 16 April–13 July 2008); Llanes, *Salón de Mayo de París en la Habana*, p. 51.
39 L. Chollet, *Grand Tableau Antifasciste Collectif* (Paris: Éditions Dagorni, 2000).
40 Leiris Michel et al., 'Pour le congrès culturel de la Havane', *Opus International*, 3, Paris, October, 1967, p. 33.
41 Participants included: Julio Cortázar, Roberto Matta, Mario Benedetti, David Alfaro Siqueiros, Adolfo Sánchez Vázquez, Aimé Césaire, Antonio Saura, Jorge Semprún, Max Aub, Blas de Otero, Carlos Barral, Luis Goytisolo, Jules Feiffer, Alain Jouffroy, Michel Leiris, Edouard Pignon, André Pieyre de Mandiargues, Yves Lacoste, Asger Jorn, Roman Karmen, Francesco Rossi and Víctor Vasarely (Y. E. Acosta Batista, *Cuba y la cultura. Primera etapa del proyecto revolucionario internacional: el Salón de Mayo y el Congreso Cultural de La Habana*, Universidad de Salamanca. Master's thesis (Advisor Paula Barreiro López), 2013).
42 *Congreso Cultural de La Habana. Reunión de intelectuales de todo el mundo sobre problemas de Asia, África y América Latina* (La Habana: Instituto del Libro, 1968).
43 Ibid.
44 Ibid.
45 J. Stites Mor, 'Rendering Armed Struggle: OSPAAAL, Cuban Poster Art, and South-South Solidarity at the United Nations', in *Anuario De Historia De América Latina*, 56 (2019), 42–65; L. Hanna, '"Tricontinental's International Solidarity". Emotion in OSPAAAL as Tactic to Catalyze Support of Revolution', in *Radical History Review*, 136 (2020), 169–84.
46 M. Berríos, 'Now History Happens Here. Del Tercer Mundo', in Vijay Prashad (ed.), *The East Was Read. Socialist Culture in the Third World* (New Delhi: Left World, 2019), pp. 101–19.
47 Fanon, *Les damnés de la terre*.
48 Declaration of the Atelier Populaire quoted in Catherine Flood and Gavin Grindon, *Disobedient objects* (London: V&A Publishing, Londres, 2014), p. 20).
49 The artists involved in the ocuppation were the Argentineans Antonio Seguí, Julio Le Parc, Durante, Demarco, Copi, Alicia Penalba, Rómulo Maccio y Luis Tomasello, the Chilean Roberto Matta and the Belgian Pierre Alechinsky.

50 P. Barreiro López, 'General! La patria agradecida. Acción y reacción en la Maison d'Argentine en mayo de 1968', *Ensemble*, 2 (2009).
51 A. Longoni and M. Mestman, *Del Di Tella a Tucumán Arde. Vanguardia artística y política en el 68 argentino* (Buenos Aires: Eudeba, 2013), p. 101.
52 Longoni and Mestman, *Del Di Tella a Tucumán Arde*; J. Vindel, *La Vida por asalto: arte, política e historia en Argentina entre 1965 y 2001* (Madrid: Brumaria, 2014).
53 Ana Longoni, *Vanguardia y revolución. Arte e izquierdas en la Argentina de los sesenta-setenta* (Buenos Aires: Ariel, 2014).
54 This was the case of Pistoletto, see J. Galimberti, 'A Third-Worldist Art? Germano Celant's invention of Arte Povera', *Art History*, 36 (Wiley Online Library, 2013), 422, but also of other intellectuals close to the Cuban revolution (Fornet, *El 71*).
55 A. Longoni, 'La pasión según Eduardo Favario. La militancia revolucionaria como ética del sacrificio', *El Rodaballo*, VI:11/12, Buenos Aires, 2000.
56 Vaneigem, 1967, quoted in David Crowley, 'In the Image of Revolution', in D. Crowley and J. Pavitt (eds), *Cold War Modern: Design 1945–1970* (London: V&A Publishing, 2008), pp. 205–27.
57 Roberto Jacoby (Buenos Aires 1944) is an Argentinian conceptual artist and sociologist, member of the Buenos Aires avant-garde of the 1960s. After being one of the Di Tella Institute's artists, he founded the group Arte de los Medios (with Eduardo Costa and Raùl Escari) and he was a key figure of Tucuman Arde. see A. Longoni, *Roberto Jacoby. El deseo nace del derrumbe* (Madrid: Museo Reina Sofía, Red Conceptualismos del Sur, Adriana Hidalgo y La Central, 2011).
58 K. Ross, *May 68 and Its Afterlives* (Chicago: University of Chicago Press, 2002).
59 Ibid., p. 81.

Appendix to Chapter 4

Figure 4.4a Pamphlet cover, 'Three continents, one common enemy, a unified struggle, a new world!!!' Tricontinentale Sorbonne, Comité des Trois Continents, 1968.

SOMMAIRE

- Plate forme d'orientation ....
- Les travailleurs immigrés, exploités par les exploités .1
- L'ennemi commun : L'Exploiteur 5
- Le Mouvement Révolutionnaire dans les Pays Capitalistes
  et la lutte Révolutionnaire des Peuples Opprimés 7
- Répercussions du Mouvement Etudiants en Afrique, Asie,
  et Amérique Latine 10
- Répression : En Afrique aussi 14
- La Lutte Continue 17
- Halte à l'expulsion de nos camarades étrangers 19
- Créer deux, trois, de nombreux Viet-Nam - Voilà le
  mot d'ordre -   CHE GUEVARA 21
- Le vrai visage de la Francophonie 35
- Langues et langage en Afrique Noire 35
- Soutien moral et matériel au peuple du Zimbabué 40
- Culture et oppression ....43 - 45
- Détruisons les derniers vestiges du colonialisme ... 46
- Activités du Comité des Trois Continents 55
- Poèmes 34bis
                                                    45bis

Prix minimum 2,50 F.

Sur chaque bulletin une résolution de la Tricontinental.

Figure 4.4b Table of contents, 'Three continents' pamphlet, 1968.

Contents

- Orientation platform
- Immigrant workers, exploited by the exploited
- The common enemy: The Exploiter
- The Revolutionary Movement in the Capitalist Countries and the Revolutionary struggle of the Oppressed Countries
- Repercussions of the Student Movement in Africa, Asia and Latin America
- Repression: In Africa too
- The struggle continues
- Stop the expulsion of our foreign comrades
- Create two, three, many Vietnam – This is the watchword – CHE GUEVARA
- The true face of La Francophonie
- Languages and language in Black Africa
- Moral and material support to the people of Zimbabwe
- Culture and oppression
- Let's destroy the last vestiges of colonialism
- Activities of the Committee of the Three Continents
- Poems.

Minimum Price 2,50 F

POUR LE CONGRES CULTUREL DE LA HAVANE

Les artistes et les intellectuels soussignés ont perçu, à Cuba, combien est étroite la liaison entre Culture et Révolution. Le combat révolutionnaire du peuple cubain vise non seulement à obtenir, pour l'ensemble du Tiers-Monde, de meilleures conditions matérielles de vie, mais à créer des conditions telles que chaque culture puisse atteindre son complet épanouissement et que chaque groupe humain affirme ainsi son existence. De plus, il suffit de circuler à La Havane ou dans le reste de l'île pour constater que la Révolution cubaine, serait-ce par les seules affiches qui en sont l'expression verbale et imagée, fait littéralement descendre la poésie dans la rue.

Du 4 au 11 janvier 1968, doit se tenir le Congrès Culturel de La Havane, réunion d'intellectuels du monde entier pour discuter des problèmes qui se posent quant à la culture dans les pays sous-développés.

En cette époque où en Asie, en Amérique Latine et en Afrique une lutte armée oppose des hommes à des gouvernements avides de maintenir la domination anachronique d'une classe privilégiée, artistes et intellectuels ne peuvent que prendre parti pour ces hommes lucides et courageux. Un peuple opprimé est, en effet, empêché de développer sa culture et, tant que l'oppression existe, le monde se trouve privé de la richesse inestimable qu'est le libre exercice de la pensée. Si l'on veut que la culture vivante, au-delà du savoir accumulé, se manifeste comme une exigence aussi générale et aussi fondamentale que celle de vivre libre, il faut que les intellectuels des pays développés se solidarisent, comme ceux des pays sous-développés, avec tous les révolutionnaires qui ont pris les armes pour faire la révolution.

Qu'un Régis Debray, philosophe et écrivain, se soit solidarisé avec les guérilleros d'Amérique Latine et qu'il soit emprisonné par un Barrientos montre à quel point la Culture est liée à la Révolution et à quel point elle est aujourd'hui en danger.

Face aux problèmes du monde sous-développé, l'intellectuel occidental porte une responsabilité qui dépasse la sienne propre : elle est celle de tous les hommes dotés de ces moyens de s'affirmer que les puissances impérialistes refusent aux peuples qu'elles dominent.

Rôle de la culture dans la lutte révolutionnaire, culture et moyens d'information, rapport entre la création artistique et la science qu'aucun fossé ne devrait séparer, passage de l'homme actuellement divisé et mutilé à l'homme total, comptent parmi les thèmes dont traitera le Congrès Culturel de La Havane. Et c'est pourquoi nous apporterons tout notre appui à cette initiative d'un pays dont nous avons pu mesurer l'immense volonté qu'il a de porter le travail de l'intelligence à son degré le plus brûlant. La Havane, 30 juillet 1967.

Michel LEIRIS, Maurice NADEAU, Wifredo LAM, Alain JOUFFROY, Eduardo ARROYO, Auguste THESEE, Alain GHEERBRANT, Pierre GUYOTAT, Philippe HIQUILY, Piotr KOWALSKI, R. E. GILLET, MESSAGIER, REBEYROLLE, MONORY, Roland PENROSE, Luigi CARLUCCIO, CATTY, Jorge SEMPRUN, Colette SEMPRUN, Ezio GRIBAUDO, Georges FALL, Gilles EHRMANN, Marc de ROSNY, Ausgan ELDE, K. S. KAROL, Harold SZEEMANN, E. ALLEYN, Denys CHEVALIER, FELTRINELLI, Edward LUCIE-SMITH, Antonio RECALCATI, Irène DOMINGUEZ, Marguerite DURAS, Gérald GASSIOT-TALABOT, Gilles AILLAUD, Dyonis MASCOLO, Jean SCHUSTER, Peter WEISS, Harry MULISCH, Lucio MUNOZ, Ewan PHILLIPS, Jean-Jacques LEVEQUE, Pierre DESCARGUES, Georges BOUDAILLE, Louise LEIRIS, José PIERRE, Gherasim LUCA, Jorge CAMACHO, COUTURIER, GILLY, César BALDACCINI, Monique LANGE, CARDENAS, Van der ELSKEN, Rossana ROSSANDA, Juan GOYTISOLO, Georges LIMBOUR, Lasse SODERBORG, L. OSKOK, de WILDE, Giorgio UPIGLIO, Jean LEYMARIE, Valerio RIVA, N. LILENSTEIN, Gundmundur ERRO, Anik SINE, A. BITRAN, César PEVERELLI, RANCILLAC, GOLENDORF, CORNEILLE, Jacqueline SELZ, Yvon TAILLANDIER, Gunilla PALMSTIERNA-WEISS, Anne ZEMIRE, Nicole PIERRE.

S'associent à cet appel :
Raoul-Jean MOULIN, Jean-Clarence LAMBERT, Jean-Luc GODARD, Jérôme PEIGNOT, Daniel POMMEREULLE, François DI DIO, Jean-Pierre FAYE.

Figure 4.5 Manifesto, 'For the cultural congress of Havana', published in *Opus International* 3 (1967).

For the Cultural Congress of Havana[1]

The undersigned artists and intellectuals have observed how closely linked Culture and Revolution are in Cuba. The Cuban people's revolutionary struggle not only aims to achieve better material conditions for the entirety of the Third World, but to create conditions through which every culture can attain its total development and for each human group to assert its existence. Furthermore, one need only stroll around Havana or the rest of the island to realise that the Cuban Revolution, if only through its posters that reflect it verbally and visually, literally brings poetry to the streets.

The Cultural Congress of Havana is slated to take place on the 4th until the 11th of January 1968 and will reunite intellectuals from around the world to discuss the problem of culture in underdeveloped countries.

In a time when armed struggles in Asia, Latin America and Africa oppose men against governments eager to uphold the anachronistic domination of a privileged class, artists and intellectuals have no choice but to take a stand with these lucid and courageous men. An oppressed people is in fact prevented from developing their culture and as long as oppression exists, everyone is deprived of the invaluable richness of the freedom of thought. If we want living culture, which goes beyond accumulated knowledge, to become as general and as fundamental a demand as the right to freedom, the intellectuals of the developed world must then stand in solidarity, as did those in underdeveloped countries, with all revolutionaries who took up arms to start the revolution.

If a philosopher and writer like Régis Debray came in solidarity with the fighters of Latin America and was imprisoned by Barrientos,[2] it shows how connected Culture is with the Revolution and to what extent it is in danger today.

Facing the problems of underdeveloped countries, the Western intellectual has a responsibility that surpasses himself; it is the responsibility of all men with means to assert themselves against the imperialist powers that deprive those of the people they dominate.

The role of culture in the revolutionary struggle, its tools of information, the rapport between artistic creation and science, which no rift can separate, as well as the transformation of the currently divided and mutilated man into the whole man (l'homme total), are some of the themes that the Cultural Congress of Havana will engage. And that is why we strongly support this initiative that was started by a country in which we saw a willingness to undertake the intellectual work to its most passionate degree.

Havana, 30 July 1967

Michel LEIRIS, Maurice NADEAU, Wifredo LAM, Alain JOUFFROY, Eduardo ARROYO, Auguste THESEE, Alain GHEERBRANT, Pierre GUYOTAT, Philippe HIQUILY, Piotr KOWALSKI, R. E. GILLET, MESSAGIER, REBEYROLLE, MONORY, Roland PENROSE, Luigi CARLUCCIO, CATTY, Jorge SEMPRUN, Colette SEMPRUN, Ezio GRIBAUDO, Georges FALL, Gilles EHRMANN, Marc de ROSNY, Ausgan ELDE, K. S. KAROL, Harold SZEEMANN, E. ALLEYN, Denys CHEVALIER, FELTRINELLI, Edward LUCIE-SMITH, Antonio RECALCATI, Irène DOMINGUEZ, Marguerite DURAS, Gérald GASSIOT-TALABOT, Gilles AILLAUD, Dyonis MASCOLO, Jean SCHUSTER, Peter WEISS, Harry MULISCH, Lucio MUNOZ, Ewan PHILLIPS, Jean-Jacques LEVEQUE, Pierre DESCARGUES, Georges BOUDAILLE, Louise LEIRIS, José PIERRE, Gherasim LUCA, Jorge CAMACHO, COUTURIER, GILLY, César BALDACCINI, Monique LANGE, CARDENAS, Van der ELŞKEN, Rossana ROSSANDA, Juan GOYTISOLO, Georges LIMBOUR, Lasse SODERBORG, L. OSKOK, de WILDE, Giorgio UPIGLIO, Jean LEYMARIE, Valerio RIVA, N. LILENSTEIN, Gund mundur ERRO, Anik SINE, A. BITRAN, César PEVERELLI, RANCILLAC, GOLENDORF, COR NEILLE, Jacqueline SELZ, Yvon TAILLANDIER, Gunilla PALMSTIERNA-WEISS, Anne ZEMIRE, Nicole PIERRE.

Those who endorse this call: Raoul-Jean MOULIN, Jean-Clarence LAMBERT, Jean-Luc GODARD, Jérôme PEIGNOT, Daniel POMMEREULLE, François DI DIO, Jean-Pierre FAYE.

Notes

1 Translated by Rayya Badran.
2 Editors: In reference to President Rene Barrientos Ortuno of Bolivia. Régis Debray is the author of *Revolution in the Revolution?* (1967) which presents an assessment of revolutionary guerilla tactics in 1960s Latin America building from the Cuban model. Debray was imprisoned in Bolivia and sentenced to thirty years in prison but was released in 1970 thanks to an international campaign mounted in his support.

5

New Left encounters in Latin America: transnational revolutionaries, exiles and the formation of the Tupamaros in early 1960s Montevideo

Marina Cardozo

Para El Negro, Grauert Lezama.

This study seeks to deepen the knowledge of political nodes of dialogic exchange about revolutionary action between the emerging Uruguayan armed left and various transnational networks of left militants in transit in Montevideo during the 1960s. This was a key moment for the configuration of revolutionary thought, as well as for the consolidation of a new radical left in Uruguay and, more broadly, in Latin America.

The chapter examines an aspect scarcely touched in the historiography of the Uruguayan armed left, contributing to the study of transnational links between New Left movements during the years of the Latin American Cold War. Here, the origin of the Uruguayan armed left is studied within the framework of the global sixties, focusing on the encounters between revolutionary militants and ideas about transnational activism that converged in the city of Montevideo in 1964. These encounters, as the chapter will go on to demonstrate, nurtured political praxis and influenced the formation of new militant subjectivities that formed the first generation of Tupamaros,[1] an Uruguay-based radical leftist urban guerrilla organisation of international repute.

The new armed left arose in contestation of what was then perceived as the revolutionary apathy of the Left and was also linked to the rich local anarchist, socialist and communist traditions: many of the first Tupamaros were, in the early 1960s, members of the 'traditional' left parties. In addition to the wealth of diverse political trajectories, the initial militancy of the Tupamaros movement brought together a network of communications, interactions and exchanges that were significant in their formation as a political group and as militants in an armed organisation. From different parts of the Americas and the world, and under different circumstances, clandestine visitors, fugitives, political exiles, or activists observing political processes in the making, converged in the city of Montevideo during the key year of 1964. Particularly noteworthy were the exchanges with political activists from other revolutionary experiences in Latin America and, at the same time, with political exiles from Brazil due to the civil-military dictatorship established there in March 1964. These exchanges will be the subject of my focused analysis in this chapter.

Over the past three decades the Movimiento de Liberación Nacional-Tupamaros – the official name of the guerrilla movement since 1965–66 – has been the subject of considerable attention, especially from the point of view of a testimonial literature written by protagonists and also by journalists who have reconstructed stories, biographies or fictionalised biographies.[2] There has also been a political and sociological interest in the subject, offering an explanatory framework,[3] which coincided with the rise of political science as a disciplinary field in Uruguay in the last decade of the twentieth century.[4] However, the historiographical literature on the subject is much smaller, and even more so in English, with some fundamental works standing out.[5]

This chapter focuses specifically on the period of genesis of the MLN-Tupamaros in the Montevideo enclave and in relation to other transnational agents of the period. It is important to highlight the relevance of focusing on the period up to 1967; the vast majority of the existing literature on the guerrilla focuses on the period after 1968, when Latin American guerrillas became institutionalised. The period up to 1968 has its own contingency and its own particular richness that is practically unexplored, especially in terms of the transnational dimension of the new armed left organisations in Latin America. My chapter also contributes to a growing literature in English on the global sixties by shedding light on the understudied foundational experience of the Tupamaros in this critical conjuncture.

In order to carry out this task, my study relies on documentary sources from the period (press, written testimonies) and, above all, oral testimonies. It is worth emphasising the importance of oral history in this study, which enables the reconstruction of aspects that are difficult to access insofar as we are studying political sectors that carried out underground militancy. These sources, in turn, allow us to address aspects that have been little explored in relation to the subject under analysis, in particular to delve more deeply into the militant subjectivities, their sociabilities and the cultural constructs that gave shape to their political choices.

The term New Left has been used in recent historiography to examine the birth of different ways of doing politics from those utilised and often developed by the 'traditional' left (essentially communists, socialists and anarchists). The term also refers to a political thought and praxis that advocated for a third space, decentred from the two axes of power, Soviet and US, at the beginning of the Cold War. In a similar vein, recent historiography on the New Left is part of emerging studies on the Cold War that examine, among other things, transnational actors in the Global South and Third Worldist socio-political movements, thus favouring a transnational perspective of the 1960s, as a global moment of contestation and unrest. Hence, the concept of the global sixties has been used to understand local dynamics in a framework which, according to Eric Zolov, includes, among other aspects: the consideration of the long-term impact of the Cold War as an 'ideological project'; the rich web of the political left and its trajectories; national liberation movements and the rise of the Global South as new political actor on the world stage; the link between politics and counterculture on a global level; and the importance of liberation theology. In Zolov's view, this would make it possible to 'provincialise' the North and to grasp the autonomy of the revolt in the South, as well as the richness of South-South interlocutions.[6]

At the same time, the 'New Left' as a concept constitutes a native notion, emerging from radical left militants, activists and intellectuals themselves in the 1960s. During the long sixties, the New Left was an expression used in militant jargon as well as in radical left publications all over the world. It alluded to a new way of acting politically and, in particular, to a new sensibility nourished by a strongly anti-imperialist component, which in Latin America continued the tradition of anticolonial American thought from José Martí (1853–95) onwards.[7] Simultaneously, this broad movement linked the Global South as re-signified through the Cuban Revolution, with anticolonial national liberation movements in Africa and Asia, from Bandung onwards.[8]

In Latin Americanist historiography,[9] the concept of the 'New Left' includes the study not only of its political-ideological manifestations but also of the interplay between this activism and the various counter-cultural manifestations that accompanied (or came into conflict with) these manifestations, in a sort of political-cultural-generational amalgam in conflict but also in dialogue with the classical left tradition.[10]

The New Left can be characterised, thus, as a polyphonic movement on different scales and geographies combining the political and the cultural, which determined circulations and exchanges between North and South. Many of these circulations and exchanges remain unexplored because of restricted historiographical perspectives that underestimated the contributions of historical processes of the Global South to the radical decade. In the words of Elizabeth Jelin analysing the Latin American 1968: 'decentring the centre – not taking Europe as the centre from which everything radiates, but proposing a model of networks and multiple centres – makes it possible to exclude Eurocentric views and enrich global analyses of '68.[11]

The Coordinador

Towards the end of 1962, the first meetings of political militants took place in Montevideo, giving rise in 1963 to the formation of the so-called Coordinador, a network of political groups that operated armed actions. This network was made up of members of the Movimiento de Apoyo al Campesino (MAC);[12] the Movimiento de Izquierda Revolucionaria (MIR);[13] militants of the Partido Socialista del Uruguay (PSU), the Federación Anarquista Uruguaya (FAU); unorganised anarchist militants and some independent members.[14]

Between 1963 and 1965, the Coordinador carried out a number of militant direct actions and armed propaganda operations including the notorious assault on the Club de Tiro Suizo (considered a foundational event),[15] 'bank expropriations', stealing of weapons, helping to organise the escape of Raúl Sendic (leader of the

Tupamaros) from prison (in Paso de los Libres, Argentina), attacks with firecrackers or explosives against significant buildings,[16] and finally, the expropriation of foodstuffs and toys for distribution in the *cantegriles*.[17] Actions involving explosive devices often did not achieve coordinated support, and were carried out autonomously by the groups that integrated the Coordinador. Never targetting the civilians, the latter are, however, the most 'forgotten' or least mentioned actions in my interviewees' memories.

The backdrop to these events was the economic crisis that began in Uruguay in the mid-1950s. In 1958 the Partido Nacional was elected, promising to address the country's economic problems and unseating the Partido Colorado (which had held power for more than ninety years). Amid increasing difficulties and the chronic stagnation of material production, new liberal economic policies were implemented. These policies restricted the role of the Uruguayan 'Welfare State' (or *Estado Social*[18] to be more precise), whose foundations were established in the first half of the twentieth century. The state consequently lost its capacity to protect the most disadvantaged sectors of society. The industrialist policies of the *second Batllismo*[19] were reduced and from 1960, the government's economic position was aligned with the policies of the International Monetary Fund. Agricultural and industrial production stagnation, combined with the onset of a constant inflationary process, had a negative impact on wage earners' incomes. As Jaime Yaffé points out in relation to the general feeling of deterioration in welfare levels derived from the progressive erosion of the *Estado Social*: 'in a few years, the imaginary of a *happy Uruguay* was replaced by the imaginary of a *Uruguay in crisis*',[20] an imaginary that would become predominant as the 1960s progressed.

All of this was part of the economic, cultural and foreign policy interventions by the United States vis-à-vis Latin American governments during the 1950s and 1960s. These interventions were clearly reinforced in the wake of the Cuban Revolution, which had aroused the sympathy and solidarity of left parties, movements and organisations across the continent.[21] Seeking to curtail and 'contain' any communist threat in Latin America during the Cold War, the United States launched the Alliance for Progress in 1961 from Punta del Este, in Uruguay. This project entailed a set of counter-revolutionary initiatives framed around the idea of modernising

Latin America so as to prevent the advent of new revolutionary experiences and to guard against progressive governments coming to power. The Alliance for Progress would also lead to a strengthening of US military aid in the region, setting the stage for an increase in authoritarianism that would take shape after the aforementioned military coup d'état in Brazil in 1964.

In direct response to the economic crisis, trade union demands intensified and the process of unifying the workers' movement gathered pace, culminating in 1966 with the creation of the Convención Nacional de Trabajadores (CNT, 'National Convention of Workers'). Meanwhile, at the level of the political left, substantial transformations took place in both the Communist Party (PCU) and the Socialist Party (PSU) of Uruguay. The former, after abandoning the Stalinist line and under the leadership of Rodney Arismendi, devoted itself to the constitution of a democratic front committed to social transformation through parliamentary means. Meanwhile, the PSU under the leadership of Vivián Trías was radicalised, leaving behind the social-democratic imprint of its historic leader Emilio Frugoni, and deepened its Third Worldist profile, pointing to the need for a national socialist revolution. The election results, however, were not favourable for the Left, which as a whole only obtained 5.6 per cent of the total votes in the 1962 national elections. The electoral disapointment was a key factor in encouraging an important segment of the radical youth militancy, which considered the electoral path incapable of leading to necessary social change. This resulted in a number of splits and the organisation of the so-called Coordinador, the beginning of the experience of the local armed left.

Certain radicalised, university-educated youth sectors were central to the transformation of the PSU, which resigned from the Socialist International in 1960, rejecting the role of French socialism during the Algerian Revolution. This is key to understanding, first, the impact of the Algerian Revolution on the budding new local left, and second, the presence of the *literal and aspirational connections*[22] that linked these radicalised Uruguayan socialist militants – some of whom would later join the armed left – to transnational activism for the liberation of Third World peoples: what was happening in Algeria was part of their own political praxis. Among these young militants was Raúl Sendic, one of the historic leaders of the Tupamaros movement. Sendic was a key figure in the organisation of the sugar cane cutters' union in the northern Department of Artigas. The sugar cane workers' (*cañeros*) union, Unión de Trabajadores Azucareros de Artigas (UTAA, 'Sugar Workers Union of Artigas'), was fundamental in the formation of the armed left in Uruguay and in the generation of a rupture with the social imaginary of a 'European' and exceptional Uruguay.[23] Several *cañeros* were active members of the Tupamaros movement, even though the latter, while proclaiming its identification with the 'peasant' cause, maintained a strong urban imprint, largely due to the composition of its initial militancy.

The Coordinador disintegrated in 1965, giving way to a new organisation (which many of the initial groups in the network decided not to join), called Movimiento de Liberación Nacional-Tupamaros (MLN-Tupamaros), the 'official' name of the guerrilla movement, known worldwide. The creation of the MLN-Tupamaros took place between 1965 and 1966. Before that, however, many members of the groups that made up the Coordinador were known as Tupamaros.[24] The Coordinador expressed the political and ideological diversity of the Uruguayan left in the early 1960s, a formative period in which multiple alternatives were possible.

Transnational connections

The emergence of Latin American guerrillas in the 1960s was a determining factor in the growth of US interventionism during the Cold War. A catalytic element was the triumph of the Cuban Revolution, even though there had been previous experiences, all of which were marked by specific local logics. International events such as the Vietnam War had an important impact on the revolutionary imaginary. Among the common elements of these New Left-wing political movements which proposed the armed path in opposition to the parliamentary political praxis of the classical left, were a strong anti-imperialism and a Latin American and Third World consciousness.

In 1964, the Coordinador began to establish links with other Latin American armed experiences, based on direct contacts with members of movements and organisations in the region, some of whom were temporary refugees in Montevideo. Among these contacts were ex-combatants of the Ejército Guerrillero del Pueblo (EGP, 'People's Guerrilla Army') which operated in Salta, Argentina in 1963–64, and important members of the Argentinean Movimiento Nacionalista Revolucionario Tacuara (MNRT, 'Revolutionary Nationalist Movement Tacuara').[25] In the first case mentioned, the connections arguably strengthened the appeal to revolutionary continentality, which constituted a central idea of the groups that made up the coordinating network. In the second case, exchanges between members of the leftist side of Tacuara exiled in Montevideo and the militants of the Coordinador focused on matters of an operational nature. They were concerned with developing practical knowledge around concrete actions and activities of revolutionary praxis. Nonetheless, this practical focus was accompanied by theoretical discussions, as for example during the visit of French activist Régis Debray to Montevideo in 1965.[26]

Between late August and early September 1964, Ciro Bustos was in Montevideo. One of the few survivors of the frustrated EGP, Bustos, known as 'Lieutenant Laureano', was also a member of Ernesto 'Che' Guevara's guerrilla movement in Bolivia. Bustos had been in charge of the EGP's links with nearby urban centres and abroad.[27] The EGP, commanded by Jorge Ricardo Masetti and supported from Cuba, had finally been defeated in Salta, in April 1964. The following month, Bustos and José María Aricó travelled to Havana to meet Guevara and to present their version of what had happened. Weeks later, Bustos arrived in Montevideo, where a few ex-combatants, survivors of the EGP experience, had settled.[28] Two socialist activists close to Tupamaros leader, Raúl Sendic, Javier Guridi (administrator of the newspaper *El Sol* of the PSU and a militant of singular importance in the web of informal ties that constituted the beginning of the armed left) and young Eduardo Galeano (journalist and writer in the famous weekly *Marcha* and in the newspaper *Época*) contacted Sendic with Ciro Bustos. According to Bustos, during the conversation with Sendic, the Tupamaros leader expressed his interest in learning about the vicissitudes suffered by the Argentinean armed group, and asked Bustos about the possibility of having some weapons from the EGP and training in militant security and intelligence. Some time later, during another trip by Ciro Bustos to Montevideo, both requests were fulfilled and Bustos personally trained a trusted Sendic militant in security practices.

At the same time, while diplomatic relations between Uruguay and Cuba were ruptured following a vote by the Uruguayan government (on 8 September 1964), a small number of firearms were clandestinely obtained through a contact in the Cuban Embassy, stored in a commercial place, and then transferred to the Uruguayan armed militants.[29] The Cuban mediation, clearly sponsored by Bustos' contacts, is of particular interest. It also indicates the Coordinador's resolution to equip itself for armed action, despite competing memories among the protagonists about the real intention behind the use of political violence, whether it was for a defensive strategy or for a revolutionary horizon, or both.

The link between militants of the Coordinador and members of the MNRT extended for a longer time. The Tacuaristas of the MNRT defined themselves as 'Peronists and revolutionaries',[30] and had emerged in the aftermath of the Cuban Revolution, inspired by the latter as well as by the anti-imperialist experiences of Algeria and Egypt.[31] In April 1964, after the trial of the MNRT for the assault on the Policlínico Bancario ('Banking Polyclinic Hospital', on 29 August 1963), some of its best-known members, such as Joe Baxter (the principal leader although not directly involved in the events of the Policlínico), Jorge Cataldo, Alfredo Roca and Ruben Rodríguez, were able to escape, largely thanks to the help of the Peronist Resistance, and settle in Montevideo.[32] José Luis Nell Tacchi, wanted for his role in the Policlínico operation, arrived in Montevideo a few months later, after his unprecedented escape from the Palacio de Tribunales (Courthouse) in Buenos Aires. All of them lived for a significant amount of time as refugees in Uruguay, between 1964 and 1966. During their Uruguayan exile, Baxter, Cataldo, Nell and Rodríguez made several clandestine trips in and out of the country. Other members of the MNRT such as Luis Alfredo Zarattini, remained refugees in Montevideo just in 1964, and only intermittently, as they travelled to Argentina on several occasions.

Meanwhile, equally relevant here is the fact that the Argentinean revolutionary leader Ángel 'Vasco' Bengochea gave two clandestine talks in Montevideo, between late 1963 and early 1964, which were published in 1970 under the title *Guerra de Guerrillas* ('Guerrilla Warfare', co-authored with Juan José López Silveira).[33] This allows us to presume connections between the finally frustrated guerrilla attempt of the Fuerzas Armadas de la Revolución Nacional (FARN, 'Armed Forces of the National Revolution') led by Bengochea himself, and the Uruguayan armed militants who were part of the coordinating network. The FARN constituted an armed movement identified with Peronism, whose origins, however, can be found in the entrist activities developed by Trotskyism, and in particular by the group Palabra Obrera ('Worker's Voice'). This group was created from the weekly publication of the same name, initiated in 1957.[34] Bengochea, in turn, strongly influenced by the Cuban Revolution, had travelled to Havana in 1962, where he maintained frequent contacts with Guevara. He died as a result of an explosives accident in Buenos Aires in July 1964, along with four other militants.

In Cuba, in 1962, 'Vasco' Bengochea and other militants of Palabra Obrera, had carried out political-military training courses together with those of diverse tendencies on the radical left who converged there at the behest of John William Cooke, Alicia Eguren and Abraham Guillén, three central figures in the shaping of the notion of revolution and armed struggle in the 1960s. Among other militants, these training courses were attended by members of the Peronist armed group Uturuncos, which operated in Tucumán in 1959 and later in 1963 and for whom Cooke and Guillén were ideologues. According to Salas,[35] Masetti's EGP – centre of attention in Havana between 1963 and 1964 – Uturuncos in their second attempt in 1963, and the FARN of 'Vasco' Bengochea, were linked to each other. This nexus constituted the support nuclei for the EGP in Tucumán (on behalf of Uturuncos and FARN), and in Buenos Aires (on behalf of FARN).

To complete the circle of contacts and exchanges in Montevideo in 1964, it is worth mentioning the frequent conversations between two key revolutionary figures: Joe Baxter (MNRT leader) and Abraham Guillén (former republican fighter in the Spanish Civil War, and later a theorist of guerrilla warfare in Latin America), who had met years before in Cuba.[36] According to Gutman,[37] Ruben Rodríguez and José Luis Nell Tacchi had also built a close relationship with Guillén. The latter was also in contact with some members of the Coordinador. Under the pseudonym Arapey, Guillén wrote in the Uruguayan newspaper *Acción*. Meanwhile, he frequently met with Raúl Sendic and other militants of the Coordinador, such as

Jorge Torres and Mario Navillat, with whom he exchanged ideas about the possibilities of urban guerrilla activities in Uruguay.

As Jorge Torres (leader of the MIR, founder of the Coordinador and later a member of MLN-Tupamaros) recalls, one of the key events in the history of the Coordinador was the founding of a press organ in 1964. Although short-lived, it represented the network's political positions. The magazine *Barricada*, of which only two issues were published, was, for Torres, concrete proof of the existence of the Coordinador, which afterwards leaders like Guillermo Chifflet of the PSU were determined to deny.[38] For Torres, who was the editor of the publication, it is important to reaffirm the revolutionary vocation and the identity of the Coordinador as well as his theoretical and political-strategic profile. From the pages of the two issues of *Barricada*, we see him setting out his analyses of the coup d'état in Brazil under the pseudonym Rolando Castro (his middle name and second surname).[39]

Abraham Guillén presents himself as a 'tactical and strategic inspirer' of the Tupamaros movement:

> Only in 1965, when I published *Estrategia de la Guerrilla Urbana* ['Strategy of the Urban Guerrilla'], did the Tupamaros see the light, because I said that 'cement forests are safer than real forests'. And that cities have more logistical resources than the countryside. And (since our civilisation is capitalist and concentrates capital and populations in the cities at an even-increasing pace), in countries like Uruguay with more than 80% of the urban population, it was absurd to go and wage revolutionary war in the countryside, where there are more cows and sheep than rural population.[40]

However, Jorge Torres[41] makes the contrary claim that Guillén was inspired to write his book *Estrategia de la Guerrilla Urbana* (first published in Buenos Aires in 1965), from the thesis elaborated by Torres and Navillat in 1964, within the framework of the Coordinador. It is quite plausible that Guillén was not behind the famous thesis of the urban guerrilla, but Torres himself. However due to Guillén's greater visibility, the idea was attributed to him.

Guillén's discussions with Régis Debray, in fact, have to do with Guillén's distrust of armed struggle as the only viable route to revolutionary change. In this sense, both the initial rejection of the Guevarist foco theory and the rural guerrilla strategy were aspects that Guillén shared with Torres. It is interesting to note that, both during the period in which the Coordinador functioned and later, after the founding of the MLN-Tupamaros, Torres was recognised by his comrades as an outstanding militant with an exceptional theoretical background.

In any case, in the clandestine talks of 'Vasco' Bengochea mentioned above, the notion of urban struggle that Bengochea would discuss with Guevara during his visit to Cuba in 1962 was already present. Beyond this specific aspect, although the testimonies of the militants underline the autonomy of their political project with respect to possible support from the Cuban Revolution and other aid linked to regional guerrillas, the existence of a nourished network of contacts, of which the armed militants of the Coordinador's groups were a very active part, is undeniable.

Between 1964 and 1967, Uruguay became the focus of the political activities of the Brazilian exile.[42] Among the most well known of these were Brazil's ousted president, Joao Goulart, and Labour leader and federal deputy, Leonel Brizola, who fled to Montevideo in 1964. From the Left, important efforts were made to denounce the dictatorship, as well as to support the Brazilian exiles who continued to take refuge in the country. For example, the Movimiento Uruguayo de Solidaridad con el Pueblo Brasileño ('Uruguayan Movement in Solidarity with the Brazilian People') was created with the support of the Asociación de Prensa ('Press Association'), the Federación Uruguaya de Magisterio ('Uruguayan Teachers' Federation') and the newspaper *Época*. Likewise, the weekly newspaper *Marcha*, banned in Brazil, constituted a platform from which prominent Brazilian politicians exiled in Uruguay could express themselves and from which permanent denunciations were made in relation to the dictatorship in that country.[43] According to the testimony of Fernández Huidobro – who participated in the Coordinador – the April 1964 coup d'état in Brazil raised great concern on the Uruguayan left, with the fear of invasion spreading during 1964. On the other hand, the rumours of a coup d'état in Uruguay did not contribute to generate tranquillity either, as Huidobro noted:

> The border began to be a focus of attention. At first, with the hope of getting into Brazil to help the resistance that was about to break out, then when we bitterly witnessed the consolidation of the dictatorship, and the border began to be the place to go to help our comrades to find a safe place in our territory.[44]

A few years earlier, between 1960 and 1961, there had been a transformation in the programme of the Brazilian Ligas Camponesas ('Peasant Leagues').[45] The previous position of an agrarian reform 'within the law' was abandoned and, under the influence of the Cuban Revolution (including through key Ligas Camponesas leaders such as Francisco Julião travelling to Cuba and participating in military training courses), the political contents of their demands were changed to claim land 'by law or by force'. This process, in turn, led to the rupture between some Ligas Camponesas leaders with political sectors of the peasant movement linked to the Partido Comunista Brasileiro (PCB, 'Brazilian Communist Party').[46] The 1964 coup d'état accelerated the growth of a New Left that questioned the previous hegemony of the PCB and promoted armed struggle against the military dictatorship.[47]

Among the Brazilian guerrilla groups, the Ação Libertadora Nacional (ALN, 'National Liberation Action'), under the leadership of Carlos Marighella, would stand out in the subsequent years. One fact makes it possible to trace the establishment of contacts between the militancy of the Uruguayan radical left and the resistance to dictatorship in Brazil, which is counted among other activities carried out by the Uruguayan armed militants in that year. The weapons from the EGP, that through the mediation of Bustos had initially been given to Sendic in September 1964, soon crossed the Uruguayan-Brazilian border. These were then handed over in Rio Grande do Sul to militants linked to Leonel Brizola, to serve the resistance to the dictatorship in Brazil.[48]

Many of the meetings, discussions and exchanges of information, books and ideas, took place in the editorial offices of Montevideo newspapers and publications. *Marcha* is undoubtedly a paradigmatic example, due to its influence (both in Uruguay and more broadly in Latin America) and the significance of its critical, anti-fascist and anti-imperialist intellectual trajectory since 1939.[49] However, at the time studied, and for the New Left, the newspaper *Época* was indispensable as a vehicle for transnational sociability and solidarity, and as a centre for contacts between radical militants. Between 1962 and 1967 *Época*, the morning newspaper of the self-considered independent or non-communist left, was a key experience to the nucleation, exchange, debate and sociability among militancy of the socialist and anarchist left, and particularly of the new groups mentioned above (especially the MAC, the MIR and later the MLN-Tupamaros). Since 1964, significant militants of the Coordinador participated in *Época*, as authors and graphic designers, or by collaborating in various ways. This was the case of Raúl Sendic, Andrés Cultelli, Germán Vidal, Gerardo Gatti,[50] Julio Marenales and Jorge Manera.[51]

The Cuban Revolution represented a key link in the early 1960s between Latin American movements that supported armed revolution. In April 1963, *Época* took part in the frustrated Continental Congress of Solidarity with Cuba (suspended in Rio de Janeiro, Brazil, by Governor Carlos Lacerda). Despite the ban, the trip to Rio de Janeiro by Guillermo Chifflet, an important leader of the PSU close to Raúl Sendic and correspondent of *Época*, was one of many experiences of contact between Chilean, Argentinean, Peruvian, Paraguayan and Bolivian delegations. On that occasion, Chifflet interviewed Francisco Julião, who pointed out the importance of a 'radical agrarian reform' and the struggle 'in favour of the Cuban Revolution and against Yankee imperialism'.[52] At the beginning of 1964, *Época* received an invitation to the International Workers Day's celebrations in Cuba, which subsequently generated a link with the *Prensa Latina* news agency, created in 1959 by Massetti in Cuba. Incidentally, on the same days that journalist Ángel Ruocco travelled to Cuba as a correspondent for *Época* the EGP, led by Massetti, was annihilated in Salta, Argentina.[53]

Conclusion

In 1964, Montevideo constituted a place of encounter and dialogue for international revolutionary militancy. It became a node of multiple connections and solidarity networks throughout the 1960s and 1970s, especially when dictatorial repression intensified in the Latin American Southern Cone. This network of transnational activism articulated the individual and collective life trajectories of New Left militancy.

Ciro Bustos, a survivor of the EGP, arrived in Montevideo in 1964 and made contact with militants of the Uruguayan armed left, linked to the Coordinador. Bustos, a member of Che's guerrilla movement in Bolivia, and also a survivor, spent a good part of his life in Malmö, Sweden. Gutemberg Charquero, who fled from the National Security dictatorship established in Uruguay in 1973, also lived in exile in that city. He acted as one of the directors of the newspaper *Época*. Charquero was also a socialist, as were Raúl Sendic, Julio Marenales, Ismael Bassini and Elsa Garreiro, all militants who founded the *Coordinador* in 1963. Garreiro would die in the Escuela de Mecánica de la Armada ('Navy Mechanics School', Buenos Aires, Argentina) in 1979, one of the thousands of disappeared people during the state terrorism under the Argentinian dictatorship (1976–83). This was not the end of José Luis Nell Tacchi, who after joining the MNR Tacuara, fled from Buenos Aires to Montevideo in 1964, subsequently joined the MLN-Tupamaros and escaped from the Punta Carretas prison in 1971, in one of the most spectacular prison escapes in history. Injured by gunshot in the Ezeiza Massacre (in Buenos Aires in June 1973), he committed suicide shortly afterwards.

In Argentina, the fate of Masetti, lost in the Salta's jungle in 1964 while leading the Ejército Guerrillero del Pueblo, is unknown. The same Masetti who had written a diary about the impressions of his travels in Algeria in 1962. The Algeria that had inspired the first *Tupamaros*, from Jean-Paul Sartre's 1961 prologue to Frantz Fanon's *The Wretched of the Earth*. The Algeria narrated by the Argentinian journalist Carlos Aguirre, bedside book of the first *Tupamaros*. The same Algeria that inspired Gillo Pontecorvo's 1966 film *The Battle of Algiers*, while Cuba inspired his compatriot Giangiacomo Feltrinelli to publish an Italian edition of the *Tricontinental* magazine. The *Tricontinental* was the press organ of the Cuban-based Organisation of Solidarity of the Peoples of Africa, Asia and Latin America (OSPAAAL). Established following the First Tricontinental Conference in Havana (in January 1966), OSPAAAL's task was to support and co-ordinate anticolonial struggle across three continents. This was one of the key moments of transnational activism and solidarity of the decade. Three months earlier, the Moroccan leader Mehdi Ben Barka, President of the Preparatory Committee for the First Tricontinental Conference, was assassinated in Paris. Ben Barka did much to inspire its political agenda, a synthesis of Marxist-Leninist thought with the activism of the national liberation movements. Feltrinelli died in 1972 on the outskirts of Milan, while handling explosives, just as 'Vasco'

Bengochea had died years earlier in Buenos Aires. Both had written, acted and dreamt of revolution. Both were part of a new transnational left.

In Paris in 1961, the editor of the French version of the *Tricontinental* magazine, François Maspero, was a friend of José Martínez, an anarchist, editor of *Ruedo Ibérico*, the anti-Francoist publishing house par excellence of the Spanish Republican exile. Exiled from a dictatorship, like Abraham Guillén's exile in Montevideo in 1964, who thought up guerrilla warfare and influenced the Uruguayan and Argentinean armed left. Or like the Brazilian exile of Darcy Ribeiro after the military coup in his country, in 1964, together with other Brazilian exiles who had contacts and exchanges with the Uruguayan left. Brazilian exiles such as the parents of Flavia Schilling, who was twelve years old in 1964, and later, as a Tupamara militant, was imprisoned in the women's prison of Punta de Rieles (Montevideo) between 1972 and 1980.

The proximity of so many actors linked to the exercise of armed struggle in Latin America, inexorably placed the Coordinador, in 1964, in one of the regional vortices of political discussion and theoretical and practical exchange in relation to revolutionary armed struggle.

These global radical 1960s, whose multiple processes produced convergent and divergent political itineraries, generated dialogues and discrepancies, as well as diverse forms of protest, did not have a unidirectional origin from North to South. Rather, as we have seen, the period engendered varied and complex dynamics where dissimilar paths complemented and communicated with others. In this rich transnational panorama, the Tupamaros experience and its trajectory in the unique Montevideo of 1964 has a significant place.

Notes

1 The word tupamaro refers to the name by which the Spaniards, during the end of the colonial period in the Banda Oriental del Uruguay, referred to those who mobilised for the revolutionary cause of independence and against the royal authority. The name Tupamaro comes from the revolt against the Spanish Empire in 1780, led by José Gabriel

Condorcanqui (Tupac Amaru II) and his followers, which ended with their executions in Cuzco, Peru, in 1781.
2 Among the testimonial, biographical and autobiographical literature: S. Blixen, *Sendic* (Montevideo: Trilce, 2000); N. Caula and A. Silva, *Ana la guerrillera. Una historia de Lucía Topolansky* (Montevideo: Ediciones B, 2011); A. Cultelli, *La revolución necesaria. Contribución a la autocrítica del MLN-Tupamaros* (Montevideo: Colihue, 2006); E. Fernández Huidobro, *Historia de los Tupamaros* (Montevideo: Tupac Amaru Ediciones, 1986/87); L. Haberkorn, *Historias Tupamaras* (Montevideo: Fin de Siglo, 2008); F. Leicht, *Cero a la izquierda. Una biografía de Jorge Zabalza* (Montevideo: Letraeñe, 2007); S. Márquez Zacchino, *Marenales* (Montevideo: Argumento, 2010); H. Mejías Collazo, *Volvería a hacerlo* (Montevideo: Urubú, 2011); S. Mosquera (ed.), *Adolfo Wasem. El Tupamaro* (Montevideo: Banda Oriental, 2006); W. Pernas, *Comandante Facundo. El revolucionario Pepe Mujica* (Montevideo: Aguilar, 2013); R. Sasso, *Tupamaros. Los comienzos* (Montevideo: Fin de Siglo, 2010); S. Soler, *La leyenda de Yessie Macchi* (Montevideo: Fin de Siglo, 2000); G. Tagliaferro, *Adiós Robin Hood. 7 tupamaros, 40 años después* (Montevideo: Fin de siglo, 2008); J. Torres, Jorge, *Tupamaros: La derrota en la mira* (Montevideo: Fin de Siglo, 2002).
3 See for example: F. Arocena, *Violencia Política en el Uruguay de los 60. El caso de los tupamaros* (Montevideo: CIESU, 1989); L. Costa Bonino, *Crisis de los partidos tradicionales y movimiento revolucionario en el Uruguay* (Montevideo: Editorial Banda Oriental, 1985); A. Garcé, *Donde hubo fuego. El proceso de adaptación del MLN-Tupamaros a la legalidad y a la competencia electoral (1985-2004)* (Montevideo: Fin de Siglo, 2006); H. Gatto, *El cielo por asalto: El MLN-T y la izquierda uruguaya (1963-1972)* (Montevideo: Taurus, 2004); A. Lessa, *La Revolución imposible* (Montevideo: Fin de siglo, 2006).
4 The *Instituto de Ciencia Política* of the *Universidad de la República* was created in the late 1980s in Uruguay.
5 In Spanish, these include: the significant reconstruction of the *MLN-Tupamaros* trajectory by C. Aldrighi, *La izquierda armada. Ideología, ética e identidad en el MLN Tupamaros* (Montevideo: Trilce, 2002), the valuable panoramic review of the organisations of the Uruguayan radical left in this period, by E. Rey Tristán, *La izquierda revolucionaria uruguaya, 1955–73* (Sevilla: CSIC/Universidad de Sevilla, 2005) and N. Duffau's pertinent research on the socialist dimension of the *Coordinator, El Coordinador (1963–1965): La participación de los militantes del Partido Socialista en los inicios de la violencia revolucionaria en Uruguay* (Montevideo: FHUCE-UDELAR, 2008).

In English, the most relevant research on the *Cono Sur* revolutionary movements in a transnational perspective, is the book by A. Marchesi, *Latin America's Radical Left: Rebellion and Cold War in the Global 1960s* (Cambridge: Cambridge University Press, 2017).

6 Cited in M. Klimke and M. Nolan, 'Introduction. The Globalization of the Sixties', in C. Jian, M. Klimke, M. Kirasirova, M. Nolan, M. Young, J. Waley-Cohen (eds), *The Routledge Handbook of the Global Sixties. Between Protest and Nation-Building* (New York: Routledge, 2018) pp. 2–9.

7 On the anti-imperialist idea and its praxis in the first half of the twentieth century in Latin America, see P. Funes, *Historia mínima de las ideas políticas en América Latina* (Madrid/México, Turner/El Colegio de México, 2014) pp. 129–45.

8 R. Young 'Disseminating the Tricontinental' in Jian et al., *The Routledge Handbook of the Global Sixties*, pp. 517–47.

9 Namely in the works of Latin American Cold War experts such as Greg Grandin, Daniela Spencer, Friedrich Katz, Richard Saull, Gilbert Joseph, among others. There is a significant number of works by the aforementioned authors, including Greg Grandin's landmark book *The Last Colonial Massacre: Latin America in the Cold War* (Chicago: Chicago University Press, 2004) and the important work coordinated by Daniela Spencer, *Espejos de la Guerra Fría: México, América Central y el Caribe* (México: Ciesas/SER/Miguel Porrúa, 2004) . On the idea of revolution throughout the Cold War in Latin America, examined from the stimulating perspective of Arno Mayer, see G. Grandin and G.M. Joseph (eds), *A Century of Revolution. Insurgent and Counterinsurgent Violence During Latin America's Long Cold War* (Durham, NC & London: Duke University Press, 2010).

10 M. C. Tortti, 'La nueva izquierda a principios de los '60: socialistas y comunistas en la revista 'Che', *Estudios Sociales* 22–23 (2002). E. Zolov, 'Expandiendo nuestros horizontes conceptuales: El pasaje de una "vieja" a una "nueva izquierda" en América Latina en los años sesenta', *Aletheia*, 2:4 (2012), 1–25. N. Dip (ed.), 'La nueva izquierda en la historia reciente de América Latina. Un diálogo entre Eric Zolov, Rafael Rojas, Elisa Servín, María Cristina Tortti y Aldo Marchesi', *Escripta* 2:4 (2020), 290–323.

11 E. Jelin, 'Il '68 visto dal Sud: storia e memoria in America Latina', in Donatella della Porta (ed.), *Sessantotto. Passato e presente dell'anno ribelle* (Milano: Feltrinelli, 2018) p. 187 (Author's translation).

12 The group was made up of young militants in the traditional working-class neighbourhood of La Teja in Montevideo, in support of trade union struggles in the Uruguayan countryside.

13 This movement was formed from a split in the Communist Party of Uruguay, which had a philo-Maoist tendency, in 1962, as a result of the Sino-Soviet controversy at world level.
14 M. Cardozo Prieto, 'Memorias del Coordinador: algunas fechas significativas en la 'formación' del MLN-Tupamaros', in E. Bohoslavsky, M. Franco, M. Iglesias and D. Lvovich, *Problemas de Historia reciente del Cono Sur* (Buenos Aires: Prometeo/UNGS, 2010) p. 151.
15 This action took place at night in July 1963, in Nueva Helvecia, a small town in the Department of Colonia, in the southwest of Uruguay, in a private shooting club, known to one of the *Coordinator's* activists, Mario Navillat, who was a native of the town. It involved some members of the MAC such as Luis Omar Puime and others, and also some 'peludos' (workers of the sugar cane in the north of the country), who had organised themselves into the Unión de Trabajadores Azucareros de Artigas (UTAA) thanks to the influence of the socialist militant and later leader of the MLN-Tupamaros, Raúl Sendic coordinated the operation, and a large part of the rifles were discovered as a result of an accident with one of the vehicles in which the militants were transporting weapons into the country.
16 For example the Montevidean offices of the international company Bayer, in protest against the use of 'Agent Orange' during the Vietnam War.
17 Popular urban neighbourhoods located in marginal areas, with precarious housing and lack of urban services.
18 See the essay by A. Frega, '*Como el Uruguay no hay*. Apuntes en torno al Estado en los años cincuenta y su crisis', *Encuentros* 2 (1993), 91–103.
19 The period between 1946 and 1958, when through the leadership of Luis Batlle Berres in the Colorado Party, social and economic measures inspired by the thinking of José Batlle y Ordóñez (President of Uruguay between 1903–07 and 1911–15) were implemented. Initial *batllismo* was characterised by a radical humanist republicanism which, without disputing the foundations of capitalist society, defended the ideal of social justice. That is why Batlle y Ordóñez proposed an interventionist and protectionist state, while at the same time promoting advanced labour and social security legislation. These reforms were opposed by the conservative sectors of society, especially the landowners, and by foreign capital, in particular, British capital. Years later, in a similar direction, José Batlle y Ordóñez's nephew, Luis Batlle Berres, strengthened the role of the interventionist state and favoured national industry.
20 J. Yaffé, 'El proceso económico', in Caetano Gerardo (ed.), *Uruguay. El País modelo y sus crisis 1930/2010* (Montevideo: Planeta/Fundación MAPFRE, 2015) pp. 169–70.
21 See Tristán, *La izquierda revolucionaria uruguaya*, 81–90.

22 Langland, 'Transnational connections of the Global Sixties as seen by a historian of Brazil', in Jian et al., *The Routledge Handbook of the Global Sixties*, pp. 15–26.
23 This persisted in what the Uruguayan sociologist Germán Rama (1932–2020) has conceptualised as a 'hyper-integrated society' to describe Uruguayan society integrated around middle-class values, as a social sector on the rise between the first and second half of the twentieth century, and also regarding the formation of democratic institutions since the beginning of the twentieth century. See. G. Rama, *La democracia en Uruguay* (Buenos Aires: Grupo Editor Latinoamericano, 1987).
24 Author's interviews with Germán Vidal, Montevideo, 22 October, 2006 and Hebert Mejías Collazo, Canelones, 23 September 2007.
25 In contrast to the Movimiento Nacionalista Tacuara, founded in 1957 in Argentina, where a right-wing Catholic stamp prevailed, the Movimiento Nacionalista Revolucionario Tacuara, a split of the former in 1963, adhered to the defence of the Cuban Revolution, rejecting the right-wing tradition and the Catholic orientation of the original Tacuara.
26 Blixen, *Sendic*, pp. 122–4.
27 G. Rot, *Los orígenes perdidos de la guerrilla en Argentina* (Buenos Aires: Waldhuter, 2010), p. 199.
28 C. Bustos, *El Che quiere verte. La historia jamás contada del Che* (Buenos Aires: Vergara, 2007), pp. 221–6.
29 Ibid., pp. 233–4; Blixen, *Sendic*, pp. 108–11.
30 R. Bardini, *Tacuara. La pólvora y la sangre* (México: Océano, 2002) p. 98.
31 Rot, *Los orígenes perdidos de la guerrilla*, p. 21.
32 A. Dandan and S. Heguy, *Joe Baxter. Del nazismo a la extrema izquierda. La historia secreta de un guerrillero* (Buenos Aires: Norma, 2006), pp. 203–12; D. Gutman, *Tacuara Historia de la primera guerrilla urbana argentina* (Buenos Aires: Vergara, 2003), pp. 248–9.
33 S. Nicanoff and A. Castellano, *Las primeras experiencias guerrilleras en la Argentina. Cuadernos de Trabajo 29* (Buenos Aires: Ediciones del Instituto Movilizador de Fondos Cooperativos, 2004), p. 62.
34 Ibid., 30.
35 E. Salas, Ernesto, *Uturuncos: el origen de la guerrilla peronista* (Buenos Aires: Biblos, 2003), pp. 114–77.
36 Dandan and Heguy, *Joe Baxter*, 246; H. Reyes, 'Abraham Guillén: teórico de la lucha armada', *Lucha armada en la Argentina*, 1:4 (2005), 59.
37 Gutman, *Tacuara*, p. 165.

38 Author's interview with Guillermo Chifflet, Montevideo, 20 September 2006.
39 R. Castro, 'Gorillas against history. An analysis of the coup d'état in Brazil', *Barricada* (September 1964), pp. 22–6.
40 "Interview with Abraham Guillén, tireless libertarian militant" *Revista Bicicleta* 1:9 (1978).
41 Author's interview with Jorge Torres, Montevideo, 5 September 2007.
42 T. Marques Schneider, *Ditadura, exílio e oposição: os exiliados brasileiros no Uruguay (1964–1967)* (MA dissertation, Universidade Federal de Mato Grosso, 2006) p. 24.
43 Ibid., pp. 83–94.
44 Huidobro, *Historia de los Tupamaros*, p. 129.
45 The Ligas Camponesas emerged in the mid-1940s in Brazil as a way of organising the peasant class. However, in the mid-1950s, they began to radicalise their programme, proposing the implementation of a profound agrarian reform in the country.
46 J. Rodrigues Sales, *A luta armada contra a ditadura militar. A esquerda brasileira e a influencia da revolucao cubana* (Sao Paulo: Editora Fundacao Perseu Abramo, 2007) pp. 38–45.
47 Ibid., p. 67.
48 Blixen, *Sendic*, pp. 108–11.
49 *Marcha* was founded in 1939 by the Uruguayan economist and intellectual Carlos Quijano. With an independent political position and great influence on Uruguayan and Latin American culture, it embodied among its political principles the generation of critical thought and the defence of anti-imperialism and democracy against fascist ideas. Some of its most important collaborators were the philosopher Arturo Ardao and the educator Julio Castro, who was assassinated by the dictatorial repression in 1977. *Marcha* was banned by the Uruguayan civil-military dictatorship in 1974, and Quijano died in political exile in Mexico shortly before the recovery of democracy in Uruguay, in 1984. From the literary point of view, *Marcha* was one of the most important tribunes on a continental level for the dissemination of the *Generation of '45*, which included among its main exponents such well-known writers and artists as: Mario Benedetti, Ángel Rama, Amanda Berenguer, Ida Vitale, Idea Vilariño, Carlos Real de Azúa, José Luis Invernizzi and Carlos Martínez Moreno.
50 Communications with Gutemberg Charquero, Malmo/Montevideo, November 2011 (by Marina Cardozo).
51 M. Cardozo, 'Ese momento no ha de tardar': *Época, la construcción de sentidos acerca de la revolución y los nexos con la izquierda armada*

uruguaya en formación (1962–1964)', *Contemporánea. Historia y problemas del siglo XX*, 8 (2017), 150.
52 J. Chagas and G. Trullen, *Guillermo Chifflet. El combate de la pluma* (Montevideo: Rumbo, 2011), pp. 177–9.
53 Cardozo, 'Ese momento no ha de tardar', 153.

6

Connected struggles: networks of anticolonial solidarity and the liberation movements of the Portuguese colonies in Africa

Víctor Barros

Introduction

The struggle for independence headed by the liberation movements of the Portuguese colonies in Africa combined several international and transnational dimensions of solidarity. This chapter analyses how three interconnected transnational arenas – the Khartoum Conference (January 1969), the Netherlands Meeting (March 1970) and the Rome Solidarity Conference (June 1970) – strengthened networks of anticolonial solidarity with the independence struggles in Portugal's African colonies. These solidarity meetings were significant for several reasons. First, because they took place in an international context characterised by the intense public condemnation of Portuguese colonial war in Africa (in Angola, Mozambique and in the so-called 'Portuguese Guinea'[1]). Second, because despite the distance between their locations, these solidarity events were closely linked; indeed, the Khartoum Conference was the key stage and incentive for organising the two subsequent international solidarity meetings. Furthermore, and most significantly, these encounters were sponsored by anticolonial militants and non-state agents to express solidarity with the liberation movements struggling for national independence in the Portuguese colonies: the PAIGC (Partido Africano da Independência da Guiné e Cabo Verde) – African Party for the Independence of Guinea and Cabo Verde, the MPLA (Movimento Popular de Libertação de Angola) – Popular Movement for the Liberation of Angola, and the FRELIMO (Frente de Libertação de Moçambique) – Liberation

Front of Mozambique. The leading figures of these movements combated colonialism in different ways, both militarily and politically.

This chapter scrutinises how these transnational solidarity events encouraged the growth of European anticolonial support vis-à-vis the African liberation movements of the Portuguese colonies and contributed to internationalising their demands for independence. In addition, it explores how the discourses of leading figures in the movements inaugurated an interpretative framework that extended the understanding of the concept of solidarity, placing these struggles in a global context. This chapter draws on contemporary printed and archival primary sources from the Mário Soares Foundation in Lisbon. Namely, documents produced by the liberation movements, the speeches delivered by the liberation leaders, resolutions released in the aftermath of those three solidarity meetings, preparatory documents and reports published by the organisers of the events, and speeches and writings provided by some delegates who took part in the gatherings.

The struggle for independence in Portugal's African colonies was shaped by many factors and multiple interactions.[2] Recently, scholars have emphasised the role of diverse forms of support (material, military, technical, medical, moral, among others) that were provided by different allies to these liberation movements.[3] This chapter builds on this emerging research by investigating international and transnational solidarity encounters that were designed to declare moral, diplomatic and political support for the liberation movements. In scholarship on the radical 1960s, transnational solidarity with African movements seeking liberation from Portuguese colonial rule remains understudied. Exploring this solidarity through the lens of the international meetings sponsored by anticolonial militants, anticolonial support committees and other non-state agents reveals the dynamic transnational connections and imaginaries which were forged.

The first section of this chapter will explore the Khartoum Conference and will show how this meeting combined African demands for emancipation from colonial occupation and oppression with the need to construct anticolonial solidarity connections around the world. The second section will examine the impact of the Khartoum Conference and how it contributed to the creation and expansion of anticolonial solidarity movements from Africa to Europe, exemplified through the Netherlands Meeting and the Rome Conference. Key here is how struggles waged in Africa influenced political interactions among anticolonial activists, political actors and solidarity groups in Europe. Thus questions about the agency and the impact of these struggles are considered within a global context in which solidarity engendered by anticolonial activists spoke well beyond the parameters of the 'local'.

The armed struggle against Portuguese colonialism in Africa was launched in the beginning of the 1960s – in Angola from 1961, in Guinea from 1963 and in Mozambique from 1964 – and continued until 1974. These movements were not detached from the global history of decolonisation that vividly gained momentum in the second half of the twentieth century.[4] Despite the late chronology in comparison with the end of other European colonial empires in Africa and Asia, the struggles for national independence in the Portuguese colonies in Africa constituted part of the global history of the 'long sixties'. As has been increasingly recognised, the period of the 'long sixties' corresponded with the emergence of the Third World and its influence over several hybrid and fragmented events across the globe.[5] These events include but are not limited to: the campaign for decolonisation and the development of a new global anticolonial consciousness; the emergence of the New Radical Left and its numerous social, political and cultural contestations; worldwide ramifications of the Cold War; the Cuban Revolution of 1959 and the ambition of its leaders to disseminate their model of guerrilla struggle; the Vietnam War; the emergence of the Non-Aligned Movement in 1961; the entrance of the newly independent Asian and African states as actors in the international political order; Algerian independence; the civil rights movement in the United States; student insurrections; and the fight against apartheid in South Africa.[6] The struggles in Africa, Asia and Latin America reinvigorated the transnational stance of solidarity, and revolutionary movements in the Third World became a guide and inspired lessons for the young Western radicals.[7] Sietse Bosgra, for example, was a Dutch activist who campaigned in the Netherlands solidarity movement supporting independence movements from Algeria to Angola and was a member of the Holland Committee on Southern Africa; he insisted that Western youth were influenced in the long sixties by many events occurring in the Third World. Cuba and its leaders Fidel Castro and Che Guevara, as well as the Vietnam War, developed public awareness and brought tens of thousands of young people into the streets.[8]

The actions of liberation movements, as well as the anticolonial solidarity networks nurtured throughout the 1960s by some of their African leaders, placed the struggles for independence from Portugal's colonial rule in the European public imagination.[9] Influenced by African demands for independence, activists formed different solidarity groups across and beyond Europe to assist the anticolonial revolution in the Portuguese colonies in Africa. Solidarity took a number of forms: material and financial aid; political and moral support; medical assistance and information campaigns.[10] As this chapter will elucidate, the promotion of international conferences was one of the specific solidarity activities, integrated within the broader repertoire of political, material and moral support.

Expanding solidarity: the Khartoum Conference

The independence struggles point to the crucial role played by solidarity networks in helping the Southern African liberation movements by various means.[11] In particular, through the solidarity links they established across the globe, the struggles for liberation in the Portuguese colonies in Africa should be understood as multidimensional and transnational phenomena. The Khartoum Conference, which took place in Sudan between 18–20 January 1969, was a crucial event in internationalising the demand for independence. From the beginning, the conference was envisioned as an example of transnational solidarity. The two preliminary meetings of the International Preparatory Committee were conducted in Cairo, Egypt and a third meeting in Lahti, Finland, with the participation of representatives from African liberation movements and organisations struggling for the same commitments. Those preparatory meetings worked out the details of the administrative programme. Key here was the appeal for support, to provide messages to the African heads of state and to produce an organisational resolution for the 'International Conference in Support of the Peoples of the Portuguese Colonies in Africa and of Southern Africa', planned to take place in Sudan.[12]

The Khartoum Conference was promoted by the Afro-Asian Peoples' Solidarity Organization and the World Peace Council, in cooperation with the African liberation movements. The event had wide international involvement. Delegates from Vietnam to Brazil, from Western European to Eastern socialist countries attended, and several progressive organisations were represented (such as the International Democratic Federation of Women, the World Union Federation, the International Association of Democratic Jurists, the International Journalists' Organization, the International Student Union, Tricontinental, among others): 400 delegates from sixty-four countries from all the continents were present in Khartoum as the expression of international solidarity towards the combatants of the liberation movements of the Portuguese colonies (PAIGC, MPLA, FRELIMO). In addition, solidarity was expressed in relation to Southern Africa movements (the ANC – African National Congress, from South Africa, SWAPO – South West Africa People's Organization, from South West Africa, present-day Namibia, and ZAPU – Zimbabwe African People's Union).[13]

According to the report published by Portuguese delegates, the Khartoum Conference was like a court bringing to judgement Portuguese colonialism and the imperialist forces that fuelled the colonial war with weapons and money. The event denounced and condemned the dangers that the fascist alliance between the governments of Portugal, South Africa and Rhodesia represented for the peace in Africa and in the world.[14] Besides the solidarity declared with the PAIGC, MPLA and FRELIMO, the conference encouraged ties of solidarity to support other struggles being waged across the world. For instance, the conference condemned the

> dastardly aggression of US imperialism, supported by its lackeys, in Vietnam, against Arab peoples and elsewhere, and the growing fascist and racist repression of elementary freedom and suppression of legitimate aspirations carried out by the minority ruling regimes, supported by West Germany and other NATO powers, against the peoples of Southern Africa and the Portuguese colonies.[15]

From this view, the Khartoum event was considered by the promoters and delegates as a step towards enlisting the support of broader sections of global public opinion and mobilising worldwide solidarity for the liberation movements. As the Portuguese delegates put it:

> The conference unanimously approved a general resolution stating that Africa and the world should provide more effective support to the liberation movements that are fighting for independence in their countries. The conference launched an appeal to all democratic organisations, to all progressive forces in the world, to develop a broad mobilising action and a broad campaign of material, political and moral support for the liberation movements of Portuguese colonies and Southern Africa.[16]

The final resolutions also recommended the creation of national support committees to inform the public about their governments' role in supporting Portuguese colonialism in Africa. While the specific tasks, and the degree to which they were pursued, varied among committees according to the characteristics of their respective countries, resources and possibilities of action, they shared a series of common goals. These mutual objectives included: intensifying the campaign to end Portuguese colonial oppression; elevating popular mobilisation in each country in order to provide material and financial aid to the liberation movements; collecting resources for medical assistance to the sick and those injured in war; and collecting school supplies for children in liberated areas.[17]

After Khartoum, European public interest in Southern Africa and the liberation movements in the Portuguese colonies intensified.[18] The conference had encouraged the formation of anticolonial solidarity groups in Europe.[19] In 1969 activists in Belgium founded the Support Committee for the Struggle Against Colonialism and Apartheid. Likewise, in May 1969 the International Mobilization Committee was created in Berlin, as well as the World Peace Assembly. According to the Secretary General of the Mobilization Committee, the Egyptian writer Youssef El-Sebai, the key goal of this committee was to stimulate the formation of national committees and specialised sub-committees in Western countries and in Africa and Asia. The other main goal was to execute the Khartoum resolutions in terms of solidarity demands regarding the liberation movements of the Portuguese colonies and Southern Africa. The Mobilization Committee also served to reinforce solidarity contacts with other organisations and to manage the political work of propaganda which would serve the goals of the struggles headed by anticolonial activists from these regions. To this end, the committee produced materials that were designed to inform international public opinion about events in the Portuguese colonies, as well as the goals of the liberation struggles. Similarly, in France in December 1969, in the aftermath of Khartoum, militants instituted the National Support Committee for the Liberation Struggle in Portuguese Colonies.[20]

The support committees served to engage the public in solidarity against colonial war and for the people's struggle for independence in Angola, Guinea and Mozambique. The rise of these anticolonial solidarity movements between 1969–70 reinforced public criticism in Europe against the Portuguese colonial war in Africa. This was a period of momentous social and cultural change in Europe regarding attitudes towards the Portuguese dictatorship.[21] For instance, after February 1969, most Dutch members of parliament were critical of their government's policy towards Southern Africa as well as their friendly relations with the Portuguese regime.[22] In West Germany, public solidarity shown towards the Southern African struggles, the wider Third World and the nationalist liberation movements in African Portuguese colonies gradually expanded to different activist groups, political actors and non-state organisations from civil society.[23] According to Rui Lopes, student activism in West Germany had become highly visible and militant. Political organisations recruited students who brought with them a passion for the cause of African liberation. 'The cause proved attractive to religious associations and to groups involved in development work which were critical of colonialism and neo-colonialism. They crucially helped the solidarity movement gain national attention in 1970.'[24]

Solidarity connections: Khartoum, the Netherlands and Rome

The resolutions passed in Khartoum contributed to strengthening international networks of anticolonial solidarity in Europe.[25] Influenced by the Khartoum Conference, on 22 January 1970 activists from various political traditions within the Left and beyond assembled in Rome to build the momentum of anticolonial solidarity with the liberation movements of the Portuguese colonies. The event was a preparatory meeting for the 'Solidarity Conference for the Peoples of the Portuguese Colonies', that would take place in Rome from 27–29 June 1970. This preparatory meeting was sponsored and organised by Italian political parties and trade union forces (the Communist Party, the Socialist Party, the Socialist Party of Proletarian Unity of Italy, the Italian General Confederation of Labour, the Christian Associations of Italian Workers) and other groups. Also present at this event were representatives of solidarity groups from several other countries – Belgium, Bulgaria, the Federal Republic of Germany, France, India, Iraq, Japan, Madagascar, the Netherlands, Palestine, Poland, Romania, Senegal and the UK. Portugal was represented by Pedro Soares, a militant of the Portuguese Communist Party, by supporters of the Patriotic Front of National Liberation and by Portugal's Peace Movement. And the liberation movements were represented by Marcelino dos Santos, a FRELIMO member.[26]

A few months after this meeting another event echoed Khartoum's claim for transnational solidarity, focusing again on the upcoming Rome Conference. From 28 to 30 March 1970, numerous groups and Western European anticolonial committees supporting the liberation movements in the Portuguese colonies convened in De Horst, Driebergen, in the Netherlands, to declare their solidarity with the movements fighting against Portuguese colonialism in Africa. The activist Sietse Bosgra, who coordinated the Dutch Angola Committee, played a key role by formally opening the event on 28 March and delivering the welcoming address to delegates. According to a contemporary report published by the event organisers, this gathering at Driebergen was a great congregation of Western European groups supporting African independence struggles in the Portuguese colonies, with at least fifteen European anticolonial support committees participating.[27] During the meeting, each solidarity committee introduced a brief account of its organisation and activities. In the following discussions, delegates highlighted topics relevant to each of the territories (Angola, Guinea and Mozambique) and their respective liberation movement's concerns. These included issues of leadership and reasons for supporting liberation movements. There were debates about the need to consolidate the existing liberated areas and to expand the autonomous areas by bringing the struggle to the whole country. Delegates deliberated how to counteract propaganda that portrayed liberation movement members in negative terms. This would mean rebuilding the image of the liberation movements, emphasising that the national liberation struggles were part of the larger global struggle against imperialism, thus improving the representation of the liberation movements in Europe. In addition, delegates who had travelled to liberated areas in Angola, Guinea and Mozambique gave accounts of their visits. They reported on military life and civil affairs, on villages destroyed by bombing and the difficulty of the population to collect their harvests under bombing raids. They recounted the work of army cadres with the populations, the organisation of village schools and the teaching process aimed at overcoming differences between tribes. Important here was the creation of village committees, particularly in Guinea, composed of five people, at least two of which should be women. These committees met regularly to organise social and political aspects of village life, including the election of judges for people's tribunals (which gave advice in all kinds of civil disputes).[28]

To support these oral accounts, slides taken in the liberated areas by different visitors (journalists, filmmakers, photographers) reporting on the abovementioned issues were shown; as well as films portraying interviews with leaders of the liberation movements and with Portuguese military deserters. There were also films about the aid provided by Portugal's allies that was used to continue the colonial war in Africa, and films showing all kind of activities (training of soldiers, schools, theatre in the bush) and social developments accomplished in liberated areas.[29] Interconnected within these subjects, activists emphasised the need to further inform European public opinion about the nature of the Portuguese political regime.

In sum, the key goal of the Netherlands Meeting was to publicise and enable debate with three main aims: first, to critically discuss Portugal's political regime; second, to examine the Portuguese colonial war in Angola, Guinea and Mozambique, as well as the broader situation in Southern Africa. Finally, with an expanded scope and an interconnected focus, to approach the global importance and meaning of African liberation struggles. Thus, the African struggle for liberty and independence should be understood as being closely related to the cause for the liberty throughout the world.[30] The conference also saw itself as part of a series of anticolonial events and a key goal was making final preparations for the Solidarity Conference for the Peoples of the Portuguese Colonies, planned to take place in Rome.

The Rome Conference of June 1970 saw the participation of numerous activists, representatives of international institutions (such as OAU and UN), political parties and members of groups from civil society who travelled from all parts of the globe to Italy to declare their solidarity with the PAIGC, MPLA and FRELIMO. The meeting generated synergy amongst anticolonial activists from different realms. About 177 mass organisations from sixty-four countries were present at the conference.[31] The meeting was organised by and received great political solidarity from various Italian leftist youth groups, left-wing political parties and prominent figures on the Italian left. One of these figures was the Vice-President of the Chamber of Deputies of Italy, Lucio Luzzatto, who was also the member of the Italian Socialist Party of Proletarian Unity (known as PSIUP).[32]

The timing of the conference was also significant as it took place shortly after Italian industry had withdrawn (in May 1970) its economic participation from the Cahora Bassa hydroelectric dam, planned by the Portuguese government in the colony of Mozambique.[33] The Portuguese government launched the construction of the Cahora Bassa project in 1968, some years after the beginning of the armed war in Mozambique initiated by FRELIMO on 25 September 1964. The economic involvement of some of Portugal's European partners (such as France, Italy and West Germany) in the project was strongly criticised by anticolonial activists. According to Keith Middlemas, Cahora Bassa was stigmatised as a fascist-colonialist plot, that was based on international cooperation between capitalist interests rather than being a project intended for Mozambique or for Mozambicans. It promised profits for the capitalists who built it, the Government of Portugal, the white settlers in Mozambique and the racist white regimes in South Africa and Rhodesia.[34]

The campaigns against this hydroelectric dam served to set up pressure groups, instruct public opinion and internationalise the liberation movements' cause.[35] The high-profile campaign organised by solidarity movements in Europe made the Cahora Bassa a domestic concern in European states as well as an international one.³⁶ At the Rome Conference, three African independence leaders – Agostinho Neto, Amílcar Cabral and Marcelino dos Santos – endorsed the criticism against the Cahora Bassa colonial project. In this way, and many others, the Rome Conference affected the public image of the Portuguese dictatorship and strengthened the political reputation of the liberation movements, as well as increasing the visibility of their leaders and the cause of their struggles. For instance, on 1 July 1970, in the event's aftermath, Neto, Cabral and dos Santos, representing respectively MPLA, PAIGC and FRELIMO, met with the head of the Catholic Church, Pope Paul VI. According to Ada Milani and Vincenzo Russo, the result of this episode was to put Portuguese colonialism under the spotlight of international attention.³⁷

The Rome Conference resolved to work to isolate the Portuguese regime through concrete actions. This included a commitment to building solidarity links with anti-imperial and anticolonial movements across the world. As well as criticising the supply of arms and all other forms of assistance provided to Portugal by its Western allies (namely by NATO members), delegates made clear their determination to increase the nature and diversity of aid to anticolonial combatants in Portuguese colonies. In addition, they undertook to inform international public opinion and mobilise progressive forces (political parties, youth groups, trade unions, committees of solidarity in capitalist countries) with regular news about Portuguese colonial atrocities. When further disseminating information about the peoples of the Portuguese colonies, they would condemn the illegal nature of Portugal's colonial presence in Africa and publicise the liberation movements' victories. Delegates at the Rome Conference also insisted that the warfare in the Portuguese colonies was part of a strategy of global imperialism, the effects of which could be felt in Vietnam, Cambodia, Laos, Middle East, among other places.³⁸ Both dos Santos and Cabral emphasised that the Third World comrades who populated the conference testified to the fraternity in arms that connected them with African combatants in the Portuguese colonies. Moreover, their presence, as well as the solidarity they addressed towards the African struggles encouraged the hopes of liberation movements. The Rome Conference was used as a front of struggle to increase collaboration and solidarity between all anticolonial and anti-imperialist activists.³⁹

The word solidarity:
'*la solidarité ici n'est pas une œuvre de charité*'

The word 'solidarity' was a core concept elaborated on and used during the Rome Conference by African independence leaders. They knew that solidarity (translated into concrete practice and expanded through transnational networks) was an important element of the liberation process. Such solidarity was imagined as antithetical to charity. In other words, solidarity was an operative expression and practice charged by political and moral significance, principally in terms of its anticolonial connotations and anti-imperialist implications. African independence leaders managed the moral and political understanding of the term in order to connect the liberation struggles in a global perspective: to link the liberation process in Africa with other struggles in the world against colonial exploitation and Western domination. The meaning of solidarity extended the framework of the concept, interconnecting local fronts of combat with other transnational political branches that transcended the national borders of the African struggles.

Their claim for solidarity stressed support for the domestic concerns that had been established in the agenda of the liberation movements, not least material, financial and health assistance to reconstruct military and civil life in liberated areas. As Marcelino dos Santos affirmed, solidarity 'must contribute to the realization of our national liberation program'.[40] Crucially, at the conference, solidarity was a way to interpret liberation struggles in Portuguese colonies in Africa as part of the global struggle against colonialism, racism, Western imperialism and all forms of exploitation and domination in the world. As Cabral proclaimed, the struggle was an act of solidarity with all peoples struggling for national liberation. In this general struggle against imperialism, the liberation movements were trying 'to do the best we can to drive Portuguese colonialism out of our country'.[41]

Solidarity with the global anticolonial independence cause was a way to fight imperialism and its supporters who prolonged Portuguese colonial domination in Africa. Thus, liberation leaders in Angola, Mozambique, Guinea and Cabo Verde considered the Portuguese colonial war and the increase of Western imperial influence as an entrenched phenomenon. After all, Portugal was dependent upon its NATO allies (France, the Federal Republic of Germany, the USA and the UK) and thus closely linked to the political and economic interests of Western imperialism.[42] Both the solidarity groups and the liberation leaders defined Portugal as a colonialist and 'underdeveloped' country whose economy was sustained by the exploitation of colonial resources and the foreign capital invested in the processing of the products extracted from the colonies.[43] This interpretation of the precarious nature of Portuguese colonial rule was informed by Cabral's understanding of colonialism and imperialism. Since 1963, Cabral had framed the actions of the PAIGC and other African liberation movements as an international struggle of 'underdeveloped' peoples against imperialism.[44] On the occasion of the 1966 Solidarity Conference of the Peoples of Africa, Asia and Latin America, known as the Tricontinental Conference (hosted in Havana during 3–15 January of that year), Cabral drew a committed distinction between imperialism and imperialist domination. On one hand, he considered that imperialism could be defined as a worldwide expression of the search for profits and the ever-increasing accumulation of surplus value by monopoly financial capital, centred in two parts of the world: first in Europe, and then in North America. On the other hand, Cabral outlined imperialist domination as a violent usurpation of the freedom of the productive forces of the dominated socio-economic whole, whatever its forms. Therefore, he concluded that national liberation exists only when the national productive forces have been completely freed from every kind of foreign domination.[45]

Continuing this same analysis in another context, Cabral argued that Portugal was not an imperialist country but, through its colonialism, the Portuguese government practised imperialist domination. This was because, he insisted, Portuguese colonialism did not have economic infrastructure that would allow it to compete with the other imperial powers. This fact, according to Cabral and other anticolonial leaders, explained the complicity of political, military and economic interests between the Portuguese government and several Western powers.[46] In fact, as some scholars have emphasised, the assistance that the Portuguese government received from its NATO partners became one of the most important spheres of Portugal's political-military diplomacy during the period of the colonial war (1961–74). For instance, West Germany and

France comprised the main source of military equipment, technical support, the formation and training of infantry units, and the renovation of armaments used by Portugal in Africa.[47] By furnishing these war supplies, they were arming the Portuguese colonial regime against the liberation movements. As Marcelino dos Santos stated, this complicity between Portugal and its partners internationalised military aid in the Portuguese colonial conflict; and due to the supply of military support, the Portuguese government reinforced its aggression against the liberation movements. From this perspective, Dos Santos insisted that anticolonial solidarity actions must be internationalised too.[48]

This was also the reason why at the Rome Conference the Republic of Guinea delegate, S. E. Keita Mamadou, argued that solidarity was a necessity that could be explained dialectally. For Mamadou, imperialism and colonialism formed a single structure in their fundamental interests and, consequently, engendered the same exploitative enemy in Africa, Asia, Latin America, as well as in Western Europe. If the exploiter was the same, but manifested in diverse ways, then the exploited were also the same. Thus, solidarity from all the progressive forces was crucial to African peoples struggling to eliminate exploitation and social injustice. According to Mamadou, from this point of view, solidarity was not an act of charity but an internationalist duty. 'This is what makes the unity of progressive forces necessary and indispensable.'[49] And as Cabral emphasised, the internationalisation of solidarity was a useful means to determine who were 'our friends' and who were 'our enemies'.[50] For this reason, according to Neto, the Rome Conference constituted a new step in extending the solidarity with people struggling in the Portuguese colonial territories in Africa.[51]

For liberation leaders, solidarity was essential to the interpretation of the independence cause as well as a tactic for anticolonial resistance. Solidarity was configured within a global framework as a radical historical phenomenon that contributed to human progress. For Cabral, these African liberation movements were fighting for all peoples and for the liberation of the whole of humanity. The meaning and the practice of liberation was, in all its dimensions, the global human quest for liberty, justice, improvement and well-being for all peoples in the world who still lived under colonial domination.[52]

Conclusion

The liberation movements struggling for national independence in Portuguese colonial territories in Africa influenced networks of anticolonial solidarity in Europe. These struggles were part of the global history of decolonisation and the emergence of the so-called Third World. Liberation movements from the Global South encouraged agency and affected the interactions of activists and political actors particularly in Western Europe. The actions of these liberation movements also expanded the meaning and the practice of the concept of solidarity. They inspired and persuaded worldwide networks of transnational solidarity with the struggles for independence underway in Portugal's African colonies during the 'long sixties'. As part of the global history of the long sixties, the struggles for independence in Portugal's African colonies exemplified how liberation movements in Angola, Guinea and Mozambique impressed anticolonial militants across the globe. Activists in the struggle against Portuguese colonialism participated within networks of anticolonial solidarity in different transnational meetings, of which the Khartoum, Netherlands and Rome conferences are key examples.

As I have highlighted elsewhere, European solidarity with the liberation struggles in Portugal's African colonies emerged gradually in the aftermath of the armed insurrection launched in Angola in 1961.[53] As the Rome Conference's preparatory document attests, the Khartoum meeting opened a new way to mobilise public opinion against Portuguese colonialism.[54] The impact of Khartoum mobilised networks of solidarity and resulted in subsequent solidarity meetings held in Driebergen and Rome, gatherings motivated and informed by demands of the African independence movements.

By denouncing the relationship between the colonial war and military and financial assistance provided by Portugal's Western allies, the independence leaders located the liberation cause as part of the global struggles against colonialism, racism, exploitation and Western imperialism. As noted above, they endorsed an understanding which situated the national liberation struggles of Portugal's African colonies within the global human quest for liberty, justice and well-being for all peoples: in sum, for the liberation of humanity. The struggles of the liberation leaders also contributed to expanding the meaning of the concept of solidarity as globally inclusive, namely with its anticolonial, Third Worldist and anti-imperialist references. As Gil Tchernia (the Secretary of the French National Support Committee for the Liberation Struggle in the Portuguese Colonies[55]) declared, 'the struggle for national independence was led by Africans conscious about the particularities of their countries and their peoples', and thus 'all support, wherever it comes from, will be accepted'.[56]

These movements also helped to strengthen transnational anticolonial solidarity networks and activities, generating political effects beyond their respective geographical African borders. Their actions influenced the international order, promoted significant interactions among diverse political actors and, ultimately, led to the overthrow of the Portuguese socio-political structure which had been ruled for four decades by an authoritarian dictatorship.[57] For this reason, the liberation movements' activities should not be viewed in isolation or by focusing on a narrow domestic context. Rather they need to be viewed through the lens of their transnational dimensions and their wider ramifications that transcended the framework of the nation-state analyses.

More than part of a 'local' history of Angola, Cabo Verde, Guinea-Bissau and Mozambique, these struggles are best understood through the transnational connections and networks of solidarity they generated. The mechanisms and practices through which these liberation movements forged solidarity in the service of transnational fronts of struggle disseminated forms of resistance, and stimulated a new political imagination and visions of future possibilities.

Acknowledgements

This paper was supported by and contributes to the research project Amílcar Cabral: from Political History to the Politics of Memory (PTDC/EPH-HIS/6964/2014), funded by the Foundation for Science and Technology (FCT) and hosted at the Institute of Contemporary History – NOVA University of Lisbon, Portugal. Thanks to the members of this project. Thanks also to the participants of the workshop Radical Sixties: Aesthetics, Politics and Histories of Solidarity, held on 11-12 June 2020 at the University of Brighton, UK, in the context of which the first draft of this paper was discussed. Many thanks to Branwen Gruffydd Jones and Rui Lopes for their incisive readings and comments. Last but not least, my special gratitude to Joke Langens who was kind enough to offer encouragement and sound advice.

Notes

1. Named after independence as Guinea-Bissau.
2. J-M. Mabeko-Tali, 'Dreaming Together, Fighting for Freedom Together: African Progressive Nationalism and the Ideology of Unity in Portugal's African Colonies in the 1950s and 1960s', *Journal of Southern African Studies*, 46:5 (2020), 829–844.
3. S. V. Borges, *Militant Education, Liberation Struggle, Consciousness: The PAIGC Education in Guinea Bissau 1963–1978* (Berlin: Peter Lang, 2019); L. Dallywater, C. Saunders and H. A. Fonseca (eds), *Southern African Liberation Movements and the Global Cold War 'East': Transnational Activism 1960–1990* (Berlin: Walter de Gruyter GmbH, 2019); C. Tornimbeni, 'Nationalism and Internationalism in the Liberation Struggle in Mozambique: The Role of the FRELIMO's Solidarity Network in Italy', *South African Historical Journal*, lxx (2018), 194–214; N. Telepneva, 'Mediators of Liberation: Eastern-Bloc Officials, Mozambican Diplomacy and the Origins of Soviet Support for Frelimo, 1958–1965', *Journal of Southern African Studies*, xliii (2017), 67–81; D. Kaiser, '"Makers of the Bonds and Ties": Transnational Socialisation and National Liberation in Mozambique', *Journal of Southern African Studies*, xliii (2017), 29–48.
4. A. Getachew, *Worldmaking after Empire: The Rise and Fall of Self-Determination* (Princeton Oxford: Princeton University Press, 2019); R. Craggs and C. Wintle (eds), *Cultures of Decolonisation: Transnational Productions and Practices 1945–1970* (Manchester: Manchester University Press, 2016); G. Wilder, *Freedom Time: Negritude, Decolonization, and the Future of the World* (Durham, NC & London: Duke University Press, 2015); F. Cooper, *Africa Since 1940: The Past of the Present* (New York: Cambridge University Press, 2002).
5. C. Kalter, *The Discovery of the Third World: Decolonization and the Rise of the New Left in France, c.1950–1976*, trans. T. Dunlap

(Cambridge: Cambridge University Press, 2016); S. Christiansen and Z. A. Scarlett (eds), *The Third World in the Global 1960s* (New York & Oxford: Berghahn Books, 2013), pp. 1–20.

6 R. Bruno-Jofré, 'The "Long 1960s" in a Global Arena of Contention: Re-defining Assumptions of Self, Morality, Race, Gender and Justice, and Questioning Education', *Espacio, Tiempo y Educación*, 6:1 (2019), 5–27; C. Jian et al. (eds), *The Routledge Handbook of the Global Sixties: Between Protest and Nation-Building* (New York: Routledge, 2018); M. Thomas and A. S. Thompson (eds), *The Oxford Handbook of the Ends of Empire* (New York: Oxford University Press, 2018); Kalter, *The Discovery of the Third*, p. viii; J. J. Byrne, *Mecca of Revolution: Algeria, Decolonization, and the Third World Order* (New York: Oxford University Press, 2016); M. Shipway, *Decolonization and its Impact: A Comparative Approach to the End of the Colonial Empires* (Oxford: Blackwell, 2008); M. Thomas, B. Moore and L. J. Butler, *Crises of Empires: Decolonization and Europe's Imperial States, 1918–1975* (London: Bloomsbury Academic, 2008); O. A. Westad, *The Global Cold War: Third World Interventions and the Making of Our Times* (Cambridge: Cambridge University Press, 2005); P. Duara (ed.), *Decolonization: Perspectives from Now and Then* (London & New York: Routledge, 2004); D. Rothermund, *The Routledge Companion to Decolonization* (London & New York: Routledge, 2000).

7 K. Christiaens, 'Europe at the Crossroads of Three Worlds: Alternative Histories and Connections of European Solidarity with the Third World, 1950s–80s', *European Review of History: Revue Européenne d'Histoire*, 24:6 (2017), 932–54; K. Kornetis, '"Cuban Europe"? Greek and Iberian *tiersmondisme* in the "Long 1960s"', *Journal of Contemporary History*, 50:3 (2015), 486–87; K. Christiaens, 'From the East to the South, and Back? International Solidarity Movements in Belgium and New Histories of Cold War, 1950s–1970s', *Dutch Crossing. Journal of Low Countries Studies*, 39:3 (2015), 215–31; A. Dirlik, 'Foreword: The Third Word in 1968', in Christiansen and Scarlett (eds), *The Third World in the Global 1960s*, vii–ix.

8 S. Bosgra, 'The Influence of the Liberation Movements on Political Opinion in Europe', in *Continuar Cabral: Simpósio Internacional Amílcar Cabral, Cabo Verde, 17 a 20 de Janeiro* (Praia: Grafediro/Prelo-Estampa, 1984), p. 574.

9 V. Barros, 'The French Anticolonial Solidarity Movement and the Liberation of Guinea-Bissau and Cape Verde', *The International History Review*, 42:6 (2020) 1297–1318.

10 V. Barros, 'The French Anticolonial Solidarity'; H. Sapire and C. Saunders 'Liberation Struggles in Southern Africa in Context', in H. Sapire and C. Saunders (eds), *Southern African Struggles: New Local, Regional and Global Perspectives* (Claremont, South Africa: UCT Press, 2013), p. 4.
11 J. Alexander, J. McGregor and B-M. Tendi, 'The Transnational Histories of Southern African Liberation Movements: An Introduction', *Journal of Southern African Studies*, 43:1 (2017), 1–12; J. Alexander and J. McGregor, 'African Soldiers in the URSS: Oral Histories of ZAPU Intelligence Cadres' Soviet Training, 1964–1979', *Journal of Southern African Studies*, 43:1 (2017), 49–66; see the chapters authored by C. Bundy, C. Gurney, E. M. Williams and C. Saunders in the rich volume edited by Sapire and Saunders, *Southern African Struggles: New Local, Regional and Global Perspectives*, pp. 212–89; J. K. Kuhn, 'Liberation Struggle and Humanitarian Aid: International Solidarity Movements and the "Third World" in the 1960s', in Christiansen and Scarlett (eds), *The Third World in the Global 1960s*, pp. 69–85; T. Weis, 'The Politics Machine: On the Concept of "Solidarity" in East German Support for SWAPO', *Journal of Southern African Studies*, 37:2 (2011), 351–67; H. Thörn, 'The Meaning(s) of Solidarity: Narratives of Anti-Apartheid Activism', *Journal of Southern African Studies*, 35:2 (2009), 417–36.
12 Archive from Fundação Mário Soares (FMS), Lisbon, Folder 09701.002.007: *Victory to the Peoples of the Portuguese Colonies and Southern Africa*, November, 1968, 1–15.
13 Archive from FMS, Lisbon, Folder 09701.002.003: *A F.P.L.N. em Khartum. Guiné, Angola, Moçambique*, 18–20 January, 1969, p. 2; Folder 09701.002.007: *Victory to the Peoples*, November, 1968, pp. 1–15; Folder 02970.001.017: *FPLN Portugal. Khartum, Encontro de Solidariedade Actuante*, 1969.
14 Archive from FMS, Lisbon, Folder 09701.002.003: *A F.P.L.N. em Khartum. Guiné, Angola, Moçambique*, 18–20 January, 1969, p. 2.
15 Archive from FMS, Lisbon, Folder 09701.002.007: *Victory to the Peoples*, November, 1968, pp. 1–15.
16 Archive from FMS, Lisbon, Folder 09701.002.003: *A F.P.L.N. em Khartum. Guiné, Angola, Moçambique*, 18–20 January, 1969, pp. 2–3.
17 Archive from FMS, Lisbon, Folder 02970.001.002: *Conferência de Roma. Apoio Internacional aos Povos de Angola, Guiné, Moçambique*, 1970, pp. 11–12; Folder 09701.002.003: *A FPLN em Khartum. Guiné, Angola, Moçambique*, 1969, p. 2; Folder 09621.001.003: *Declaração do Comité Nationale Soutien de la Lutte de Libération des Peuples des Colonies Portugaises*, Paris, May, 1970, p. 2; Folder 04322.002.004: *MSACP (Mouvement de Soutien aux Peuples de*

l'Angola e des autres Colonies Portugaises), December, 1969; Folder 04322.001.031: *Première Conférence Internationale de Soutien à la Lutte de Libération des Peuples des Colonies Portugaises et de l'Afrique Australe*, Khartoum, January, 1969; Folder 09701.002.007: *Victory to the Peoples*, November, 1968, pp. 1–15.

18 Archive from CIDAC (*Centro de Intervenção para o Desenvolvimento Amílcar Cabral*), Lisbon, Folder BAC-0290, NC/58: *Activities of the Dutch Angola Committee*. See also N. Schliehe, 'West German Solidarity Movements and the Struggle for the Decolonization of Lusophone Africa', *Revista Crítica de Ciências Sociais*, 118 (2019), 173–94; F. Clara, 'Notes on Twentieth-Century German Public Opinion, Colonialism, and the Portuguese Colonies (a Tentative Approach)', *Revista Crítica de Ciências Sociais*, 118 (2019), 151–72; V. Barros, 'The French Anticolonial Solidarity.'

19 Archive from FMS, Lisbon, Folder 02970.001.002: *Conferência de Roma. Apoio Internacional aos Povos de Angola, Guiné, Moçambique*, 1970, p. 11; *A F.P.L.N. em Khartum. Guiné, Angola, Moçambique*, 18–20 January, 1969, pp. 2–5.

20 Archive from FMS, Lisbon, Folder: 02970.001.012: *Conferência de Roma. Apoio*, 1970, pp. 1–2; Folder: 04307.003.007: *CNSLCP – Bulletin D'Information*, n° 2, December, Paris, 1970, p. 1; Folder 04322.001.031: *Première Conférence Internationale de Soutien à la Lutte de Libération des Peuples des Colonies Portugaises et de l'Afrique Australe*, Khartoum, January, 1969, pp. 1–5.

21 P. A. Oliveira, 'A Sense of Hopelessness? Portuguese Oppositionists Abroad in the Final Years of the Estado Novo, 1968–1974', *Contemporary European History*, 26:3 (2017), 465–86; R. Lopes, 'Accommodating and Confronting the Portuguese Dictatorship within NATO, 1970–74', *The International History Review*, 38:3 (2015), 505–26.

22 Archive from CIDAC, Lisbon, Folder BAC – 0290, NC/41: *Angola Comité*; NC/43: *Activities Concerning the Supply of Three War-Ships to Portugal by West Germany*.

23 N. Schliehe, 'West German Solidarity Movement'; F. Clara, 'Notes on Twentieth-Century Public Opinion'.

24 R. Lopes, *West Germany and the Portuguese Dictatorship, 1968–1974* (Basingstoke: Palgrave Macmillan, 2014), pp. 88, 66–91.

25 Archive from FMS, Lisbon, Folder 02970.001.012: *Conferência de Roma. Apoio*, 1970, p. 5.

26 Archive from FMS, Lisbon, Folder 02970.001.012: *Conferência de Roma. Apoio*, 1970, pp. 1–15.

27 Archive from CIDAC, Lisbon, Folder BAC – 0290, NC/57: *Meeting of the West-European committees, supporting the liberation movements*

in the Portuguese Colonies, 28, 29, 30 March 1970, De Horst Driebergen, Holland.
28 Archive from CIDAC, Lisbon, Folder BAC – 0290, NC/57: *Meeting of the West-European committees, supporting the liberation movements in the Portuguese Colonies*, 28, 29, 30 March 1970, De Horst Driebergen, Holland; Archive from FMS, Lisbon, Folder 04322.001.032: *CNSLCP – Déclaration (Conférence Internationale d'Appui aux Peuples des Colonies Portugaises, à Rome, 27–29 Juin,* 1970), pp. 1–3; Folder 02970.001.012: *Conferência de Roma. Apoio,* 1970, pp. 1–13; Folder 04322.001.031: *Première Conférence Internationale de Soutien à la Lutte de Libération des Peuples des Colonies Portugaises et de l'Afrique Australe*, Khartoum, January 1969, pp. 1–5.
29 Archive from CIDAC, Lisbon, Folder BAC – 0290, NC/57: *Meeting of the West-European committees*
30 Archive from CIDAC, Lisbon, Folder BAC – 0290, NC/57: *Meeting of the West-European committees*; Archive from FMS, Lisboan, Folder 02970.001.012: *Conferência de Roma. Apoio,* 1970, p. 4.
31 Archive from FMS, Lisbon, Folder 04307.002.002: *Conférence Internationale de Soutien aux Peuples des Colonies Portugaises*, Rome, 27–29 June, 1970; Folder: 04321.003.005: *Conférence Internationale d'Appui aux Peuples des Colonies Portugaises*, Rome, 27–29 June, 1970, p. 4; Folder 09621.001.005: *Programa da Conferência de Roma e Lista de Participantes*, June 1970.
32 See other Italian left-wing supporters in Archive from FMS, Lisbon, Folder: 04321.003.005: *Conférence Internationale d'Appui*, Rome, 27–29 June, 1970; Folder 04341.001.011: *PAIGC – Notre Lutte est aussi un Acte de Solidarité*, 1970, p. 2.
33 Lopes, *West Germany*, 25; Archive FMS, Lisbon, Folder 04341.001.011: *PAIGC – Notre Lutte est aussi un Acte de Solidarité*, 1970, pp. 11–12.
34 K. Middlemas, *Cabora Bassa: Engineering and Politics in Southern Africa* (London: Weidenfeld and Nicolson, 1975), p. 161; M. Patrício, 'Cahora Bassa nas relações bilaterais entre Portugal e Moçambique: 1975–2007', *Revista Portuguesa de Ciência Política*, 2 (2012), 149–58.
35 S. Bosgra, *Cabora Bassa* (Gottingen: Horst Ahlbrecht, 1969).
36 Lopes, *West Germany*, 66, 108–14.
37 A. Milani and V. Russo, '1.º de Julho de 1970: O Encontro Entre Paulo VI e os 'Rebeldes' das Colônias Portuguesas de África: A Receção da Imprensa Italiana', *Revista Polifonia*, 19:26 (2012/2), 218–34. For more details on the Italian support towards the liberation movements in the Portuguese colonies see, V. Russo, *La Resistenza Continua. Il Colonialismo Portoghese, le Lotte di Liberazione e gli Intellettuali Italiani* (Milano: Meltemi, 2020).

38 Archive from FMS, Lisbon, Folder 04321.003.005: *Conférence Internationale d'Appui*, Rome, 27–29 June, 1970, respectively pp. 1–3.
39 Archive from FMS, Lisbon, Folder 04341.001.011: *PAIGC – Notre Lutte est aussiun Acte de Solidarité*, 1970, p. 3; Folder 09621.001.006: *Relatório do Presidente da CONCP, Marcelino dos Santos*, 1970, p. 13.
40 Archive from FMS, Lisbon, Folder 09621.001.006: *Relatório do Presidente da CONCP*, 1970, p. 12.
41 Archive from FMS, Lisbon, Folder 04341.001.011: *PAIGC – Notre Lutte*, 1970, p. 14.
42 Archive from FMS, Lisbon, Folder 04341.001.011: *PAIGC – Notre Lutte*, 1970, pp. 10–15; Folder 09621.001.006: *Relatório do Presidente da CONCP*, 1970, pp. 1–14.
43 Archive from La Contemporaine – Nanterre University, Paris, Folder: *Boletim – Comité da Luta Anti-Colonial na Emigração (CLACs na Emigração)*, May, 1973, pp. 1–8; Comité de Soutien a la Lutte des Peuples de Guinee, d'Angola et du Mozambique, *Abattre le Colonialisme Portugais*, Toulouse, April, 1973, pp. 9–31; *Lutte – Bulletin du Comité de Soutien aux Deserteurs Portugais en France*, n° 2, October, 1972, pp. 12–24; Archive from FMS, Lisbon, Folder 09621.001.003: *Declaração do Comité National de Soutien de la Lutte de Libération des Peuples des Colonies Portugaises*, Paris, May, 1970, pp. 2–3.
44 Archive from FMS, Lisbon, Folder 07177.031: *Libertação*, 31 (June, 1963), 6.
45 Archive from FMS, Lisbon, Folder 04602.042: *Fundamentos e Objetivos da Libertação Nacional em Relação com a Estrutura Social*, January, 1966, pp. 10–14.
46 Archive from FMS, Lisbon, Folder 04344.003.005: *M. Amílcar Cabral, SG du PAIGC a Visité la Finland*, 1971.
47 M. K. Byrnes, 'Diplomacy at the End of Empire: Evolving French Perspectives on Portuguese Colonialism in the 1950s and 1960s', *Cold War History* (2019), 1–15; R. Lopes, *West Germany*; A. M. Fonseca and D. Marcos, 'Cold War Constraints: France, West Germany and Portuguese Decolonization', *Portuguese Studies*, 2 (2013), 209–26; A. da S. Lala, *L'Enjeux Colonial dans les Relations Franco-Portugaises 1944–1974* (PhD dissertation, Institut d'Etudes Politiques de Paris, 2007); A. J. Telo, *Portugal e a NATO: o Reencontro da Tradição Atlântica* (Lisboa: Edições Cosmos, 1996), pp. 321–34; E. de S. Ferreira, *Portuguese Colonialism from South Africa to Europe. Economic and Political Studies on the Portuguese Colonies*, South Africa and Namibia (Göttingen, Levinstr: Aktion Dritte Welt, Freiburg i. Br., Lorettostr, 1972).

48 Archive from FMS, Lisbon, Folder 09621.001.006: *Relatório do Presidente da CONCP*, June 1970, pp. 6–12.
49 Archive from FMS, Lisbon, Folder 04321.003.005: *Conférence Internationale d'Appui*, Rome, 27–29 June, 1970, pp. 1–2.
50 Archive from FMS, Lisbon, Folder 04341.001.011: *PAIGC – Notre Lutte*, 1970, p. 7.
51 Archive from FMS, Lisbon, Folder 04321.003.005: *Conférence Internationale d'Appui*, Rome, 27–29 June, 1970, p. 1.
52 Archive from FMS, Lisbon, Folder 04341.001.011: *PAIGC – Notre Lutte*, 1970, pp. 1–14; Folder 04321.003.005: *Conférence Internationale d'Appui*, Rome, 27–29 June, 1970, pp. 1–5; Folder 09621.001.006: *Relatório do Presidente da CONCP*, June, 1970, pp. 1–14.
53 Barros, 'The French Anticolonial Solidarity'.
54 Archive from FMS, Lisbon, Folder 02970.001.012: *Conferência de Roma. Apoio*, 1970, p. 11.
55 In French: *Comité National de Soutien de la Lutte de Libération dans les Colonies Portugaises*, located at 6 Rue Emile-Dubois, Paris, 14ème.
56 G. Tchernia, 'La Responsabilité de l'Occident dans la Guerre Coloniale Portugaise', *Le Monde*, 27 June, 1970, p. 3. On Gil Tchernia's solidarity towards the liberation movements of the Portuguese colonies in Africa see, Barros, 'The French Anticolonial Solidarity'.
57 The Portuguese dictatorship regime well-known as *Estado Novo* – New State – was officially instituted by António Oliveira Salazar in 1933. Salazar ruled until 1968 when, after an illness, he was replaced by Marcelo Caetano (1968–74). The New State as well as the Portuguese colonial empire collapsed on 25 April 1974 as a consequence of the Carnation Revolution, pressed by the weight of the liberation wars in Portugal's African colonies.

7

'Action needed': the American Committee on Africa and solidarity with Angola

Aurora Almada e Santos

The struggle to end Portuguese colonialism in Angola, Mozambique, Guinea, Cabo Verde and São Tome and Principe, waged between 1961 and 1974, generated a wide range of transnational solidarity activities as well as attracting humanitarian aid from around the globe. Yet research into these solidarity networks has so far been relatively meagre[1] and among US transnational solidarity groups, the American Committee of Africa (ACOA) is perhaps the only one that has been analysed.[2] The first accounts on ACOA were published by George Houser, the civil rights activist and Methodist Minister who was the Executive Director of the organisation from 1955 until 1981.[3] Much of the existing academic literature has appeared in the last decade and does not display a broad understanding of ACOA's solidarity with the Portuguese colonies, thus maintaining many of the historiographical silences that still exist in relation to this subject.[4] There is little information about the origins of the organisation, how it built on previously existing networks and movements, the evolution of its activities, the relationship it established with anticolonial organisations and whether it succeeded or not in having an impact on public opinion and US government policy.

This chapter explores the complexity of ACOA's solidarity with the Portuguese colonies, examining its assistance to the National Front for the Liberation of Angola (Frente Nacional de Libertação de Angola–FNLA) through the Emergency Relief to Angola (ERA) programme which operated between 1962 and 1965. The investigation of the ERA programme is guided by the following questions: why was the programme initiated, how was it implemented and why did it become inactive? The analysis is based on primary sources and seeks to contribute to the growing scholarship on the transnational solidarity networks with Portuguese colonies. By broadening the scope of research on ACOA, it also complicates the prevailing narratives on how this organisation helped liberation movements. It will argue that ERA was a pilot project that had as much to do with helping the struggle for independence of Angola as with ACOA's intent of promoting its own ideas on solidarity. As such, the chapter highlights how different interests helped to create and implement transnational solidarity initiatives by non-state actors.

'Our help is sought and expected'

Why, then, did ACOA establish the ERA programme? The official genealogy of ACOA traces its origins to the Americans for South African Resistance (AFSAR), a group established in 1952 by activists connected to organisations such as the Fellowship of Reconciliation, the War Resisters League, the International League for the Rights of Man and the Congress of Racial Equality.[5] AFSAR's aim was to support the Defiance Campaign promoted by the African National Congress (ANC) and the South African Indian Congress (SAIC) against the racial laws of apartheid. AFSAR's members used the rhetoric of the domestic struggle against racism to support a similar struggle in Southern Africa, helping to intertwine the opposition to racial inequality at home and the anti-apartheid/anticolonial cause abroad.[6] After the decline of the campaign, and stressing the need to react to the lack of interest shown in Africa by US institutions and public opinion, AFSAR expanded its scope, renaming itself ACOA in 1953.[7]

Operating under the slogan 'Action Needed', ACOA pioneered a style of transnational activism with the victims of colonialism and racism in Africa, modelling the strategies and tactics adopted later by other activists.[8] The committee's intent was to become a key external player in the support for struggles that were little known in the US at the time. The organisational strategy included providing support for the independence of African territories and assistance to the national liberation movements, as well as promoting the transformation of US government policies on Africa, the education of public opinion and the dissemination of accurate information about the continent.[9] To accomplish these goals, the committee created networks at both national and international levels, engaging in joint actions with political, religious and business institutions, trade unions, congressmen, civil servants and grassroots organisations.[10]

From a small volunteer organisation, ACOA would become one of the most influential solidarity organisation in the US lobbying for anticolonialism and black majority rule in Africa.[11] ACOA's support for the liberation struggle in the Portuguese colonies was not an isolated phenomenon but rather was linked to the events that took place during the so-called 'long sixties'.[12] Together with the civil rights movement in the US, the protests against the Vietnam War and the youth rebellions across the globe, as well as the ecology, peace and women's movements, the struggle to end Portuguese colonialism was an integral part of the politics and the transnational solidarity networks of that period.[13] The activism directed against Portuguese colonialism was an illustration of both the wide range of transnational solidarity networks and the multiple entanglements that shaped exchanges between the First, Second and Third Worlds.[14] Indeed, not only did a wide variety of actors from across the globe voluntarily engage in complex relationships with the anticolonialists from the Portuguese colonies, but the anticolonial organisations themselves also actively sought to mobilise activists in numerous countries in order to internationalise the liberation struggle.[15] In many circumstances, the activists became the centre of campaigns to support the anticolonial organisations, and sometimes they brought with them a dense web of transnational connections, helping to create formal and informal networks of assistance.[16]

From its beginnings, ACOA sought to influence the debate on Portuguese colonialism, but the organisation had only a modest participation in the international campaign against Portugal's colonial rule in the 1950s. After establishing contact with anticolonial organisations from the Portuguese colonies, George Houser concluded that 'our help is sought and expected', pointing to the agency of the liberation movements in developing relationships with a broad array of groups.[17] Even though the committee engaged with different Angolan organisations, the contacts with the Union of the Peoples of Angola (União dos Povos de Angola–UPA) were more intimate, being conducted on a personal level, and particularly so between Houser and the movement's leader, Holden Roberto.[18] ACOA's preference for the UPA depended largely on the friendship between Houser and Roberto, as well as on Cold War considerations due to this liberation movement's professed anti-communism.[19] Houser had met Roberto while travelling to the Belgian Congo in 1954, providing an opening for ACOA to become a target of the UPA's diplomatic offensives directed towards external actors such as governments, international organisations and non-state actors. Through the application of different methods, ranging from personal contacts to letter-writing, trips and participation in conferences and other meetings, diplomacy was an important tool for the liberation movement to garner both material and non-material support. In addition, diplomatic relations were used by the movement to strengthen its image as a politically active organisation, neutralise adversaries in the context of a fragmented anticolonial struggle and help to isolate Portugal in the international arena.[20]

The use of diplomacy by the UPA to mobilise key transnational allies translated into ACOA's support for the liberation movement even before the Portuguese colonies were placed at the forefront of the international debate on decolonisation. The committee became more active in combating Portuguese colonialism in response to events in Angola in 1961, when the UPA launched the armed struggle.[21] With the outbreak of war, ACOA took part in the rhetorical battle being waged worldwide against Portugal.[22] As the public discussion became even broader, the committee became increasingly concerned with the Angolan refugees who had fled to neighbouring countries such as the Republic of the Congo (Leopoldville).[23] In dialogue with the UPA, the committee conceived the idea of giving emergency assistance to the refugees – officially numbering 150,000 in December 1961 – and to Angola.[24] Holden Roberto was asked by the committee to comment on the medical needs of the refugees and those Angolans who were unable to cross the border into Congo.[25] ACOA engaged in a collaborative effort to meet those needs, working with the African Technical Assistance Foundation, the International Rescue Committee, the United States Committee for Refugees and MEDICO to collect medicines.[26] Although American voluntary agencies, the International Red

Cross and the United Nations High Commissioner for Refugees (UNHCR) were already providing relief to the refugees, ACOA understood that no duplication of efforts would occur if its own aid was delivered directly to displaced people inside Angola.[27]

It was after a trip to the Congo and Northern Angola, undertaken by Houser and John Marcum[28] between December 1961 and January 1962 to assess the situation on the ground and deliver medicines, that ACOA embarked on a full medical aid project for the refugees.[29] Houser and Marcum's fact-finding trip was a vehicle for learning about events in Angola and thus bringing a new emphasis and fresh directions to the committee's work.[30] In his confidential report detailing the journey, Houser recommended that the medical relief programme (initiated with the medicines delivered during the trip) should be expanded to meet the existing needs.[31] Stressing that no initiative existed at that time to assist internally displaced people inside Angola, in March 1962 the committee announced it was initiating the ERA programme. Scheduled to launch on 15 April, the programme would raise funds to transport medicines and medical equipment to Leopoldville, to send medical personnel to Angola, and to receive, package and transport medical supplies that had been delivered directly to ACOA's office.[32]

The ERA programme, intended to be humanitarian and not political, can be linked to ACOA's interests, as well as to forms of resistance against Portuguese colonialism adopted by the UPA. Joanna Tague has demonstrated that ACOA did not provide medical relief out of sheer altruism, since its aid was strategic and targeted.[33] ACOA's agenda certainly played an important role in the implementation of the programme. The background of the programme was the desire to raise ACOA's visibility as an organisation committed with the struggle against colonialism.[34] ERA was a way for the committee to cultivate proximity with the situation on the ground, enabling ACOA not to disperse its limited funds, but to work more efficiently in partnership with a liberation movement that was already embedded among the refugees. Instead of the committee being dependent on isolated actions, ERA represented a chance to provide greater humanitarian relief and to have an apparatus to manage the funds collected for the refugees' assistance.[35] The ERA programme was also implemented for financial reasons, since the committee was burdened with a large deficit.[36] ERA was to fulfil ACOA's desire to have a specific programme for fundraising, and, in the short run, the committee expected it would help sustain its work through an overhead charge.[37]

For the UPA, ERA was an opportunity to help make its concept of state-building programmes more tangible. After an association with the Democratic Party of Angola (Partido Democrático de Angola–PDA), the UPA renamed itself in early 1962 as the FNLA and established the Revolutionary Government of Angola in Exile (Governo Revolucionário de Angola no Exílio–GRAE). While waging the war against Portugal, behind the lines in those areas proclaimed to have been liberated in Angola and across the border in the Congo, the FNLA organised assistance programmes, giving special prominence to education and health care. The establishment of such programmes was regularly presented by the movement as an attempt to build a proto-state, laying the foundations for a new society to be created after independence.[38] The movement created its state-building programmes not only to gain the goodwill of the populations in Angola and the refugees, but also to demonstrate that the FNLA had adopted normative paradigms of statehood. The FNLA used the state-building programmes to sideline competing anticolonial organisations, such as the Movement for the Liberation of Angola (Movimento para a Libertação de Angola–MPLA), which also had its own educational and health programmes, as well as to attract assistance from networks of solidarity on humanitarian grounds. In this context, ERA was an attractive resource for the Service of Assistance to the Refugees of Angola (Serviço de Assistência aos Refugiados Angolanos–SARA) established by the FNLA to run its medical activities. ERA had the potential to help legitimise the FNLA and to demonstrate its capacity, its power of organisation and its administration on behalf of the people.[39]

'Much more than scratched the surface'

ERA's first step was to raise funds by appealing to donors and, in the same way with other ACOA initiatives, the programme used methods borrowed from domestic social movements, in a quite familiar process as the work of Charles Tilly on social movements repertoires evinces.⁴⁰ Like other transnational networks of activity, ACOA used a myriad of strategies and methods, including public meetings, rallies, workshops and conferences, pamphleteering, statements to media, dissemination of publications, boycotts, lobbying, field work and so on. Combining and adapting previously established practices, ERA printed and distributed brochures and sent letters to contributors on behalf of the Angolan refugees.⁴¹ Although ACOA's mailing was sometimes centred exclusively on the programme, ERA's fundraising efforts were only modestly successful. Other concerns, like the civil rights movement, competed for the attention of the public opinion, creating difficulties in raising funds for ERA.⁴² Besides targeting anonymous donors, ERA sought to stimulate other organisations and encourage cooperative efforts in order to secure financial contributions and medicines. Plans were drawn up to seek funds, medicines, and medical supplies from pharmaceutical companies and doctors.⁴³ Similarly, the programme attempted to attract organised groups in the general community to support the initiative through campaigns in churches, trade unions, student associations and universities. ERA also sought to involve tax-exempt agencies, such as the Congo Protestant Relief Agency, the Africa Service Institute (ASI) and the Manhattan Central Medical Association, to help with the cost of the programme.⁴⁴

Besides preparing shipments of medicines and medical supplies, ERA raised funds to send medical personnel to work at SARA's Angolan clinic in Leopoldville, to help refugees at the border, and to provide medical assistance inside Angola. Initially, SARA gave priority to solving the lack of transportation, which was limiting contacts with refugees at the border over having skilled medical help.⁴⁵ Only after ACOA's determined insistence was F. Ian Gilchrist, a Canadian doctor, able to arrive in the Congo. Sending Gilchrist to Leopoldville was important because other than providing relief to refugees, ACOA's sights were set on its own interests and constituencies. The organisation was trying to push its own concept of solidarity which included the intent of dispatching people to work with the liberation movement to improve the health and education conditions of refugees. Similarly, ACOA hoped that Gilchrist's experience with SARA would enable ERA to acquire a sense of greater intimacy and urgency, since his personal accounts could be used for publicity and fundraising.⁴⁶ According to Houser, people would respond more readily to a personalised appeal, thus making it possible for ERA to raise larger sums of money. In addition, Gilchrist's presence in the Congo would be useful in opening a channel of direct contact between ACOA and the situation on the ground. Instead of continuing to be largely dependent on sporadic reports, ACOA saw Gilchrist as an opportunity for gathering information, monitoring the fighting inside Angola, and gaining greater knowledge of the relationship between the contending liberation movements.[47]

The son of a medical missionary in Angola, Ian Gilchrist had volunteered to work with SARA, moving to Leopoldville in January 1963. Like many other activists, Gilchrist's activist biography reveals the importance of family history and a personal experience of Portuguese colonialism in forging a commitment to the anticolonial struggle.[48] Born in Halifax, Canada, into a family with an international outlook, Gilchrist lived in Angola for ten years before returning to Canada, where he finished his medical training in 1961.[49] After spending a short period in Angola and Sierra Leone, he went to Leopoldville, where his wife and two children joined him. Gilchrist was one of many Third World advocates who fell into the category of 'key activists', defined as being a node in the solidarity networks, coordinating and articulating actions, as well as communicating the flows of information.[50] His path mirrored that of many other activists who forged links with the liberation movements and leveraged their professional skills – as journalists, academics, filmmakers, missionaries, priests, doctors and intellectuals – in support of the Portuguese colonies' struggle for independence.[51]

Despite being a sympathiser of the cause of Angolan independence and claiming to view the situation from an African perspective, Gilchrist was unable to escape the influence either of the colonial paternalism or of the Cold War mentality.[52] Such behaviour was not uncommon, since other activists, like Houser himself, sometimes revealed a paternalistic and ethnocentric appreciation of African culture and agency and were not free from the constraints imposed by the Cold War.[53] Furthermore, Gilchrist seems to have belonged to the category of those activists who often romanticised their projections and dreams about the liberation movements.[54] His enthusiasm towards the cause for independence was at times naïve, as revealed by the affirmation that 'the first Angolan rebel was a man with only the power of Right' and by the portrayal of the war in Angola as 'the obvious right versus the obvious wrong'.[55]

Based at SARA's compound in Leopoldville, he became one of the four doctors working for the FNLA's medical relief programme for refugees. Together with ACOA, the International Rescue Committee (IRC) and the ASI also appointed doctors to help SARA, revealing the breadth of the international involvement in providing assistance to Angolan refugees.[56] Gilchrist's primary objective was to help Angolan refugees, while trying to separate the humanitarian assistance from the FNLA's armed struggle, since he objected to the programme's resources being used for military purposes.[57] His efforts were directed towards administering treatment to patients; travelling to settlements on the Angolan border to work among refugees and distribute medicines; establishing dispensaries staffed with nurses; sending supplies into Angola; treating wounded fighters; and training medical volunteers to improve the local treatment administered in the field.[58] In addition, Gilchrist combined his medical activities with other initiatives designed to meet the urgent needs of refugees, especially from a nutritional point of view, and with assisting them in becoming self-supporting.[59] Since, according to the UNHCR, the flow of refugees from Angola reached 200,000 by 1965, it is difficult to assess Gilchrist's precise contribution to the solution of their problems.[60] Evidence provided by Gilchrist himself suggests that ERA was unable to do 'much more than scratched the surface'.[61]

Whenever possible, Gilchrist took advantage of his privileged position within the FNLA to provide ACOA with first-hand information, supplied either voluntarily or on request.[62] As mentioned above, the flow of information originating from Gilchrist reflected one of the priorities established by the committee for his presence in the Congo. Because Portugal had imposed a wall of silence around its colonies, ACOA had become one of the channels for gathering knowledge about Portuguese colonialism in Africa.[63] It was partly because of Gilchrist that ACOA continued to serve as an expert body that other organisations looked to for information. The content of the information provided by Gilchrist was wide-ranging, covering such areas as: the number of refugees, the medical assistance that was in place for them, their health, living conditions, and needs;

day-to-day developments in the power struggle among the liberation movements; the status of the fighting inside Angola; stories of acts of brutality credited to Portuguese troops; and the internal situation in the Congo. Most of the time, these descriptions, coupled with pictures taken by Gilchrist himself, employed a language very similar to the one used by the FNLA's, repeating the liberation movement arguments about Portuguese colonialism and the war in Angola. ACOA made use of Gilchrist's descriptions in various ways: as publicity to attract new contributors; for the preparation of publications; disseminating information to the public opinion; lobbying the US government and the United Nations (UN); and exchanging data with other organisations. The information was not only an important component of the ERA programme, but it also paved the way for concrete initiatives.

As had been planned from the beginning, Gilchrist was encouraged by ACOA to share his experience in a well-publicised tour, designed to strengthen the committee's solidarity.[64] During the speaking tour – the most extensive ACOA tour at the time – Gilchrist spent two months in the US and Canada in the spring of 1964, where he undertook several engagements, addressing groups of students, workers and church members, and helping to raise the funds needed to sustain ACOA's ability to continue the ERA programme.[65] Gilchrist's tour included interviews for radio, television and newspapers, using the space opened up by the media to express the anticolonial message and demonstrate solidarity towards Angolan refugees. Appearances at institutions such as the California Institute of Technology, Claremont College, the International Relations Association and the International Student Center further cemented ACOA's strategy of keeping the Angolan situation in the public light.[66] Besides the tour's usefulness in supporting ACOA's public information and educational activities, Gilchrist brought the refugees' problem in the Congo and the situation in Angola to the attention of the UN.[67]

In order to mobilise donors, Gilchrist painted the war in Angola in moral terms, denouncing Portugal's colonial rule.[68] In keeping with ACOA's critical view of Portuguese colonialism, two fundamentally different images of the situation in Angola emerged from his discourse. First, he depicted the Angolans as the victims of the situation, enduring harsh living conditions, racial discrimination and Portugal's manoeuvres to divide the population.[69] Second, Gilchrist evoked the Angolan masses as heroes who, even though they were ill-prepared to wage a modern war, were ready and willing to fight against Portugal. As a result, he criticised the involvement of Western countries in the war in Angola, exposing both the material and moral support they gave to Portuguese colonialism in Africa.[70] A close examination of Gilchrist's words shows that, while emphasising ERA's material limitations, he avoided any reference either to the problems affecting the Angolan struggle for independence or to the real difficulties that the relief programme was facing. He described ERA as 'our small part of the Revolution. It is our beginning, for we know that we have much to do, that it is not easy to do more, and that the end yet seems a long way off.'[71] In the end, Gilchrist's account resonated with the donors, helping to improve ERA fundraising and to secure the resources needed to continue the project.[72]

'Basically humanitarian rather than political'

If resources were available, why, then, was the ERA programme so short-lived? After almost three years, ACOA suspended ERA, while still maintaining the hope that the programme could be reactivated when possible. According to the timeline of events, in early 1964, Gilchrist started to voice criticism of Roberto's strategy for achieving Angolan independence.[73] As suspicion grew on all sides, the relationship between Gilchrist and the FNLA leaders, including Roberto, deteriorated. The crisis dragged on for almost a year and a half and, during that period, Gilchrist questioned the value of his presence in Leopoldville.[74] Both he and ACOA drew up plans for his departure, but the final decision was postponed on various occasions. In June 1965, following accusations of interference in political events related to the fight for Angolan independence, he and his family left Leopoldville returning to Canada.[75]

Events in the Congo certainly affected ERA's experiment, limiting the provision of humanitarian aid to the Angolan refugees in the country. The Congolese situation remained fluid following the crises that had arisen in the wake of Patrice Lumumba's assassination in 1961, culminating in the Mobutu Sese Seko coup d'état in 1965. Besides these underlying factors, there were many other motives for suspending the ERA programme, including the power struggle between the liberation movements. Soon after arriving in Leopoldville, Gilchrist asked ACOA how close his association with SARA should be, because he thought that a valuable impetus could be lost if the programme remained directly under the FNLA's supervision.[76] ACOA's answer tried to take into account the fragmented nature of the struggle for Angolan independence, avoiding intervening directly in what was regarded as an African debate among the liberation movements. The reality proved how difficult it was to approach the question of providing assistance to the Angolan refugees from a 'basically humanitarian rather than political' and partisan point of view, as ACOA intended.[77] Far from achieving its aim of not being a politicised programme, ERA was neither impartial, nor neutral or independent.[78] In many ways, this was not surprising, since the two key anticolonial organisations, the FNLA and the MPLA, operated their relief services as branches of their political activities. While trying to cultivate good relations with different organisations, Gilchrist was not able to free himself from the complications of being in either one camp or the other.[79]

We should also add to this Gilchrist's difficulties in avoiding becoming involved in the FNLA's infighting. Competing factions within the movement engendered plots, intrigues and counterplots, sometimes resorting to violence. During his time in Leopoldville, Gilchrist was implicated in various intrigues, and different factions among the FNLA regarded him with suspicion, requesting his removal from SARA.[80] One of the major factional struggles within the FNLA took place in 1964, in which Roberto was challenged by Jonas Savimbi, an Ovimbundu raised by foreign missionaries in Angola and the GRAE's Minister of External Affairs.[81] In his correspondence with ACOA, Gilchrist, whose family lived in the Ovimbundu area in Angola, did not conceal his favourable opinion of Savimbi and his judgement that he was the best option to replace Roberto in the leadership of the FNLA.[82] Gilchrist's problems with Roberto, against whom he was becoming more and more vocal in his criticisms, seem to have increased as a result of Savimbi's split from the movement. When Savimbi left the FNLA in July 1964, convincing other militants to follow him, Roberto suspected Gilchrist of being implicated and began to make accusations against him.[83]

Perhaps the accusations were related to Gilchrist's decision to carry with him a list of soldiers who were ready to leave the FNLA and join Savimbi.[84] Although the accusations did not have any direct consequences, Gilchrist was unable to restore a relationship of trust with Roberto during the remainder of his period of cooperation with SARA.

Much of the tension that existed between Gilchrist and the FNLA was related to their disagreements about how the relief assistance should be implemented by SARA. Gilchrist understood that the extent of SARA's relief assistance was almost completely limited to the clinic in Leopoldville, and that it did not reach the refugees.[85] Despite constant insistence, all his requests to be allowed to make a trip to Angola were turned down by the FNLA, and the ERA's plan for getting relief into the territory never came to fruition. Gilchrist felt severely handicapped, believing that SARA was giving too much emphasis to the refugees from the Angolan Bakongo ethnic group (among whom Roberto had his family roots), while disregarding the non-Bakongos living in places like Katanga, Rhodesia and Bechuanaland.[86] He voiced his disappointment that, over time, the visits to the frontier became far too infrequent, due to the limitations of transportation, thereby preventing the supply of relief and medical treatment. Arguing that none of his suggestions were ever acted upon, in his last year and a half in Leopoldville, Gilchrist's grievances about SARA's internal organisation multiplied.[87] His list was quite extensive, including accusations of obstruction in the access to medicines and medical supplies, political interference by the FNLA, the use of ERA's humanitarian assistance for military purposes, the misappropriation of funds and the appointment of Roberto's relatives to SARA. The turning point for Gilchrist was the resignation of the head of SARA, José Liahuca, who left to join the MPLA, following Savimbi's split from the movement.[88] After such an event and the consequent reorganisation that took place, Gilchrist's commitment to SARA's operations became ever weaker.[89]

By and large, the FNLA and ACOA's different understandings of solidarity played an important role in dictating the suspension of the ERA programme. When he arrived in Leopoldville, Gilchrist was exposed to the accusation that he was a tool of American imperialism.[90] On different occasions, Roberto gave the impression that the FNLA was wary of accepting foreign technicians, and particularly Americans, for fear that charges of American imperialism would imperil the provision of aid from other sources.[91] This was a clear illustration of the fact that the FNLA's interpretation of solidarity was based more on the material provision of assistance and less on having foreigners participating in the state-building programmes, as was the intention of ACOA. This situation did not only affect the ERA programme, for the IRC also had to reconsider its medical project with SARA, summoning its physician, Louis Wellington, back to the head office.[92] After Gilchrist and Wellington's departures, SARA's relief programme was placed in the hands of two African doctors: an Angolan and a Congolese. The FNLA would continue to ask for ACOA's assistance, requesting medicines, medical equipment and other supplies.[93] As in the past, the committee provided the assistance needed, but not without adjusting its definition of solidarity, dropping the idea of sending people to work with the liberation movement. In the end, ERA functioned as a formative event for ACOA's solidarity, shaping the committee's views on how to engage with the liberation movements.

Conclusion

How does exploring the ERA programme increase our understanding of the transnational networks of solidarity in the 1960s? Tracing the trajectory of ERA highlights several familiar aspects of the transnational networks of solidarity. As in many other case studies, ERA shows how solidarity groups connected with one another, sponsored special trips for face-to-face interaction with 'distant others', transferred resources for humanitarian assistance, mobilised donors for fundraising, created flows of communication, played the role of public opinion makers through the media and lobbied governments and international organisations in order to raise awareness about a particular cause. These striking commonalities between ERA and other initiatives are reinforced when we look at the diversity of participants and activists, as well as at the role of individuals and their 'professional activism' in the context of transnational networks of solidarity.

Not only does this chapter illustrate how solidarity was performed, but it also confirms that it was a dynamic process and not a unilateral one. ERA provides an excellent example of the intersections between different interests that helped to create and implement solidarity initiatives. This ERA case study also raises questions about how the connections between the solidarity networks in the North and the Third World liberation movements led to misunderstandings and engendered tensions. Another aspect of the complex interactions between actors displayed by the history of ERA is that different concepts of solidarity were to be found at the core of the relationship between providers and beneficiaries. ERA can be understood as having been one of the mobile, highly malleable and far from monolithic, transnational networks of solidarity that were fuelled in the 1960s by organisations such as ACOA.

Notes

1 For references of existing publications see: A. A. Santos, B. C. André, C. Tornimbeni and I. Vasile (eds), 'International Solidarities and the Liberation of the Portuguese Colonies', *Africhi e Orienti*, 3 (2017), 1–146; I. Vasile, A. A. Santos, C. Tornimbeni (eds), 'What Solidarity? Networks of Cooperation with the Liberation Movements from Portuguese Colonies', *Revista Crítica de Ciências Sociais*, 118 (2019), 125–212.

2 Other solidarity groups in the US in this period included the Chicago Committee for the Liberation of Angola, the Angola Support Conference, the Mozambique Support Network, and the Mozambique Solidarity Office.

3 Born into a family of Methodist missionaries, George Houser spent his early childhood in the Philippines. He graduated from the University of Denver and entered the ministry. As a seminarian, in 1940, he served a prison term for disobeying peace-time conscription. He worked with several organisations: Fellowship of Reconciliation and the Committee of Racial Equality. G. Houser, *No One Can Stop the Rain. Glimpses of Africa's Liberation Struggle* (New York: The Pilgrim Press, 1989), pp. 5–9.

4 C. Stephens, *The People Mobilized. The Mozambican Liberation Movement and American Activism (1960–1975)* (PhD Dissertation,

Temple University, 2011); R. J. Parrott, *Struggle for Solidarity: The New Left, Portuguese African Decolonization, and the End of the Cold War Consensus* (PhD Dissertation, University of Texas at Austin, 2016); R. J. Parrott, '"We Are an African People": The Development of Black American Solidarity with Portuguese Africa' (Master Thesis, University of Texas at Austin, 2014); J. Tague, *Displaced Mozambicans in Postcolonial Tanzania: Refugee Power, Mobility, Education, and Rural Development* (New York: Routledge, 2019); J. Tague, 'American Humanitarianism and the End of Portugal's African Empire: Institutional and Governmental Interests in Assisting Angolan Refugees in Congo, 1961–74', *Portuguese Journal of Social Science*, 14:3 (September 2015), 343–59.
5 Stephens, *The People Mobilized*, 170–2.
6 Ibid.
7 Ibid.
8 S. D. Collins, *Ubuntu: George Houser and the Struggle for Peace and Freedom in Two Continents* (Athens: Ohio University Press, 2020), p. 2.
9 African Activist Archive (AAA) at Michigan State University, ACOA, The Programme and Purposes of the American Committee on Africa, p. 4.
10 AAA, ACOA, Report from the American Committee on Africa to the Conference of the International Defense and Aid Fund, 25–27 April 1969, pp. 1–2.
11 Collins, *Ubuntu: George M. Houser*, p. 119.
12 M. Klimke and M. Nolan, 'Introduction: The Globalization of the Sixties', in C. Jian, M. Klimke, M. Kirasirova, M. Nolan, M. Young, J. Waley-Cohen (eds), *The Routledge Handbook of the Global Sixties: Between Protest and Nation-Building* (London & New York: Routledge, 2018), p. 5.
13 Ibid.
14 K. Kuhn, 'Liberation Struggle and Humanitarian Aid: International Solidarity Movements and the "Third World" in the 1960s', in S. Christiansen and Z. Scarlett (eds), *The Third World in the Global 1960s* (New York & Oxford: Berghahn Books, 2013), p. 6.
15 Vasile et al. (eds), 'What Solidarity?'; Santos et al. (eds), 'International Solidarities'.
16 V. Barros, 'The French Anticolonial Solidarity Movement and the Liberation of Guinea-Bissau and Cape Verde', *The International History Review*, 2020, 1–22.
17 Ibid.
18 Houser, *No One Can Stop the Rain*, p. 42.
19 Parrott, *Struggle for Solidarity*, 152–3.

20 A. D. Amado, 'The PAIGC "Congratulatory" Diplomacy towards Communist States, 1960–1964', *Lusotopie*, 19 (2020), 57–60.
21 Stephens, *The People Mobilized*, 182–3.
22 Arquivo Nacional Torre do Tombo (ANTT), Arquivo Oliveira Salazar, AOS/CO/NE–30B–14, Minutes of the Conversation between J. H. Themido and Xanthaky, Counselor of the US Embassy in Lisbon, 4 October 1962, pp. 78–80; AOS/COE–2-2-7, Minutes of Conversation between Franco Nogueira and George Anderson held at the Ministry of Foreign Affairs, 6 July 1964, pp. 27–80. Parrott, *Struggle for Solidarity*.
23 Amistad Research Center (ARC) at Tulane University, ACOA Papers, Part 1, Executive Committee Minutes and National Office Memoranda, 1952–75, 2/15, Executive Committee Minutes June–December 1961, Draft, 14 November 1961, Microfilm 5, pp. 5–6.
24 United Nations General Assembly Official Records: Seventeenth Session, *Report of the United Nations High Commissioner for Refugees Supplement No. 11 (A/5211/Rev.1)* (S.l: s.n, 1963).
25 ARC, ACOA Papers, Archives 1948–88, Series III, Programmes and Activities in African Countries, Box 80, Angola–Collected Items–Gulf–Portugal, 1956–76, 80/5, Angola–African Relief Services Committee–Brochures–Press Releases–African Research Foundation–Memorandum 1961, Memorandum for the Record by James L. Monroe of the African Research Foundation, 12 December 1961.
26 Ibid.
27 ARC, ACOA Papers, Series I, Administration, Interoffice Memorandums, 1952–55, 1/6, Interoffice Memorandums 1961, Memorandum on Fundraising for ACOA by James R. Robinson, 20 October 1961, Microfilm 1, pp. 311–12.
28 John Marcum was an African scholar and an ACOA member, being involved in the struggle against colonialism and apartheid in Africa. He was the author of *The Angolan Revolution: The Anatomy of an Explosion (1950–1962)* (Cambridge, MA & London: MIT Press, 1969).
29 AAA, ACOA, A Report on a Journey Through Rebel Angola by George M. Houser, February 1962, p. 11.
30 Collins, *Ubuntu: George M. Houser*, p. 169.
31 Ibid.
32 ARC, ACOA Papers, Series I, Administration, Interoffice Memorandums, 1952–55, 1/8, Interoffice Memorandum March–July 1962, Memorandum to Elsie Carrington, Dr Charles Brown, Dr George D. Thorne, and Alan Morrison from George Houser, 14 March 1962, Microfilm 1, p. 399.
33 Tague, 'American Humanitarianism', 346.

34 Stephens, *The People Mobilized*, 174–5.
35 Tague, *Displaced Mozambicans*, p. 87.
36 ARC, ACOA Papers, Series I, Administration, Interoffice Memorandums, 1952–55, 1/8, Interoffice Memorandum March–July 1962, Memorandum to George Houser from James R. Robinson, 8 May 1962, Microfilm 1, pp. 412–13.
37 ARC, ACOA Papers, Series I, Administration, Interoffice Memorandums, 1952–55, 1/6, Interoffice Memorandums 1961, Memorandum on Fundraising for ACOA by James R. Robinson, 20 October 1961, Microfilm 1, pp. 311–12.
38 Nations Unies, A/C.4/SR 1398. *Quatrième Commission, 1398e Séance. Mardi 27 Novembre 1962, à 10h55* (New York: General Assembly, 1962).
39 ARC, ACOA Papers, 1948–8, Series III, Programmes and Activities in African Countries, Box 79, Angola–Correspondence–Miscellany, 1954–78, File 4, Letter from SARA,14 August 1962.
40 See for instance C. Tilly, 'Introduction to Part II: Invention, Diffusion, and Transformation of the Social Movement Repertoire', *European Review of History: Revue europeenne d'histoire*, 12:2 (2005), 307–20.
41 AAA, ACOA, 1963 Report, 1 January 1963 through 31 December 1963.
42 ARC, ACOA Papers, Part 1, ACOA Executive Committee Minutes and National Office Memoranda, 1952–75, 2/17, Executive Committee Minutes 1963, Executive Board, 16 September 1963, Microfilm 5, pp. 149–51.
43 ARC, ACOA Papers, Series I, Administration, Interoffice Memorandums, 1952–55, 1/8, Interoffice Memorandum March–July 1962, Memorandum to Elsie Carrington, Dr Charles Brown, Dr George D. Thorne, and Alan Morrison from George Houser, 14 March 1962, Microfilm 1, p. 399.
44 Ibid.
45 ARC, ACOA Papers, 1948–88, Series III, Programmes and Activities in African Countries, Box 79, Angola–Correspondence–Miscellany, 1954–78, File 4, SARA, Leopoldville, 14 August 1962.
46 ARC, ACOA Papers, Series I, Administration, Interoffice Memorandums, 1952–55, 1/9, Interoffice Memorandums, August–November 1962, Memo to Daniel J. Bernstein, Treasurer, from James R. Robinson, Assistant Director, 29 August 1962, Microfilm 1, pp. 443–5.
47 ARC, ACOA Papers, 1948–88, Series III, Programmes and Activities in African Countries, Box 79, Angola–Correspondence–Miscellany, 1954–78, File 5, Letter from ACOA to José J. Liahuca, 19 October 1962.
48 Ian Gilchrist's father, William Sidney Gilchrist, a specialist in public health and preventative medicine, was appointed by the United

Church as medical missionary to Angola in 1928. He arrived in Angola in 1930 and worked among the Ovimbundos for 37 years, leaving the territory in 1966 after being interrogated by the police. ANTT, Arquivos da PIDE/DGS, Del A, P Sec, N° Processo 1124, William Sidney Gilchrist.

49 AAA, ACOA, Background on Dr. F. Ian Gilchrist and the Situation in Angola, April–May 1964, p. 1.
50 H. Thörn, 'The Meaning(s) of Solidarity: Narratives of Anti-Apartheid Activism', *Journal of Southern African Studies*, 35:2 (2009), 422.
51 Several examples can illustrate how individual activism was instrumental for the solidarity towards the struggle for independence in the Portuguese colonies. Basil Davidson, a British journalist, took interest in African history from 1951 onward and went on to write about the struggle of the national liberation movements from Portuguese colonies. In 1967, at a dinner in Kenia, the African-American lawyer Robert van Lierop met Eduardo Mondlane and together they conceived the idea of producing the film *A Luta Continua* about the armed struggle in Mozambique for American audiences.
52 In Gilchrist's own words: 'Our sympathy and understanding for the Angolan rebel then, does not blind us to the fact that he is sometimes a rascal, a liar and a thief, unambitious and lazy by virtue of his long indoctrination of worthlessness by the colonial master, and no longer possessing the standards and values of the tribe to moralize him.' ARC, ACOA Papers, Archives 1948–88, Series III, Programmes and Activities in African Countries, Box 80, Angola–Collected Items–Gulf–Portugal, 1956–76, 80/41, Angola: Emergency Relief Fund to Angola (SARA), Ian Gilchrist Tour, Clippings, Notes, Fliers, Agenda, Writing, Photographies [1964], The Hardest Revolution–Ian Gilchrist.
53 Collins, *Ubuntu: George M. Houser*, p. 106; Parrott, *Struggle for Solidarity*; Parrott, '"We Are an African People"'.
54 Ibid.; Kuhn, 'Liberation Struggle', 78.
55 ARC, ACOA Papers, Archives 1948–88, Series III, Programmes and Activities in African Countries, Box 80, Angola–Collected Items–Gulf–Portugal, 1956–76, 80/41, Angola: Emergency Relief Fund to Angola (SARA), Ian Gilchrist Tour, Clippings, Notes, Fliers, Agenda, Writing, Photographies [1964], The Hardest Revolution–Ian Gilchrist.
56 ARC, ACOA Papers, Archives 1948–88, Series III, Programmes and Activities in African Countries, Box 79, Angola–Correspondence–Miscellany, 1954–78, File 6, 79/8, Angola–Correspondence–April 1963–June 1963, Letter from George Houser to Ian Gilchrist, 27 June 1963.
57 After arriving in Leopoldville, Gilchrist admitted that he encountered a reality different from what he had imagined: 'I have had several

talks and meetings with Holden during the past week. He has been helpful, but is perhaps not quite the little tin god I had thought him to be. Things do not always run smoothly in his office and several people are not just too happy with him, but I expect that this is just the normal human variation.' ARC, ACOA Papers, Archives 1948–88, Series III, Programmes and Activities in African Countries, Box 79, Angola–Correspondence–Miscellany, 1954–78, File 6, 79/6, Angola–Correspondence January 1963–February1963, Letter from Ian Gilchrist to George Houser, 8 February 1963.

58 AAA, ACOA, 1962 Report, 1 January 1962 through 31 December 1962; 1963 Report, 1 January 1963 through 31 December 1963; 1964 Report, 1 January 1964 through 31 December 1964.

59 ARC, ACOA Papers, Archives 1948–88, Series III, Programmes and Activities in African Countries, Box 79, Angola–Correspondence–Miscellany, 1954–78, File 6, 79/9, Angola–Correspondence July 1963–August 1963, Letter from George Houser to Ian Gilchrist, 30 August 1963.

60 United Nations General Assembly Official Records: Twenty-First Session, *Report of the United Nations High Commissioner for Refugees. Supplement No.11 (A/6311/Rev.1)* (S.l.: s.n., 1966).

61 AAA, ACOA, Background on Dr. F. Ian Gilchrist and the situation in Angola, April–May 1964, pp. 2–3.

62 ARC, ACOA Papers, Archives 1948–88, Series III, Programmes and Activities in African Countries, Box 79, Angola–Correspondence–Miscellany, 1954–78, File 6, Letter from George Houser to Ian Gilchrist, 7 February 1963.

63 A. A. Santos, *A Organização das Nações Unidas e a Questão Colonial Portuguesa (1960–1974)* (Lisbon: Instituto de Defesa Nacional, 2017).

64 ARC, ACOA Papers, Archives 1948–88, Series III, Programmes and Activities in African Countries, Box 7, Angola–Correspondence–Miscellany, 1954–78, 79/12, Angola–Correspondence March 1964–April 1964, Letter from James Robinson to Ian Gilchrist, 4 April 1964.

65 ARC, ACOA Papers, Part 1, Executive Committee Minutes and National Office Memoranda, 1952–75, 2/18, Minutes Executive Board, 20 January 1964, Microfilm 5, pp. 159–60.

66 ARC, ACOA Papers, Part 1, Executive Committee Minutes and National Office Memoranda, 1952–75, 2/18, Executive Committee Minutes, 1964, Comments by James R. Robinson to Executive Board, Gilchrist Tour, 15 June 1964, Microfilm 5, pp. 18–83.

67 Santos, *A Organização das Nações Unidas*.

68 ARC, ACOA Papers, Archives 1948–88, Series III, Programmes and Activities in African Countries, Box 80, Angola–Collected Items–Gulf–Portugal, 1956–76, 80/41, Angola: Emergency Relief Fund to Angola

(SARA), Ian Gilchrist Tour Clippings, Notes, Fliers, Agenda, Writing, Photographies [1964], The Hardest Revolution–Ian Gilchrist.
69 Ibid.
70 Ibid.
71 Ibid.
72 ARC, ACOA Papers, Part 1, Executive Committee Minutes and National Office Memoranda, 1952–75, 2/18, Executive Committee Minutes, 1964, Comments by James R. Robinson to ACOA Executive Board, Gilchrist Tour, 15 June 1964, Microfilm 5, pp. 182–3.
73 ARC, ACOA Papers, Archives 1948–88, Series III, Programmes and Activities in African Countries, Box 79, Angola–Correspondence–Miscellany, 1954–78, 79/11, Angola–Correspondence January 1964–February 1964, Letter from Ian Gilchrist to Holden Roberto, 9 February 1964.
74 ARC, ACOA Papers, Archives 1948–88, Series III, Programmes and Activities in African Countries, Box 79, Angola–Correspondence–Miscellany, 1954–78, 79/12, Angola–Correspondence March 1964–April 1964, Letter from Ian Gilchrist to George Houser, 14 March 1964.
75 ARC, ACOA Papers, Archives 1948–88, Series III, Programmes and Activities in African Countries, Box 80, Angola–Collected Items–Gulf–Portugal, 1956–76, 80/45, Angola: Emergency Relief Fund to Angola–Report, Excerpts, Background Info–Gilchrist, A Report on the Gilchrist Withdrawal from Leopoldville.
76 ARC, ACOA Papers, Archives 1948–88, Series III, Programmes and Activities in African Countries, Box 79, Angola–Correspondence–Miscellany, 1954–78, File 6, 79/6, Angola–Correspondence January 1963–February 1963, Letter from Ian Gilchrist to George Houser and James Robinson, 11 January 1963.
77 ARC, ACOA Papers, Archives 1948–88, Series III, Programmes and Activities in African Countries, Box 79, Angola–Correspondence–Miscellany, 1954–78, File 6, 79/6, Angola–Correspondence January 1963–February 1963, Letter from James Robinson to Ian Gilchrist, 18 January 1963.
78 Tague, 'American Humanitarianism', 343.
79 ARC, ACOA Papers, Archives 1948–88, Series III, Programmes and Activities in African Countries, Box 79, Angola–Correspondence–Miscellany, 1954–78, 79/8, Angola–Correspondence April 1963–June 1963, Letter from George Houser to Ian Gilchrist, 8 April 1963.
80 ARC, ACOA Papers, Archives 1948–88, Series III, Programmes and Activities in African Countries, Box 79, Angola–Correspondence–Miscellany, 1954–78, 79/17, Angola–Correspondence March

1965–April 1965, Letter from Ian Gilchrist to George Houser, 27 March 1965.
81 From the Ovimbundu region in Southern Angola, Jonas Savimbi received his education through Protestant missions and attended university in Switzerland. He became a senior member of the FNLA's government in exile, supervising its international strategy. After leaving the FNLA, Savimbi established, in March 1966, the National Union for the Total Independence of Angola (União Nacional para a Independência Total de Angola–UNITA), based in Zambia and supported by the People's Republic of China.
82 ARC, ACOA Papers, Archives 1948–88, Series III, Programmes and Activities in African Countries, Box 79, Angola–Correspondence–Miscellany, 1954–78, 79/13, Angola–Correspondence May 1964–August 1964, Letter from Ian Gilchrist to Deborah Kallen, 20 July 1964.
83 ARC, ACOA Papers, Archives 1948–88, Series III, Programmes and Activities in African Countries, Box 79, Angola–Correspondence–Miscellany, 1954–78, 79/13, Angola–Correspondence May 1964–August 1964, Letter from Ian Gilchrist to George Houser, 26 July 1964.
84 ARC, ACOA Papers, Archives 1948–88, Series III, Programmes and Activities in African Countries, Box 79, Angola–Correspondence–Miscellany, 1954–78, 79/12, Angola–Correspondence March 1964–April 1964, Letter from Ian Gilchrist to George Houser, 7 March 1964.
85 ARC, ACOA Papers, Archives 1948–88, Series III, Programmes and Activities in African Countries, Box 79, Angola–Correspondence–Miscellany, 1954–78, 79/12, Angola–Correspondence March 1964–April 1964, Letter from Ian Gilchrist to George Houser, 14 March 1964.
86 Ibid.
87 ARC, ACOA Papers, Archives 1948–88, Series III, Programmes and Activities in African Countries, Box 80, Angola–Collected Items–Gulf–Portugal, 1956–76, An Analysis of Certain Factors in the Angolan Resolution.
88 Born in Angola, José Liahaca was one of the African students that fled from Portugal in 1961 to enroll in the struggle against Portuguese colonialism. As a doctor, he became head of SARA, until his departure to join the MPLA in 1964. See www.museudoaljube.pt/wp-content/uploads/2020/06/Dossier-do-M%c3%aas_Opera%c3%a7%c3%a3o-Angola.pdf.
89 ARC, ACOA Papers, Archives 1948–88, Series III, Programmes and Activities in African Countries, Box 80, Angola–Collected Items–Gulf–Portugal, 1956–76, 80/45, Angola: Emergency Relief Fund to Angola–Report, Excerpts, Background Info–Gilchrist, A Report on the Gilchrist Withdrawal from Leopoldville.

90 ARC, ACOA Papers, Archives 1948–88, Series III, Programmes and Activities in African Countries, Box 79, Angola–Correspondence–Miscellany, 1954–78, File 6, 79/6, Angola–Correspondence January 1963–February 1963, Letter from Ian Gilchrist to George Houser, 8 February 1963.
91 ARC, ACOA Papers, Archives 1948–88, Series III, Programmes and Activities in African Countries, Box 79, Angola–Correspondence–Miscellany, 1954–78, 79/7, Angola–Correspondence March 1963, Letter from Ian Gilchrist to George Houser, 10 March 1963.
92 ARC, ACOA Papers, Archives 1948–88, Series III, Programmes and Activities in African Countries, Box 79, Angola–Correspondence–Miscellany, 1954–78, 79/16, Angola–Correspondence January 1965–February 1965, Letter from Ian Gilchrist to George Houser, 4 January 1965.
93 ARC, ACOA Papers, Archives 1948–88, Series III, Programmes and Activities in African Countries, Box 79, Angola–Correspondence–Miscellany, 1954–78, 79/20, Angola–Correspondence 1967, Letter from Manuel Barros Necaca, Director of SARA, to George Houser, 21 August 1967.

Appendix to Chapter 6

Figures 7.1a and 7.1b (overleaf) Booklet cover and inside flap *Sun of Our Freedom: The Independence of Guinea-Bissau*. Publisher: Chicago Committee for the Liberation of Angola, Mozambique and Guinea (CCLAMG), 1/1974.

The material in this booklet was originally presented as a program to celebrate the victory of the people of Guinea Bissau, following the declaration of independence. A collection of quotations, poems, proverbs, photos and official statements, it is offered as a celebration of a victorious people's struggle against colonialism and imperialism.

We are producing the booklet on the first anniversary of the assassination of PAIGC leader Amilcar Cabral, whose writings on the significance of culture to Revolution inspired our original program.

The Chicago Committee for the Liberation of Angola, Mozambique and Guinea (CCLAMG) is organized to provide material and financial aid to MPLA, FRELIMO, and PAIGC; to work to end U.S. military and economic support of Portuguese colonialism in Africa; and to help clarify the links between the struggle of people in Africa and our struggles for a better life in the United States.

January, 1974   CCLAMG
                     2546 N. Halsted St.
                     Chicago, Illinois 60614
                     (312-348-3370)

The title of this booklet comes from the poem, "Our Sure Road" by the Cape Verdian poet, Sampajudo.

> *"Our sure road is pain and blood*
> *Straight road to the sun*
> *The sun of our freedom..."*

Figure 7.1b (continued)

SOLIDARITY

Freedom-loving people all over the world support the struggle of PAIGC against Portuguese colonialism and their imperialist allies. This support takes many forms – military materials, educational supplies, agricultural equipment. But an equally important expression of solidarity, especially from people within the countries allied with Portugal, is political support and actions to expose and end complicity with Portuguese colonialism.

Here in the United States, solidarity is expressed by actions directed against those forces which seek to oppress working people here as well as the people in Guinea Bissau – the military, big business, and corrupt political leaders.

"To end up with, I should like to make one last point about solidarity between the international working class movement and our national liberation struggle. There are two alternatives: either we admit that there really is a struggle against imperialism which interests everybody, or we deny it. If, as would seem from all the evidence, imperialism exists and is trying simultaneously to dominate the working class in all the advanced countries and smother the national liberation movements in all the underdeveloped countries, then there is only one enemy against whom we are fighting. If we are fighting together, then I think the main aspect of our solidarity is extremely simple: it is to fight – I don't think there is any need to discuss this very much. We are struggling in Guinea with guns in our hands, you must struggle in your countries as well – I don't say with guns in your hands, I'm not going to tell you how to struggle, that's your business; but you must find the best means and the best forms of fighting against our common enemy: this is the best form of solidarity.

There are, of course, other secondary forms of solidarity: publishing material, sending medicine, etc; I can guarantee you that if tomorrow we make a breakthrough and you are engaged in an armed struggle against imperialism...we will send you some medicine too.

— A. Cabral, Revolution in Guinea

****

THE STRUGGLE CONTINUES

The Portuguese still cling desperately to their strongholds in the mainland of Guinea Bissau, and they still control the Cape Verde Islands. PAIGC will continue to fight for the total liberation and eventual unification of the mainland and the islands.

The liberation struggle in Guinea Bissau continues... the struggle for land, for education, for health care, for equality and justice...the struggle to grow enough food, the struggle to read and write, the struggle to live beyond the age of five, the struggle to expel a foreign occupying power... the struggle to control ones own destiny. That is the history that the people of Guinea Bissau are making.

A Luta Continua!   The Struggle Continues!

No Pintcha!   Forward!

Figure 7.1c From *Sun of Our Freedom* (pp. 30–31), featuring a statement on solidarity by Amílcar Cabral.

8

On transnational feminist solidarity: the case of Angela Davis in Egypt[1]

Sara Salem

In the early 1980s Angela Davis, one of the most visible faces in US Marxist, anti-racist and feminist activism, visited Egypt. The result of the trip was not only a fascinating account of her experiences, published as a chapter in her book *Women, Culture, and Politics*,[2] but it also marked the formation of new transnational connections of solidarity between Davis and numerous Egyptian feminists. This visit and her account of it shed light on the 1950s–80s as a particular moment in global feminist organising, one influenced not only by the wave of decolonisation across the Third World but also by the radical movements of the Global North. It was a moment of a new form of solidarity for many, including feminists, and this solidarity was forged on the basis of analysis and activism against the material realities of capitalist expansion and emerging forms of imperialism. For Egyptian feminists, this solidarity was distinct from previous forms and was articulated through the lens of nationalist anticolonialism.

I want to use Davis' visit as a framework through which to raise several lines of inquiry that in turn can shed light on the subject of transnational feminist solidarity. The first focuses on the shared experiences between Egyptian and African American women based on the ways in which white Western feminists have represented them. The second line of inquiry focuses on the possibility of forging transnational solidarity based on shared material oppression. Davis looked to contextualise gender oppression within multiple structures, including globalised capitalism, and for this reason she was able to make connections with the experiences of women in other parts of the world.[3] This coincided with the focus of many

Egyptian feminists from the 1950s to the 1980s on questions of imperial capitalism and national independence, as opposed to a focus on culture.[4] The final line of inquiry revolves around the feminist practice of forging connections. Throughout the text, Davis questions her assumptions about Egypt and Egyptian gender relations in a productive way that does not create distance between her and the people with whom she interacts, but rather brings them closer. This raises interesting questions about the role of difference in feminist organising.

By addressing these three lines of inquiry I aim to recapture Davis' visit as a moment within which feminists could imagine solidarities in new ways and to suggest that by contextualising gender relations within the dynamics of capitalist modernity and class, these connections fostered solidarity. This meant a shift away from creating solidarity based on the notion that we are all women (and therefore we are all oppressed by men): it is, rather, basing solidarity on the notion that we as women are dominated in a variety of different ways, but that at the global level it is the experience of capitalism – which is always gendered and racialised – that creates divisions among women. I argue that in order to understand the uniqueness of this visit and locate it within its temporal context, we must trace the Egyptian feminist movement back to its inception and understand what happened to this movement in the 1970s and 1980s.

Theorising solidarity: transnational feminism and the Egyptian feminist movement through time

Transnational feminism can be seen as a paradigm that aims to understand the ways in which capitalist modernity affects gender relations. The concept emerged in the 1970s, which should come as no surprise given the dominance of radical movements and the lingering excitement and energy of the decolonisation period. Transnational feminism provided a means through which feminists could come together in solidarity without assuming that the differences among them did not exist or that they were not potentially divisive. Audre Lorde has been central in framing difference as powerful, writing, 'advocating the mere tolerance of difference between women is the grossest reformism. It is a total denial of the creative function of difference in our lives. For difference must be not merely tolerated, but seen as a fund of necessary polarities between which our creativity can spark like a dialectic.'[5] Similarly, in their book *Feminist Genealogies, Colonial Legacies, Democratic Futures*, Chandra Talpade Mohanty and M. Jacqui Alexander write:

> *Feminist Genealogies* drew attention to three important elements in our definition of the transnational: 1) a way of thinking about women in similar contexts across the world, in different geographical spaces, rather than as all women across the world; 2) an understanding of a set of unequal relationships among and between peoples, rather than as a set of traits embodied in all non-U.S. citizens (particularly because U.S. citizenship continues to be premised within a white, Eurocentric, masculinist, heretosexist regime); and 3) a consideration of the term international in relation to an analysis of economic, political, and ideological processes that would therefore require taking critical antiracist, anticapitalist positions that would make feminist solidarity work possible.[6]

Transnational connections between feminist movements had been occurring for decades in places like Egypt. Starting in the late 1800s and accelerating with the spread of literacy and the printing press, Egyptian women and men began to articulate visions of womanhood that tied modernity and progress to the achievement of certain rights for women. Huda Sha'rawi, Nabawiya Moussa, Malak Hifni Nassef and Saiza Nabarawi are a few of the pioneering women who fought for gender equality, focusing on women's right to work and be educated, the issues of seclusion and veiling, and the questions of marriage and divorce. Indeed, these were the issues that collectively became known as the 'woman question'.[7] Most of the pioneering feminists came from the upper or upper-middle classes, spoke foreign languages and travelled extensively, which could explain the ease with which they forged connections with Western feminists. Nevertheless, these connections with US and Europe-based feminists would ultimately suffer due to disagreements over the question of imperialism.

These interactions must be placed within the context in which they occurred: Egypt was occupied by the British, and a modern state and expanding capitalism were becoming an undeniable reality. As Margot Badran has written, in the second half of the nineteenth century Egypt experienced growing encroachment by the West in its economic life. British colonial rule interrupted the process of economic and social development begun under the direction of the previously autonomous Egyptian state. The political economy was redirected to serve British needs.[8]

Many feminists saw Egyptian independence and progress as tied to gender equality. This is unsurprising, given the colonial situation these men and women were in. It also led to important confrontations between Egyptian feminists and Western feminists over the question of imperialism, a question not all Western feminists were comfortable confronting.[9]

It is precisely this contradiction that led Egyptian feminists to look elsewhere for solidarity. This had already begun in the 1940s, as Egyptian feminists began to shift their focus from solidarity with European feminists to solidarity with Middle Eastern feminists and – later – other Third World feminists. International feminists were accused of not upholding the democratic and equal principles they constantly spoke of.[10,11] Egyptian feminists noted that democratic countries such as Britain were never criticised for colonial rule or the treatment of Arabs in Palestine, whereas totalitarian countries were consistently criticised. At the International Association for Women (IAW) Congress in 1939 in Copenhagen the discussions revealed to Egyptian feminists the myth of a global sisterhood. Badran writes,

> this double standard made Huda Sha'rawi feel that 'it had become necessary to create an Eastern feminist union as a structure within which to consolidate our forces and help us to have an impact upon the women of the world'. Indeed, as early as 1930 Nabarawi had asserted that the path towards liberation of Eastern women was different from that of Western women, suggesting that Eastern women should unite. Meanwhile a move toward Arab unity had been growing among women and men in Egypt and other Arab countries.[12]

Badran traces the shift towards what she calls 'Arab feminism' to the emergence of the Palestinian cause.[13] The first sign of this shift was the 1944 Congress for Arab women in Cairo, based on the themes of nationalism and feminism. The 1950s–80s saw the mushrooming of other Third World organisations as well, also based on notions of anticolonialism and independence.

The Afro-Asian Conference in Bandung was the pinnacle of this era and demonstrates that transnational Third World connections among women were already developing in the 1950s. The Afro-Asian People's Solidarity Organization is another prominent example of a forum Egyptian feminists turned to in order to connect with other Third World women. Laura Bier writes,

> as new alliances were forged in the international arena, groups of women activists, writers, students, and politicians circulated within the milieu of international conferences, visiting delegations, summits, and committee meetings. The resulting exchanges and networks were part of what made possible the sorts of imaginings that overflowed the boundaries of the nation state.[14]

Tracing the shifts in this form of solidarity shows that by the 1940s Egyptian feminists were moving away from solidarity with Western feminists and towards connections with other Third World women. This shift makes it particularly interesting to focus on Davis' encounter. Not only does her work as a whole represent an important example of transnational feminism, but her trip to Egypt and her recounting of it provide an overview of some of the questions transnational feminism aims to answer.

Visiting Egypt and drawing parallels

Davis remains one of the most significant scholars and activists within the fields of feminism, anti-racism and class struggle.[15] She was a member of both the US Communist Party and associated with the Black Panthers and has published extensively on the topics of race, gender, class and capitalism. Her prominence within these radical circles renders her visit to Egypt even more salient, given the dramatic changes Egypt was undergoing in the years following independence. This chapter is based on a text Davis wrote for a book on global feminism during the UN Decade for Women (1975–85).[16] Prominent feminists, among them Davis, Maya Angelou, Nawal el Saadawi and Germaine Greer – were invited to write on the situation of women in a country not their own. The description of the book states 'ten writers – five from poor countries, five from rich countries – visited distant lands and brought back rich insights into women's lives around the world. The Third-World women reported on industrialised nations and vice versa and the result is a fascinating set of cross-cultural viewpoints.'[17] This problematic framing of the book suggests why Davis at first resisted contributing. Davis was initially approached to write a chapter on 'Egyptian women and sex', while Nawal el Saadawi was asked to write on women and politics in England. Davis writes:

> When I initially agreed to travel to Egypt for the purpose of documenting my experiences with women there, I did not yet know that the sponsors of this project expected me to focus specifically on issues relating to the sexual dimension of women's pursuit of equality. I was not aware, for example, that the practice of clitoridectemy was among the issues I would be asked to discuss. Since I was very much aware of the passionate debate still raging within international women's circles around the efforts of some Western feminists to lead a crusade against female circumcision in African and Arab countries, once I was informed about the particular emphasis of my visit, I seriously reconsidered proceeding with the project.[18]

This correlation between Egyptian women and sex is striking. It is precisely this naturalised assumption – that gender in Arab contexts should be discussed through the lens of sexual rights and autonomy – that Davis is critiquing. While gender oppression in other places, such as England, was seen as more complex and as consisting primarily of political oppression, in Egypt, women were understood primarily in bodily, sexual and cultural terms, not political or intellectual terms. Davis thus sets the scene of her visit by contextualising the dynamics between Egyptian and Western feminists within the crusade against circumcision, which is made to be the be-all and end-all of gender oppression in places like Egypt. She does not stop here, however, and connects her decision to refuse the invitation to write about Egyptian women's sexual lives to her own experiences as an African American woman:

> As an Afro-American woman familiar with the sometimes hidden dynamics of racism, I had previously questioned the myopic concentration on female circumcision in US feminist literature on African women. The dynamics here are not entirely dissimilar from those characterizing the historical campaign waged by US feminists for the right to birth control.[19]

Davis goes on to note that throughout her career of teaching at various US universities, most students did not know anything about women in Egypt other than that they were victims of genital mutilation. In this way we see how well-meaning feminist crusades serve to construct women in the Third World in ways that focus on sexual oppression and an overall lack of autonomy, just as they have with African American women in the United States. Drawing this type of parallel is not simply part of telling a story; it points to a type of solidarity that emerges from the ways in which some groups of women have been framed and represented by other groups of women. In other words, drawing parallels acts as a means of bringing to the fore power dynamics within feminist theorising and activism. These types of parallels also serve to deconstruct the myth of a universal sisterhood based on gender or sex and instead point to the possibilities of sisterhood based on shared experiences. Imperialism, racism and capitalism represent just three examples of these, and by drawing these types of parallels, Davis is suggesting that the Western feminists responsible for the crusade against circumcision are in fact part of these structures rather than fighting against them.

Here we see similarities with the experiences that Egyptian feminists of the 1930s and 1940s had with Western feminism, particularly on the question of Palestine. Nabarawi, one of the most prominent feminists of the pre-independence era, wrote this following the IAW Congress in Copenhagen:

> The congress, far from representing global views of women, was too often the echo of the political or racial preoccupations of the so-called democratic states and Zionist groups. When one waited to hear women protest energetically against injustices and condemn war, their voices were raised only to condemn certain regimes in accordance with the political interests of their governments.[20]

Nabarawi, too, is raising questions about the myth of a universal sisterhood and demonstrating that certain structures were making transnational feminist solidarity impossible. At the same time, Davis is explicitly centring solidarity as a concept. She is in no way suggesting that the dividing lines between women should prevent forms of solidarity that may produce avenues of emancipation. Rather, she is redrawing the lines along which solidarity can and should be fostered. In this way, the material conditions that situate women on different sides of the international division of labour can provide women with a basis for solidarity.

In addition to generating solidarity, Davis' tendency to draw parallels allows her to de-exoticise Egypt and render it as a place that has gender inequality just like everywhere else. For example, in her discussion on sexual violence in Egypt, she was told that when Egyptian women are raped, the men are often not held accountable because the women are framed as being sexually promiscuous. Davis notes: 'this problem, of course, is hardly peculiar to Egypt or to the Arab world. The dualistic representation of women as virgins and whores is an integral element of the ideology of womanhood associated with the Judaeo-Christian tradition.'[21] Indeed the virgin/whore dichotomy is found in many contexts across the globe, and it can be explained not only with reference to patriarchy; it must also be contextualised within racialised dynamics. As Davis notes, white womanhood is implicated in the production of this dichotomy. In the US context, whiteness is associated with virginity and innocence and blackness with promiscuity, oversexualisation and lack of morality. This recalls processes of European colonisation in Africa, where the same dichotomy was central to the colonial project itself: white European women were to be protected from oversexualised African men and to be distinguished from oversexualised African women.

Davis' parallels serve to prevent the reader from seeing gender inequality as being especially pronounced in Egypt. At the same time, they do not allow the reader to see women of colour – Egyptian or African American – as exceptionally affected by gender inequality. Instead, Davis skillfully connects the demonisation of women of colour to racialised notions such as the virgin/whore dichotomy or movements such as the crusade against female circumcision, both of which betray the position of Western feminists vis-à-vis those they claim to embrace as 'sisters'. Indeed we see that by the 1940s, Egyptian feminists had already begun to raise questions about the myth of universal sisterhood, something that was to accelerate in the decades to follow.

Gender and class: neoliberalism and Egyptian gender relations

Davis' positionality as a communist feminist means that her work is always carefully attuned to the workings of global capitalism and its production of class-based hierarchies. Thus, during her trip to Egypt her analysis did not rely on culturalist interpretations but rather tried to uncover the particular relations between class dynamics – local and international – and gender relations. On her trip from the Cairo airport to her hotel, Davis notes seeing the sprawling cemeteries in which hundreds of thousands of people lived. She writes: 'I was immediately sensitized to the fact that the issue of adequate housing was high on the list of priorities for women in Egypt.'[22] The next day, as she was taking a walk along the Nile, she again noted scenes of poverty. Her response to this, however, betrays a materialist understanding of political and economic realities: 'This was the legacy of Sadat's open-door economic policy: the transnational corporations that had greedily rushed into Egypt under the guise of promoting economic development had created more unemployment, more poverty, and more homelessness.'[23]

Egyptian feminists of the time were very sensitive to questions of class, nationalism and economic independence. In 1952 a popular revolution led to Egyptian independence from British colonial rule. Gamal Abdel Nasser was Egypt's first post-independence leader, and his project of Arab socialism, industrialisation, nationalisation and anti-imperialism provided a way out of the colonial predicament faced by most Third World nations. The Nasser era is particularly notable for the welfare state that led to free education and other social services for all Egyptians.

Many feminists, most of whom had been active in the anticolonial movement, supported Nasser to some extent. Indeed the new generation of feminists were to experience the highs of independence, which ultimately affected them greatly. During the 1950s we see the emergence of state feminism, an extensive project that must be contextualised within the broader changes occurring under the Nasser regime:

> For Egyptian women, the new welfare state offered an explicit commitment to public equality for women. It contributed to the development of state feminism as a legal, economic, and ideological strategy to introduce changes to Egyptian society and its gender relations.[24]

The key paradox of feminism under this regime was that it simultaneously gave women access to spaces in society they had long fought for – including work and education – while also closing down space for democratic politics and extending control over independent organisations. In effect, state feminism represented a contradictory project that encapsulated the goals of the new regime and suffered from the authoritarianism that resulted from the 1952 revolution. Just two decades after this revolution, the 1967 war with Israel and the declining economic situation led to a political crisis that brought about the rise of a new regime, headed by Anwar el Sadat.

By the time of Davis' visit, the shift towards a new economic system was well underway. After fourteen years of state socialism under Nasser, Sadat, elected in 1970, ushered in a neoliberal 'open-door' policy, opening the Egyptian economy to international investment and curtailing or eliminating state support that had been accessible to all Egyptians. Sadat's decision to open Egypt's markets marked the beginning of the neoliberal era. Davis makes reference to this at several points throughout the text. At one point she notes that one of her hosts, Shehida Elbaz, convincingly argued that the situation of women in Egypt had significantly worsened after Sadat's economic policies.[25] Later in the text, Davis recalls that Latifa al-Zayyat told her she would be doing Egyptian women a great service if she told people (in the United States) that Egyptian women want to be liberated and equal but from an economic point of view, not a sexual one.[26] This raises important questions about the meanings of terms such as 'liberation' and 'equality' that have become so dominant within feminism. Al-Zayyat's statement empties these words of their presumed meanings and shows that in different contexts they mean different things. As Davis notes, a focus on sexual issues alone would not solve the problem of women's exclusion from the political and economic realms, let alone the problems faced by both men and women such as economic inequality and political disenfranchisement.

The multiple critiques that Egyptian feminists in this text launched against Sadat's open-door economic policy betray a specific political positioning. Sadat's presidency brought about a complete change, starting with Egypt's economic liberalisation and an emphasis on foreign investment, and with it an influx of foreign norms and values and the establishment of a native capitalist class that reproduced itself by relying on speculation, real estate and import/export. Mervat Hatem has argued that these changes – primary among them the retreat of the state from social services – undermined the prospects of lower-middle-class and working-class women: 'They benefitted a small group of bourgeois and upper-middle-class women. The overall effect of these changes was to introduce pronounced economic, social and ideological divisions among Egyptian women.'[27] These dramatic economic changes are referred to more than once in Davis' text, with feminists decrying the social changes brought about by economic liberalisation.[28]

Despite the awareness of class on the part of the Egyptian feminists Davis met, she does observe that most of these women were urban and educated, even though some had come from poor and rural backgrounds. She notes that their lifestyles were very different from those of most Egyptian women. This type of class awareness is again on display when Davis discusses the veil. Davis attempts to connect the rise of the veil with the urban middle classes and cites writings that point to the lack of veiling and seclusion among peasant women.[29] At one point, during a trip to Mansoura, a city about 120 kilometres from Cairo, Davis noticed that many women were not only unveiled, but also not fully covered. She writes:

> The road followed the tortuous route of the Nile, where unending groups of colorfully dressed women were at work on the riverbank. Not only were they unveiled, but their dresses were frequently pulled up above their knees as they waded in the ancient waters. These images flew aggressively in the face of the notion that women's bodies are always be to camouflaged so as not to provoke sexual desire in men.[30]

These observations bring to light the heavy influence of class dynamics on women's movements in the Third World. As I note above, the first debates about women's rights and feminism in Egypt took place in the early 1890s, when Egypt was under British colonial rule and when modernism and European values were seen as progressive. Many of the arguments for women's emancipation were therefore made within a framework that took the Enlightenment as its point of departure, such as Qāsim Amīn's famous book *The New Woman*.[31] The 'woman question' therefore emerged at a particular time when upper-class men and women – educated in Western institutions and using European epistemologies – dominated definitions of feminism and emancipation. The issues they focused on, such as the veil or the harem, revealed this class bias: the veil was something worn mainly by women of a certain class, and women of the lower classes were not confined to harems because of the economic need for their labour.[32] This shifted somewhat in the 1950s, with the emergence of Nasserism and a strong state-feminist movement focused on class mobility. However, by the 1980s and 1990s, with the emergence of gender NGOs and what Islah Jad calls the 'NGO-isation' of the Arab women's movement, some have argued that we see a return to the framing of women's rights according to global liberal discourses.[33]

It is thus useful to pause and interrogate the positionality of the feminists Davis met and included in her text. As she notes, they too came from the upper or upper-middle classes, even if they focused heavily on the need for redistributive economic justice and class equality. Another division characterising the feminist movement of that era was the supposed division between secular and Islamist feminists. Some scholars, such as Laura Bier, have argued that the Nasser era was marked by a clear division between secular and Islamist visions of feminism.[34] This can be seen in the memoirs of activists such as Latifa al-Zayyat[35] and Zeinab al-Ghazali.[36] I would question, however, whether the secular-religious divide was as strong as the leftist/non-leftist divide, in which Islamists would be included in the latter.

Sexualising Egyptian women and the practice of self-reflexivity

Davis describes the first reactions when the women she met with learned of the project that she was supposedly there to complete:

> As I had expected, the response to the description of the project I had undertaken was instantaneous and incisive. The most outspoken of the group, Dr. Shehida Elbaz, hastened to point out that 'women in the West should know that we have a stand in relation to them concerning our issues and our problems. We reject their patronizing attitude. It is connected with built-in mechanisms of colonialism and their sense of superiority. They decide what problems we have, how we should face them, without even possessing the tools to know our problems'.[37]

At another event, when Davis explained to the thirty women in attendance that she had come to conduct research for a project on 'women and sex', the room exploded before she had a chance to explain that she had declined to be part of the project:

> Pandemonium erupted. The obvious hostility arising from every corner of the room made me regret not formulating my ideas in such a way as to avoid the spontaneous outrage that was apparently elicited by the very mention of the word *sex*. When I was finally able to get a word in, I reacted rather defensively. However, it soon became clear that the very idea that sex might be the focus of an article on Egyptian women was so objectionable that I could not stem the waters of anger simply by qualifying my own position on the subject.[38]

Al-Zayyat, meanwhile, had the following to say:

> If you were simply an American research worker, I wouldn't have come to see you. I would have even boycotted this meeting, because I know that through this research we are being turned into animals, into guinea pigs. I would boycott any American who is doing research on Arab women because I know that we are being tested, we are being listed in catalogues, we are being defined in terms of sexuality for reasons which are not in our own interests.[39]

Elbaz noted: 'I am outraged by the assignment of these topics. To make the topic of England "Women and Politics", and in Egypt "Women and Sex", shows that they assume that women's participation in politics in England is more important than in Egypt.'[40]

These responses raise several interesting and interrelated points. One is the particular positionality of Western researchers vis-à-vis Egyptian women,[41] which, as al-Zayyat notes, serve to construct and represent Egyptian women in particular ways – as objects – and that also serve to judge Egyptian women depending on characteristics based on external assumptions. This brings to mind the many indexes and rankings today that measure how gender progressive or regressive different countries are, with the Third World invariably at the bottom. Such rankings reify common assumptions about what gender equality signifies, and how it can be measured, in ways that are Eurocentric. Moreover, they represent women as existing in a vacuum, ignoring national economic and political contexts. Indeed al-Zayyat hints at the fact that these types of rankings – exercises of power – depend on measurements that are biased and that serve to consolidate an already established racialised hierarchy. These rankings act as a 'test', as al-Zayyat notes.[42] Similarly, Elbaz points again to the difference in Western assumptions regarding gender in the West versus in the Arab world, noting that in England the discussion centres on the role of women in politics, whereas in Egypt it is always about women and sex. Interestingly, she adds that the work of English feminists is less revolutionary because it does not threaten the international capitalist system.

And yet this is the point where we see the productive result of anger and Davis' decision to be self-reflexive even as she was being attacked:

> After all, was I not in Egypt to learn about the way Egyptian women themselves interpreted the role of sexuality in their lives and struggles? And was I not especially interested in their various responses to the unfortunate chauvinism characterizing attitudes in the capitalist countries toward the sexual dimension of Arab women's lives? I tried to persuade myself that even within these attacks, which seemed clearly directed at me, there was a significant lesson to be learned.[43]

Davis thus reflects on her initial feelings of defensiveness and interrogates them; she notes that she was not given the space to defend herself over what was ultimately a misunderstanding and then goes on to contextualise the strong reactions coming from all over the room. It is during such moments – when mistakes are made, limits are pushed, lines are crossed and feelings are hurt – that we see the productive uses of difference. These differences can only be addressed productively, however, because of both Davis' self-reflexivity and the solidarity the women feel towards one another because of shared circumstances. Here al-Zayyat's characterisation of Davis as different from an American researcher is interesting: it suggests that it is precisely Davis' positionality as someone fighting a similar struggle that makes these women reach out to her and explain their grievances. Indeed, at one point Davis mentions meeting Inji Efflatoun, a particularly famous Egyptian feminist, and recalls that Efflatoun handed her a portrait that she had painted of Davis during the time when Davis was in jail.[44] This brings to the surface the fact that Davis' struggles in the United States were known and respected among the Egyptian feminists she met. Similarly, al-Zayyat noted that Davis was known in Egypt because of her struggle.⁴⁵ This is what gave Davis her particular positionality, and this is what allowed these women to engage with her and to form bonds of solidarity across national borders, across race and across class.

The subject of race is one that does not appear in the chapter on Davis' visit to Egypt. This is in spite of the fact that the role of race and racism in the production of societal relations is an important issue in the Arab world, due to debates about erasure of lineages of racism in the region and the historical legacy of the Arab slave trade. At the same time, there is always the risk of imposing US-centric notions of race and racism onto contexts outside of the United States, even those that may appear to be similar, such as in Europe.⁴⁶ Discussions of race in Egypt must take into account complicated processes of colonisation that date back as well as the conflation between nationalism, racism and ethnicity. Similarly, the categories of race and class are not seamless or easily separable: one argument is that the formation of a native colonised class through the imposition of colonial rule shifted the racialised boundaries of societies so that this class adopted racialised views of nonelites that applied to both Egyptians and non-Egyptians.

Despite the absence of race in Davis' text – a silence that is important to note – I want to suggest that questions of racism in contexts such as Egypt represent an important division that needs further research.⁴⁷ If the aim of transnational feminism is to bring divisions and differences to the forefront in order to engage with them productively, the racialisation of women in colonised contexts such as Egypt (and North Africa broadly) is an important arena for such an engagement. The space for more scholarly work on legacies of race and racism in Egypt and the silence on the subject in Davis' text may point to something interesting: whereas today feminists have taken to exploring the intersections of race, gender and class in postcolonial contexts, this may not have been the case in the 1970s, when notions of solidarity between women of colour in the West and women in postcolonial countries served to hide the divisions among women in postcolonial countries.

A further social divide that becomes apparent is that between the cosmopolitan 'urban' women and the rest of Egyptian women in the countryside. This divide becomes tangible during Davis' visit to a village near Mansoura:

> This was one of the most difficult moments of my visit. The masses of women in Egypt are peasants, yet I had only a few hours to spend attempting to communicate with these women, whose language was completely unfamiliar to me. How could I honestly view these as anything more than token encounters?[48]

The particular position of the peasant woman in Egyptian feminist activism is important to touch on. Many feminists used the motif of the peasant woman as a symbol of freedom[49] (without deeply interrogating the ways in which their own economic advantage was dependent upon the poverty of these very women). As Beth Baron has noted,

> many nationalisms celebrate male and female peasants as 'culturally authentic', in opposition to urbanites, who are somewhat suspect in cultural terms, because they tend to be more cosmopolitan or westernized. Peasants have a concrete tie to the land, which is, after all, central to the claims of territorial nationalists.[50]

Similarly, many feminists looked at peasants as women who were not tied down by urban restrictions such as seclusion or veiling. Nawal el Saadawi has made a clear class critique by pointing to the ways in which history remembers the actions of upper-class feminists and ignores those of peasant women: 'Little has been said about the masses of poor women who rushed into the national struggle without counting the cost, and who lost their lives, whereas the lesser contributions of aristocratic women leaders have been noisily acclaimed and brought to the forefront.'[51] Additionally, Baron has argued that it was middle-class Egyptian women who pushed for political rights, since they did not have the same access to power as upper-class women.[52] These nuances show how complicated the picture of the Egyptian feminist movement becomes when we take intersections of identity into consideration.

It is precisely these types of questions that highlight Davis' knowledge of power dynamics within gender relations. Not all Egyptian women are the same, and indeed the majority of women are very different from the women who organised her tour in Egypt. Moreover, she could not communicate with most Egyptian women, and it is for this reason that she does not claim to speak for them or their realities. Indeed, there seems to be an implicit critique of the women who organised her tour. Because of the limited time spent in

Mansoura, her encounters with peasant women could not be more than token encounters, encounters that could be used to show that Davis *did* meet different types of women but that she never got to know the realities of these women, realities that were no doubt very different from those of the feminists she was visiting.

Contextualising gender solidarity: 1950–80

In an article on transnational feminisms, Breny Mendoza argues that transnational feminism has failed to do what it set out to do – 'deliver the bases for political solidarity between women across class, race, ethnicity, sexuality and national borders'.[53] What texts like Davis' and the experiences of Egyptian feminists suggest is that the conditions for creating a truly transnational form of feminist solidarity based on anti-imperialism and anticapitalism existed from the 1950s to the 1980s, even if our contemporary moment does not seem to hold the same potential. The waning of these types of solidarity can be attributed to multiple factors. Within Egypt, the changes following Sadat's open-market shift as well as the shift towards civil society as a space of contestation were key. Globally, broader changes in feminist organising and within the academy suggest why the decline in this form of transnational feminist solidarity occurred. I argue that these two developments are tied to the neoliberalisation that has been under way for several decades and will be the subject of this section.

The effects of Sadat's open-door policy were far-reaching. This era saw the decline of Nasserist state feminism and the rise of civil society, which became the key site for feminist organising. Some scholars have spoken of the 'NGO-isation' of the Arab women's movement,[54] suggesting that this has resulted in Arab women framing gender equality in ways that match the global liberal common sense of major donor institutions. There is little doubt that there is a power dynamic between donors and local NGOs and that this has material and ideological effects on the ways in which projects are conceptualised and implemented. At the same time, the demise of state feminism and of an Egyptian regime interested in national development along gendered lines left little space for feminist organising outside of civil society. Moreover, the 1990s–2000s saw the creation of local NGOs that contested these power dynamics, even if they remained enmeshed within them.

The types of theorising found in the academy often mirror changes happening within the multiple political and economic contexts within which scholars find themselves. This was particularly noticeable during the 1950s–80s, a period in which radical movements around the globe were being fought relentlessly, after which neoliberalism firmly set in. At the global level, changes both within the academy and feminist organising began to materialise in the 1980s. The rise of neoliberalism has been suggested as a prime reason for the decline in structural analysis, which has in turn influenced gender analysis.[55] Some scholars have pointed to postmodernism as connected to this process. Chandra Talpade Mohanty asks, 'What happens to the key feminist construct of "the personal is political" when the political (the collective public domain of politics) is reduced to the personal?'[56] Mohanty brings in a materialist analysis when she points out that the representational politics of gender, class, race, and so on are detached from their materialist underpinnings and difference is thereby flattened.[57]

The shift away from the structural has particular effects on countries in the Global South, where structures of imperialism and capitalism continue to determine life-and-death reality for millions of people. Calls for fluidity and nuance become tricky in a context where the very real and material effects of neoliberalism hit people the hardest. It is in these spaces that a materialist analysis that looks to the systemic is crucial if we want, as feminists, to unpack the multiple structures producing and reproducing gender relations. The point here is not to engage in a full-fledged critique of postmodernism and its many variants but rather to point to its dominance within feminist theorising today. Sara Ahmed has noted the need for feminists to 'speak back to postmodernism' following postmodernism's increasing tendency to dictate feminist priorities.[58] This speaking back must include a revisiting of structural forms of critique, which seems to me an important way to bring the Global South into the picture.[59] Throughout Davis' text, we see the process of locating identity within the material: what it means to be an Egyptian woman is connected to imperialism, to the rise of neoliberalism in Sadat's Egypt, to the position of Egypt globally, and so on. It is never a given that being an Egyptian woman means being oppressed; it is always contextualised. This work of contextualisation is precisely what makes the solidarity between these women and Davis possible. By contextualising identity within material structures that affect both Egyptian women and African American women, the text uses identity as a political means of forging solidarity rather than as a division that prevents solidarity.

Conclusion

The idea that differences among women can be engaged productively is one of the main arguments of this chapter. Tracing the way different generations of Egyptian feminists have engaged with transnational feminism shows that by locating identity within the material, they were often able to make difference productive. Transnational feminism allowed feminists to counter the simplistic notion of a universal sisterhood by pointing to the multiple divisions that separate women from one another while at the same time not seeing these divisions as barriers to solidarity.

The argument that transnational feminist solidarity was possible at a certain moment in time under certain conditions is itself an indication that structural analysis is important. Throughout this chapter I have pointed to the 1970s as a time when radical movements and decolonisation processes were challenging old forms of imperialism. On the other hand, the 1980s was a time of backlash: the rise of neoliberalism and conservatism, as well as the spread of structural adjustment and austerity, meant that the hope and resistance of the 1950s–70s were destroyed. The effects of this continue today, even as new forms of resistance have emerged. As Alexander and Mohanty write, global processes require global alliances. It is only by looking at the transnational level that feminists can make sense of what divides us and what unites us in order to create solidarity.

Notes

1. An earlier version of this chapter originally appeared in *Signs* 43:2 (2018). Republished by permission of the University of Chicago Press.)
2. Angela Y. Davis, *Women, Race, and Class* (New York: Random House, 1981).
3. Angela Y. Davis, 'Radical Perspectives on the Empowerment of Afro-American Women: Lessons for the 1980s'. *Harvard Educational Review* 58:3 (1988), 348–54.
4. Lila Abu-Lughod, 'Review: "Orientalism" and Middle East Feminist Studies'. *Feminist Studies* 27:1 (2001), 101–13.
5. Audre Lorde, *Sister Outsider: Essays and Speeches* (Freedom, CA: Crossing, 1984), p. 99.
6. M. Jacqui Alexander and Chandra Talpade Mohanty, 'Introduction: Genealogies, Legacies, Movements', in *Feminist Genealogies, Colonial Legacies, Democratic Futures* (London: Routledge, 1997), pp. xiii–xlii (xix).
7. Beth Baron, *Egypt as a Woman: Nationalism, Gender, and Politics* (Berkeley: University of California Press, 2005), p. 31.
8. Margot Badran, *Feminists, Islam, and Nation: Gender and the Making of Modern Egypt* (Princeton: Princeton University Press, 1996), p. 11.
9. Ibid., p. 13.
10. Ibid., p. 223.
11. Interestingly, one exception to this came when Irish feminists expressed their support for Egypt's struggle against the British in a letter to Safiyyah Zaghloul, a prominent feminist activist who campaigned extensively for Egyptian independence after her husband – Prime Minister Saad Zaghloul – was exiled to Malta by the British for demanding Egyptian autonomy. She was the leader of the women's branch of the Wafd Party. Baron, *Egypt as a Woman*, p. 148.
12. Badran, *Feminists, Islam, and Nation*, p. 238.
13. Ibid., p. 223.
14. Laura Bier, *Revolutionary Womanhood: Feminisms, Modernity, and the State in Nasser's Egypt* (Stanford: Stanford University Press, 2011), p. 159.
15. Davis' most prominent work – *Women, Race, and Class* – remains a classic that marks her as one of the most important figures in the fields of postcolonial, black and Third World feminism.
16. The report was published as a book. See: Debbie Taylor (ed.), *Women: A World Report: A New Internationalist Book* (Oxford: Oxford University Press, 1985).
17. This quotation is taken from the publisher's online description of the text, available at www.abebooks.co.uk/Women-World-Report-New-Internationalist-Book/1024158141/bd.

18 Angela Y. Davis, 'Women in Egypt: A Personal View', in *Women, Culture, and Politics* (New York: Vintage, 1990), pp. 116–54 (117).
19 Ibid., p. 129.
20 Saiza Nabarawi, 'La delegation égyptienne au Congrès de Copenhague' [The Egyptian delegation at the Copenhagen congress], *E* (1939), 2–9 (3).
21 Davis, *Women in Egypt*, p. 149.
22 Ibid., 128.
23 Ibid., 132.
24 Mervat F. Hatem, 'Economic and Political Liberation in Egypt and the Demise of State Feminism', *International Journal of Middle East Studies* 24:2 (1992), 231–51 (231).
25 Davis, *Women in Egypt*, p. 134.
26 Ibid., p. 137.
27 Hatem, *Economic and Political Liberation in Egypt*, 231.
28 This type of critique has become less dominant in current scholarly writing on Egyptian gender relations, with some key exceptions: see Homa Hoodfar, *Between Marriage and the Market: Intimate Politics and Survival in Cairo* (Berkeley: University of California Press, 1997); Farha Ghannam, *Remaking the Modern: Space, Relocation, and the Politics of Identity in a Global Cairo* (Berkeley: University of California Press, 2002); Julia Elyachar, *Markets of Dispossession: NGOs, Economic Development, and the State in Cairo* (Durham, NC: Duke University Press, 2005).
29 Davis, *Women in Egypt*, p. 150.
30 Ibid., p. 153.
31 Qāsim Amīn, *'The Liberation of Women' and 'The New Woman': Two Documents in the History of Egyptian Feminism*, trans. Samiha Sidhom Peterson (Cairo: American University in Cairo Press, 2000 [1990]).
32 Badran, *Feminists, Islam, and Nation*, p. 4.
33 Islah Jad, 'The NGO-isation of Arab Women's Movements', *IDS Bulletin* 35:4 (2014), 34–42.
34 Bier, *Revolutionary Womanhood*, p. 43.
35 Latifa al-Zayyat, *The Open Door* (Oxford: Oxford University Press, 2004).
36 Zeinab al-Ghazali, *Return of the Pharaoh: Memoir in Nasir's Prison*, trans. Mokrane Guezzou (Leicester: Islamic Foundation Press 1994).
37 Davis, *Women in Egypt*, p. 133.
38 Ibid., p. 136.
39 Ibid., p. 137.
40 Ibid., p. 138.
41 This raises an interesting question about Davis' own positionality as a US citizen, which, on the one hand, gave her certain privileges over the

Egyptian feminists she was meeting but, on the other hand, located her in a particular racial hierarchy that complicates the notion that she was privileged compared to the women she encountered.

42 Davis, *Women in Egypt*.
43 Ibid., p. 136.
44 Ibid., p. 134. Davis was arrested in the United States after a judge accused her of having contact with Jonathan Jackson, a member of the Black Panther Party, who held a courtroom at gunpoint in 1970. The gun he used had been purchased by Davis. She was found not guilty after her trial in 1972.
45 Ibid., p. 136.
46 Sara Salem and Vanessa Eileen Thompson, 'Old Racisms, New Masks: On the Continuing Discontinuities of Racism and the Erasure of Race in European Contexts', *nineteen sixty-nine: an ethnic studies journal* 3:1 (2016), 1–24.
47 Recent incisive works include: E. T. Powell, *A Different Shade of Colonialism: Egypt, Great Britain, and the Mastery of the Sudan* (Berkeley: University of California Press, 2003); E. M. T. Powell, *Tell this in My Memory: Stories of Enslavement from Egypt, Sudan, and the Ottoman Empire* (Stanford: Stanford University Press, 2012).
48 Davis, *Women in Egypt*, p. 142.
49 Badran, *Feminists, Islam, and Nation*, p. 92.
50 Baron, *Egypt as a Woman*, p. 68.
51 Nawal el-Saadawi, *The Hidden Face of Eve: Women in the Arab World* (London: Zed, 1980), p. 176.
52 Baron, *Egypt as a Woman*, p. 187.
53 Breny Mendoza, 'Transnational Feminisms in Question', *Feminist Theory* 3:3 (2002), 295–314 (310).
54 Jad, *The NGO-isation of Arab Women's Movements*.
55 Nancy Fraser, 'Heterosexism, Misrecognition, and Capitalism: A Response to Judith Butler', *Social Text 52/53* 15:3/4 (1997), 279–89; Chandra Talpade Mohanty, 'Transnational Feminist Crossings: On Neoliberalism and Radical Critique', *Signs: Journal of Women in Culture and Society* 38:4 (2013), 967–91.
56 Mohanty, *Transnational Feminist Crossings*, p. 971.
57 Ibid., p. 972.
58 Sara Ahmed, *Differences That Matter: Feminist Theory and Postmodernism* (Cambridge: Cambridge University Press, 1998).
59 Sara Ahmed, 'The Language of Diversity', *Ethnic and Racial Studies* 30:2 (2007), 235–56; Sara Ahmed, *On Being Included: Racism and Diversity in Institutional Life* (Durham, NC: Duke University Press, 2012).

9

'Don't play with apartheid': anti-racist solidarity in Britain with South African sports

Christian Høgsbjerg

Introduction

Anti-racist resistance against the apartheid regime in South Africa was one of the critical points of solidarity for the British (and international) Left during the long 'radical sixties'. Black resistance in South Africa itself was at a low ebb in the aftermath of the Sharpeville massacre in the Transvaal on 21 March 1960, when police opened fire on a crowd of thousands peacefully protesting against the oppressive pass laws; sixty-nine people, including women and children, were killed and around 180 injured.[1] In the words of Ronnie Kasrils, a founding member of Umkhonto we Sizwe (MK), the armed wing of the African National Congress (ANC), the 1960s were 'possibly the darkest days of apartheid, following the South African security police crackdown of 1963–66, which led to an entire liberation movement leadership being incarcerated in prison or driven into exile'. Kasrils himself would escape to London in 1965, where he would engage radical British students to undertake 'underground work' delivering propaganda for the ANC back in South Africa (the 'London Recruits').[2]

In words later made famous by Bob Marley, Haile Selassie described apartheid South Africa at the UN in 1963 as one of those 'ignoble and unhappy regimes that holds our brothers ... in subhuman bondage', which needed to be 'toppled and destroyed'. This call was heard in Britain as it was internationally.[3] Many young anti-apartheid activists internationally were inspired by the advance of guerrilla fighters in Mozambique and Angola, and in 1967 and 1968 by the Wankie and Sipolilo campaigns, when MK joined fighters from ZAPU (Zimbabwe African People's Union) to fight their way through Zimbabwe into South Africa. The dialectical relationship between the internal struggle against apartheid in Southern Africa and the external struggle in Britain – a key international ally of the apartheid regime – has parallels with the relationship between anticolonial resistance in the British Empire and anti-imperialist dissent in the imperial metropole of Britain itself as elucidated by Priyamvada Gopal. Indeed, as we will see, anti-apartheid activism in Britain itself had roots in this earlier anticolonialist tradition.[4]

This chapter explores how South African anti-apartheid activists in exile worked with British activists and campaigners to build up anti-racist solidarity with black South Africans in one critical area – the field of sports. In the process, it will illuminate how sport can act as a site of political struggle, and so expand our understanding of forms and cultures of solidarity. What began as a limited liberal campaign based on a strategy of 'respectability' and appeals to British ideas of 'fair play' by elite figures in the world of British politics, sport and civil society became a grassroots mass movement of international solidarity. Amid the wider radicalisation and politicisation of the late 1960s, this movement included non-violent civil disobedience and militant direct action on a scale not previously seen in Britain in the world of sport.

The organisation at the heart of this new movement in Britain was the Stop the Seventy Tour Committee (STST), founded in 1969. Focused mainly on the protests against the South African rugby union tour of Britain in 1969–70, the STST was a campaign that, in defiance of police brutality and violent racist intimidation, successfully achieved its aim of halting the white South African cricket tour of England in 1970, a remarkable victory for anti-racist politics. As leading STST activist Peter Hain (whose family's anti-apartheid activism had exiled them to Britain in the 1960s) once recalled:

> for the first time in ten long bitter years since Sharpeville, black South Africans and whites involved in the resistance had something to cheer about. There were people abroad prepared to risk a great deal in standing up for their rights. This was a clarion call in the wilderness, a flash of light in the dark.[5]

The STST campaign has been somewhat neglected by scholarship on 'the radical sixties' and, indeed, histories of anti-racism in

Britain. Hain wrote about the campaign in its immediate aftermath, and the fiftieth anniversary of the STST victory in 2020 prompted a number of new studies, although we still arguably lack a definitive history of the campaign itself.[6] Yet the STST was to anti-racism in this period in Britain what the Vietnam Solidarity Campaign was to anti-imperialism, and the Miss World protests in 1970 were to women's liberation. This chapter will not dwell on the STST itself but attempt to recover what David Featherstone has called 'the hidden histories and geographies of internationalism' in relation to the politics of South African sport in 1960s Britain.[7] It will recover the roots of the STST campaign in earlier struggles, such as the West Indian Campaign Against Apartheid in Cricket, the Campaign Against Race Discrimination in Sports (CARDS) and the Movement for Colonial Freedom (MCF) which – like the STST – remain generally marginalised in the scholarly literature.

'A slow coal train coming': the roots of STST

The history of racism in sport, and protests and boycotts against it, is a long one. There was a struggle against racist sport in South Africa before the apartheid era. But when thinking about international solidarity with black South Africans under apartheid in the field of sport in Britain, the high point of militancy of the STST was, with apologies to both Bob Dylan and Hugh Masekela, 'a slow coal train coming'. It rested on over a decade of prior campaigning and activism.

During the 1950s, there had been successes in some minor sports most notably table tennis. Here, thanks to the work of former table tennis champion (and left-wing filmmaker) Ivor Montagu, the International Table Tennis Federation removed the all-white South African Table Tennis Union from membership and recognised the non-racial South African Table Tennis Board as the sole controlling body in South Africa.[8] Yet when it came to major sports like rugby union, cricket and football, it was not until the late 1950s, after Father Trevor Huddleston raised this as an issue in Britain, that the Campaign Against Racial Discrimination in Sport (CARDS) was formed in 1958.[9]

Trevor Huddleston was an English priest who had lived in South Africa from 1943–56 and had won respect through challenging apartheid, while CARDS was established by figures around the MCF which had itself been formed in Britain in 1954. The MCF (later called Liberation) involved leading members of the Labour Party including later party leader and Prime Minister Harold Wilson, Barbara Castle and Tony Benn. Its leading figure was the veteran socialist, campaigner and Labour MP, Fenner Brockway, who later recalled 'South Africa represented everything to which we were opposed'.:

> Though independent it was an occupied country, a white minority denying the non-white any political rights. The distinction between its racism and the rest of the world was that, though many nations practised some discrimination, most were ashamed of it, whilst South Africa on the other hand boasted of apartheid, applauding it as the basic precept of her political philosophy ... Sport was crucial because to white South Africans rugby, football and cricket are a religion.[10]

The liberal objectives of CARDS were set out by its secretary Anthony Steel in 1959, who wrote of 'the contribution that the Campaign hopes to make towards the recognition by South Africa of the international principle that the only criterion for judging a sportsman is ability and keenness, and not the colour of his skin'.:

> The first step in establishing our Campaign was to gain the support of distinguished British people, so that it would have a considerable status. The first to lend their names as sponsors were Fenner Brockway M.P., J. P. W. Mallalieu M.P. (both Labour), Jo Grimond M.P. (Liberal), E. Bullus M.P. (Conservative), [the novelist] J. B. Priestley, Prof. A. J. Ayer (Professor of Philosophy at London University), Sir Julian Huxley, the Archbishop of York, the Roman Catholic Archbishop of Liverpool, and the Chief Rabbi. We then felt able to approach leading British sportsmen with the suggestion that they sign a letter which would be sent to the *Times*, condemning the colour-bar in South African sport, as reflected at the Empire Games; and calling upon all sportsmen to work to persuade the international federations controlling each sport to adopt the Olympic principle. Twenty great sportsmen, known to millions all over the world, signed the letter published in the *Times* on 17th July 1958, two days before the start of the Empire Games.[11]

This CARDS letter in *The Times* deplored the presence of the exclusively white South Africans at the British Empire and Commonwealth Games in Cardiff which meant that 'the policy of *apartheid* should be extended even into international sport' and urged 'athletes and sportsmen in this and other countries should take active steps through their clubs and their national associations to obtain the endorsement by their international federation of the principle of racial equality which is embodied in the Declaration of the Olympic Games'. The famous sports stars who signed were leading footballers Walley Barnes, Danny Blanchflower, Johnny Haynes, Jimmy Hill, George Knight, Stanley Matthews and Don Revie, the motor racing champion G.E. Duke, athletes Geoff Elliott, Mike Ellis, Thelma Hopkins, Derek Ibbotson, Ken Norris and Frank Sando, the boxer Joe Erskine, the cricketers David Sheppard, M.J.K. Smith, Maurice Tremlett and Alan Wharton and tennis player Bobby Wilson.[12]

As Dennis Brutus, the South African poet and anti-racist campaigner, noted in 1959,:

> At the time of the Commonwealth Games at Cardiff last year, a protest was organized by Mrs Gladys Griffiths of Penarth, and more than a thousand signatories protested at the exclusion of non-Whites from the South African team ... the Movement for Colonial Freedom held a meeting in Cardiff on the eve of the Games. Through the valiant efforts of Welsh sportsmen, the matter was placed on the agenda at the meeting of the [Olympic] Federation, but London officials suppressed it in 'the interests of harmony', and the absence of representatives of four-fifths of the South African population was ignored at this meeting of the 'great family of nations'.[13]

CARDS lobbied British football clubs to adopt the Olympic principle, and then lobbied the International Olympics Committee (IOC) to press for the expulsion of white South Africa. As Anthony Steel recalled,:

> At the meeting of the I.O.C., India, Egypt and the Soviet Union strongly supported the memorandum sent by the South African Sports Association and by this Campaign. To avert the possibility of expulsion, the South African official representative gave an undertaking (since confirmed by the South African Olympic and Commonwealth Games Association – SAOCGA) that his association would do all it could to further the interests of non-white sportsmen in the Union, and would certainly have no objection to their inclusion in future South African Olympic teams, if they were good enough.[14]

One athlete, Nicholas Stacey, wrote to explain why he had joined CARDS:

> I recently accepted an invitation to join the Committee of the Campaign Against Race Discrimination in Sport for two reasons: As an ex-International and Olympic athlete, I know that international sport becomes a farce and mockery unless in the words of the Olympic Charter 'no discrimination is permitted on grounds of race, religion or politics'. If a national team is not made up of the best possible sportsmen available it ceases to be a truly national team. The aim of every aspiring sportsman is to represent his country. That some people should be denied this honour simply on grounds of their colour is as unfair as it is nonsensical. For years I ran fairly consistently second to one of the greatest sprinters in the world – Mr. Macdonald Bailey, a coloured man. Because of him I was denied almost every major athletic honour. But I would not have had it any other way. He was a better runner than I was. If we had had race discrimination in sport in England, I should have won many titles, but they would have been hollow and valueless victories. Race discrimination in sport is really a misnomer, because if there is race discrimination it ceases to be sport. In sport there should be only one criterion; that of ability.[15]

A dialectic of protest was now in play. From above, celebrities and leading figures in the world of sport and civil society lobbied elite sports officials via open letters, and from below mass petitions against a betrayal of 'sporting' or 'Olympic values' were organised, at times backed up by protests outside the grounds. In response, representatives of white South African sport would try to promise inclusion of black sports players 'if they were good enough'. This of course was a promise never realised given the white supremacy underpinning South African sports policy, one which echoed those of Nazi Germany. Ritter von Halt, the Nazi sports official, when explaining why the German Olympic team was exclusively Aryan had said 'the reason that no Jew was selected to participate in the Games was always because of the fact that no Jew was able to qualify by his ability for the Olympic team'.[16] In fact, the link to Nazism was even more direct, as politicians who had been members of the Afrikaner Broederbond – apologists for Nazism – at the time of the Second World War in South Africa (when they had been imprisoned for sabotage and subversion), were now in positions of power and authority in apartheid South Africa in the highest posts of government and their brutal security apparatus, the Bureau of State Security.

Protesting the 1960 South African cricket tour

Soon three new factors emerged, which emboldened the small but growing campaign in Britain. First, there was a developing movement among black South Africans in sports activism, spearheaded by Dennis Brutus. In October 1958, Brutus had helped form the South African Sports Association (SASA), with the writer Alan Paton, author of *Cry, the Beloved Country*, as patron, and the inaugural conference of SASA was held in South Africa in January 1959. In October 1959, SASA successfully blocked an all-black West Indian international team led by Frank Worrell from touring and playing against a set of black teams in South Africa. This was a controversial move by the SASA, as defenders of the idea of the Worrell tour (including the West Indian Marxist C. L. R. James) argued that it would allow black cricketers in South Africa the opportunity to play against a world-class international Test team, the West Indies, led by an inspiring black captain. The successful blocking of the Worrell tour laid down an important marker about the importance of rejecting anything that could be interpreted as legitimising the apartheid division of South African sport.[17]

Second, the Indian government also took a position against the Worrell tour, and so pressure from newly independent countries was now another new critical dimension that opened up amid the wider process of decolonisation underway. This force was growing in power and would later be harnessed by the formation of the South Africa Non-Racial Olympics Committee (SANROC) by Dennis Brutus in 1962. Both SANROC and Brutus would be based in London by 1966.[18] The rise of new independent black African states and the rise of African stars in fields like athletics culminated in the formation of the Supreme Council for Sport in Africa in 1966 at the Bamako conference, shaped by Brutus and the white South African weightlifter and treasurer of SANROC, Chris de Broglio. Black American athletes were also coming to fore in the 1960s, symbolised by the courageous and inspiring stance in solidarity with the wider Black Power movement taken by Tommy Smith and John Carlos at the 1968 Mexico Olympics, and the prospect of black American stars boycotting future Olympic Games if white South Africans were present became another new factor.[19]

Third, the bloody Sharpeville massacre on 21 March 1960 exposed the brutal, barbaric nature of the apartheid system worldwide. When the white South African cricket team toured England in June–August 1960, in the immediate aftermath of the massacre, CARDS were therefore pushing at an open door when they began to think about raising voices in protest. By this time, CARDS had as its President His Grace the Archbishop of Cape Town (Joost de Blank), Professor A. J. Ayer as chairman, Anthony Steel and Derrick Silvester from MCF serving as joint secretaries, and headquarters at the London surgery of black civil rights activist and doctor David Pitt. The Rev David Sheppard – an English Test cricketer – made a pioneering stand by refusing to play against the South Africans. The Rev Nicholas Stacey, the former Olympic athlete, also declined to preach the 'sportsman's service' before the first Test at Edgbaston.[20] CARDS did not call for people to boycott the matches, perhaps fearing this would be going too far against the mainstream of public cricket-going opinion, but they did organise a petition to Marylebone Cricket Club (MCC), then the governing body of English cricket.:

> We the undersigned regret that the South African Cricket Association did not see fit to consider for inclusion in the touring side players of non-European stock and urge the M.C.C., not to support fixture tours conducted on such a basis. We are sorry that the M.C.C. should have appeared to condone the application of the principle of Apartheid in sport.[21]

As at the British Empire and Commonwealth Games in Cardiff, there were some protests and leafletting organised outside grounds before matches, asking spectators to protest to the South African Cricket Association at its selection of an all-white team. There was also the embryo of a more militant approach emerging amongst some activists. In Sheffield, a group of activists prepared to paint anti-apartheid slogans on the walls of the stadium one night, but the police were waiting as they arrived and arrested many of them.[22] There was some labour movement support, particularly in

Wales where the Welsh Council of Labour and the South Wales National Union of Mineworkers (NUM) called on Glamorgan to cancel their match.

However, the level of protest at this tour (and also at the South African rugby union team – the 'Springboks' – tour of England of the autumn of 1960 and spring of 1961) was in general very low, certainly compared to, say, the tens of thousands who attended contemporary protest marches organised by the Campaign for Nuclear Disarmament in this period. CARDS did make a small impact however, perhaps if only through their novelty. For example, the young white South African journalist Donald Woods recalls being surprised at the protests and arguing with protesters outside Lords, defending the segregation of South African sport and questioning whether it was right to target the matches given the players were arguably not the main enemy, 'they are sportsmen not politicians'. It was only when the former South African cricketer Jackie McGlew joined the ruling apartheid National Party and stood as their parliamentary candidate in the late 1960s, that Woods started to question the doctrine of 'keeping politics separate from sport'. As Woods put it in retrospect, this doctrine was 'a lunatic view, since sports is a part of life, and all life is connected to politics'.[23] Perhaps less as a result of the protests and more as a result of the wider feeling of public disgust among many cricket supporters after Sharpeville, the 1960 tour was the first tour of England by South Africa since 1912 to make a financial loss, suggesting a limited informal boycott had taken place.[24]

The Anti-Apartheid Movement and the 1965 South African cricket tour

In the early 1960s, the formation of the Anti-Apartheid Movement (AAM) in Britain, in which many South African exiles played a leading role, meant the campaign against racist sport begun by CARDS was now waged under the banner of the AAM.[25] The AAM already utilised a range of tactics including boycotts and protests, but now sport became a site of struggle as well. As Christabel Gurney – a AAM activist herself from 1969 – records,:

Throughout the 1960s AAM supporters demonstrated at sports events involving South Africans. Cardiff and Glasgow City Councils refused to entertain a South African bowls team, there were protests against tours of South Africa by the Welsh Rugby Union and Arsenal Football Club ... At an international level the AAM worked with the South African Non-Racial Olympic Committee (SANROC) to ensure that South Africa was excluded from the Olympic Games. It wrote to 118 national Olympic committees and [AAM secretary] Abdul Minty lobbied at the International Olympic Committee's 1963 conference in Baden-Baden. As a result South Africa was excluded from the 1964 Tokyo Olympics.[26]

With the successful reimposition of South Africa's ban from FIFA membership in 1964, international football as well as the Olympics were effectively closed off to apartheid South Africa. In South Africa, the Riviona Trial saw ANC leader Nelson Mandela and others imprisoned for life, leading to a growing number of student protests in Britain over the question of apartheid. For example, at Oxford University, on the 12 June 1964, 500 people, mostly students (including the Pakistan-born radical Tariq Ali, later a leader of the wider student revolt in Britain), joined a picket organised by the local AAM group with the support of the Labour Party after the South African Ambassador, Carel de Wet, had been invited to speak by the Oxford University Conservatives. This meeting took place on the very day Mandela was imprisoned, and as Ian Birchall recalled, 'students organised a large demonstration against the ambassador. The Oxford Union's hall was plunged into darkness when a future editor of *International Socialism* journal [Peter Binns] removed the fuses'.[27] As Binns recalls,:

> the ambassador had been invited to speak at the Union and that was the reason why I and others thought that sabotaging the event by plunging it into darkness was the thing to do. Removing the fuses (which were in an ancient fuse box and irreplaceable) made sure that the event could not just be postponed to later in the evening but had to be abandoned altogether.[28]

As Birchall remembered:

> A 'mob' – which I am proud to have been part of – surrounded the ambassador's car and let the tyres down ... The response of the University proctors was to place concern for petty regulations before

justice in South Africa. A number of students (including Tariq Ali) were victimised by suspension ... These events led to the launching of a campaign for student rights, which was the first stage of a movement that was to reach culmination in 1967 and 1968.[29]

October 1964 saw the election of a Labour government under Harold Wilson, a supporter of the AAM, though nominally overseeing a British capitalist state with historic trade and military links to the apartheid South African regime. This would, in time, lead to a tension over approaches within the AAM, between lobbying the Labour government 'behind the scenes' and campaigning through 'respectable' protest on the one hand, and the need to hold the Wilson government to account through grassroots pressure and direct action. In response to the 1965 South African rugby union tour of Ireland and Scotland, the AAM put out a public statement in April 1965 urging a boycott signed by figures including Oliver Tambo, acting president of the ANC, leading parliamentarians like David Ennals MP (chair of the AAM), Jeremy Thorpe MP (the future Liberal Party leader), Lord Brockway and Eric Heffer, and the writers Basil Davidson, Ethel Mannin, Bertrand Russell and Leonard Woolf.[30]

In the summer of 1965, the AAM advocated a boycott of the South African cricket tour, organising protests and pickets outside every tour centre – the most effective intervention around sport by the AAM to that point. A mass protest petition, posters stating 'Going to see the South African "Whites Only" Cricket Team? (It's Not Cricket)', campaign badges, leaflets, stickers and balloons all circulated.[31] This had the feel of a movement getting under way, but as the potential ability of students to mobilise *en masse* during the summer months was limited, it fell mainly on established Left networks in various localities to organise opposition. In Derby for example, Tom Pendry, then a young trade unionist with National Union of Public Employees (now UNISON), helped co-ordinate a hundred-strong picket in Chesterfield with the local Derbyshire branch of the National Union of Miners when the South Africans played Derbyshire on 28 June 1965 after being contacted by the AAM executive secretary Ethel de Keyser. 'The line not only had miners, with Dennis Skinner at the fore, but other workers in the area, as well as Anti Apartheid supporters from Derbyshire and Yorkshire', Pendry recalls. De Keyser then invited Pendry to speak the next day at a national AAM rally in London's Trafalgar Square alongside national and international figures such as Nobel Peace Prize winner Philip Noel-Baker MP, the former Bishop of Johannesburg Ambrose Reeves, David Ennals MP, the actor Patrick Wymark, Jeremy Thorpe MP and the South African communist activist, scholar and campaigning journalist Ruth First.:

> My part in the rally was small but well received, as it demonstrated that sport-loving people were prepared to forego their natural desire to attend a favoured sport in the interest of a greater ideal – namely, the conquering of racism in sport, and we would do so wherever racism reared its ugly head.

But Pendry remembers Ruth First's 'eloquence and passion, saying that South Africa was isolating itself from the world':

> 'You must pass from verbal condemnation to practical action,' she urged. 'The people of Britain must see that their government stops dragging its feet at the United Nations whenever the question of South Africa comes up. The guilty men of apartheid are not only those who make the laws in South Africa, they are among us here in Britain – those who draw the profits from apartheid.'[32]

As with David Sheppard before, one cricketer in 1965 publicly refused to play the white South Africans, Stanley Jayasinghe, from Sri Lanka. 'I'm a bit of a rebel', he told *Anti-Apartheid News*, 'I decided five years ago I'd never play the SA team again' after his experiences in 1960, when:

> afterwards, at the socials, they were standoffish with a lot of us chaps from the Commonwealth. I'd been boycotting South African goods even before that, but decided this wasn't enough ... You can call it childish but I think of millions of dark fellows in South Africa who get no chance to exercise their rights, who carry passbooks around like dogs wearing a collar, of the torture in the jails, and I used my freedom to express my disapproval of the whole SA system.[33]

As well as a higher level of public protest, another new dynamic began to emerge in the mid-1960s as black Britons start to organise against apartheid. In November 1966, a 'West Indian Committee Against Apartheid' led by W. Wilkie organised a protest about the 'Rest of the World' against Barbados match set for March 1967 as the 'Rest of the World' included a Rhodesian player and two white

South Africans in its team. Their leaflets quoted the West Indian former cricketer and civil rights campaigner Sir Learie Constantine,: 'Must we be hosts to people whose guests we can never be?'[34] Rising black British protest amid the growth of 'Black Power' would play an increasingly important role in the AAM, linking the struggle against racism in South Africa with the need to fight racism and break the 'colour bar' of institutional racism closer to home.

The 'spirit of 1968' and the turn towards direct action

The year 1968 was famously marked by a series of demonstrations in Britain, with students at their heart, from the Hornsey College of Art occupation to the growing anti-Vietnam War demonstrations, including a march on the US embassy in Grosvenor Square in March 1968 which saw violent clashes with the police.[35] Some of the earliest student protests that year in Britain took place against apartheid, and in their new militant tactics epitomised the wider revolutionary 'spirit of 1968'.

In January 1968, the white-only University of the Orange Free State rugby union team, known as the Shimlas, arrived from South Africa for what was originally scheduled to be a tour of ten different rugby university teams. Campaigning by student unions and anti-apartheid students meant most of these were cancelled before their arrival, and only three games remained lined up to play.[36] The first was scheduled for 31 January 1968 against Newcastle University at Gosforth. Fifty students from Newcastle and Durham led by one young student with a megaphone organised a protest with placards, but about fifty police placed on duty ensured they were kept away from the game itself unless they discarded their placards. Frustrated that they were unable to prevent the match from going ahead, students bought tickets and entered the ground. During the match Ian Taylor, a member of the International Socialists (IS) and student from Durham, said to his fellow Durham student IS member Anna Paczuska, 'It will be no more than ten pound fine to run on the pitch and stop this. Are you up for it?' Yes, came the answer. 'Good. Pass it along.' Five minutes later, thirty student protesters, including several black students, then did something up to that point unheard of – they rushed onto the pitch – and again twice more during the game as well.[37] They made the national TV news. The *Daily Telegraph* reported 'the semi-comic atmosphere of siege' in which the game was played, and that:

> the incident provided the crowd with some light relief as young men and girls in jeans and miniskirts played a game of 'catch me if you can' with burly, heavy-coated policemen ... In the second half a girl dressed in green tights and jumper with a snappy red waistcoat ran onto the pitch and almost playfully, invited half a dozen young policemen to catch her. She led them a merry dance until she tripped and then was transported bodily to the sidelines. The crowd watched it all with good humour.[38]

There were no arrests. About thirty protesters were escorted out of the ground by police, and one publication reported how 'fifty policemen stood by while the demonstrators chanted "apartheid is nasty" and paraded with banners saying "for pity's sake stop it" and "we must oppose" '.[39]

The second Shimlas game was up at the University of St Andrews in Scotland on 2 February 1968, despite the public opposition of David Steel, the Liberal MP and AAM President, and the university rector-elect, Sir Learie Constantine. Constantine wrote a telegram to St Andrews students:

> Fixture with South Africans deplorable. Government which by legislation reduces human beings to lower animals unworthy associate with decent governments and people. Statement that our attitude brings politics into sport highfalutin nonsense. South African government began by taking away discretion sporting bodies by legislation.[40]

Once again about one hundred student protesters from across Scotland and the North of England mobilised, with banners declaring the match was 'a disgrace' to 'human rights' and slogans including 'we say no to apartheid every time', 'the rugby club does not represent us', 'Anti-Apartheid' and 'this match is deplorable'. The Durham University student paper, the *Palatinate*, reported how, after the second scrum which was the signal agreed on beforehand, fifty student protesters ran onto the pitch, occupied it and so halted play, supported by scores of St Andrews students in their red gowns on the touchline (St Andrews University students had been threatened with severe disciplinary action if they invaded the pitch themselves). After the pitch invasion, the vice-principal Professor

Norman Gash, a Conservative historian, strode onto the pitch and requested the students to leave: 'I fancy you are not members of this university. You are guests. I would like you to behave as guests. You have made your demonstration and will you now please go? I don't want to have to bring in the police.' *The Palatinate* reported how 'the professor's voice was drowned in shouts of refusal'. Gash threatened the protesters with police dogs. Protesters jeered, asking how the dogs would know the difference between protesters and players. Gash called for the police and left the pitch. At this point, a section of the wider rugby-supporting crowd (including a racist element who called the protesters 'nigger lovers', a sign of the wider racist backlash which would receive encouragement from the Conservative MP Enoch Powell's infamous anti-immigration 'Rivers of Blood' speech two months later) began shouting 'Off, off' at the protesters. Declaring 'let us rush them off the pitch', this element proceeded to linking arms and charging the protesters. While many demonstrators were violently cleared from the field in this manner (with one Durham female protester assaulted in the process), a minority of the protesters managed to re-assemble again in the middle of the pitch, disrupting the game for twenty-five minutes in total before the police arrived and arrests were made.[41] Even after the match finally re-started, individual protesters tried to interrupt play at various times by running onto the pitch but they were ignored by the players, who even knocked one such protester to the ground. Twelve students in total were arrested from a range of universities including Durham, Newcastle, Edinburgh and Dundee, and were held for four hours, charged with trespass and breaching the peace under Scottish law. Funds were raised to pay for their fines, though it seems all charges were eventually dropped.[42] In the aftermath of these two disrupted matches, both which achieved a high level of media attention due to the new tactics of direct action, the third match set to be held in Lancaster was abandoned. This cancellation signalled a clear victory for the protesters.

If David Sheppard was right to describe cricket's relationship to apartheid and racism as the biggest challenge to face cricket in its history, this relationship was now in the national spotlight as a result of the controversy around the South African 'Cape Coloured' player Basil D'Oliveira. D'Oliveira had been unable to further his career under apartheid and so moved to England, where in 1966 he was selected to play in the Test side for England against the West Indies. In September 1968, D'Oliveira was refused permission to enter South Africa with the MCC team as part of a tour, with South African Prime Minister John Vorster declaring that with D'Oliveira in the side: 'it is not the MCC team – it's the team of the anti-apartheid movement'.[43] This provoked a diplomatic incident of sorts, and British Prime Minister Harold Wilson condemned the D'Oliveira decision, which had led to the cancellation of that tour, stating: 'Once the South Africans had said that they were not taking a player we wanted to send, I would have rather thought that put them beyond the pale of civilised cricket.'[44] Yet in December 1968, the MCC voted 4,664 to 1,214 to continue hosting tours from South Africa, even if there was still no meaningful progress being made towards non-racial cricket in the country.[45]

In 1969, with another cricket tour from South Africa planned for the summer of 1970, the AAM once again initiated a protest petition. By mid-July 1969, some 2,000 signatures had been collected, but there was a growing mood among many younger activists that more militant action was needed.[46] Peter Hain, a leading member on the radical wing of the Young Liberals (the youth group of the Liberal Party), and other students, mostly around the Young Liberals and AAM networks, had led disruptive pitch invasions against the white South African Wilf Isaacs Invitation cricketing XI in July 1969, and also protests at the tennis Davis Cup between Britain and South Africa in Bristol.[47] In a press release issued during these Wilf Isaacs protests, Hain wrote:

> our protest will take the form of a non-violent token disruption. Its aim will be to demonstrate the seriousness of our intention to massively disrupt the 1970 tour, and at the same time to give the MCC an opportunity to call off the tour. We regard the tour of the white South African team to Britain as an outright capitulation to racialism and an affront to Britain's coloured community. And we will do all in our power to ensure that this tour is a failure, should it take place.[48]

Their sense that there was now the need for a formal organisation to co-ordinate such militant direct action would culminate in September 1969 with the formation of a new group, the Stop the Seventy Tour Committee (STST), with one aim: to stop the cricket tour next summer, and by any means necessary.

The Stop the Seventy Tour Committee

This is not the place to discuss the subsequent history of the STST, and the important anti-racist victory it achieved in 1970 through protests and direct action during the Springboks rugby tour of 1969–70. There were of course wider factors than simply the STST campaigning which forced the British government to cancel the 1970 South African cricket tour, including the deepening anger among Britain's black community at apartheid (as evidenced by the formation of the West Indian Campaign Against Apartheid in Cricket). On 3 February 1970, the trade union leader Frank Cousins, Chair of the Community Relations Commission, said in a letter to the Home Secretary the tour would do 'untold damage to community relations'.[49] The West Indian Campaign Against Apartheid in Cricket discussed one day strike on London transport by black West Indian workers to coincide with the first match at Lord's.[50] Ethel de Keyser argued that black British pressure 'tipped the balance at Lord's' in favour of the protesters among officials.[51] Finally, growing international pressure in the arena of international sport amid decolonisation so brilliantly mobilised by Brutus and SANROC was also increasingly making itself felt. In March 1970, the general assembly of the Supreme Council for Sport in Africa met – and this led to a coordinated boycott threat of the upcoming Commonwealth Games in Edinburgh by many independent African states.[52]

Nonetheless the militancy, creativity and scale of the STST was central to the victory, with an estimated 50,000 people taking part in protests at twenty-two venues during the Springboks tour from 30 October 1969 to 2 February 1970 across Britain and Ireland. Up to 100,000 people were expected to march on Lord's in the event of the 1970 cricket tour going ahead. Though the STST prioritised direct action, it also attempted to build alliances with other organisations where possible, and its partnership with the AAM, which produced around 200,000 leaflets and posters, was particularly important.[53]

In short, the AAM and STST worked together to build a mass movement, which mushroomed to the extent that, at its height, there were some 400 local action groups.[54] The STST's eye-catching direct actions on the sports field meant it made a massive impact on the mass media, while the AAM's poster highlighting South African police brutality against women at Cato Manor in Durban in 1959 – 'if you could see their national sport, you might be less keen to see their cricket' – was hugely popular and powerful.

The radical Jamaican-born sociologist Stuart Hall and his co-authors of *Policing the Crisis* (1978) evocatively analysed the 'tactically brilliant' STST campaign, noting it was part of 'the transmission of the spark of student politics to a wider constituency and field of contestation – the "politics of the street"' underway at the time, which 'somewhat resembled some wild anarcho-libertarian scenario' where 'in truth there was no recipe' in 'the classical revolutionary cook-books'. For Hall and his co-thinkers, STST 'exhibited all the concentrated force of a single-issue campaign, limited in scope, but wide enough to involve young liberal people'.:

> It provoked – such was the atmosphere of the moment – a vigorous and on some occasions a vicious response (at Swansea the police appeared to make room for anti-demonstrator vigilantes to roughhouse the protesters; the Home Secretary had subsequently to intervene to limit the scope of the rugby 'stewards'). STST was a strange enough coalition of forces, to be sure. The South African paper, *Die Beeld*, classically described it as a 'bunch of left-wing, workshy, refugee long hairs', neatly catching all the clichés. But very considerable numbers of young people, sensitised by the events of 1968, were recruited into the politics of the demonstration by the clarity of its anti-apartheid appeal.[55]

Hall and his co-thinkers were correct that 'there was no recipe' for 'the transmission of the spark of student politics to a wider constituency and field of contestation' in 'the classical revolutionary cook-books' – for the simple reason that until the 1960s, students in Britain (and across Western Europe) had been a very privileged layer comparatively and so in general 'student politics' had tended to be as much associated with reaction (as in the 1926 General Strike in Britain) as revolution. But the presence of revolutionary students within STST activism and indeed throughout wider AAM activism, and with the protests backed by the National Union of Students, testifies to how student politics had been transformed in the aftermath of 1968, but also to the revolutionary creativity and audacity of the best of this radical generation.[56]

Critically, as Peter Hain later wrote of the STST, 'the most important factor in its development and amazing depth of support and commitment was that it gave expression to a deep and almost enraged opposition to racialism amongst many people in Britain'.[57] For the first time since Enoch Powell's racist speech in 1968 there was mass militant anti-racist resistance on the streets. The STST victory inspired further anti-apartheid activism internationally and future anti-racist and anti-fascist activism in Britain. Hain would go onto form the short-lived Action Committee Against Racialism and then help found the Anti-Nazi League in 1977 which played a critical role in confronting and defeating the rising threat of the fascist National Front. STST proved to be a model for the Australian Campaign Against Racialism in Sport (CARIS), which (alongside activists in New Zealand) organised mass protests against the Springboks rugby union tour of 1971, successfully stopped the 1971 cricket tour of Australia and made an impact directly on South African sportsmen who now came to understand full reality of apartheid situation once isolated.[58]

The STST protests therefore helped pave the way for the future victories of multiracial sporting teams in South Africa after apartheid's fall, including the Springbok's inspirational Rugby World Cup victory in 2019 with black captain Siya Kolisi. Yet perhaps the most vital impact was made at the time among those in South Africa fighting apartheid on the front line. As Tennyson Makiwane of the ANC told a meeting of Surrey AAM activists in London in December 1969, Africans rejoiced at seeing the 'White supermen' of the Springboks ridiculed by the protesters.[59] The protests gave a huge morale boost to prisoners of the apartheid regime. The white liberal Hugh Lewin, imprisoned in Pretoria for his activism in the African Resistance Movement, had a news blackout, but heard his rugby-supporting warders swear about the *betogers* (demonstrators) and 'that bastard Peter Hain'.[60] Moses Garoeb, a leading freedom fighter in the South West African People's Organisation (SWAPO), later told Hain that STST had been an inspiration to SWAPO cadres in the African bush as they heard the news on their radios. Hain's reply, that 'it was the dedication and sacrifices of people like them which inspired us to campaign even more vigorously', might stand as testament to the bonds of solidarity forged during the anti-apartheid struggle during the radical 1960s.[61]

Acknowledgements

With very many thanks to all those who helped with my researches into the STST (and who are thanked in the acknowledgements of the co-written booklet *Apartheid is not a game*), or heard me present aspects of this research in different forums and provided helpful comments and feedback. My special thanks for help with this chapter to Talat Ahmed, Cathy Bergin, Geoff Brown, Fran Burke, Zeina Maasri, Marc Keech, Anna Paczuska, the late Ed Rooksby, Aurora Almada e Santos and Stuart Sweeney.

Notes

1 T. Lodge, *Sharpeville: An Apartheid Massacre and its Consequences* (Oxford: Oxford University Press, 2011).
2 R. Kasrils, 'Introduction', to K. Keable (ed.) *London Recruits: The Secret War Against Apartheid* (Pontypool: Merlin Press, 2012), p. 1.
3 B. Marley, 'War', *Rastaman Vibration* (1976).
4 P. Gopal, *Insurgent Empire: Anticolonial Resistance and British Dissent* (London: Verso, 2019).
5 P. Hain, *Sing the Beloved Country: The Struggle for the New South Africa* (London: Pluto, 1996), p. 61.
6 P. Hain, *Don't Play with Apartheid: The Background to the Stop the Seventy Tour Campaign* (London: George Allen and Unwin, 1971), and P. Hain and A. Odendaal, *Pitch Battles: Protest, Play and Prejudice* (London: Rowman and Littlefield, 2020). The Anti-Apartheid Movement Archives at the Weston Library, University of Oxford (afterwards listed as AAM) contain many relevant documents, some of which are digitalised online at www.aamarchives.org/. See also G. Brown and C. Høgsbjerg, *Apartheid is Not a Game: Remembering the Stop The Seventy Tour Campaign* (London: Redwords, 2020); G. Brown, 'Not just Peterloo: The Anti-Apartheid march to the Springbok match, Manchester, 26 November 1969', *Socialist History*, 56 (2019); C. Schoeman, *Rugby Behind Barbed Wire: The 1969/70 Springboks Tour of Britain and Ireland* (Stroud: Amberley, 2020); A. Sengupta, *Apartheid: A Point to Cover* (Amstelveen: CricketMASH, 2020); C. Shindler, *Barbed Wire and Cucumber Sandwiches: The Controversial South Africa Cricket Tour of 1970* (Worthing: Pitch Publishing, 2020). The STST was also infiltrated by undercover police in Britain, and the website of the Undercover Policing Inquiry, set up

in 2015 to get to the truth about undercover policing across England and Wales since 1968, has begun to publish a number of files relating to STST activists. See www.ucpi.org.uk/
7 D. Featherstone, *Solidarity: Hidden Histories and Geographies of Internationalism* (London: Zed Books, 2012).
8 S. Sweeney, 'Ivor Montagu, Table Tennis and Apartheid South Africa', *Table Tennis History Journal*, 92 (October 2020), 45–50.
9 Hain, *Don't Play with Apartheid*, p. 106.
10 F. Brockway, *Towards Tomorrow: The Autobiography of Fenner Brockway* (London: Hart-Davis, MacGibbon, 1977), p. 212.
11 A. Steel, 'Sports Leads the Way', *Africa South*, 4:1 (1959), 114–15.
12 'Race Discrimination in Athletics', *The Times*, 17 July 1958.
13 D. Brutus, 'Sports Test for South Africa', *Africa South*, 3:4 (1959), 35–9.
14 Steel, 'Sports Leads the Way', 114–15.
15 N. Stacey, 'The One Criterion', *Africa South*, 4:1 (1959), 116.
16 Hain, *Don't Play with Apartheid*, p. 45.
17 L. Sustar, and A. Karim (eds) *Poetry and Protest: A Dennis Brutus Reader* (Chicago: Haymarket, 2006), pp. 129–130. See also J. Winch, 'Should the West Indies have toured South Africa in 1959? C. L. R. James versus Learie Constantine', in B. Murray, R. Parry and J. Winch (eds), *Cricket and Society in South Africa, 1910–1971* (London: Palgrave Macmillan, 2018).
18 M. P. Llewellyn and T. C. Rider, 'Dennis Brutus and the South African Non-Racial Olympic Committee in Exile, 1966–1970', *South African Historical Journal*, 72:2 (2020), pp. 246–71.
19 Hain, *Don't Play with Apartheid*, 98–100; Sustar and Karim (eds) *Poetry and Protest*, 133–4. See also M. Keech, 'The Ties that Bind: South Africa and Sports Diplomacy, 1958–1963', *The Sports Historian*, 21:1 (2001).
20 J. Gemmell, *The Politics of South African Cricket* (London: Routledge, 2004), p. 120.
21 AAM and CARDS leaflet, 1960, AAM 2227, www.aamarchives.org/archive/campaigns/sport/spo01-south-african-cricket-tour-1960.html.
22 A. Burchardt, 'Memories', www.aamarchives.org/archive/campaigns/sport/mem04-andrew-burchardt.html
23 M. Bose, *The Spirit of the Game: How Sport Made the Modern World* (London: Constable, 2012), p. 325. Donald Woods would famously befriend black activist Steve Biko.
24 Gemmell, *The Politics of South African Cricket*, p. 120.
25 Brockway, *Towards Tomorrow*, p. 212.
26 C. Gurney, 'In the Heart of the Beast: The British Anti-Apartheid Movement, 1959–1994', in *The Road to Democracy in South Africa,*

Volume 3, International Solidarity (Pretoria: South African Democracy Education Trust, Unisa Press, 2008).

27 I. Birchall, 'Oxford Mandela Demo 1964', http://grimanddim.org/historical-writings/19952007-oxford-mandela-demo-1964/.
28 P. Binns, personal communication with author, 23 September 2019.
29 Birchall, 'Oxford Mandela Demo 1964'. See also T. Ali, *Street Fighting Years: An Autobiography of the Sixties* (London: Verso, 2018), pp. 102–3.
30 AAM Press Release, 3 April 1965, AAM 1433.
31 On the popularity of AAM badges with the young, see AAM 1439. The 1965 AAM poster 'It's Not Cricket' is online at www.aamarchives.org/archive/campaigns/sport/po193-'it's-not-cricket',-1965.html.
32 T. Pendry, *Taking It On the Chin: Memoirs of a Parliamentary Bruiser* (London: Biteback Publishing, 2016), pp. 248–50.
33 AAM 1439.
34 AAM 1429/AAM 1439.
35 For discussion of one small example of British student militancy at the University of Leeds in 1968, see M. Farrar, C. Høgsbjerg, L. Lavender, M. McGrath, S. Perrigo and T. Steele, ' "Paris today, Leeds tomorrow!" Remembering 1968 in Leeds', *Northern History*, 57:2 (2020), 291–317.
36 *Natal Witness*, 28 November 1967; *Palatinate*, 30 November 1967. Cuttings here (and in publications listed below with respect to these protests) in AAM 1433 and courtesy of the private collection of Anna Paczuska.
37 *Northern Echo*, 1 February 1968, which includes a photo of Ian Taylor being carried off by police, and information from Anna Paczuska, 15 September 2019. See also *The Times*, 1 February 1968, and J. Young, 'Ian Taylor (1944–2001)', *Guardian*, 24 January 2001.
38 *Daily Telegraph*, 1 February 1968.
39 *The Journal*, 1 February 1968; *Guardian*, 1 February 1968.
40 'Sir Learie condemns match', *AIEN*, 31 January 1968.
41 *Palatinate*, 8 February 1968; *The Courier and Advertiser*, 3 February 1968.
42 *The Courier and Advertiser*, 3 February 1968.
43 Hain, *Don't Play with Apartheid*, pp. 78, 82. On D'Olivera, see M. Brearley, M. *On Cricket* (London: Constable, 2019), pp. 119–34; P. Oborne, *Basil D'Oliveira: Cricket and Conspiracy* (London: Time Warner Books, 2005).
44 D. Booth, 'Hitting Apartheid for Six? The Politics of the South African Sports Boycott', *Journal of Contemporary History*, 38:3 (2003), 480.
45 *Britain and Apartheid Sport: Breaking the Links* (AAM, June 1983), p. 2.

46 S Abdul to chair of International Cricket Conference, Lords, 11 June 1969, AAM 1439.
47 Hain like some other radical Young Liberals saw himself as a 'libertarian socialist' by this time. See P. Hain, *Outside In* (London: Biteback Publishing, 2012), p. 46.
48 Young Liberals News Press release, 5 July 1969, AAM 1439.
49 Hain, *Don't Play with Apartheid*, p. 168.
50 Ibid., p. 175.
51 E. M. Williams, *The Politics of Race in Britain and South Africa: Black British Solidarity and the Anti-Apartheid Struggle* (London: I.B. Taurus, 2017), p. 127.
52 Hain, *Don't Play with Apartheid*, p. 174.
53 Gurney, 'In the Heart of the Beast'.
54 Hain, *Don't Play with Apartheid*, p. 196.
55 S. Hall, C. Critcher, T. Jefferson, J. Clarke and B. Roberts, *Policing the Crisis: Mugging, the State and Law and Order* (Basingstoke: Macmillan, 1978), pp. 251–2.
56 On the 'London Recruits', see K. Keable (ed.) *London Recruits: The Secret War against Apartheid* (Pontypool: The Merlin Press, 2012).
57 Hain, *Don't Play with Apartheid*, p. 195.
58 Hain and Odendaal, *Pitch Battles*, pp. 47–54.
59 *Morning Star*, 18 December 1969.
60 Hain, *Outside In*, pp. 56–7.
61 Ibid., pp. 65–6.

10

The Gulf Committee: interview with Helen Lackner, September 2020

What were the political contexts of activism and solidarity that you were involved in?

The 1960s were a period marked by anticolonial and anti-imperialist struggles in what were then described as Third World countries, all of which were part of the new revolutionary movements focused on 1968. In the UK, France and elsewhere in Europe, support for such struggles was perceived as part of the responsibilities for left-wing, progressive individuals and groups. A multiplicity of solidarity groups was established, some larger than others: for example, solidarity with the Vietnamese people against US aggression involved thousands and produced really large and impressive mass demonstrations in the streets of London twice in 1968. Other solidarity groups were far less successful, for example support for the East Timor liberation movement or the Gulf Committee with which I was involved.

SOAS, then known by its full name the School of Oriental and African Studies at the University of London was, unsurprisingly, the base for many such groupings, supporting anti-British and anti-US movements including East Timor, Hong Kong and of course South East Asia, mainly Vietnam and Cambodia. In the Middle East, the 1967 June War marked the beginning of a shift away from support for Israel in the UK left which had previously successfully projected an image of a socialist country, run by a labour party (Mapai) and with the kibbutz model of community-based socialism. This was presented as a contrast to the Arab monarchies and dictatorial regimes, an image which was not entirely devoid of anti-Arab racism. Israel's expansionism and rapid defeat of the Arab armies in that war, followed by the early military resistance activities of the

Palestine Liberation Organisation, encouraged this shift and helped initiate the emergence of solidarity groups with Palestine and the Palestinian liberation movements.

Among the student body in SOAS were a few Marxists from different Arab states, including future academics like Walid Kazziha, Fawwaz Traboulsi and others who encouraged UK students to develop an interest in the anti-imperialist struggles of the Arab world. While Palestine got the most attention, we also learned about the left-wing movements and groupings throughout the region, and in particular the revolution in Oman against the British-supported Sultan. This was a war which directly involved Britain, which had senior officers leading the army, and members of the SAS (Special Air Service, a Special Forces unit of the British army) involved both in training and in operations against the revolutionaries who, by 1970, were in control of most of the rural south-western Dhofar region of the country. Solidarity with that movement seemed imperative for people living in the UK.

What did solidarity mean to you then and what does it mean to you now?

I don't think my understanding of solidarity has changed. Solidarity meant understanding the hopes and ambitions of ordinary Omanis, who were living under a very oppressive regime and were deprived of access to modern facilities which they craved. We also believed the leadership of the Front was committed to the same ideals. Our support came by increasing awareness of the situation through media articles, our publications and demonstrations usually in front of the Omani or Iranian embassies or Downing Street, where we held small pickets and occasional marches, though we never managed to bring together more than a few hundred participants.

It was also important for us to demonstrate our solidarity directly to improve living conditions for the people of Oman: we set up an account to collect funds and sent money for medical supplies. When we collected donations at meetings it was for the medical aid fund.

As members of the Gulf Committee, all our work was voluntary, and we paid ourselves nothing. Our limited funds were used to pay for office supplies and printing our publications (which we did ourselves on Roneo machines). We were given free office space by Peggy

Duff, then Secretary General of the International Confederation for Disarmament and Peace (ICDP) at 6 Endsleigh Street, London, in a building owned by the Peace Pledge Union, where she had (presumably cheap or free) space on the top floor.

Tell us about your lived experience as a political activist
I have been a politically motivated person from childhood onwards, brought up to believe that I must do my best to contribute to equality and social justice. From a family of refugees, I always felt committed to marginalised and ignored communities. When in SOAS as an undergraduate (a minority, as undergraduates were only about 200 out of a total of 800 students), I joined the active 'non-denominational' Marxist Group and got involved initially in solidarity with Palestine. When that took off and became popular and I found out about the war in Oman, I shifted my activism there for two main reasons: first, that it was almost unknown and therefore I perceived it as a neglected cause, and second, because it directly involved the government of the country where I was living.

We formed the Gulf Committee in 1971 after a first trip to the revolutionaries in Oman by Fred Halliday and Fawwaz Traboulsi. We were determined to focus our activism on support to the Omani revolution and we remained a small committee of less than ten members; for most of us it was our main political activism as it took as much time as we could spare from our jobs or studies or whatever we did as a 'day job'.

What were the high points of your experience?
There is no doubt that the high point of the experience was the visit to the liberated areas of Dhofar in the spring of 1973. A conference of support groups attended by solidarity groups from various European and Arab countries as well as the USA was held in Aden, the capital of the People's Democratic Republic of Yemen (PDRY), whose regime supported the Popular Front for the Liberation of Oman and the Arabian Gulf (PFLOAG). This opportunity to meet others with the same priorities and exchange experiences was a boost to morale. The highlights of our time in Aden included detailed briefings on PFLOAG and all aspects of the situation in Oman alongside formal meetings with the leadership of the Yemeni revolution where we learned something of the regime's experience shortly after its independence from Britain.

Figure 10.1 'Britain and U.S. out of the Gulf – Down with all Shahs and Sultans – Victory to the PFLOAG [Popular Front for the Liberation of Oman and the Arab Gulf]', the Gulf Committee, c.1972. The poster features a film still from *The Hour of Liberation has Arrived* by the Lebanese director Heiny Srour.

With Fred Halliday, I was then privileged to visit the westernmost part of the liberated areas and spent a few days in the Front's school and its medical facilities in the hills near the coast. All located in totally rural areas, without communications with the outside world (this was the era pre-internet and pre-mobile phones), with only short-wave radios to remind us of the news alongside occasional flyovers by British-Omani military aircraft. The week I spent with the students and the movement in the mountains of Dhofar, alongside the trip there and back from Aden, remain amongst outstanding memories of my life.

What were the challenges?

The Gulf Committee faced two main challenges: first, the successful UK government effort to keep this war secret. We had great difficulty getting information published in the press about what was going on in Oman, and only very occasionally managed to get an article in the mainstream press. Hence, ignorance of the struggle remained widespread, even among the more progressive left-wing circles.

The second challenge was dealing with the multiple left-wing factions in the Marxist movements in the UK. Divided between a multiplicity of Trotskyist and Maoist factions, each with its own organisation, the movement was as much involved in internal struggles as in any activities focused either on action in Britain or on solidarity movements internationally. Each group was keen to cooperate with us but wanted to have 'representatives' on the committee. Further to our experience of other solidarity groups and other activism, we were firmly determined to focus our work on solidarity with the Omanis and to avoid the type of intra-movement factional fighting over historical developments in the Soviet Union or the then still lively Sino-Soviet dispute. So, we told all of them that we were keen to cooperate, write for their publications, talk at their meetings and in any other way help increase knowledge of the situation in Oman, but that we refused to have representatives of any organisation as committee members. This helped us avoid the abovementioned problems, but it also meant that we got less interest and involvement from these various factions. It may be worth pointing out that none of the European committee members was affiliated to any of these organisations.

The situation in Oman, and the gradual weakening of the PFLO (renamed in 1973) in the face of the massive military onslaught of British-led forces, assisted by Jordanians and Iranians, also, of course, had an impact on our work. As we were more successful in increasing public interest in the struggle, the Front was being defeated militarily. Eventually, the committee closed down in early 1978, when I was in the PDRY working as a language teacher.

Did gender impact your activism in any way?

In the late 1960s and 1970s, the women's movement was emerging and increasingly active. I was the only female member of the committee. Formally, gender issues did not feature insofar as we were all meant to implement most activities: in practice I was the office manager and the person most involved in the production of our publications, writing, editing, typing and producing. Although others encouraged me to speak at meetings, I was very reluctant to do so, and thus the other members did most of the speaking at public meetings. To be fair to my colleagues, I believe that there was no gender discrimination within the committee as other members certainly encouraged me to have a more high-profile public presence, and it was my reluctance which prevented me from being more of a public figure in the committee.

Though at a broader level, and outside of the Gulf Committee, I was involved in the early days of the women's movement and joined the Arsenal Women's Liberation Group, and I attended the first national women's conferences in Oxford, Manchester and London. Interestingly the Arsenal group was mainly composed of former Oxford students and included some members who were then, and remained, prominent in public life, particularly focused on women's issues. I probably felt more intimidated there than I did in the Gulf Committee.

How would you compare activism in the 1960s with today's movements?

The modern social media, internet and so on have transformed some aspects of activism, but it is interesting to note that, regardless, ultimately, movements only have a real impact when people move out of the virtual world and develop a physical presence in the streets, as was seen in the 2011 'Arab spring', recently in

Belarus, and XR (Extinction Rebellion) in the UK or even the Black Lives Matter protests in 2020. This is not to decry the fantastic contribution social media and the web have made in bringing people together worldwide, and enabling both organisation and increased involvement of people in a wider range of movements.

Another fundamental difference is that activism in the 1960s was managed and organised mainly by nationally based political organisations, parties and factions. The notable exception was the women's movement which was the first major one based on 'identity' politics. Though we saw some of this at the time, we did not imagine that identity politics would so successfully replace issues of political economy and actual power. This change successfully undermined 'class' and economic-based issues and prevented the emergence of any fundamental threat to the capitalist system, and allowed finance capitalism to dominate not only the economy but also the state and its institutions throughout the world. This is not to diminish the importance of the 'identity'-based movements, whose successes are essential to a society with real social equality and human rights for all. At the time of the PFLO and the work of the Gulf Committee, women's rights were recognised. The Front itself, as well as the regime in the PDRY, promoted support for women's equality and rights, and focused on women's education and access to employment, thus followed an 'East European' model. But issues such as gay rights in the broadest sense were, at best, ignored by these movements.

Today activism is more focused on world issues (global warming, racism) and nationally around identity issues, neglecting power structures and failing to challenge them. The decline of far-left political groups is certainly largely due to their inability to offer innovative and relevant solutions to today's problems, including those of capitalism, but it is also largely due to the success of the capitalist soft media structures to divert people's attention away from the fundamental issues of control of power.

11

'The brilliant sun of revolt' rising in the East: solidarity in Britain with the uprising in Pakistan of 1968–69

Talat Ahmed

In November 1966, Ayub Khan, President of Pakistan, arrived in London for a state visit over five days. The affair was fully regaled with the fanfare and pomp associated with such occasions. Ayub was guest of Queen Elizabeth II, stayed at Buckingham Palace and met with a range of British figures from Prime Minister Harold Wilson, opposition leader Edward Heath and the Archbishop of Canterbury (Michael Ramsey). He was accompanied by the Queen in an open carriage to the 'warm hearts' of thousands of British Pakistanis from all across London waving British and Pakistani flags. Some carried homemade placards with Ayub's picture, a portrait that became emblematic of such UK visits. Ayub visited the Science Museum where he and the Queen opened the Engineers' Day exhibition in the company of the Minister of Energy, Tony Benn, and laid a wreath to commemorate Commonwealth soldiers of both World Wars at the Grave of the Unknown Warrior. Ayub visited Edinburgh and as a royal guest stayed in the state apartments in Holyrood Palace. At the time there were about 7,000 Pakistanis in Scotland, who cheerfully waved and cheered his entourage in the streets of Edinburgh. At Holyrood Palace, Ayub received guests from various Pakistani societies in Scotland in the throne room. The Scottish leg of his tour included a visit to Sighthill Laboratories to view the latest nuclear detecting equipment and to Glenrothes, then a new town development, where again cheering crowds of well-wishers gave him a warm welcome. His tour took in Dundee, which as centre of the jute industry had historic and contemporary trading connections with Pakistan, and was also the biggest supplier of raw jute. Ayub visited Calder Hall to see the wonders of British technology as this beautiful Cumbrian site was home to the

Sellafield plant, the first industrial-scale nuclear power station in the world. In Manchester, Ayub was guest of honour at a reception given by the city's Pakistan Society. On his final day, Ayub was welcomed to London's Guildhall by the Lord Mayor for a lavish feast. The welcome address was presented in a casket engraved with the Pakistan Coat of Arms and the City of London Crest. The Lord Mayor expressed admiration for Pakistan's development under Ayub.[1] The UK state visit, as is evident, was a full itinerary, which is why Ayub joked in his speech at the final evening that he had been 'walked off his feet'.

The visit clearly demonstrates close political, economic and military ties between Britain and Pakistan. State visits were designed to elicit sales of British technology and military equipment to Pakistan. Indeed, as President, Ayub regularly visited London, attending the annual Commonwealth leaders' conferences at Marlborough House, while Prince Philip had toured Pakistan in 1959 and the Queen made a full state visit in 1961. This underlines the political alliance between ruling elites who shared common class interests. A vision of calm and constancy was projected through official news reportage, which created the appearance of great pride and support for Ayub amongst the majority of the 200,000-strong Pakistani community settled in the UK. As Ahmed Shaikh writes, at the beginning of 1968, Ayub Khan seemed to preside over one of the most stable regimes in the world.[2] Ayub's rule seemed impregnable and in autumn 1968, he celebrated his tenth year as President of Pakistan. He had been feted by world leaders with the US government hailing Pakistan as a model of economic success and political stability and a dynamic model for capitalist development in the Global South. And yet, just two years after this state visit, Ayub's regime was in its deepest crisis ever, with a revolt by students, workers and rural communities underway, one that would eventually bring about the end of his dictatorship by March 1969.

Tariq Ali refers to 1968 as 'momentous' and one key factor behind this was his native Pakistan – though the student rebellion here is often missed out of popular histories of '68 as a revolutionary year. As Ali writes, 'by December [1968] it had become clear that the student rebellion in Pakistan was on a much larger scale than France and was spreading from city to city quite spontaneously'.[3] This chapter charts how protests against Ayub in Pakistan developed into a fully-fledged revolution against his regime. Crucially, it also explores a much-neglected transnational aspect of the anti-Ayub movement through examining the solidarity undertaken by migratory Pakistani students and other South Asian communities and labour movement activists in the UK. This movement took time to develop. When Ayub visited the UK in 1965 he had been greeted at London airport by hundreds of cheering Pakistani nationalists, as was customary. Some were waving handmade banners, one saying, 'We shall dig India's grave in Kashmir', carrying pictures of Ayub and chanting '*Pakistan Zindabad*' (Long Live Pakistan). This in part was probably due to a sense of ethnic and national pride for the country of their birth; in part it was also due to the nationalism whipped up amid the deadlock over Kashmir following the war with India earlier that year. But the *Birmingham Post* also reported a protest against Ayub by Kashmiris at the same time and place. Its front page had a photo of a protester being arrested by police, as noisy demonstrators shouted slogans of 'Independence for Kashmir'.[4] Yet by 1968 a more significant anti-Ayub movement in the UK was developing, and the new bonds of solidarity constructed from below by British-based Pakistani students, first-generation Indians and Pakistanis settled in the UK with the revolutionary movement in Pakistan – and supported by some British socialists and revolutionaries – reveals diasporic connections across continents and important intersections of subaltern agency.

The Ayub regime

General Ayub Khan had come to power in a military coup in October 1958. In a scathing attack on the 1956 constitution, which had re-labelled the country as the Islamic Republic of Pakistan, and which Ayub castigated as 'the selling of religion for political gains', he created the Republic of Pakistan. In 1960 Ayub argued that 'Pakistan was not achieved to create a priest-ridden culture but was created to evolve an enlightened society', adding 'it is a great injustice to both life and religion to impose on twentieth century man the condition that he must go back several centuries in order to prove his credentials as a true Muslim'.[5] This underlined his contention that Pakistan was to be a modern political state, not a theological entity. In honour of this anniversary, in 1968 he declared his reign the 'Decade of Development'.

Ayub Khan was a Sandhurst-trained colonial officer, and after taking power addressed the bewildered nation in a radio broadcast: 'we must understand that democracy cannot work in a hot climate. To have democracy we must have a cold climate like Britain.' The Law (Continuance in Force) Order 1958 was promulgated, stripping the courts' powers of judicial review. Ayub banned all political parties, took over opposition newspapers and told the first meeting of his cabinet: 'As far as you are concerned there is only one embassy that matters in this country: the American Embassy.' This clearly outlined his political priorities on the domestic and global front, where Pakistan was a key US ally in the Cold War. He described the 1958 takeover not as a coup but as a revolution, but the fact it was directed from above through the military was evident enough from his own 1967 memoir, *Friends Not Masters*:

> Revolutions take long and painstaking preparation, detailed planning, clandestine meetings, and country-wide movement of troops. In our case there was very little preparation. It was handled as military operation. What happened was that a Brigade was moved. Actually, two Brigades.[6]

Ayub's assumption of power was not viewed as any kind of revolution by ordinary people, as they fell victim to state-orchestrated repression. In Baluchistan, an insurgency had begun following its forced incorporation into Pakistan in 1948. Abdul Karim Khan had launched a rebellion in May 1948, and two years later he was arrested and sentenced to seven years' imprisonment.[7] Ayub responded through aerial bombardment of cities.[8] In the UK, reports surfaced of further atrocities such as 400 Baluchis being taken to a concentration camp. In the camp semi-naked people were hung by their feet and tortured and seven were hanged at Hyderabad prison. There was also the arrest, torture and disappearance of Hassan Nasir, a well-known communist militant from Karachi.[9]

By 1962, Ayub had promoted himself to field-marshal and decided that the time had come to widen his appeal. He took off his uniform, put on native gear and addressed a public meeting (a forced gathering of peasants assembled by their landlords) at which he announced that there would soon be presidential elections and he hoped people would support him. The bureaucracy organised a political organisation, the Convention of Muslim League, as Ayub's political party. In 1963, martial law was suspended, however on 28 March 1963 a new Press Ordinance was issued, banning the publication of any news relating to strikes or industrial unrest. In September 1963, another ordinance stipulated that no assembly proceedings that were not 'authorised by the Speaker or court proceedings not authorised by the Chief Justice or the presiding authority shall be published'.[10] The new Governor in East Pakistan, an Ayub appointee, Monem Khan, summarily dismissed the vice-chancellor of Dacca University, Dr Mahmoud Hussain, an old-fashioned liberal academic, who took exception to being ordered around like a police lackey.

The election took place in 1965 and the electoral system was designed to ensure the field-marshal's victory.[11] His opponent, Fatima Jinnah (the sister of the state's founder), fought a spirited campaign but to no avail given she was up against the bureaucracy and the police state, who pilloried her as an agent of India and attacked her modesty.[12] Yet beneath the apparent calm of political stability, there was growing economic inequality as a result of the Ayub regime's model of capitalist development and 'modernisation from above', embracing private-sector industrialisation and free-market principles. The benefits of this so-called economic miracle failed to reach the mass of ordinary citizens, and the early 1960s saw a steady decline in wages. The share of wages in the value-added manufacturing industry had been 45 per cent in 1959 but dropped to 25 per cent in 1967.[13] The regime's own chief economist, Dr Mahbub ul Haq, calculated that 66 per cent of the country's industrial capital, 80 per cent of banking and 79 per cent of insurance assets was concentrated in the hands of just twenty-two families.[14] Economic expansion and growth in national income had occurred simultaneously with a deterioration in the living standards of the majority of the population, whose food consumption had actually declined over the preceding five years. In 1965, war with India further aggravated the burgeoning gap between rapid economic growth and sluggish social development. Opposition initially came from unemployed graduates and students. Their frustration brimmed over to burning their degree certificates.[15] Any nationalism or jingoism felt in Pakistan itself as a result of the war with

India was destined to be short-lived, as material reality hit home. In the urban areas, trade union activity was held in check, as all strikes were banned, aspects of martial law were re-imposed and several union leaders put on the regime's payroll.

'Ayub must go': Pakistani student protest in Britain

With opposition crushed at home, it was among the Pakistani diaspora abroad that murmurs of dissent found expression. The Pakistani-born activist Tariq Ali, who would emerge as one of the leaders of the student revolt in Britain during 1968, recalls a meeting he had a few years before with the then Pakistan Ambassador to France, J. A. Rahim. Over a lavish lunch in Paris, Rahim referred to Ayub as the 'bastard' and believed it was time to remove him, not by conventional political methods but through a more 'permanent' solution. Ali recalls that:

> The Ambassador to France had actually suggested assassinating the President. When regimes begin to crack up at the top it is usually the case that the more farsighted among them have realised that trouble from below is not far away. So Pakistan in 1966–68.[16]

In the summer of 1968, the Pakistan Students' Federation (PSF) in Britain held a meeting to plan a march to the Pakistan High Commission in London. Led by their 29-year-old president, Subid Ali, they were protesting against detention without trial of 'more than 2000 political prisoners in jails' across the country.[17] A hundred students took part in the demonstration where a portrait of Ayub Khan was destroyed. Once there, they went up to the door and demanded to be let in. The door was opened by a stunned official who stood aside as the students stormed in and occupied the building. Refusing appeals to leave from the High Commissioner, police were called in and removed thirty students. No-one was arrested or injured. The PSF declared their intention to conduct more protests during Ayub's visit later that month. And they did.

On 22 July 1968, Ayub arrived in London for a ten-day visit, including a reception at the residence of the Pakistani Ambassador to the UK.[18] Explaining the purpose of the visit, Ayub stated it was for a rest, a medical check-up, and 'his first real holiday in

30 years'. But his first day proved to be anything but, as some 150 students belonging to the PSF organised a rowdy reception as he arrived at Claridge's Hotel. The protest was jointly sponsored by the East Pakistan Defence Front as demands from the Pakistan student movement included opposition to the arrest and trail of Sheikh Mujib and thirty-five others in East Pakistan. Mujib was the leader of the Awami League in the eastern wing of the country. The students carried torches, chanted slogans of 'Ayub must go' in English and Urdu and burnt a portrait of him. They clashed with police brought in to provide extra protection for a visiting Head of State, but again there were no arrests.[19]

This holiday entailed dining with the Queen, a meeting at 10 Downing Street with Prime Minister Harold Wilson and a visit to a model farm in Kent to look at combine harvesters. Considering this was a private trip, the farm visit was as a guest of the Ministry of Agriculture. *The Guardian* reported that Ayub would be seeking defence equipment, including navy vessels, thus demonstrating the business nature of his visit and underlining the close partnership between Ayub's regime and the British state.[20]

The British Pakistani community by 1968 was split over Ayub's rule. Most seemed to still admire him and wished to express their support. So as before, he was greeted with a warm welcome by British Pakistanis at the airport and similarly on his departure, where crowds gathered to cheer and wave him off. The homemade placards of the Pakistan Ex-Servicemen's Association UK read 'Long Live Ayub'.[21]

The contrasting reaction in London at this time demonstrates migratory transnational solidarities and questions of identity albeit in two directions. First-generation settled Pakistanis generally identified with their country of birth and its political institutions. In 1951 there were an estimated 5,000 Pakistanis in Britain. In 1961 the estimated number of Pakistanis had reached 25,000 and by 1966 it had grown to 119,700. Similarly, migrants from India numbered an estimated 31,000 in 1951, rising to 81,000 in 1961 and reaching an estimated 375,000 by 1971.[22] In the post-war era, Britain relied on its former colonies to help fill labour shortages in textiles, manufacturing, the National Health Service, transport, car production, food processing and the retail sector.[23] Their labour was required to help rebuild a war-shattered economy and the Indian subcontinent was fertile territory for this. Solidarity with the Ayub regime was constructed via ethnic pride at independent Pakistan and its close ties with the UK government. Such visits seemed to correspond with and reaffirm the experiences of a settled, law-abiding and respectable newly immigrant community.

Yet for Pakistani students, the UK was a place of study not settlement. Unencumbered by financial necessities of paid employment and family responsibility these students enjoyed a certain freedom to engage in political activity with relative impunity. State repression at home meant London became a key site for dissent and expression of support for those wishing to challenge Ayub in their native land.

The class dimension of this Pakistani diaspora was also quite pronounced. The overwhelming majority of settled Pakistani immigrants came from Pakistani Kashmir and rural Punjab with some Pashtuns, Baluchis and Sindhis with few formal qualifications. They were recruited to work in unskilled and semi-skilled manual industries involving long hours, poor pay and, at times, hostility from some white Britons. Conversely students were drawn predominantly from an English-speaking, urban, highly educated upper middle-class milieu. Their class privilege provided some degree of shielding from the worst excesses of racism and economic hardship. The above social and political context of Pakistani communities in Britain was decisive in determining their outlook and aspirations, thus demonstrating how positionality was critical to shaping responses to the Ayub regime. In both cases solidarity was rooted in pre-existing commonality. Here bonds of cultural association informed by a Pakistani identity compelled both settled immigrant communities and international students to demonstrate solidarity. But class positionality and privilege meant these were forged in quite distinctive contexts and histories of the Pakistani diaspora.

The rising 'brilliant sun of revolt' in Pakistan

October 1968 marked the tenth anniversary of General Ayub Khan's coup. Coming as it did during a tumultuous year of revolt on a global scale, it was not surprising that amid Ayub's official celebration of his 'Decade of Development', the occasion would spark an outbreak of protests against the state by students in Pakistan. The chief organisational vehicle for these protests was the National Student Federation (NSF), a left-wing organisation with links to the Maoist faction of the Communist Party of West Pakistan. This union was the combination of several regional student federations in Sindh and Punjab which together labelled Ayub's ten years as the 'Decade of Decadence' and planned a week of demands and a protest campaign to expose the so-called 'development'.[24] The NSF Demands Week started on 7 October 1968 and the first demonstration took place in front of the Board of Secondary Education in Karachi.

In early November 1968 about seventy students from Gordon College in Rawalpindi, an elite colonial era institution established in 1893 initially as a church school, visited Landi Kotal, about 25 miles north of Peshawar in the North West Frontier Province (NWFP). This was one of several designated 'tribal areas' where normal state laws did not apply, such as no restriction on imports. The students bought about Rs 5,000 of goods. When they returned, their goods were confiscated at the customs checkpoints and the students charged. On the night of 6 November 1968, a group of these students met in one of their hostels and decided to hold a demonstration in Rawalpindi the next day, to be led by Raja Anwar, Vice-President of the Students Union of Gordon College. The next morning, on 7 November, a general assembly was called and 3,000 students gathered. Their protest was against the Landi Kotal arrests, but the students also railed against Ayub's government, pointing out that while Ayub and his family had been enriching themselves for the last ten years, the seventy students had been arrested after only purchasing goods worth Rs 5,000. They marched to the offices of the local commissioner. They stopped every car with a flag, removed the flag and shouted anti-Ayub slogans. A limousine carrying the Chief Election Commissioner was stopped and the bureaucrat's ears were pulled. There was no reaction from the police. The commissioner fled and appointed his deputy commissioner to deal with the students.

Zulfikar Ali Bhutto, leader of the Pakistan People's Party (PPP)[25] and critical of the Ayub regime, was holding a rally in Rawalpindi at the Hotel Intercontinental where the students wanted to march but they were stopped by police. They threw a few stones at police who backed down to let them through. Bhutto had not been allowed to address the students at the local Polytechnic, which enraged the crowds of students. It was at this point that police armed with rifles, batons and tear gas opened fire. One bullet hit Abdul Hamid, a seventeen-year-old first-year student from Rawalpindi Polytechnic College. He died immediately. Angered students fought the police with bricks and paving stones. Some students broke into the hotel lobby but police tear-gassed them. Four police were wounded as were many students. This incident is considered as pivotal in the downfall of Ayub.[26]

On 8 November 1968, over 10,000 students gathered at Government College in Rawalpindi, as Gordon College had been sealed off by police who used tear gas to disperse students assembling. That day Ayub's portraits were burnt publicly. Every shop window displaying his picture was smashed; private cars were stopped and passengers forced to get out and shout anti-Ayub slogans and kicked in the backside if they refused. As the students marched into the city centre, they demanded the lowering of sugar and flour prices; and they were joined by unemployed workers and others in a generalised outpouring of grievances. The demonstrators attacked symbols of power, including banks and the large houses of the rich. The action of the students was tapping into and articulating a widespread hatred of the Ayub regime. By 8 pm that night, the entire city of Rawalpindi was in revolt and out of governmental control. The next day police killed two people who they recognised as being on the demonstration the previous day; their corpses were dragged through the streets in the hopes of deterring further protests. But the rebellion deepened as protesters painted stray dogs with 'Ayub' that then became a target for armed police. A rent-strike occurred, and many shop owners and passengers refused to pay bus and railway fares. Just how out of touch the ruling elite were with the popular mood of anger on the streets can be seen from the comments of the Chief Justice of Pakistan Supreme Court, Fazle Akbar, who told protesting students to instead 'devote part of their time in the services of the Red Cross'.[27]

From protest to rebellion

In the capital city of Dacca in East Pakistan, auto-rickshaw drivers, harassed by police responded with a series of lightning strikes which spread to cycle rickshaw drivers. On 6 December 1968, the Dacca

National Awami Party headed by Maulana Abdul Hamid Khan Bhashani, eighty-two-year-old activist, called a meeting attended by thousands of workers and students. He demanded regional autonomy, lambasted Ayub and stated that the rights of people will never be achieved without mass movements. On 7 December, a general strike took place in Dacca, completely shutting down the city. Police and the East Pakistan Rifles opened fire at picketers. Twenty-three workers were injured, six seriously, and Abdul Majid, a twenty-eight-year-old worker, was killed. Grievances felt in the east wing ran deep due to the virtual second-class status of east Pakistanis in this new country. Bhashani had spent time in Europe and was due to attend the World Peace Conference in Berlin on 28 May 1954 but was unable to due to visa problems. He was a seasoned activist leading protests of farmers in Bhashan Char in Assam, part of Sylhet district, and was the founder and President of the Pakistan Awami League (later to become the Awami League (AL)). Due to his left-wing politics (he was referred to as the 'Red Maulana') he parted company with the AL and formed the National Awami Party, a more radical outfit. While in London, he had meetings with Marxist intellectuals such as the communist Raj Palme Dutt, editor of *Labour Monthly*. He was popular amongst UK Pakistanis from the Sylhet region who flocked to see him and supported his opposition to the Ayub regime as well as calls for greater autonomy for East Pakistan.[28] Such transnational conversations are indicative of global connections between activists in the West and Global South as well as South Asian actors across the diaspora.

In East Pakistan, students mounted successful campaigns and activity amongst the local population. A Student Action Committee (SAC) was established which adopted an eleven-point programme.[29] The first point aimed to deal with educational demands. The ten remaining points included broader political demands pertaining to democracy, representation and injustice. This included the sub-federation of Baluchistan, North West Frontier Province and Sindh demanding regional autonomy for each unit; nationalisation of banks, insurance companies and all major industries; calls to quit the Pakistan-US military pacts.[30] This programme came to symbolise the programme of the people.

Agitation started by industrial workers soon acquired a more radical shape as workers adopted a range of tactics such as the *gherao*, the encirclement of factories and mills. Workers had used this technique before in Pakistan, indeed Communists of Indian Bengal, Bihar and East Pakistan had been using it since 1954. Previously militant workers had encircled a number of factories including Mohini Textile Mill and People's Jute Mills in Khulna, for twelve days in 1964. In April 1965, workers encircled Amin Jute Mills in Chittagong and a huge *gherao* occurred in Tongi industrial area the same year. In most of these actions the state used police and paramilitary forces on the demand of industrialists to crush them. However, its use in the 1968–69 protests was unique. In the rebellion against Ayub Khan, workers united and protested not just at one specific mill, but all over major industrial zones of East Pakistan. Moreover, these *gheraos* were unique because workers were not just concerned with their own interests; they drew their strength from the mass movement. In response to these *gheraos* in 1968, the government once again relied on police and paramilitary forces to use against the growing demands of the industrial workers. Often, the use of these forces resulted in many killings.

The protests extended beyond urban areas into rural ones where peasants began to protest against the conditions they were subjected to. The situation in the rural areas had been deteriorating for the previous three to four years due to the exploitative tactics of *jotadrs* (landowners) and *mahajans* (moneylenders). From the mid-1960s peasants attacked their oppressors, killing landowners, moneylenders, cattle rustlers (hired thugs employed by landowners) and police officers. This violence led to further repression from the government. On 19 December 1968 there was a province wide general strike in East Pakistan, following on from another general strike in Dacca. In Rawalpindi Nadeem Shahid, a journalist, was shot and seriously wounded by Ayub's thugs. This led to a strike by journalists on 11 December in both East and West Pakistan, meaning no newspapers appeared that day.

In addition to protests from students, peasants and industrial workers there was the involvement of intellectuals and journalists. When the government tried to ban weeklies, the Pakistan Federal Union of Journalists met. From 15 December to 17 December 1968, the Pakistan Federal Union of Journalists reviewed the situation of Pakistani journalism. This union concluded that, due to the government's involvement, the national press was no longer constructive, nor was it a democratic instrument of public opinion. Later in December, journalists, writers and poets rallied together. Members of the public joined in the public procession, and the entire mass wore red turbans and shawls to symbolise the rising socialist and communist trend. Journalists continued to resist the government's oppression, as did intellectuals. Musicians wrote songs symbolising resistance. Political theatre expanded as dramas inspired by female student sit-ins took to the stage, including the play, *Jaloos* (political rally) containing revolutionary lyrics.[31] The 1969 film *Zerqa*, purportedly based on a sympathetic portrayal of armed Palestinian resistance, offered a left critique of Ayub's regime as it refracted Pakistan's political crisis through the question of Palestine.[32]

Towards the end of December 1968 Bhashani announced a *gherao* programme for the peasants and asked them to encircle village *hats* (weekly rural markets), police stations and government offices. This was intended to be a rural substitute for urban strikes. Accordingly, in a number of rural areas, including Hatirdia near Narsingdi in the district of Dhaka, encirclement took place. While *gheraoing* the local *hat*, villagers clashed with the police who opened fire, killing several people.[33] It was unsurprising that in a countrywide uprising the peasantry would become involved. Thus, in late 1968 and early 1969 peasants and other working people from rural areas began to attack their oppressors and the state officials who supported them. Major conflict occurred in many areas including Chandpur, Tangail, Jamalpur and Chittagong and peasants came out in thousands joining the protests and encircled police stations and local administrative offices. The killing of large numbers of landowners, moneylenders, cattle rustlers and police officials was reported.[34] In many villages the peasants, following communist commune principles, elected their own village committees, established local courts and began to try landowners, moneylenders, cattle rustlers and police officials, and to settle local disputes and punish criminals. Although this peasant uprising was very much part of the general uprising, the peasant association (Krishak Samity) under Bhashani and particularly the pro-Peking communists played an active role in shaping its political character. All over Pakistan peasants adopted the slogan: 'land to the tillers, establish the rule of peasants and workers'.[35]

In January 1969, several opposition parties formed the Democratic Action Committee (DAC) with the declared aim of restoring democracy through a mass movement. On 17 January 1969 there was a coordinated strike day in both East and West Pakistan. On 25 January 1969 furious street battles in Karachi, the country's largest industrial city, lasted over eight hours as workers, students and unemployed youth burnt buses, trams, petrol pumps, oil stations and government offices. Workers raided banks, bringing safes out into streets and blowing them open. Hundreds were injured and over 500 arrested. Over 1,000 students marched on the house of a prominent member of Ayub's government. Police shot and critically wounded a student, and this led to further protests the next day. Apparently, a young officer of an army unit stationed outside one mansion was confronted by students and, when they explained their grievances, he ordered his unit elsewhere; the students then burnt the mansion to the ground. In Lahore, students attacked the offices of a pro-Ayub newspaper and set it ablaze. Further, 50,000 students and workers marched in the city setting alight to cars, fighting the police street by street and taking over government offices. Even the Supreme Court of Pakistan building was set on fire.

On 13 February 1969, students, workers and intelligentsia marched to the offices of Oxford University Press, publisher of Ayub's autobiography, *Friends Not Masters*. Every copy of the book was destroyed and the offices were damaged to the tune of 20,000 pounds. On the same day over 30,000 railway workers struck and marched in the city centre carrying red flags chanting 'Destroy capitalism' and 'Keep religion out of politics'. As a British journalist observed: 'With the entry of the working class into the revolt, hitherto limited to students and political parties, observers are beginning to doubt whether the government or the opposition can control the forces unleashed in Pakistan.'[36]

On 18 February, a curfew was imposed in Dacca but challenged. The first group to defy the army were slum dwellers – misery had hardened them to face anything and they had nothing to lose. They linked up with others among the city poor and finally students joined in too. Dacca became a city of revolt and a number of army officers deserted. But others behaved like any occupying force, and shot dead protesters in cold blood. Workers sabotaged railway lines. By 1am that night even government officials with curfew passes were not allowed onto the streets. Unofficial estimates were that over 100 people were killed that night.

The end of Ayub

On 19 February 1969, Ayub summoned his three Commanders in Chief of the armed forces. He demanded they impose martial law in all cities of East and West Pakistan but army chief General Yahya Khan refused point blank. He had received a report from his officers in Dacca, which stipulated that if martial law was imposed, they might be able to hold Dacca but could not be confident about the rest of East Pakistan. The officers made it clear that they were not opposed to martial law to 'save the country' but it would have to be a martial law without Ayub. Yahya persuaded Ayub to accept all demands of the DAC and withdraw from politics. On 20 February the curfew ended, and on 21 February Ayub announced his forthcoming exit from Pakistani politics.

The violence of the state to attempt to crush the revolt was creating an unimaginable catastrophe in both wings of Pakistan. In Dacca alone, from 7–21 March 1969, thirty-nine people were killed in various affrays that government authorities could not quell. In Laksam in East Pakistan, four policemen were beaten to death.[37] The same paper reported several clashes in Jamalpur, in the same province, with seven people killed and two burnt alive.[38] Industrial unrest had reached such a boiling point in Karachi that on 20 March the President of the Federation of the Pakistan Chambers of Commerce and Industry asked the government to deploy troops in industrial areas.[39] The ferocity of violence, including wanton violence in some cases, was bordering at the level of gang fights, particularly on university campuses. One report described Dacca University campus as being reduced to 'an intellectual slum'.[40] The deterioration of the situation for the regime was untenable, as tensions were exacerbated by internal feuding within Ayub's Convention Muslim League where loyalists demanded that the regime intervene directly to bring the situation under control.[41]

Ayub had once characterised student protests as typical in newly independent countries where 'traditions of responsibility are not sufficiently developed; irresponsibility comes easy, since it so often goes unpunished'.[42] As his regime was collapsing, he told former ministers, 'I am sorry we have come to this pass. We are a very difficult country structurally. Perhaps I pushed it too hard into the modern age. We are not ready for reforms. Quite frankly, I have failed. I must admit that clearly. Our laws were for a sophisticated society.'[43] However, a former civil servant in Ayub's government, Roedad Khan, has a more plausible explanation: 'the Revolution – the real Revolution because it involved the masses – had gathered such momentum that nothing Ayub did could have averted it'.[44] Indeed, even Ayub had been forced to bitterly concede how the movement had paralysed the functioning of the state and society.:

> The civilian labour force in Karachi dockyards had struck and stopped work. No loading or unloading of ships was being done. In one case a ship went back empty as it could not be loaded with cotton. Bhashani has been in Karachi and elsewhere spreading disaffection. Expectations were that the situation was likely to deteriorate.[45]

On 25 March 1969, Ayub Khan announced his resignation and Yahya Khan assumed the presidency. Yahya Khan soon promised free elections within a year on the basis of adult franchise to the National Assembly, which would draw up a new constitution. The 1970 general election (the first in Pakistan's history) resulted in a landslide victory for the Awami League, Bengali nationalists from East Pakistan (now Bangladesh).

Migratory transnational solidarity with the revolution in Britain

The Pakistan 1968 movement inspired radicals internationally, particularly in Britain, where there was a dialectical interplay between activists across the Indian subcontinental diaspora. Since 1950, Pakistani students in Britain, both UK citizens and Pakistani nationals, had had an organised presence. At Pakistan's inception, there was the inheritance of the communist-aligned student group, now called the Democratic Students Federation (DSF). In 1953, the DSF drew up a charter of demands that included issues pertinent to students: tuition fees, library facilities and improved classrooms.[46] Following its left origins and leanings, the DSF also opposed the growing shift of Pakistan towards the Western camp in the Cold War, which had begun even before Ayub's coup in 1958. In May 1954, Pakistan had signed the Mutual Defence Assistance Agreement with the United States. In the same year it became a member of the South East Asia Treaty Organisation (SEATO) along with the United States, Britain, France, Thailand, the Philippines, Australia and New Zealand. By 1955, Pakistan joined the Baghdad Pact, another mutual defence organisation, with Britain, Turkey, Iran and Iraq. The United States did not join this organisation but was closely associated with it. After Iraq's departure in 1958, it was renamed CENTO (Central Treaty Organisation). In 1959, Pakistan (alongside Turkey and Iran) signed a bilateral Agreement of Cooperation with the US, which was designed to reinforce the defensive purposes of CENTO. In 1954 the Pakistan state proscribed the Communist Party of Pakistan (CPP) and its associated organisations, including the DSF. The only possibility of organising activism was to relaunch the movement under a new name and so the National Student Federation was born in 1955. Initially set up as a government student front, it was quickly infiltrated by former DSF members who became a majority and began to articulate opposition to the government. When Ayub took command in his military coup in 1958, the NSF was proscribed.

Banned in Pakistan itself, the NSF shifted its focus to Pakistani students based in the UK as well as inspiring young British Pakistanis. The annual Commonwealth conferences became a target for student solidarity protests against Ayub throughout the 1960s. In July 1964, members of the East Pakistan House students, comprising those Pakistani students who stood for regional autonomy for the eastern wing and supported by some west Pakistani students, published a leaflet titled 'Ayub Exposed'. The leaflet was posted to all the secretaries of the Commonwealth leaders attending the conference at Marlborough House, and distributed by students on the day outside, making it the first successful initiative to challenge and expose Ayub outside of Pakistan.[47] These were students who had direct experience of the dictatorship and its opposition. By the late 1960s, their activities in the UK helped to inform an earlier generation of settled communities, some of whom initially had romanticised Ayub, of the inspirational uprisings against his regime.

So solidarity was expressed by more established communities of British South Asians, mostly formed by those of the wider

'Windrush generation' of British colonial or Commonwealth subjects who had come to work and settled in the UK in the 1950s and early 1960s. Amongst trade unionists and workers, through the Pakistani Workers Association (PWA) and Indian Workers Association (IWA), there were active mobilisations for this conference and subsequent conferences and visits by Ayub Khan. In 1965, both the PWA and IWA jointly authored and published a leaflet opposing the war between India and Pakistan over Kashmir and called for peace and Kashmiri autonomy.[48] Avtar Singh Jouhl of the IWA also recalls how IWA members moved resolutions to support the anti-Ayub movement in their trade unions.[49] This would seem to suggest that there was some limited British trade union support for the Pakistan movement.

Tariq Ali himself during 1968 in Britain edited the radical student paper *Black Dwarf* and its front page from June that year was headlined 'We Shall Fight, We Shall Win: Paris, London, Rome, Berlin'.[50] The headline was clearly internationalist, but Europe-focused. However, the transnational dimensions of the publication can be gleaned from the reports it carried. So in October 1968, arguably the most intense period in Europe, *Black Dwarf* had coverage of Britain but also articles on Portugal, Mexico, an international student conference in New York City, the Students for a Democratic Society (SDS) conference in Frankfurt and the Japanese revolutionary students' movement.[51] The front page headline was 'Workers and Students, Don't Demand, Occupy, your schools and factories. All Power to Campus Soviets'. But it carried nothing on Pakistan, even though the student movement was certainly quite vibrant from the late 1950s onwards. Once the student revolt broke out in Pakistan in October–November 1968, *Black Dwarf* carried a series of articles in early 1969. Radical students in Rawalpindi led by Raja Anwar issued invitations on behalf of the local Students Action Committee for Ali to come and join them in the struggle. This he did in early January 1969.[52]

While in Pakistan, Tariq Ali travelled across the country speaking to huge crowds of students, workers and peasant leaders in Lyallpur (now Faisalabad), Lahore, Karachi, Hyderabad and Baluchistan. But more fundamentally, Ali was invited to the eastern wing, where huge crowds flocked to hear about events in Europe and discuss what needed to be done in Pakistan at this stage. Ali was always a popular hero for activists in the West but an indication of the warmth and solidarity Pakistanis in the East felt towards him is illustrated by the reception that awaited him in Dacca University. Addressing thousands of students under the famous *Amtala* tree on campus, Ali asked in Urdu, 'Which language should I speak in, Urdu or Punjabi? I don't know how to speak Bengali.' '*English! English! English! English! English!*' the crowd chanted.[53] Ali spoke at meetings organised by the Awami League and met with Sheikh Mujib to convey solidarity from the UK and also to discuss the state of the movement. At another mass gathering of workers and peasants an animated discussion on democracy from below engaged Ali with the audience, as Ali talked about a workers' and peasants' government. The hesitancy of some was apparent when peasant leaders stated, '*Hamari zindagi inn kay haathon mein hai*' ('our lives are in their hands'). And '*maar deyn gay humeyn*' ('they will kill us'). Ali responded, '*Ab nahin maareyn gay. Ye mauqa hai*' ('Not anymore. This is the opportunity').

Ali summed up his experience of the Pakistan movement thus: 'I learnt a lot, much more than one learns from books, just by talking to ordinary people, listening, and replying to questions ... It was very formative and educative for me.'[54] This recollection underlines what David Featherstone refers to as the transformative impact of solidarity, where mutual recognition and respect across borders are forged in the course of a mass struggle.[55] The lived experiences of Pakistani students, workers and peasants acted as a detonator for Ali to reflect upon his own social position and understanding of the process of rebellion and revolution. The role of peasant communities and workers exercising such agency placed their concerns, grievances and demands on a par with the revolts in Europe. Similarly, in Britain revolutionary activists supported the democratic demands raised by the Pakistani student and workers' movement, of releasing all political prisoners, freedom of speech and the press and 'one man one vote'.[56] British radical activists were excited by the upheaval in Pakistan as it reinforced the belief that global revolution was possible and, in the words of Chris Harman, one leading activist at the LSE, '1968 is a year of international revolution no less than 1793, 1830, 1848, 1917 and 1936'.[57] So helping to transform self-perceptions and subjectivities about 1968 in the process. Here solidarity from below was not contingent upon a pre-set list of demands from either side, but flowed organically from a sense of common purpose of shared interests in overthrowing the established order.

Conclusion

The Pakistan student movement of 1968–69 galvanised an entire population to revolt against the Ayub regime and ultimately made the country ungovernable so that Ayub had no choice but to relinquish power in March 1969. In less than six months, one of the world's most powerful dictatorships had crashed to a humiliating end. Some have argued that though the movement garnered the participation of a wide spectrum of the population – students, workers, intellectuals, professionals and also peasants – it 'failed to bring any fundamental change in the socio-economic structure or radical reforms'.[58] However, Tariq Ali cites Pakistan as the one place that the radical sixties scored a spectacular victory. A military dictator was toppled, free elections were held and a new era of democratic politics began to open up which eventually led to national liberation in East Bengal and the creation of Bangladesh.

The student protests and government repression that occurred during October and early November of 1968 were part of a much larger movement that gained momentum characterised by extra parliamentary activity on the streets, in workplaces, campuses and, critically, also industrial action by workers and peasants. Geopolitical alliances from above by ruling elites as demonstrated at the beginning ensured Ayub's survival for a decade. But common cause from below by students, workers and peasants in conflict with the regime proved far stronger and led to his demise by March 1969. When students come out of the bounded zones of the academy and interact with wider constituencies, a social and political explosion becomes a real possibility.

For too long Pakistan has been neglected in the histories of radicalism. As a students' and workers' struggle in a postcolonial state it complicates the popular romantic image of 'Third World' struggle – with the possible exception of events in the eastern wing and the struggle for Bangladeshi independence. Second, there is the issue of presentism. Pakistan is framed through the lens of Western modernity, and seen as quintessentially anti-modern with a propensity for military regimes and Islamist extremism. Yet Pakistan's '1968' demonstrates the deep democratic impulse that is endemic to Pakistani civil society. Contrary to Ayub's assertion, democracy is a human impulse, not the preserve of the West. To suggest otherwise is to orientalise non-Western peoples.

Finally, we should remember that transformative alliances of solidarity were forged by Pakistanis in Britain (and others such as the British far Left) with those on the front line of the mass struggle in Pakistan. As Tariq Ali – whose presence in Pakistan symbolised that transnational solidarity – has recalled of those heady months: 'you got a real feeling of how political consciousness changes. I've never got that feeling anywhere else, never on that scale. People were *incredibly* radicalised … All their questions came up – why do we live like this? … you know, from ordinary people.'[59]

Notes

1 Amazing 14.53 minutes of footage from Pathé News, titled 'Britain Welcomes President of Pakistan (1966) on his state visit'. BFI National Archives. www.youtube.com/watch?v=nd1KT8CBiVc
2 A. Shaikh, '1968: Was it Really a Year of Social Change in Pakistan', in B. Jones and M. O'Donnell (eds), *Sixties Radicalism and Social Movement Activism: Retreat or Resurgence?* (New York: Anthem Press, 2012), p. 73.
3 T. Ali, *Street Fighting Years: An Autobiography of the Sixties* (London: William Collins Sons & Co, 1987), p. 308. For a popular account of '1968' that ignores events in Pakistan entirely, see Kurlansky, *1968: The Year That Rocked the World* (New York: Ballantine Books, 2004).
4 *Birmingham Post*, 17 June 1965.
5 Speech delivered in 1960.
6 A. Khan, *Friends Not Masters* (New York: Oxford University Press, 1967), p. 71.
7 A. Khan, 'Baloch Ethnic Nationalism in Pakistan: From Guerrilla War to Nowhere?' *Asian Ethnicity*, 4:2 (2003), 286.
8 I. Ali, 'The Balochistan Problem', *Pakistan Horizon*, 58:2 (2005), 47.
9 Reported in *Black Dwarf*, 10 January 1969, p. 12.
10 *Civil and Military Gazette*, Lahore, 3 September 1963.

11 The electoral system was referred to as the 'Basic Democracies' scheme, a blatant initiative to install loyalists willing to vote for Ayub in an indirect presidential election. Eighty thousand Basic Democrats constituted the Electoral College for the election. See Aasim Sajjad Akhtar, *Dawn*, 12 July 2019.
12 'Pakistan: Trouble with Mother', *Time*, 25 December 1964.
13 I. Hussain, *Pakistan –The Economy of an Elitist State* (Karachi: Oxford University Press, 1999).
14 *The Times*, London, 22 March 1973.
15 K. Siddiqui, *Conflict, Crisis and War in Pakistan. Conflict* (London: The Macmillan Press Ltd, 1972).
16 Ali, *Street Fighting Years*, pp. 308–9.
17 *Evening News*, 8 July 1968, p. 3.
18 Issue date 30 July 1968, Reuters, British Pathé.
19 *The Illustrated London News*, 27 July 1968, p. 6.
20 *Guardian*, 24 July 1968.
21 Issue date 30 July 1968, Reuters, British Pathé.
22 Office of National Statistics.
23 R. Richardson and A. Wood, *The Achievement of British Pakistani Learners* (Stoke on Trent: Trentham Books Limited, 2004), pp. 2, 1–17.
24 A. Saleem and N. Abbas, *Jam Saqi: Chale Chalo Ke Who Manzil Abhi Nahin Aaei* (Lahore: Jamhoori Publications, 2017), p. 42.
25 Bhutto had been a member of Ayub Khan's government from 1958–66, when he left to take charge of the PPP.
26 A. Khwaja, *People's Movements in Pakistan* (Karachi: Kitab Publishers, 2017), p. 616.
27 *Pakistan Times*, 11 November 1968.
28 F. Ahmed, *Bengal Politics in Britain: Logic, Dynamics and Disharmony* (New York: Creation, 2013), pp. 43, 47.
29 Khwaja, *People's Movements in Pakistan*, p. 618.
30 T. Ali, *Pakistan: Military Rule or People's Power* (New York: William Morrow Company, Inc., 1970), p. 260.
31 Shaikh, '1968', p. 81.
32 A. Petiwala, '*Falasteen Ka Matlab Kya?*' (What Does Palestine Mean?) in Riaz Shahid's *Zerqa* (1969)', *Film History*, 32:3 (2020), 95–8. See also chapter by Sabah Haider in this volume.
33 B. Umar, *The Political Objectives of the Gherao Call* (Dacca: Mowla Brothers, 1974).
34 R. Khan, *The American Papers: Secret and Confidential India-Pakistan-Bangladesh Documents* (Dacca: University Press Ltd, 1999).
35 B. Umar, *The Emergence of Bangladesh* (Karachi: Oxford University Press, 2006).

36 *The Times*, London, 14 February 1969.
37 *Pakistan Observer*, 17 and 18 March 1969.
38 *Pakistan Observer*, 18 and 20 March 1969.
39 *Pakistan Observer*, 21 March 1969.
40 *Pakistan Observer*, 6 March 1969.
41 *Pakistan Observer*, 2 February 1969.
42 Khan, *Friends Not Masters*, 101.
43 Quoted in Gauhar, *Ayub Khan, Pakistan's First Military Ruler* (Lahore: Sang-e-Meel Publications, 1994), p. 479.
44 R. Khan, *Pakistan: A Dream Gone Sour* (Karachi: Oxford University Press, 1997), p. 44.
45 9 March 1969. Quoted in A. Khan, *Diaries of Field Marshal Mohammad Ayub Khan, Ayub Khan, 1966–1972* (Oxford: Oxford University Press, 2008), p. 305.
46 N. F. Paracha, *End of the Past: Ayub Khan, 1966–1972* (Oxford: Oxford University Press, 2008), p. 69.
47 Ahmed, *Bengal Politics in Britain*, pp. 91–2.
48 Interview with Avtar Singh Jouhl, leader of IWA in Birmingham, 19 May 2020.
49 On Jouhl, see also the 2019 interview, Jouhl 'Life-long Class Fighter Against Racism', *International Socialism*, 164 (2019).
50 *Black Dwarf*, 1 June 1968.
51 Ibid., 15 October 1968.
52 Jiwani and Mallick, '1968 and Ever Since: An Interview with Tariq Ali (Part 1)', *Jamhoor*, 30 January 2019, www.jamhoor.org/read/2019/1/10/1968-and-ever-since-part-one
53 Ibid.
54 Ibid.
55 D. Featherstone, *Solidarity: Hidden Histories and Geographies of Internationalism* (London: Zed Books, 2012), p. 37.
56 'Pakistan: the crisis and its origins', *Black Dwarf*, 10 January 1969, p. 12.
57 Quoted in D. Widgery (ed.) *The Left in Britain 1956–1968* (London: Penguin, 1976), p. 341.
58 Shaikh, '1968', p. 85.
59 Jiwani and Mallick, '1968 and Ever Since'.

12

Palestine through the prism of Pakistani cinema: imagining sameness and solidarity through *Zerqa* (1969)

Sabah Haider

> Research into memory is perhaps most interesting when paired with retrieval and analysis of concrete historical realities and lost worlds.[1]
> – Ali Nobil Ahmad in 'Film and Cinephilia in Pakistan: Beyond Life and Death'

Introduction

In the winter of 2014, I was in Pakistan to conduct fieldwork tracing the history of Pakistani volunteer fighters in the Palestine Liberation Organisation (PLO) in the 1970s. One afternoon I found myself sitting in a café in Lahore, chatting with an elderly screenwriter about the intersections of culture and politics in Pakistan at that time. He had started his career in the late 1960s in Lahore – the hub of Pakistan's film industry, known as Lollywood. He described the city as a vibrant and energetic scene of artists, intellectuals and filmmakers who increasingly watched and took inspiration from foreign films, largely because Indian cinema was banned in Pakistan at the time. The café where we sat that afternoon was on a bustling street in an older part of the city and, as a Lahore native, the screenwriter was completely at ease, conversing freely and without hesitation against the backdrop of the chaotic soundscape. At one point he paused in the middle of our conversation to listen attentively to some of the noise around us and smiled. He pointed towards a nearby vegetable cart where an elderly seller was singing as he went about his work arranging his produce. My companion looked at me and remarked, 'Listen! It's a song from *Zerqa*.' I was unfamiliar with the film at the time but, as I tuned in to listen to the words, I caught, '*Eh Falasteen!*' (Oh Palestine!).

Eh Falasteen! was a song from the 1969 film *Zerqa* which became an anthem for armed struggle against imperialism. The message in the song, to take up arms and join the struggle, was clear:

> Oh Palestine!
> We have faith that this night of injustice will end in Palestine
> Every victim of this injustice has heard our message, oh Palestine!
> The oppressors will not remain
> Our blood will not go in vain
> Even as we die as martyrs, we sing your name, oh Palestine!
> Until we remove every trace of the coloniser from our country,
> We swear on the greatness of our Prophet, that we will not rest.
> Oh Palestine, oh Palestine!

On 17 October 1969, Pakistan's then thriving film industry, released the film *Zerqa*, an Urdu-language epic drama named after its title character and set against the backdrop of the atrocities and losses of the Palestinian *Nakba* – the Arabic word for 'catastrophe' which is used to describe the annexation of Palestinian land and displacement of Palestinian people as a result of the establishment of the State of Israel in 1948. At first glance, the song-and-dance-laced film could be mistaken for any popular Pakistani feature film of that period. Lollywood in 1969 was booming and *Zerqa* featured Pakistan's biggest film stars of the era. The widely popular and sultry Neelo, who was also the wife of the director Riaz Shahid, played the title role of the film. As 'Zerqa', she played the daughter of a revolutionary who was martyred defending his position and resisting Israeli forces in his village. Her co-star and love interest in the film was Alauddin, a megastar of the era. The film was accessible to the Pakistani public not only because it featured movie stars Neelo and Alauddin, and because it was in Urdu, but also as it featured culturally, visually and ideologically relatable characters, plenty of singable songs (a total of seven), dance and the distinctly theatrical/melodramatic acting styles that were used in Pakistani cinema at the time. The 1960s and early 1970s are known as the 'golden days' of Pakistani cinema when the industry had a high output of films, with more than two hundred films produced annually. Cinema enjoyed wide popularity, and there were at least seven hundred cinemas operating in the country.[2] *Zerqa* was a mega-hit and became the first film in the country to achieve 'Diamond-Jubilee' status by being screened in cinemas for more than one hundred weeks straight.

Zerqa offers a fascinating cultural text to study not only visually and narratively, but also ideologically in terms of how transnational solidarity with the Palestinian liberation struggle was imagined and constructed in Pakistan. This chapter examines how *Zerqa* directly functioned as a call to action and mobilised solidarity with the Palestinian struggle. Moreover, the particularities and political conveniences of the timing of *Zerqa*'s release in October 1969 also had the effect of serving to distract Pakistanis from their own domestic political crises. Throughout the 1970s, thousands of Pakistani civilian men volunteered as *fida'iyeen* fighters in the Palestinian liberation struggle under the PLO, in Lebanon. They arrived independently, ready to die for Palestine. Indeed my research explores the social relations and kinship ties between these Pakistani *fida'iyeen* as they met in Lebanon and formed a community that became essential to their survival in life and in martyrdom. This film gives us a lens through which to understand Pakistani cultural history in the late 1960s and early 1970s and thus better situate the motivations for Pakistani participation in the Palestinian armed struggle. My analysis is grounded in ethnographic fieldwork I conducted in Lebanon between 2011 and 2018, and in Pakistan in 2014 and 2015. In this chapter I will argue that *Zerqa* directly functioned as a call to action and served to situate Palestine in the Pakistani public eye, popularising the Palestinian struggle and stimulating a widespread ethical imperative of solidarity and action.

The film

The film *Zerqa* is named after its main character.[3] In Palestine, 1948, a beautiful young woman named Zerqa is turned into a revolutionary by circumstance as the Zionist forces take power and her father, a revolutionary, is killed and deemed a martyr. In his dying words to her, he expresses his pride in her and tells her that she would be fulfilling her duty if she were also to die fighting for the liberation of her homeland from the occupying enemy. Zerqa commits herself to the liberation of Palestine and sacrifices life, love and dignity in the pursuit of freeing her homeland. Through initial scenes of Zionist violence against Palestinian peasants and villagers, the film tells the story of a violent and unjust Israeli occupation of

Palestine leading to the rise of the Palestinian liberation movement. Zerqa, the innocent woman, is depicted as someone to care about. She is someone who must be protected from pain and suffering. In other words, Zerqa is a symbol of Palestine.

Zerqa has all the defining characteristics of an epic film: a noteworthy historical event, a dramatic setting, extravagant costumes, significant music and a star-studded cast. Set in Palestine between 1948 and 1969, the film depicts Palestinians as mostly Muslims and Israelis as foreign occupiers of Palestine. Shot in Lahore, Zerqa is entirely in the Urdu language, and cast only Pakistani actors to play both the Palestinian and Israeli roles. The film relies on polarising personae, cultures, behaviours, ideologies and victim/aggressor dynamics to communicate to viewers a narrative of the differences between Palestinians and Israelis.

The story of *Zerqa* begins in 1969, in a Fatah[4] office where dozens of *keffiyeh*[5]-clad armed men depicting *fida'iyeen* (freedom fighting guerrillas) stand attentively in line, listening to their commander as he introduces them to an elderly blind Palestinian man named Shaaban Lotfi. He had also once been a *fida'i*, twenty-one years earlier in 1948, as he had fought against Zionist forces upon the creation of Israel and was blinded in the struggle. A respected figure, Lotfi comes to a Fatah office in 1969 to address and to inspire a group of *fida'iyeen* who are about to set out on an important mission. As he narrates the story of *Zerqa*, through his flashbacks, the film switches back and forth from present to past, to situate the context of the struggle and deliver the ethical imperative to fight and resist an unjust occupation. Both explicitly and immediately from the start of the film, *Zerqa* serves as a distinct call to action into the Palestinian armed struggle: the first thirty seconds of the film serve to set the terms of engagement for the viewer, as Lotfi declares:

> Before this war was only for Arabs to fight, but now this is everyone's war to fight!
>
> (*Pahalay yay jang sirf Arabon ki thi, lekin ab yay jang sab ki hai!*)

The soundtrack

In addition to the movie stars headlining its cast, music was a defining element of this film (Figures 12.1a and 12.1b). The best of Pakistan's music industry was brought together to produce the film's legendary songs, which were composed by Wajahat Attre and written by Habib Jalib.[6] The latter was a renowned left-wing activist and revered revolutionary poet in Pakistan who was in the same circle as the celebrated Marxist and PLO-affiliated intellectual, Faiz Ahmed Faiz (d. 1984).[7] Considering his political views and far-reaching popularity, it was perhaps no surprise that Jalib was asked by Shahid to write the songs for *Zerqa*. Of the seven songs in the film, four were explicitly about Palestine,[8] and the other three were about oppression and injustice:[9]

1   Dance when we can't speak
2   Chains on my dignity
3   Oh Palestine!
4   I came to sell flowers
5   I swear to God
6   My darling from Hebron
7   Oh people, wake up for humanity!

The lyrics to the song 'Oh people, wake up for humanity!' (*Qomulal Insaan*) also communicate a clear call to action, urging people to fight for justice and sacrifice their lives to guard the honour of the country, saying that only the most courageous will die as martyrs. The revolutionary language in the songs describes the occupation of Palestine as a troubling night that will end through perseverance, and that without people's participation, injustice cannot end.

These lyrics reveal a great deal about the views being communicated to the Pakistani public through cinema and music, its most popular and accessible mediums at the time. As such, it is important to note how these songs explicitly appealed for people to rise up and take up arms and in a way that transcended all layers of the Pakistani public.

Across the country, the songs swiftly became popular and were to remain so for years. According to Fayyaz Ahmed, author of the four-volume *Urdu Filmi Gaanay* (Urdu Film Songs), an exhaustive catalogue of every song in every Pakistani film made since the birth of the industry, Pakistanis continued to sing *Zerqa*'s songs for decades. During my field visits to Lahore in 2014 and 2015, I spent significant amounts of time visiting DVD shops throughout the city. Almost all of the DVD sellers knew the film and when

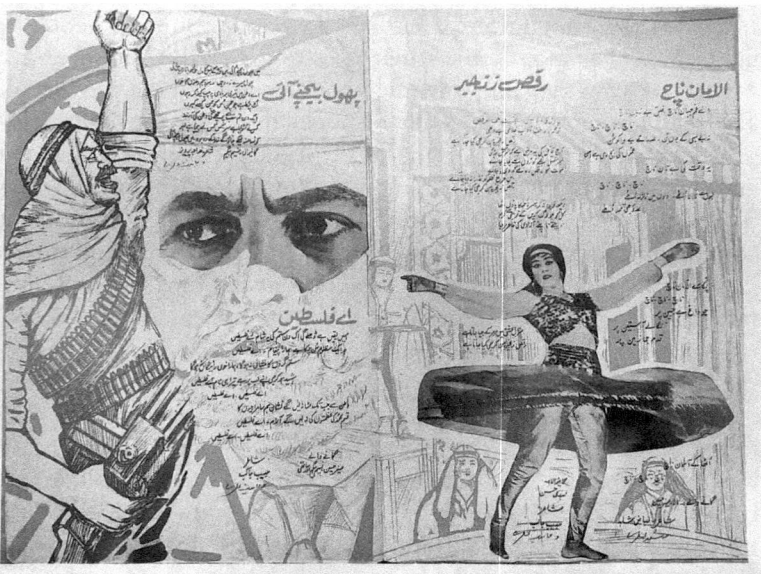

Figures 12.1a and 12.1b Double pages from the pressbook of the film *Zerqa* featuring the lyrics of its songs.

asked about it, would either start singing a song from the film or describe its soundtrack as noteworthy due to the widely respected artists behind it. Until this day, the songs of *Zerqa* are still sung by the older generation that remains linked to the popular culture of their era – everyday Pakistanis who may be long removed from the Palestinian struggle, yet remain connected to it through its music: a significant piece of cultural and political memory.

In the only historical survey of Pakistani cinema done in recent years, *Cinema and Society: Film and Social Change in Pakistan*, surprisingly, the only notable mention of the film *Zerqa* is that of the film's poster (Figure 12.2):

> Posters of the 1960s also include political and revolutionary, anti-colonial themes, most notably Riaz Shahid's *Zerqa*, which he wrote, directed and produced with the assistance of his wife and leading lady Neelo. *Zerqa* was the story of a female resistance fighter involved in the Palestinian struggle against Zionist imperialism. The iconic poster depicts Neelo bound in chains, representing both the individual and Palestinian people, and is one of the most famous images in Pakistani cinema history.[10]

As the most successful and longest-running Pakistani film at the box office in its cinematic history, it is baffling that the film did not warrant further analysis in the book. In the only other book that attempts to offer a survey of Pakistani cinema, Mushtaq Gazdar's *Pakistan Cinema, 1947–1997*,[11] *Zerqa* is not even mentioned. Nonetheless Pakistani film critic Sarfaraz Fareed Nihash has made notable efforts in recent years to bring attention to this film through numerous articles in Urdu-language newspapers and journals. He attributed the disregard for *Zerqa* to a broader problem of poor scholarship about the history of film in Pakistan. More recently, in the first English-language scholarly account of *Zerqa*, Ada Petiwala notes that it has remained invisible in film studies of the era precisely because its articulations of multiple registers and scales of cultural politics challenges the field's academic classifications and interpretations.[12] Petiwala's analysis situates *Zerqa* historically within Third Worldist solidarity films concerning Palestine and related Pakistani cultural politics in the 1950s and 1960s, focusing in particular on the nuances and tensions of religious and gender identity that the

Figure 12.2 Official poster for the film *Zerqa* (1969), by Riaz Shahed.

film's characters bring about. My chapter extends Petiwala's reading to explore other as yet unattended questions about *Zerqa*'s visuality and aurality as a cultural text and to examine the ways in which the film functioned *then* as a call to action mobilising Pakistanis to join the Palestinian struggle and its afterlives *now* in Pakistani cultural memory.

Zerqa in political context

In 1969, Pakistan as a nation-state was only twenty-two years old. India was still the key enemy – President Ayub Khan had even banned Indian films in Pakistan[13] – and Pakistan had forged strong political relationships with its allies in the Arab world. In 1973 when Zulfiqar Ali Bhutto came to power, these relationships only strengthened. Domestically, however, the government was struggling on multiple levels. Most notably, Pakistan was experiencing two separate armed revolts. In East Pakistan, which later became Bangladesh, a democratic uprising was in full swing, and in the western province of Baluchistan, separatists were engaged in a violent war with the Pakistani army. The separatist movements and violent uprisings in East Pakistan and Baluchistan caused so much concern for the Pakistani government that it implemented a media blackout on top of its already existing draconian media censorship.[14] This is worth noting, because while the state was engaged in several ethnic and political struggles, domestically the most popular cause in Pakistan was the liberation of Palestine.

At the time of the film's release in 1969, illiteracy and poverty were widespread in Pakistan. Pakistani exposure to Arabs was largely via media images and socially distant encounters during the Hajj pilgrimage in Saudi Arabia for those who were able to go.[15] After the Palestinian armed struggle gained force following the devastating losses and Arab defeat in the 1967 June War, the question of the Palestinian national struggle took a more prominent place in the international arena along with the Vietnam War and the struggle against apartheid in South Africa. Of note regarding the 1967 Arab-Israeli war is the little-known efforts of volunteer Pakistani Air Force (PAF) fighter pilots who played a key role as they downed ten Israeli aircraft without losing a single aircraft.[16] Four of those ten were by PAF fighter pilot Saiful Azam who returned to a hero's welcome in Pakistan where he was awarded the *Sitara-e-Jurat* (Star of Courage).[17] After 1967, Palestine was front and centre of the public consciousness in Pakistan. The Pakistani public could relate to the Palestinian struggle, especially after the annexation of East Jerusalem in 1967, due to its significance in the shared imagination of a Muslim community. After Mecca and Medina, Jerusalem is the third holiest city and place of pilgrimage for Muslims. Its fall under the control of the Jewish state of Israel was thus perceived as a threat not only by Palestinians but by Muslim communities beyond.[18]

Thus *Zerqa* emerged from that cultural zeitgeist but, narratively and ideologically, it carried a specific aim and message. According to the Pakistani film writer, Sarfaraz Fareed Nihash, *Zerqa* 'was the first Pakistani film that gave the people a real issue. It was not just a film, but a moment to mobilise the Muslim world.'[19] He notes that through it, 'The people were delivered a very big message in their own language.'[20] This message and ideological goal became

Figure 12.3 'Rights for Film *Zerqa* Given to Al-Fatah: Director Riaz Shahid calls for all recreation tax collected from *Zerqa* film ticket sales to be given to Al-Fatah', *Daily Jang Newspaper*, Karachi, 25 October 1969.

even more apparent when on 25 October 1969, at a launch party for the film in Karachi, *Zerqa*'s director Riaz Shahid announced that he had given the film's Middle East distribution rights to Fatah (Figure 12.3),[21] thereby giving all profits from screenings in the Arab world to support the Palestinian armed struggle.[22]

Shahid thus made clear that his film was an expression of solidarity with the Palestinian armed struggle, not only in sentiment but in material tangible support. He also called upon the Pakistani government to give tax proceeds from screenings in Pakistan to Fatah. His intent in creating *Zerqa* as a means of simultaneously raising awareness and mobilising physical and financial support for the Palestinian armed struggle was clear. At the same time, the fact that *Zerqa* served a greater goal was also made clear by Fatah. From Fatah's side, the relationship between the party and the film was made official by their endorsement of the film at the same event that Shahid announced it had given them the Middle East rights. Fatah's representative in Pakistan, Khalid Sheikh, who was in attendance at the event, said: 'We have great hopes from our Pakistani brothers for our armed struggle. The film *Zerqa* is a practical example of those hopes,' and he added: 'Pakistan is the first country to make a film on the topic of our Palestinian armed struggle. And this movie truly represents our feelings.' On behalf of Fatah, Sheikh then presented Shahid with a medal of Fatah's monogram, in honour and recognition of his support for Fatah's mission.[23] As such, *Zerqa* was not just a film that brought to light the Palestinian cause for a Pakistani public in a relatable way. It also functioned as an explicit means to an end: it was a propaganda film serving as a call to action and communicating the urgency to support the Palestinian armed struggle to express solidarity and engagement on every level, be it through taking up arms, raising the importance of challenging imperialism, initiating and calling for financial support and ultimately entering Palestine through a transnational imagination that linked Pakistanis with Palestinians.

With the biggest names in Lollywood, and its timing and message adapted for the Pakistani public, *Zerqa* served to make the Palestinian struggle popular, relatable and actionable. The film delivered an ethical imperative to the public, a call to action for Pakistanis that manifested in different social strata. On campuses around the country, Fatah had clubs where students engaged in activism and debates in solidarity with the Palestinian struggle. Around Pakistan, both students and intellectuals – artists, writers, scholars, journalists – regularly discussed and represented Palestine in the public sphere. Less than two years after the release of *Zerqa*, another Pakistani feature film on the Palestinian armed struggle was released by the director Riaz Ahmad. It was called *Al-Assifa* (1971), named after the main armed wing of Fatah which was under the direct command of Yasser Arafat. *Al-Assifa* did not achieve the same success of *Zerqa* – it was, after all, a smaller budget film with lesser-known stars – yet the goals of the film were made explicit through its promotional materials and songs. In those days film distributors sent pressbooks about new film releases to cinemas to stimulate interest in screening it and to the press to promote the film. In *Al-Assifa*'s pressbook, the film's logline is as explicit as its title: 'The real story of the Freedom Fighters of Al-Assifa who are determined to change the map of the world. The History of dedicated "FIDAYIN" [sic]. Who are sacrificing and struggling for freedom and solidarity of their homeland Palestine.'[24]

In parallel, in different corners of Pakistan, separatist foreign-backed liberation movements were fiercely fighting their own independence struggles with the Pakistani state. In what was then known as the province of East Pakistan, the Bengalis fought a violent and bloody war with the Pakistani army in their struggle for self-determination. At the same time, the provisional government of Bangladesh allied with India which, after intervening, helped lead to the surrender of Pakistan in December 1971. In the north east, in the disputed Kashmir region claimed by both Pakistan and India, even after both countries signed the 1965 Soviet Union-mediated Tashkent Declaration peace treaty, separatist guerrilla activity in Kashmir continued. According to countless media interviews and reports, Pakistani government officials admitted their support of Kashmiri guerilla groups in resisting Indian forces. At the same time, Kashmiri nationalism surged as the people of Kashmir pursued their right to self-determination. Thus, throughout the late 1960s and early 1970s, with the Bengalis, Kashmiris and Baluch all engaged in violent wars with the state, the issue of self-determination and occupation was a relatable idea for the Pakistani public. The idea resonated particularly strongly as the country had only been created in 1947 as a homeland for Muslims out of British colonial partition. Among those three independence struggles in Pakistan, the one that had most explicitly aligned with the Palestinian struggle was the Baluch struggle, as the Soviet-backed Baluch separatist groups had close relations with the PLO and the Popular Front for the Liberation of Palestine (PFLP).[25] One of the Baluch separatist groups, the Baluch Liberation Front (BLF), was created in 1964 by Jumma Khan, a radio journalist who had lost his job on national radio for raising awareness of the Baluch struggle and achieved widespread popularity among the Baluch in Iran, Pakistan and Afghanistan. Khan's BLF 'depended mainly on clandestine support from a variety of radical Arab sources'[26] and explicitly aligned itself with the Palestinian struggle 'against imperialism, colonialism and Zionism', claiming ethnic connection with Arab people.[27]

Thus, the idea of a shared collective identity, whether ethnic or religious, and common perception of the hostile enemy, as well as shared experiences of British colonisation, occupation and anticolonial struggle, seems to connect these struggles. These linkages are essential to understanding how notions of empathy and solidarity, as well as an imagined sense of duty – either religious or as colonised peoples – framed popular representations of the Palestinian struggle for the Pakistani public.

A prototypical Lollywood genre

In Pakistani society, cinema has always served as a key form of entertainment transcending class differences, especially among peasant and working-class groups. In fact, in his 1969 study of the Pakistani film industry, Alamgir Kabir started his book by observing exactly this point. He wrote: 'The very fact that people love to go to the movies – people from all strata of society – proves convincingly that art is indispensable for all and that cinema has the potential of being the most popular great art.'[28] Kabir's description of the accessibility and role of cinema points to the fluid and essential function cinema has served in a country that has struggled with immense illiteracy and social and economic inequality. At the time of *Zerqa*'s release, Pakistan had close to five hundred public cinemas (Figure 12.4) and Kabir notes that cinema was 'the only form of entertainment within the economic reach of the people'.²⁹ Understanding this helps contextualise the phenomenal reach that the film *Zerqa* had, considering it played for one hundred weeks straight at repeatedly sold-out screenings.

Films from Pakistan's golden age of cinema are distinctive in their melodramatic style and their focus on social problems. Regarding the style, Kabir wrote in his 1969 analysis of the Pakistani film industry:

> Melodrama and 'stagey' production are the two prominent characteristics of Pakistani productions in general ... the emphasis is undoubtedly on 'entertainment' but is often stretched to ludicrous limits. Keeping the censor codes at bay by having plump actresses 'technically' clad, every effort is made to exploit audience inclination for vulgarity.³⁰

Figure 12.4 A recoloured photo of the crowds upon the film's cinematic release at Lahore's now iconic Gulistan Cinema on 16 October 1969.

Here Kabir highlights the accessibility of this style of film for the Pakistani public, and *Zerqa* is no exception to this. The hyperfeminine character of Zerqa is always dressed in a way to highlight her curves and beauty, and she moves about on screen to the pleasure of the male gaze both within the film and for the public to garner their sense of desire and thus support of her. That Zerqa's struggle is a representation of the struggle of Palestine is interesting when considered in relation to the narrative being in the 'social problem film' genre, which is best described as: 'Films that dramatize some set of concerns, which they depict as broadly representative of the conditions of their historical moment ... and they usually employ a serious tone and realistic mode of representation in engaging with their subject matter.'[31]

Situating *Zerqa* within the 'social problem film' genre enables us to understand how it embodied the cultural and political zeitgeist. In the Global South, the Palestinian cause came to prominence during the long sixties especially as anticolonial liberation movements throughout the Global South increasingly established relations with the PLO, which also benefitted from support from China,[32] North Vietnam[33] and other socialist countries allied in the movement against imperialism.[34] Films of an anti-imperialist position were reflective of the director of *Zerqa*'s political views; prior to writing *Zerqa*, in 1962, Shahid had written the screenplay for the film *Shaheed*, a remake of *Lawrence of Arabia*.[35] Shahid had also worked for the Pakistani leftist journal *Layl-o-Nahar* (Night and Day) which was then edited by the revered Pakistani poet and Marxist, Faiz Ahmed Faiz.

Given Shahid's political views, it was not surprising that he would take on a film about the Palestinian struggle. Shahid was not only motivated by anti-imperialism as a theme and resistance as a maxim, he was also encouraged by international cinema. Apparently Shahid was inspired by the story of a famous Algerian revolutionary, Djamila Bouhired, a woman who had joined the Algerian National Liberation Front and fought against French colonial rule and the occupation of Algeria.[36] In 1958, the internationally renowned Egyptian filmmaker Youssef Chahine had put Bouhired's story on screen in a landmark film – *Jamila, the Algerian*.[37] According to Nihash, it was Chahine's filmic tribute to Bouhired that spurred

Shahid to adapt the figure of a female anticolonial fighter to a Palestinian context and frame it to a Pakistani audience.

The question of what stimulates such transcultural adaptations that transform one milieu into another (local) one is one that Bhaskar Sarkar considers in 'Epic Melodrama, cine-maps of the global south'. Sarkar questions the strategies and equivalences that render such transformations (or translations) possible. He asks: 'What resonances in material structures and phenomenological experiences might allow for congruent historical consciousnesses and aesthetic forms, in spite of all the differences of lifeworlds and habitus?' The answer he points to lies in the popularity and use of the epic melodrama which are common across the Global South:

> the epic melodrama counterpoises to the grandiose concerns the palpable messiness of local, quotidian struggles, thereby interrogating all those fictions that are offered as resolutions at both local and global levels ... the epic melodrama maps an entire material and intimate geography that allows us to divine otherwise opaque translocal structures, connections and processes.[38]

Sarkar's description enables an understanding of how *Zerqa* localised the Palestinian struggle and representation of Palestine and the Palestinians for Pakistani audiences through a mapping of parallel experiences of colonisation, a geography of affinities of Islam and Islamic culture. Nihash explains that people in Pakistan empathised with the film's story of martyrdom. It was easy for them to know whose side they were on: they loved Zerqa and hated Major David, the cruel Israeli general in the film. But how these emotions manifested among the Pakistani public was extraordinary:

> In the cinemas people would curse the Zionists and Major David out loud. These people went to see this film in the cinemas two or three times – maybe more. It was in the cinema for two years straight, and movie-goers in Pakistan were emotionally charged – they were standing up and cursing Israel when they watched this film.

When asked who these cinemagoers were, Nihash explained that with its ethical imperative framed by anti-imperialism and religious identity, this film transcended all strata of Pakistani society: 'All people loved this film. Even religious people watched it and liked it because the film is defending faith.'[39]

Imagining sameness and transnational solidarity on screen

Nihash, the aforementioned film critic, notes that *Zerqa* was subversive because it used the language of commercial cinema. It employed relatable ideas of oppression and Islamic identity to communicate a radical message and call to action to the Pakistani public, who were largely disengaged from global politics and unfamiliar with independent and Third Cinema. Sean Carter and Klaus Dodds argue that popular media, like films, are an intrinsic part of international politics, helping to constitute politics as a set of practices that extends to all parts of society. Further, they state that film serves to provide the public with 'ways of feeling about international politics'.[40] Notably, they say that the 'role of "distant others" can often be crucial in these particular representations of international politics as can the apparent visual imperative to be seen to be doing something to protect the border by fortifying it'.[41] For Pakistani viewers, their imagined sameness with Palestinians encompassed a sense of shared cultural and political identity through Islam and a history of colonialism, and seeing people like themselves on screen enabled an understanding that the Palestinian struggle was their struggle too. One of the key points that Carter and Dodds emphasise is the role of vision in geopolitical accounts of the world. For them, vision is the way that some things, some people or some objects are made more visible than others, highlighting how space, vision and power function together through film. Likewise, Zeina Maasri refers to 'translocal modes of visuality', to describe what is created by 'the visual field of relations produced in and through the mobility of particular sets of images ... as a force-field entangled with politics'.[42] A defining example of how translocal visuality functioned was through the image of the *fida'i*. Maasri writes:

> The revolutionary guerrilla, or 'freedom fighter' to use the rhetoric of the day, was a quintessential figure in the repertoire of signs, symbols and myths occupying the imagination of revolutionary fervour, in and through which transnational political subjectivities of the Third World were formed and actualized on the battlefront. The trope of the gun-carrying guerrilla occupied many photographs in the press, films and posters from the 1960s and on into the 1970s.[43]

From the very start of the film, these images functioned as defining elements of *Zerqa* to situate it in a very specific ideological and political objective. By adopting the visual language of Third Worldist anticolonial struggles and more specifically of the Palestinian armed struggle, Shahid made clear one week after the film's release that the film was a strong expression of solidarity with and a call to arms for the Palestinian cause in Pakistan. It is also important to note that, unlike other non-Arab volunteer fighters who were often members of allied groups and joined the Palestinian guerrilla organisations in Lebanon after 1971, the vast majority of Pakistani *fida'iyeen* were individual volunteer fighters who independently travelled from their places of origin in Pakistan to Damascus, Syria by road to join the armed struggle. In Damascus they registered at the PLO offices where they were assigned a unit and issued uniforms and a weapon, and from there they travelled to Lebanon.

It is this interweaving of anticolonial with Muslim transnational solidarity that makes it possible to understand how the Palestinian struggle was made accessible to the Pakistani public across the different communities and classes. Consequently, I argue that the narrative of *Zerqa* and its call to action is centred on a collective moral imaginary anchored in Islam, and more specifically cultural Islam, because *Zerqa* is not at all a religious film. God, martyrdom and jihad are all referenced in the film in relation to Palestine, but they are not explored as a religious duty and practice. Islam was leveraged in the narrative of this film to evoke a relevance and direct link with the Palestinian struggle by its representation of Palestinians as Muslim brothers and sisters, thereby configuring the Palestinian cause as a responsibility for all Muslims. As the film begins, 'Brothers, these Muslims ...' (*Bhaiyon, yey musulman ...*). The film evokes Islam at various points to convey conviction and the goal of justice, but Islam is represented culturally at best: various religious symbols, practices, expressions and icons form part of the mise-en-scene in the film, creating a familiar and relatable universe for Pakistani audiences. Shaaban Lotfi says to the *fida'iyeen* in the opening scene of the film: 'You are not just fighters of Fatah, but you are also snipers of God, who has adorned the greatness of martyrdom for those pursing betterment of the world.' He continues: 'My sons, you are of great destiny, that you are setting out for martyrdom. I am the unfortunate that I was only able to give my eyes to my country.'

Visually the film draws upon orientalist imagery to depict Arabs as both *keffiyeh*-clad revolutionaries and also as extravagant hedonists in robes and dishdashas – both images that reveal perhaps the limited actual exposure to Arabs and specifically Palestinians that Shahid and his art department likely had. Most texts and reference materials about the Levant and available in English in Pakistan at the time were British and thus inflected by a colonial gaze. Thus, the visual depiction of Palestinians, Palestine and Palestinian culture in this film is clearly imagined patchwork, and largely reminiscent of orientalist tropes and imagery, that is, a snake charmer in the old city of Jerusalem, Bedouin-robed men, and so on. However, while the image references and depictions may have derived from unchallenged colonial orientalist sources, it is not possible to accuse the film of orientalism because it does not hierarchically 'other' the Palestinians or Arabs as an inferior subject-race as orientalist tropes do. What it does, however, is represent them stereotypically. To this point, it is clear in the film that representations of Palestine and Palestinians are not entirely credible, not only in language and dress, but also in behaviours and manners. Even key details such as the iconic *keffiyeh* scarf are not entirely accurate in terms of the pattern, or how they are typically worn. In the opening scene in a Fatah office, amusingly the extras playing the characters of Palestinian *fida'iyeen* are wearing civilian clothes as opposed to army uniforms, and their faces are covered by *keffiyeh* scarves – something they would do when in the battlefield to hide their faces, but not among each other. In addition, these characters were not cast effectively: the men are out of shape, either overly thin or overweight, appearing middle-aged and meek as opposed to charged and trained soldiers ready to go to battle. Fatah was widely known to have training camps and its *fida'iyeen* were obliged to do physical training there. When viewed with an analytical lens on cinema, the combination of melodrama, unconvincing casting and ineffective costumes and art direction, make the film entirely unbelievable. Yet its incredible success in Pakistan and the impact it had on the Pakistani public in both influence and motivation reveals a great deal not only about the limited exposure that Pakistanis had to Palestinians and Arabs at the time, but also about how such melodramatic genres invite their audience to suspend their belief and just enjoy watching the film unroll.

All this is to reiterate that the film was made relatable to Pakistanis on every level: language, values, culture, religion, a common enemy, familiar landscapes and an enemy with distinctly Western and non-Muslim behaviours. The general in the Zionist army and his wife, also played by Pakistani actors speaking Urdu in the film, were given a distinctly inferior moral character in their behaviour towards the Palestinians. The Israelis drank alcohol, dressed in Western fashions and were clearly represented as being foreigners in the space(s) they inhabited. In one memorable scene, the wife of the villain, Israeli 'Major David', is frustrated by her adopted country and expresses her desire to go back to her country, the one she came from, as she feels like a stranger in Israel. Her husband tells her that this is her home now, although she does not seem convinced.[44]

In the film's opening scene, after saying, 'Before this war was only for Arabs to fight, but now this is everyone's war to fight!' Shaaban Lotfi tells the *fida'iyeen*: 'The flames of the fires lit by the Jews have now reached the feet of Zerqa.'[45] The intentionality of this emotional appeal could not be made more manifest. Another implicit goal of the film as text is made apparent in how Palestinians, Arabs and Palestine are represented to Pakistanis as similar (in appearance, in language, in clothing, in culture and behaviours), evoking a sense of imagined sameness – as farfetched as that may be – between the viewers and the subject. In 'Cinema and the City: The Ayub years', anthropologist Kamran Asdar Ali describes an imagined 'sameness' that emerged in post-partition Pakistan that served to foster a sense of familiarity, belonging and connection with the new physical environment of Pakistan, as well as with the new groups of people from varying origins, ethnicities and languages who now inhabited the newly configured society:

> Historians have critically analyzed this notion of 'sameness' by pointing out the genesis of Muslim nationalism as a partial resolution of the contradiction between the particularism of Muslim identity linked to locality and place and the larger construction of a Muslim moral community connected to a territorially bounded nation-state.[46]

I argue that *Zerqa* leverages the notion of sameness to a perceived Muslim identity to generate an empathy, affinity and solidarity with the Palestinian cause. Asdar Ali notes that during the struggle for Pakistan's creation after its independence, 'Pakistan's political leadership emphasized a Muslim nationalism that incorporated one language (Urdu), one religion (Islam), one people (Pakistani)'[47] as three tenets used to bridge different cultures and ethnicities through an imagined sameness to generate a collective identity or, in other words, to create an imagined nation. It is thus interesting to consider how these same tenets were used in *Zerqa* to imagine the Palestinian struggle as a Pakistani struggle too. These ideas of jihad, martyrdom, respect and freedom, all in honour of Islam, point to 'religion as the central trauma of Pakistani cinema'[48] in that they belie the idea of partition. As Hamid Dabashi wrote, 'the crisis of religion, particularly the anxiety of a perceived external threat to the state and its obsession with a dominant Islamic narrative is also one that persists within artistic ventures and can be seen as part of a formative Pakistani National Cinema'.[49] Thus, the sameness that Asdar Ali writes about is again evoked in this idea that transcends geographies and national borders. A shared religion, morality, unity and the anxiety of a perceived external threat to the state, functioned together to catalyse a transnational solidarity with the Palestinian struggle.

Conclusion: *Zerqa* as a cultural text

When I discovered *Zerqa* during my fieldwork, I initially perceived the film only as a peripheral finding. However, as I continued with my research across Pakistan and Lebanon, I could not help but reflect constantly on the cultural context that the Pakistani *fida'iyeen* emerged out of, must be framed by, and thereby remembered through. By contextualising the particularities and political conveniences of the timing of *Zerqa*'s release, this chapter's exploration of the narrative and political imaginary of the film allows an understanding of how it created the context for widespread solidarity with Palestine as a popular movement in Pakistan. In turn, my research uncovered how the film was used strategically to redirect the national gaze away from domestic politics and towards Palestine as the central moral conflict.

The film repeatedly surfaced in many different contexts and geographies in my research. In the process of connecting those dots, the film emerged as an essential dimension of my understanding. It offers a valuable contextual frame for the ethnographic observations

I made when conducting fieldwork in South Lebanon villages, and in excavating the testimonies of surviving foreign fighters. One of the most striking memories that was shared with me was by Huda,[50] an elderly Lebanese woman, in a small village near Nabatiye who recalled the story of M.S., a Pakistani *fida'i* with Fatah. M.S. had rented a room in the home of a local family who had befriended him; he would come and rest there whenever he was granted time off from the battlefield. She recounted how the villagers were fond of M.S. as he had a lively personality and was always listening to music on his portable cassette player or singing. She described him as a very proud *fida'i* who took the utmost of care of his uniform, and always wore a perfectly perched beret on his head. During the war years electricity shortages and blackouts were commonplace in the village and she reminisced how at nighttime the villagers would sit outside together, drinking tea and smoking their nargileh pipes, socialising in complete darkness in the silent, still nights. She smiled as she recalled that the villagers would always know M.S. was coming home from the frontline because they would hear him singing Pakistani songs from a mile away, and the wind would carry his voice to them. One can only imagine him singing the songs of *Zerqa*.

Since the release of *Zerqa*, across Pakistan, people of different backgrounds, classes and social groups started singing the Urdu-language revolutionary Palestinian anthems of the film. Many of these songs are still sung by older workers and shopkeepers, who may be long removed from the Palestinian struggle yet remain connected to it through a piece of cultural and political memory. *Zerqa* had the effect of triggering people's awareness and igniting a conviction. It took a popular struggle and translated it into a culturally specific language. In the summer of 2015, I went into a bootleg DVD shop in Lahore, with a list of films I was going to teach, for a course I developed, called 'Cinemas of the Middle East'. The shop was run by a man in his forties, a passionate cinephile of Pakistani cinema. As he looked over my list of mostly Arab films, he paused when he reached *Zerqa*. He was about to say I must be mistaken as it's not an Arab film, but suddenly stopped and his eyes lit up. He smiled and started singing,

> Oh Palestine! We have faith that this night of injustice will end in Palestine …
> The oppressors will not remain, our blood will not go in vain …

Notes

1 Ali Nobil Ahmad, 'Film and Cinephilia in Pakistan: Beyond Life and Death', *BioScope* 5:2 (2014), 81–98.
2 S. Faruqi, 'Pakistani Film Industry and Cinema Culture', *Dawn News* (15 December 2020), http://beta.dawn.com/news/591275/pakistans-film-industry-and-cinema-culture (21 September 2020).
3 According to Nihash, Sarfaraz Fareed, Pakistani film journalist, film director Riaz Shahid named the title character Zerqa after the name him and his wife Neelo had given their daughter. Author personal telephone interview, 4 September 2020.
4 Founded in 1959 as a political organisation, Fatah was the largest political and military faction under the Palestine Liberation Organization (PLO) under the leadership of Yasser Arafat.
5 The checkered black and white scarf traditionally worn by peasants in the Arab Middle East, and which became a symbol of Palestinian nationalism and resistance from the 1960s onwards.
6 'Zarqa', [sic] IMDB, www.imdb.com/title/tt1464797/trivia?ref_=tt_trv_trv, accessed 10 February 2016.
7 Faiz had to flee Pakistan and go into exile in 1977 after the chief of the army, General Zia-ul-Haq, staged a coup, taking control of the country from Prime Minister Zulfiqar Ali Bhutto. A longtime and close friend of PLO Chair Yasser Arafat, Faiz was granted asylum by Arafat in Beirut and was appointed editor of *Lotus*, the literary periodical published by the Afro-Asian Writers' Association from the late 1960s until the early 1990s.
8 *Zerqa* songs about Palestine: '*Eh Falasteen,*' '*Wallah Nujda,*' '*Ya Khalili, Ya Albi,*' '*Qoumulul Insan*'.
9 All titles translated from Urdu by Nudrat Haider.
10 Ali Khan and Ahmed Ali Nobil, *Cinema and Society: Film and Social Change in Pakistan* (Karachi: Oxford University Press, 2016), p. 230.
11 First published by Oxford University Press in 1997 with a second edition in 2019.
12 Ada Petiwala, '*Falasteen Ka Matlab Kya? (What does Palestine Mean?)* in Riaz Shahid's *Zerqa* (1969)', *Film History* 32:3 (2020), 75–104 (83).
13 Naila Inayat, 'Bring Back Bollywood, We Can't Watch Pakistani Films about Kulbhushan Jadhav Sabotaging CPEC' (16 January 2020), https://theprint.in/opinion/letter-from-pakistan/pakistanis-need-bollywood-films-not-ones-showing-kulbhushan-in-balochistan-sabotaging-cpec/350161/#:~:text=In%201965%2C%20after%20the%20second,decades%2C%20Pakistan's%20cinema%20industry%20collapsed (20 September 2020).

14 Abbas Zaffar, 'The Missing Pages of History: 70 Years of Pakistan and *Dawn*', *Dawn News*, 20 August 2017, www.dawn.com/news/1352579 (accessed 20 September 2020).
15 Large waves of Pakistani migrant workers to the Gulf countries only surged in the 1970s.
16 'When Pakistani Pilots Battled Israelis', *Pakistan Insider* (20 July 2014), https://insider.pk/opinion/pakistani-pilots-battled-israelis/ (accessed 6 February 2021).
17 'Legendary PAF fighter pilot Group Captain Saiful Azam passes away in Bangladesh', Dawn.com (15 June 2020), www.dawn.com/news/1563682 (accessed 6 February 2021). See also: 'Palestinians mourn death of a Bangladeshi war hero', AlJazeera.com (15 June 2020), www.aljazeera.com/news/2020/06/15/palestinians-mourn-death-of-a-bangladeshi-war-hero/ (accessed 29 September 2020).
18 Petiwala mentions how the loss of East Jerusalem was met with painful responses from leading Urdu poets in Pakistan. She also refers to an arson attack at Al-Aqsa Mosque in August 1969, resulting in the damage of the minbar of Saladin, which sparked outrage in the Muslim world. See 'Falasteen Ka Matlab Kya?' 75–6, 88. By the time *Zerqa* was released in October 1969, Palestine was already present in Pakistani public discourse.
19 Sarfaraz Fareed Nihash, Pakistani film journalist, personal telephone interview, 4 September 2020.
20 Ibid. In Urdu, Nihash said: '*In ki zaaban main ek barra pegham tha*'.
21 *Daily Jang Newspaper*, Karachi, 'Film for Rights of *Zerqa* Given to Al-Fatah: Director Riaz Shahid calls for all recreation tax collected from *Zerqa* film ticket sales to be given to Al-Fatah', 25 October 1969.
22 Nihash said the film was dubbed in Arabic among many other languages, and played in several Arab countries, most notably in Lebanon, Jordan, and the United Arab Emirates. Personal telephone interview, 4 September 2020.
23 Ibid.
24 *AL-ASSIFA* Film Promotional Brochure (Lahore, Pakistan: Riazi Films, 1971).
25 Selig S. Harrison, *In Afghanistan's Shadow: Baluch Nationalism and Soviet Temptations* (New York: Carnegie Endowment for International Peace, 1981), p. 120.
26 Ibid.
27 Ibid., p. 105–6.
28 Alamgir Kabir, *The Cinema in Pakistan* (Dacca: Sandhani Publications, 1969), p. 1.
29 Ibid., p. 175.
30 Ibid., pp. 170–1.

31 Stephen Doles, 'Social Problem Films' Entry', Oxford Bibliographies, www.oxfordbibliographies.com/view/document/obo-9780199791286/obo-9780199791286–0161.xml (accessed September 2020). DOI: 10.1093/OBO/9780199791286–0161.
32 John K. Cooley, 'China and the Palestinians', *Journal of Palestine Studies* 1:2 (1972), 19–34, www.jstor.org/stable/2535952.
33 Evyn Le Espiritu, 'Cold War Entanglements, Third World Solidarities: Vietnam and Palestine, 1967–75', *Canadian Review of American Studies/Revue Canadienne d'études Americaines* (2018). Advance online article doi: 10.3138/cras.2018.004.
34 Ibrahim Abu-Lughod, 'Altered Realities: The Palestinians since 1967', *International Journal: The Arab States and Israel* 28:4 (1973), 663.
35 Nate Rabe, 'Sound of Lollywood: In Pakistan's Version of "Lawrence of Arabia", A Stirring Lament for Love', Scroll.in, 5 August 2017, https://scroll.in/reel/846182/sound-of-lollywood-in-pakistans-version-of-lawrence-of-arabia-a-stirring-lament-for-love.
36 Nihash interview, 4 September 2020.
37 The story of Djamila Bouhired was perhaps most famously depicted in *The Battle of Algiers* (1966) by Italian filmmaker Gillo Pontecorvo.
38 Bhaskar Sarkar, 'Epic Melodrama, or Cine-Maps of the Global South', in Robert Burgoyne (ed.), *The Epic Film in World Film Culture* (New York: Routledge, 2011), p. 264.
39 Nihash interview, 4 September 2020.
40 Sean Carter and Klaus Dodds, *International Politics and Film: Space, Vision, Power* (New York: Wallflower Press, 2014), pp. 2–4.
41 Ibid., p. 5.
42 Zeina Maasri, *Cosmopolitan Radicalism: The Visual Politics of Beirut's Global Sixties* (Cambridge: Cambridge University Press, 2020), p. 16.
43 Ibid., p. 216.
44 For more insight on the tensions in representations of Jewish identity in the film see Petiwala, 'Falasteen Ka Matlab Kya?', 93–5.
45 '*Nawbat yahan tak pahonch gayi hai kya yahoudioun kay lagay vay aag kay sholay Zerqa kay ghungat tak pohanch chukay hain.*'
46 Asdar Ali, Kamran, 'Cinema and the City: The Ayub Years', in Ali Khan and Ahmed Ali Nobil, *Cinema and Society: Film and Social Change in Pakistan* (Karachi: Oxford University Press, 2016), p. 101.
47 Ibid.
48 Jaza Akil, 'Sproj Essay on *Zerqa* 1969' (2017), unpublished undergraduate essay written by one of my former students at the Lahore University of Management Sciences.
49 Dabashi in *Cinema and Society* (2016), pp. xi–xii.
50 Not her real name.

13

The long sixties and Islamist activism: radical transregional solidarities

Claudia Derichs

Introduction

In Southeast Asia, 'purifying' Islamist resurgence movements were particularly strong on university campuses in the 1970s and 1980s. Gradually, their demands gained traction in society and politics, but these movements did not appear out of the blue. Their emergence can be traced back to, and rests upon, organisational structures that were developed in the decades before, and which crossed national borders and regional zones. This is why we can indeed speak of a 'long sixties' with regard to the transformative power of religious activism in many parts of what is usually called the Muslim world. A couple of questions merit attention in this regard. What role did political Islam play in transnational and transregional activism of the 1960s and 1970s? And, in conceptual and theoretical terms, can social movement theory gain from a consequent inclusion of faith-based political movements into the narrative of radical movements of the long sixties?

This chapter seeks to explore these questions and takes transnational and transregional Islamist solidarity in Indonesia as a case in point. The first part of the text addresses the shifts in social science analyses from the 'secularization thesis' to the inclusion of 'religious actors', and the reflection of this shift in social movement theory. In the empirical part, I zoom in on Indonesia, the nation-state with the highest number of Muslim citizens on the globe. While the status of being the biggest Muslim state is a legitimating factor in itself for giving Indonesia a closer look, there is another reason which renders the country a 'must' in the research on Third World solidarity and anticolonialism: the active promotion of

Afro-Asian solidarity and the anti-communist massacres of 1965. The legacy of the latter formed the basis for Middle East-Asian Islamic cooperation in the subsequent decades. Taking Indonesia as a vantage point for tracing transnational and transregional Islamist movements in general and radical Islamic activism in particular provides insights into a perspective that demonised communism while promoting a vision of world politics that was not dominated by the (allegedly secular) West.

The foundation for effective, religiously framed, transregional (Middle East-Asia-Africa) resource mobilisation was laid in the 1960s and 1970s, particularly through non-state activism. While the power of religious non-state activism to topple a dictatorship was most clearly illustrated by the Iranian revolution of 1979, Egypt presented an effective export model as well: the Muslim Brotherhood.[1] Indonesian Islamist activists were significantly inspired by the Brotherhood's thinkers and their organisational capacities. There was state activism as well. Saudi Arabia sponsored the World Muslim League/Islamic World League,[2] which 'went to work against the growth of secularism and socialism'.[3] In doing so, Saudi Arabian state politics – presumably inadvertently – facilitated non-state actors' solidarity against oppressive regimes in other countries.

The role of Islam and the connectivity of Muslim activists across nations and regions invites a long durée perspective on the rise of political Islam in the long sixties. This resonates with critical studies that encourage us to rethink the historicisation of political Islam as a concurrent phenomenon in the wake of a failure of Arab nationalism.[4] Moreover, it cautions against notions of a globally coherent 'Islamist conspiracy' against a common enemy and instead recommends acknowledging the diversity of Islamist articulations and activist currents.[5]

Religious activism in social movement theory

For a long time, religious actors received marginal if any attention in the social sciences as agents of political change. On a conceptual level, the 'secularisation paradigm' was a major cause for neglecting the agency of religious actors in politics. It was not until the 1980s and the so-called 'religious turn' – one among admittedly many turns that we find in the social sciences and the humanities – that scholars' attention shifted. The secularisation thesis[6] claimed considerable clout in academic discourse and matched the 'classical' version of modernisation theory. Peter Berger's *Sacred Canopy* (1967)[7] counts as a standard in this regard, claiming that religion's retreat into the private sphere and hence its disappearance from the public realm was a global trait accompanying societies' modernisation. By relegating piety, religious principles and practices, religious authority and belief in God to the private sphere, religion adopted an aura of tradition (as, in this logic, opposed to modernity) and non-rationality (rational choice being a paradigm in social theory). Religion and religious actors were out of fashion as an analytical category in political science. Social movement theorists in Europe and the USA followed suit, preferring to study secular 'new social movements'[8] and post-materialism.[9] Apart for a few selected groups, such as black churches in the civil rights movement of the USA,[10] faith-based activism did not attract much attention from social movement scholars. Scholarship on religiously-inclined protest movements with a political agenda for change was remarkably limited in relation to that found on environmental, women's or peace movements. Moreover, the prominent Western theoretical approaches for analysing social movements almost exclusively focused on the national level[11] – often from a comparative perspective, but not from a transnational one.[12] On an empirical level, however, cross-border activism flourished, Muslim activism being a case in point.

A move in social theory towards stronger acknowledgement of religious actors occurred when the explicit critique of the Eurocentrism inherent in the secularisation thesis led to calls for a reassessment of the role of religion and religious actors in society and politics.[13] Political developments beyond the West underscored the relevance of religion for the mobilisation of political activism, culminating, in a way, in the Iranian revolution and subsequent establishment of the Islamic Republic of Iran in 1979. Apart from its global effect on the conception and study of faith-based political mobilisation, the events in Iran set in motion a huge wave of intra-Islamic conversion from Sunnism to Shi'ism. Southeast Asia was no exception in this regard,[14] proving the transnational and transregional mobilising power of Islam. The impact of the Iranian revolution is also remarkable in view of the intellectual currents that emphasised Islamic socialism and what is called left Islamic thinking – the Iranian-born scholar Ali Shariati (1933–77) being one of the prominent figures of this school of thought.[15] Underground activism too brought Islamic and left groups into contact. For example, the Japanese Red Army (JRA), an organisation known for its close cooperation with the Popular Front for the Liberation of Palestine (PFLP) in the struggle for Palestinian liberation, had at least indirect relations with Islamic groups.

These occasions hinted at the social, cultural and, last but not least, political function of religion and religious identity. Faith-based political mobilisation across borders was – and in some cases continues to be – an important means for organising protest and opposition towards authoritarian regimes on the national level. Religion and politics are not separated ontological entities but facets of complex relationships and, at times, geographies of belonging that escape the binary container categories of left and right or secular and religious. Transnational and transregional Islamist connectivities, as discussed below, underscore this finding. Against this backdrop, it is surprising that cross-border advocacy networks and the 'boomerang pattern' surfaced as important concepts in social movement theory only in the 1990s.[16]

In addition to the distinction between state and non-state Islamism, the one between statist and non-statist Islamism[17] is useful in analysing the spectrum of activism considered here. Islamist political parties in Pakistan (statist actors), for instance, aspire to power within the limits of the nation-state, whereas militant Islamist groups in the same country frame their goals and aspirations in settings that go beyond the nation-state (non-statist) – orientating towards a Muslim *umma*. Both are groups of activists within a religiously defined nation-state that has its religious bureaucracy, institutions and (non-violent) civil society organisations. But following Volpi and Stein, the former are statist and the latter non-statist Islamist actors, each striving for power yet on different scales. Islamist activism then is heterogeneous, as the case of Indonesia shows, too. The Islamist political party Masyumi (see below) has been a statist actor at times and at others, when banned, a non-statist Islamist actor. Its trajectory shows similar traits to what Volpi and Stein describe for the Muslim Brotherhood, that is, 'modalities of Islamist activism do not always correspond neatly to divisions between groups but can coexist within the same organization'.[18] What statist and non-statist actors of these kinds share is a religiously related identity and the stressing of this feature as an important marker and source of inspiration.

Yet in terms of terminology, there is an 'apparent difficulty in delineating the Islamist factor' and in 'identifying and explaining political Islam/Islamism'.[19] The same goes for 'Muslim'/'Islamic' as terms of choice. In the following, I use the term 'Islamism' for an ideology-political movement mobilising around Islam, and 'Islamist' in order to refer to actors within that ideology (thereby following Volpi and Stein). 'Islamic' inherently hints at the dichotomy between religious and secular – which I try to relativise – whereas 'Muslim' refers to contexts in which individuals find themselves, that is, to a certain situatedness that is dynamic and open for change, and often unrelated to the binary of religious and secular.[20] Yet the distinction is more of an analytical nature and does not reflect strict segregations in lived reality.

From Bandung to the crocodile hole

In the introduction to their book *1968 in Retrospect*, Gurminder K. Bhambra and Ipek Demir remind the reader of a vital task:

> Acknowledging the significance of '1968', then, is also to acknowledge the significance of a world structured around the dominance of the West and Western narratives. Seeing 1968 as a key moment in the history and narratives of freedom and protest is at once to privilege the actions of particular actors while also further silencing those actors and activities that are not (yet) recognized as 'world historical'.[21]

Consequently, the authors in the 2009 volume consider less visible actors and topics – Algerian immigrants in France, transgender and gay-lesbian debates, African American students and so on. Yet they nonetheless operate in a certain secular and dichotomous ideological terrain. The political Left of the 1960s is juxtaposed against 'the rise of the new right in the 1970s and 1980s'.[22] While this is no doubt a legitimate lens to look through, we may ask who else could be inspected as 'actors and activities not (yet) recognized as world historical'? Shifting our gaze towards Indonesia may serve as an entry point for the identification of such actors and activities. In doing so, I want to highlight two events that occurred in Indonesia in 1965, both of which, astonishingly, have received relatively little attention in research on transnational or international solidarity in the sixties. One is the genocide in Indonesia that erupted in October 1965, which engendered a spiral of violence in the following months and years, and is connected to a physical site called 'the crocodile hole'. The other is an event preceding this, namely the first Asia-Africa Islamic Conference (KIAA, Konferensi Islam Afrika-Asia) that took place in Bandung in March 1965, that symbolically illustrates Afro-Asian solidarity on the basis of a shared faith.

It is puzzling why Indonesia's anti-communist purge in 1965, which even at a conservative estimate caused the death of half a million people and has been described as a genocide,[23] drew so little international attention. Where was the international solidarity with the hundreds of thousands of victims, which one would have expected to be articulated in a similar manner as the solidarity with the victims of the Vietnam War? After all, the massacres happened in a country not too far away, geographically, from Vietnam, and in a period of time when political actors globally were alert towards anti-left violence and repression. In Japan, where the movement for peace in Vietnam made headlines in the middle of the sixties, Indonesia seemed to be overlooked.[24] In Western activist circles, where campaigns appealed to a strong Tricontinental solidarity the Indonesian genocide did not trigger as much activity as the Vietnam killings did. Martin van Bruinessen, who was at that time not yet engaged in Indonesian studies but alert to the politics of the era, mentions an Indonesia solidarity committee in the Netherlands that published a newsletter and organised protests. But aside from such comparatively tiny initiatives, the general public seemed to be quite unaware of what was going on in Indonesia.[25] Van Bruinessen recalls that only later 'we learned of the mass killings' and of how students had been used in 'a bloody struggle for power'.[26] As Tariq Ali observed:

> The news from the killing fields in Sumatra and Java revealed that the scale of the butchery was on a much larger scale than Shanghai 1927, but nothing moved in the capital cities of the West. The Generals in

Indonesia had, you see, succeeded in wiping out the communists ... the success was applauded in secret and many Pentagon strategists asked in public why what was possible in Jakarta was difficult in Saigon.[27]

Admittedly, the New Left in the West did not particularly appreciate then-President Sukarno's administration in Indonesia (Tariq Ali has a biting anecdote on Sukarno's machismo).[28] Sukarno's affinity to the Indonesian Communist Party (PKI) counted as somehow 'left', but not very progressive. Activists of the New Left by definition distinguished themselves from the 'old' Left, that is, usually the established communist parties on the national level. But this appears insufficient to explain the paucity of international protest. Apart from the fact that the USA's Central Intelligence Agency lent considerable support to the mass murder in Indonesia (as has become increasingly apparent with the de-classification of official documents), it remains surprising how little international condemnation there was of these massacres. Soe Tjen Marching, who collected a number of accounts of first, second and third generation victims of 1965, says 'the support of the American government was crucial to the success of the genocide, as it was able not only to justify but also to legitimate the genocide via several channels'.[29] The lack of voices of international solidarity thus poses a conundrum.

In Indonesia itself, the propaganda machinery of Sukarno's successor Suharto, the instilling of fear, and the portrayal of this brutality as a protective strategy against the evil of communism merged perfectly with the framing of communism as an atheist ideology: 'The categories "communist" and "atheist" became synonymous, and both groups were seen as betraying Pancasila,[30] Indonesia's five founding principles.'[31] What is *not* surprising then is that in a country with close to 90 per cent of the population associating with Islam as their religion (and another close to 10 per cent with other religions),[32] eradicating atheism became a service to the nation. The framing of atheism as 'anti-national' and as a threat to religion in general and Islam in particular became a persistent thread. Hence the biggest Islamic mass organisation Nahdlatul Ulama (NU) and its youth organisation Ansor actively engaged in the hunt and murder of (alleged) communists.[33] Without this kind of 'assistance', the army would not have been able to kill so many people in such a short time. In one of the most valuable

English-language publications on the propaganda of Suharto's long-lasting post-1965 administration (1965–98), Saskia Wieringa and Nursyahbani Katjasungkana relate the growth of Islamism in contemporary Indonesia to the events of 1965:

> Muslim groups, which had been helping the army to massacre hundreds of thousands of alleged communists, were shoved aside after 1965; they are now asserting their influence, calling for a hegemonic Sharia state. The Islamists, spearheaded by the aggressive Muslim militia *Front Pembela Islam* (FPI – Islam Defenders' Front), are able to organize huge street demonstrations.[34]

Was the adversarial relationship of Islamist and communist groups an inevitable one? And how different was it from the adversarial relationship between established Communist Parties and the New Left in other countries? The reasoning that the 'purge' and the concurrent rise of Islamic activism occurred just because a political identity vacuum had to be filled is inadequate. Rather, it is worth looking for accounts that explain the ways in which an antagonism between Islam and communism was actively constructed. It is also important to examine the ensuing irreparable relationship between Islamic and communist political groups that culminated in the killings and subsequent demonisation of virtually anything that could be associated with 'the Left' in Indonesia's *'années 1965'*.[35]

The Bandung conference of 1955, convened by President Sukarno, was the beacon for a new era of Asian-African effort in overcoming subjugation, domination and exploitation of peoples and nations by colonialism.[36] It was also the prelude to the formation of the Non-Aligned Movement (NAM) in 1961. A significant element of transregional unity against imperialist overtures was shaped by the building of networks between Asian and African Muslim communities. The sense of belonging based on shared faith allowed for multiple forms of collective interest articulation. One telling example of such efforts was the Asia-Africa Islamic Conference (KIAA) in, once again, Bandung in March 1965. In contrast to the 1955 Bandung conference, there is little research on the KIAA in European languages. Choirotun Chisaan is among the few who examined the event for an edited volume in English[37] on world culture and 'being Indonesian' in the crucial postcolonial period of

1950 to 1965. Chisaan's chapter pays particular attention to Islamic art and culture organisations but concedes that, inevitably, cultural associations cannot be separated from political contexts and are hence meaningful for international politics as much as for cultural exchange.[38] In the context of the KIAA, one of the key Indonesian groups hosting the conference was the Association for Islamic Arts and Culture or HSBI. Formed in 1956, HSBI was close to the Islamist political party Masyumi, which I will turn to below. After the banning of Masyumi by Sukarno in 1960, HSBI attached itself to the government's Department of Religion. A second major player was the Institute of Indonesian Muslim Artists and Cultural Figures or LESBUMI. This group was part of NU (the organisation that, as mentioned above, became actively involved in the genocide). NU had helped to initiate the KIAA, apparently in an effort to 'counter the monopoly over the formation of international movements which hitherto had been exercised by the communists'.[39]

Organising a conference that was particularly devoted to the faith-related dimension of arts and culture meant, in political terms, that it ought to stress the relevance of the element of religion (*agama*) in Sukarno's triangular ideological formula NASAKOM (*nasionalisme* [nationalism], *agama* [religion], *komunisme* [communism]). According to Chisaan, 'the guiding principle was "religion", Islamic organizations with differing approaches found themselves coming together in political alliances that overrode the differences between them'.[40] Sukarno 'welcomed the combination of the three ideological streams of nationalism, Islam and Marxism as the basis for an effective weapon against neo-colonialism and imperialism',[41] but despite the president's efforts in this regard, communism continued to be identified as 'the principal enemy of Indonesian Islam' as it had been since 1948.[42]

The Islamic Asia-Africa conference was attended by delegates from thirty-three countries of the two continents.[43] The issue of transregional solidarity was high on the agenda:

> the political concepts that were intended to lay down the guiding principles of the main event, stating that 'the basis and aims of the KIAA are to intensify solidarity and cooperation among the umma in the Africa-Asia region in concrete and positive form and in accordance with the spirit of the Ten Bandung Principles'.[44]

Zuhri mentions that several resolutions of the conference stressed solidarity with the independence struggles of peoples in different parts of the world; particular commitment was declared to solidarity with the Palestinian people's fight for liberation.[45] Among the topics of discussion that Chisaan lists, a remarkable one is the commitment to promote the use of spoken Arabic with the aim to have one language symbolising the unity of the Muslim *umma* across regions.[46] Although it is a bit speculative to suggest a causal relation between the acquisition of Arabic for the said purpose, and the enhancement of student mobility from Indonesia to the Middle East by a leading Masyumi figure, one may recognise the important role of spoken as well as written Arabic for creating transnational and transregional unity in a diversity of national/ist struggles.

Despite the rivalry between communism and Islam, political Islamists in Indonesia made some attempts to find a temporary reconciliation between Islamic and leftist politics. Collaboration between Islamic and communist forces, however, was certainly not consolidated.[47] As for Masyumi, its comprehension of democracy excluded both communist leanings and radical Islamism. In the period of 1949 to 1963, armed groups fighting for an Islamic State in Indonesia were thus met with utter rejection by Masyumi (cf. JRA and Islamist groups in the 1970s, mentioned above). The party not only criticised domestic currents of a 'retrograde Islam', but also the Gulf monarchies whose leaders it 'considered as deplorable examples of backward Islamic government'.[48] Masyumi's pledge for parliamentary democracy resulted in a regional rebellion in 1957, which failed to bear fruit. Instead, the effect was a ban of Masyumi in 1960, accompanied by the arrest of its leaders. In its concerted efforts to oppose Sukarno's 'Guided Democracy'[49] and to establish a democratic Indonesian republic (a federal state), Masyumi naturally fell from Sukarno's grace.[50] It was not until 1998 – with the resignation of Sukarno's successor Suharto – that parliamentary democracy emerged again as an option for Indonesia, and with it the chance to revive Islamic party politics.

In view of transnational Islamic connectivity during the Sukarno era, the hopes of Indonesian Muslims that had been aroused with the Bandung conferences in 1955 and 1965 were dashed in just a few months. The anti-communist massacre of *enam puluh lima* ('65') put an end to anything that might have been associated with

NASAKOM, including politico-religious cooperation. The spirit of Afro-Asian solidarity which was ignited in Bandung in 1955 and expanded, as Reem Abou-El-Fadl examines meticulously, through the Cairo Conference of 1957, did not leave a significant footprint in post-1965 Indonesia.[51] Although the KIAA had the potential to carry the Afro-Asian spirit further on an explicitly Islamic platform, the connecting threads were mostly cut under Suharto. The genocide of 1965, evoked by the term 'crocodile hole',[52] overshadowed all Bandung-inspired achievements and destroyed any chance of developing or reigniting a New Left activism in Indonesia. If it were not too cruel a metaphor, we might say in Indonesia, the spirit of Bandung ended in a crocodile pit – except, perhaps, for the branch of transnational/transregional Islamic political activism and solidarity.

Post-1965 political Islam

When the genocide of 1965 received support by many a devout Muslim in Indonesia, one might speculate that Masyumi members would have become rehabilitated and their efforts vindicated by the New Order regime of Suharto. But to the contrary, the forces of political Islam were not even recognised as allies in the creation of the demonising image of a 'communist threat'. Suharto decided that Islam had to be depoliticised, that is, a 'cultural Islam' was tolerated, but potentially influential Islamic political parties had to be constrained. The leaders of Masyumi, although released from prison, were not allowed to return to political activism. Supporters of the party hence reorganised in various shapes – engendering another transformation of Masyumi.[53] Aside from the former Masyumi affiliates, the violent Islamic groups of Sukarno's time had to find breakout spaces for their members. Here, the Darul Islam (DI) movement became highly active, both nationally and transnationally. The two currents became closer to each other in the years to come. On the one hand, a circle around former Masyumi leader Mohammad Natsir founded the Indonesian Council for Islamic Propagation (DDII) in 1967. DDII's propagation activities were legal and could be carried out publicly. On the other hand, the radical militant groups (Darul Islam being one of the most prominent) adopted semi-legal forms of organisation and activism while also conducting missionary and dissemination activities. DI and DDII faced the same 'enemy' – Suharto. Van Bruinessen points out that an increasing orientation towards the Middle East in general and Saudi Arabia in particular came along with the new organisational shape of former Masyumi:

> The DDII established close relations with the Islamic World League (Rabitat al-'Alam al-Islami, established in 1962), of which Natsir became one of the Vice Chairmen. It became the Saudi's preferred channel when they began using their oil wealth to finance the spread of conservative and puritan brands of Islamic teaching.[54]

Mohammad Natsir utilised his international contacts to build bridges between the Middle East and Southeast Asia. This move was nurtured by an increasing number of Indonesian students studying at Middle Eastern (and particularly Saudi Arabian) universities.[55] Indonesian-Malaysian connections worked well, too. Malaysia's greater tolerance for political Islamic activism allowed for the establishment of pathways for the transit of Arabic scripts from the Middle East into Indonesia. For those operating semi-underground in Indonesia, Natsir's Islamic diplomacy enabled the purchase of writings from Egypt's Muslim Brotherhood (MB). After returning from their study abroad, students were able to translate the works of Sayyid Qutb[56] and other prominent MB figures into Indonesian – making access to this literature possible for hundreds of fellow students in the country. Machmudi, however, notes that it is not clear when exactly DDII activists made their initial contacts with the Muslim Brothers. These connections could well have occurred before 1960, since several Masyumi leaders had studied in Cairo by then.[57] The writings were studied in small groups called *usroh*, which is the Indonesian reading of the Arabic term *usra* (family). As an activist interviewed by Elizabeth Fuller Collings relates:

> I myself started the first *usroh* in Salman Mosque, maybe the first *usroh* in Indonesia. I was sent to Malaysia by Imaduddin, where I found books by the Muslim Brothers. I brought them back and started translating them into Indonesian. This was in 1976–1977. It was a dangerous time to do *dakhwah*. I would translate a few pages, and they would be copied and passed around. We studied these in our *usroh*.[58]

The preaching and propagation activities of DI and DDII, called *dakwah* in Indonesian language (*da'wa* in Arabic), transformed to become a crucial tool for political Islamic mobilisation in the decades to come. Underground forms of organisation, utilised in global protest activism in the post-'68 period (that is, when the peak of significant student power movements and street fighting declined and smaller activist circles flourished – cadre groups like the German 'K-Gruppen' or *tôha* ['party factions', often called 'sects'] of the New Left in Japan being cases in point) increased. In Indonesia, small circles of activists scattered across the archipelago were organised in mosques and Islamic boarding schools (*pesantren*). Under military rule – Suharto being a high-ranking army general before his seizure of presidential power – those were the only spaces left in which political opposition could be organised and articulated. In the 1980s, students' study circles on campuses provided a major recruiting ground for Islamist activist networking.[59]

Although the first decade of the New Order regime looked bleak for political Islam,[60] the struggle was never put to rest. Even though leading activists had been imprisoned, the *usroh* system and the networks built up through *pesantren* across the country provided a stable basis for expanding the movement. Clandestine activities maintained a sense of resistance, and various networks paved the way for future mobilisation. The circles and networks in mosques and *pesantren* were indeed what social movement theorists call resources for the mobilisation of a bigger force – organisational platforms that can be mobilised when the political opportunity to do so arises.[61]

Individual activists sustained by the transnational connections that had been developed before the genocide resumed their networking efforts in the late 1970s. The rhetorical framing however was no longer that of Afro-Asian solidarity. The envisaged goals were the establishment of an Islamic state – a prime concern particularly after the Iranian revolution[62] – and the implementation of *shari'a* laws. For this purpose, linking up with fellow activists abroad was a natural endeavour. Initiating such cooperation very much depended on individual efforts. Moreover, it was difficult for Indonesian students to meet Brotherhood members in Egypt, since their operations were suppressed there. Given this, contacts largely occurred in Saudi Arabia.[63] Saudi Arabia and Malaysia both became important transit sites for Indonesian activists. Describing a wave of violent incidents carried out by militant DI groups in the 1980s, van Bruinessen points to the relevance of activists' transnational and transregional connections, enabled by transit via Malaysia: 'From Malaysia, dozens and possibly hundreds or even thousands of Indonesians travelled to Pakistan and Afghanistan, in order to engage in jihad and receive guerrilla training.'[64]

Conclusion

I began by asking what role religion played in transnational and transregional political activism of the 1960s and 1970s, and if social movement theory might gain from a consequent inclusion of transnational/transregional Islamic movements of the long sixties. The Indonesian trajectory of transnational and transregional Muslim solidarity shows that not only was religion (and especially Islam) a crucial mobilising factor for state-sponsored Afro-Asian solidarity in the 1950s and 1960s, but also for the anti-authoritarian struggle of Middle Eastern and Asian people in the 1970s and 1980s. A state's stance towards faith-based political activism may change according to regime preferences and conditions dictated by inter-governmental relations and global power politics. The political opportunity structures for faith-based opposition movements – statist and non-statist alike – no doubt depend on the liberties and repressions the state grants and exerts. Regardless of how open or closed the windows of opportunity are, however, faith-based affiliation and the sense of belonging to a community that shares particular concerns facilitates movement actors' resource mobilisation. Rooted in the belief in a religiously defined cosmos, the feeling of belonging, the sharing of a similar fate or the determination to act in solidarity for the sake of a particular cause are resources that can be mobilised for collective political action. Quite in contrast to the long-held 'secularization thesis' that relegated religion to the private realm, religion was and is political – in the same way as feminists in the 1970s stressed that the personal is political (the slogan of 1970s feminist movements). The long sixties were hence a period in which the demarcations between the religious and the secular became blurred (Muslim communists; Islamic Left) as well as juxtaposed (Islam versus communism), and in which formations surfaced that can well be captured by the concept of 'transnational advocacy networks'.[65] 'Islamism's oldest movement',[66] the Muslim Brotherhood, appealed to activists well beyond Egypt. In Indonesia under Suharto, the MB-inspired transregional solidarity served as a supplement for the waning Afro-Asian solidarity of Sukarno's times. It is this feature of transnational and transregional activism that appears to be most valuable for reviewing the main works on (Western) social movement theory of the latter part of the twentieth century. The relatively late attention and conceptualisation of the transnational in this current of theory seems to be related to a considerable neglect of religion as a resource for transnational and transregional mobilisation.

Notes

1 The Muslim Brotherhood is an organisation that was founded in 1928 by Hassan al-Banna in Egypt. It grew over the decades and formed a huge transnational movement. In the latter half of the twentieth century, the Muslim Brotherhood gained particular political mileage, although its activities in Egypt were oppressed by the government most of the time. In the West, the movement is predominantly seen as a radical Islamist organisation. For a detailed account of the genesis and unfolding of the Muslim Brotherhood see G. Kepel, *Muslim Extremism in Egypt: The Prophet and Pharaoh* (Berkeley: University of California Press, 2003); C. R. Wickham, *The Muslim Brotherhood: Evolution of an Islamist Movement-Updated Edition* (Princeton: Princeton University Press, 2nd ed., 2015).
2 The translation of the Arabic term *rabitat al-alam al-Islami* varies. A literal translation suggests Islamic World League, but the literature also has Muslim World League (e.g. in V. Prashad, *The Darker Nations: A People's History of the Third World.* (New York: The New Press, 2007). See also my remark on terminology in this text.
3 Prashad, *The Darker Nations*, p. 270.
4 Cf. S. Haugbolle, 'The New Arab Left and 1967', *British Journal of Middle Eastern Studies* 44:4 (2017), 497–512.
5 Cf. J. O. Voll, 'Relations Among Islamist Groups', in J. L. Esposito (ed.), *Political Islam: Revolution, Radicalism, or Reform.* (London: Lynne Rienner Publishers, 1997); F. Volpi and E. Stein, 'Islamism and the State After the Arab Uprisings: Between People Power and State Power', *Democratization* 22:2 (2015), 273–93.

6 K. Dobbelaere, *Secularization: An Analysis at Three Levels* (Brussels: P.I.E. Peter Lang, 2002).
7 See P. L. Berger, *The Sacred Canopy: Elements of a Sociological Theory of Religion* (New York: Random House, 1967).
8 Alberto Melucci, 'The New Social Movements: A Theoretical Approach', *Information (International Social Science Council)* 19:2 (1980), 199–226.
9 R. Inglehart, *The Silent Revolution: Changing Values and Political Styles Among Western Publics* (Princeton: Princeton University Press, 1977); R. Inglehart, 'Post-Materialism in an Environment of Insecurity', *The American Political Science Review* 75:4 (1981), 880–900.
10 D. McAdam, 'The Framing Function of Movement Tactics: Strategic Dramaturgy in the American Civil Rights Movement', in D. McAdam, J. D. McCarthy and M. N. Zald (eds), *Comparative Perspectives on Social Movements* (New York: Cambridge University Press, 1996).
11 Cf. D. McAdam, John McCarthy and Mayer N. Zald (eds), *Comparative Perspectives on Social Movements* (New York: Cambridge University Press, 1996).
12 For a more detailed tracing of the development of Western social movement theory see C. Derichs, *Japans Neue Linke. Soziale Bewegung und außerparlamentarische Opposition, 1957–1994* [Japan's New Left. Social Movement and Extra-Parliamentary Opposition, 1957–1994] (Hamburg: OAG, 1995). Another important aspect to ponder is the lack of historical enquiry or engagement in historical accounts of social and political movements of the past. Historians have addressed transnational Islamic activism of the nineteenth century. This seems to be a disciplinary blind spot as much as a Western epistemological one. (Author's communication with Zeina Maasri, 19 January 2021.)
13 G. E. Lenski, *The Religious Factor: A Sociological Study of Religion's Impact on Politics, Economics, and Family Life* (Garden City: Doubleday, 1961); David Martin (1965), 'Towards Eliminating the Concept of Secularization', in J. Gould (ed.), *Penguin Survey of the Social Sciences* (Baltimore: Penguin Books, 1965).
14 M. Van Bruinessen, 'Genealogies of Islamic Radicalism in post-Suharto Indonesia', *Southeast Asia Research* 10:2 (2002), 131.
15 The Syrian branch of the Muslim Brotherhood was engaged in the project of Islamic socialism. For more details see J. Teitelbaum, 'The Muslim Brotherhood in Syria, 1945–1958: Founding, Social Origins, Ideology', *The Middle East Journal* 65:2 (2011), 213–33. One of the books deriving from this current, *Islamic Socialism* by Mustafa al-Saba'i, was translated into Indonesian and became quite influential in Indonesian Muslim politics (Van Bruinessen, 'Genealogies of Islamic Radicalism in Post-Suharto Indonesia', 125).

16 M. E. Keck and K. Sikkink (1999), 'Transnational Advocacy Networks in International and Regional Politics', *International Social Science Journal* 51:159, 89–101. Transnational advocacy networks are 'actors working internationally on an issue, who are bound together by shared values, a common discourse, and dense exchanges of information and services' (ibid., p. 89). The 'boomerang pattern' of such networks emerges when activists establish international connections and allies to foster their concerns and thereby put pressure on their regimes at home (ibid., 93–4).
17 Volpi and Stein, 'Islamism and the State After the Arab Uprisings'.
18 Ibid., 277.
19 Ibid.
20 The literature on terminology and meaning of key terms such as Islam, political Islam, Muslim, Islamism, religion and secularism is rich. A deeper discussion and clear-cut definitions are left out here for the sake of the overarching argument. Yet the scholarship and the debates on these terms merit mention, not least because they rarely occupy centre stage in social movement theory. Among others: For a discussion of Islam and secularism see S. Zubaida, 'Islam and Secularization', *Asian Journal of Social Science* 33:3 (2005), 438–48; on Islam as discursive tradition see T. Asad, 'The Idea of an Anthropology of Islam', *Poznan Studies in the Philosophy of the Sciences and the Humanities* 48 (1996), 381–406; on Islamism and social movement theory, and the notion of 'non-movement' see A. Bayat (2005), 'Islamism and Social Movement Theory', *Third World Quarterly* 26:6 (2005), 891–908; for a thorough case study of revolutionary and post-revolutionary political Islamic thought see E. Sadeghi-Boroujerdi, *Revolution and Its Discontents: Political Thought and Reform in Iran*. Vol. 7. (Cambridge: Cambridge University Press, 2019); on the question of perception ('terrorism', 'Islamism') see the case study of the Lebanese Hezbollah by M. Harb and R. Leenders (2005), 'Know Thy Enemy: Hizbullah, "Terrorism" and the Politics of Perception', *Third World Quarterly* 26:1(2005), 173–97.
21 G. K. Bhambra and I. Demir (eds), *1968 in Retrospect: History, Theory, Alterity* (Basingstoke: Palgrave Macmillan, 2009), p. xiv.
22 Ibid., p. xii.
23 R. Cribb, 'Genocide in Indonesia, 1965–1966', *Journal of Genocide Research* 3:2 (2002), 219–39; S. T. Marching, *The End of Silence: Accounts of the 1965 Genocide in Indonesia*. With original photography by Angus Nicholls. (Amsterdam: Amsterdam University Press, 2017), pp. 20–5.
24 The Japanese movement is known by the acronym *Beheiren*, meaning 'Citizen's League for Peace in Vietnam' (Betonamu ni heiwa wo shimin

rengô), a comparatively loosely organised but impressive civil society force (1965 to 1974).
25 M. Van Bruinessen (2015), 'In the Tradition Or Outside? Reflections on Teachers and Influences', *Al-Jāmi'ah: Journal of Islamic Studies* 53:1 (2015), 62–3.
26 Ibid., 62.
27 T. Ali, *Street Fighting Years: An Autobiography of the Sixties.* (London: Verso, 2018 [2005]), p. 130.
28 Ali, *Street Fighting Years*, p. 128.
29 Marching, *The End of Silence*, p. 23.
30 Pancasila is also called the 'national ideology' of Indonesia. Its five principles are belief in God, humanism/internationalism, unity, democracy, and social justice.
31 Marching, *The End of Silence*, p. 27.
32 Number taken from CIA world factbook: 87.2 per cent Muslims, Protestant 7 per cent, Roman Catholic 2.9 per cent, Hindu 1.7 per cent, other 0.9 per cent (includes Buddhist and Confucian), unspecified 0.4 per cent. (www.cia.gov/the-world-factbook/countries/indonesia/#people-and-society, accessed 25 January 2021)
33 Cf. S. E. Wieringa and N. Katjasungkana, *Propaganda and the Genocide in Indonesia: Imagined Evil* (London: Routledge, 2019).
34 Ibid., p. 7.
35 I borrow here from G. Dreyfus-Armand et al. (eds), *Les années 68: Le Temps de la Contestation* (Brussels: Complexe, 2000), who reflect on 'les années 1968'.
36 See The Ministry of Foreign Affairs Republic of Indonesia (ed.), *Asia-Africa Speaks from Bandung.* (Jakarta: Ministry of Foreign Affairs, 1955). This compendium contains a number of speeches given at the conference, the final communique, and material on the participating delegations. The need for addressing the problems of dependent peoples and colonialism is spelled out explicitly in the final communique.
37 J. Lindsay and M. H. T. Liem (eds), *Heirs to World Culture: Being Indonesian 1950–1965* (Leiden: KITLV Press, 2012).
38 C. Chisaan (2012), 'In Search of an Indonesian Islamic Cultural Identity, 1956–1965', in J. Lindsay and M. H. T. Liem (eds), *Heirs to World Culture* (Leiden: KITLV Press, 2012).
39 S. Zuhri, *Sejarah kebangkitan Islam dan perkembangannya di Indonesia* [History of Islamic resurgence and Development in Indonesia]. (Bandung: al-Ma'arif, 1981), p. 654, cited in Chisaan, 'In Search of an Indonesian Islamic Cultural Identity', p. 289.
40 Ibid., p. 285.
41 Ibid., p. 287.

42 A. Feillard and R. Madinier, *The End of Innocence? Indonesian Islam and the Temptations of Radicalism* (Honolulu: University of Hawai'i Press, 2011), p. 19.
43 See Chisaan, 'In Search of an Indonesian Islamic Cultural Identity', p. 288 for a full list of participating countries.
44 Ibid., p. 289.
45 Zuhri, *Sejarah kebangkitan Islam dan perkembangannya di Indonesia*, 655, cited in Chisaan, 'In Search of an Indonesian Islamic Cultural Identity', p. 294.
46 Ibid., p. 295. Arabic is the language and script of the Quran; its use as an official language between non-Arabic speaking countries reaffirms a shared Muslim identity across regions.
47 A fact that should not be ignored here is that many communists in Indonesia were Muslims (see my remark on terminology in this text). The distinction made here between Islam and communism relates to the explicit commissioning of Islam for fostering anti-communist sentiments.
48 Feillard and Madinier, *The End of Innocence?*, p. 20. Van Bruinessen, sees Masyumi in the 1950s as 'much like a European social democratic party' because of its favour of Western ideas of democracy. 'Genealogies of Islamic Radicalism in Post- Suharto Indonesia', 121.
49 This opposition Masyumi to Guided Democracy was shared by the Indonesian Socialist Party.
50 Although not leading to a success, this rebellion is remarkable for the support it gained from the CIA (Van Bruinessen, 'Genealogies of Islamic Radicalism inPost-Suharto Indonesia', 122). The anti-communism of Masyumi in the 1950s was thus stronger than its anti-Americanism, which became a trait later.
51 R. Abou-El-Fadl, 'Building Egypt's Afro-Asian Hub: Infrastructures of Solidarity and the 1957 Cairo Conference', *Journal of World History*, 30:1 (2019), 157–92.
52 The 'crocodile hole' was a pit on the training ground of the Indonesian air force in a Southeastern suburb of Jakarta. It was the spot where the seven army members were killed on 30 September 1965 – the occasion triggering the genocide. See also S. Wieringa's novel *The Crocodile Hole* (Jakarta: Yayasan Jurnal Perempuan, 2015).
53 For a detailed account of Masyumi's transformations see Van Bruinessen, 'Genealogies of Islamic Radicalism in Post-Suharto Indonesia'.
54 Ibid., 123.
55 For numbers of student mobility to Middle Eastern universities see Y. Machmudi, *Islamising Indonesia: The Rise of Jemaah Tarbiyah and the Prosperous Justice Party (PKS)* (Canberra: ANU E Press, 2008),

p. 175. See also M. Abaza, *Indonesian Students in Cairo: Islamic Education, Perception and Exchanges* (Paris: Association Archipel, 1994), for a study of Indonesian students in Cairo.
56 Sayyid Qutb (1906–66) was an Egyptian journalist who became one of the most influential ideological leaders of the Muslim Brotherhood and their followers all over the world. He was hanged after being convicted of taking part in a conspiracy against then-President Gamal Abdul Nasser. Qutb's writings continue to influence Islamist formations around the globe.
57 Machmudi, *Islamising Indonesia*, p. 94.
58 H. Dipoyono, cited in E. Fuller Collins, *Indonesia Betrayed: How development Failed* (Honolulu: University of Hawai'i Press, 2007), p. 156. According to Van Bruinessen, the works of the following authors were particularly appreciated in Indonesia: 'Later al-Banna became the leading authority, along with the Pakistani Abu'l-A'la Mawdudi. Several of Sayyid Qutb's works were also translated, including *Ma'alim fi'l-tariq* (Signposts on the Road) but his more radical political ideas appear not to have made the impact in Indonesia that they made elsewhere. It was the non-revolutionary, Saudi-sponsored brand of Brotherhood materials that became most influential in former Masyumi circles in the 1980s and 1990s' (Van Bruinessen, 'Genealogies of Islamic Radicalism in Post-Suharto Indonesia', 125).
59 Cf. Machmudi, *Islamising Indonesia*.
60 On this and the subsequent decades of (militant) Muslim activism in Indonesia see Feillard and Madinier, *The End of Innocence?*, pp. 104–23.
61 J. D. McCarthy and M. N. Zald, 'Resource Mobilization and Social Movements: A Partial Theory', *American Journal of Sociology* 82:6 (1977), 1, 212–41. For resource mobilization, opportunity structures, and framing as analytical concepts in social movement theory see McAdam, McCarthy and Zald, *Comparative Perspectives on Social Movements*.
62 Volpi and Stein, 'Islamism and the State After the Arab Uprisings', 278.
63 Machmudi, *Islamising Indonesia*, 180. For examples of important individuals who served the transnational and transregional cooperation between Muslim activists in Indonesia and the Middle East see Machmudi, *Islamising Indonesia*, pp. 170–90.
64 Van Bruinessen,' Genealogies of Islamic Radicalism in Post-Suharto Indonesia', 130.
65 Keck and Sikkink, 'Transnational Advocacy Networks in International and Regional'.
66 Volpi and Stein, 'Islamism and the State After the Arab Uprisings', 280.

14

A Witness of Our Time (1972): drawings by Dia al-Azzawi

Selected and introduced by Zeina Maasri

Figures 14.1a–14k Artist's book by Dia al-Azzawi: *Shahid min hatha al'asr: yawmiyyat shaheed qutila fi majzarat al-urdun aylul 1970* (Baghdad: Iraqi Ministry of Information, 1972).

A Witness of Our Time: The Journal of a Fidayee Killed in the Jordan Massacre of 1970 is a bilingual book (Arabic and English), edited and illustrated by the Iraqi artist Dia al-Azzawi (b. 1939) with a translation into English by the renowned Palestinian-Iraqi novelist and literary critic Jabra Ibrahim Jabra (1919–94). It was published by the Iraqi Ministry of Information in 1972, in a print run of 5,000 copies. The book is based on the diary of a *fida'i* (guerrilla combatant) killed during the crackdown by the Jordanian Armed Forces against the Palestine Liberation Organization (PLO) in September 1970, referred to in Palestinian history as Black September.

Palestinian guerrilla warfare had been on the rise as a popular armed struggle against Israel, particularly in the aftermath of the devasting Arab-Israeli war in 1967. Precipitated by the success of the 'Battle of al-Karama' in 1968, a Palestinian anticolonial liberation movement was in full sway, spearheading an Arab revolutionary struggle and gaining others for its cause, both regionally concerning Palestine, and globally in countering the forces of imperialism. Its revolutionary momentum threatened the Jordanian monarchy of King Hussein, who proceeded violently to suppress the PLO in a military assault beginning on 16 September 1970 that targeted both Palestinian guerrilla bases and refugee camps in Jordan, resulting in the expulsion of thousands of refugees from the country and the relocation of the PLO to Lebanon. Black September dealt a major blow to the Palestinian liberation struggle; it was perceived as a harsh betrayal by a compliant Arab regime enacting imperialist and Israeli strategies to maintain its power. Nonetheless, the events galvanised international solidarity and gave further ideological impetus to a revolutionary Arab Left's rise at once against the repression of post-independence Arab states locally and against imperialism on the world stage.

Azzawi was among a number of Iraqi artists and intellectuals on the Left – mostly members of the Iraqi Communist Party, repressed with the coming to power of the Baath Party in 1963 – who were drawn to the Palestinian liberation movement. While some joined the ranks of the Palestinian guerrilla organisations, others, such as Azzawi, drew inspiration from its revolutionary promise to reconfigure art's radical political potential in the post-1967 Arab conjuncture. Centred on the figure of the *fida'i* as the new revolutionary Arab subject, *A Witness of Our Time* is one of Azzawi's earliest artworks in solidarity with the Palestinian cause. Several more followed it, and his artistic career came to be marked by a concern with the ongoing plight of Palestinians in the face of Israeli colonial occupation and further Arab betrayals.

The diary entries, attributed to a fallen combatant referred to by his *nom de guerre*, Bassem, relate the day-to-day brutality of the battle and siege of al-Hussein refugee camp, from 16 September until its seizure by the Jordanian Armed Forces on the 23rd.

Azzawi's drawings accompany the diary entries and fill the majority of the book's ninety-six pages, interspersed occasionally with press reports and revolutionary songs. The diary closes poetically with a peculiar posthumous entry headed 'a day after death', which raises a doubt in the reader about the authenticity of the actual diary and leaves open the possibility of its being a work of fiction. Azzawi claims that the original text was passed on to him by another Iraqi author, but does not deny that it might have been fictitious. But would it matter? Rather than a textual document acting as historical evidence, it is here the artist, by way of the imagined figure of the *fida'i*, who bears witness. *A Witness of Our Time* is neither material evidence in a court of law nor an ordinary document in the archive. It is an artistic expression of solidarity that invites another reading of history.

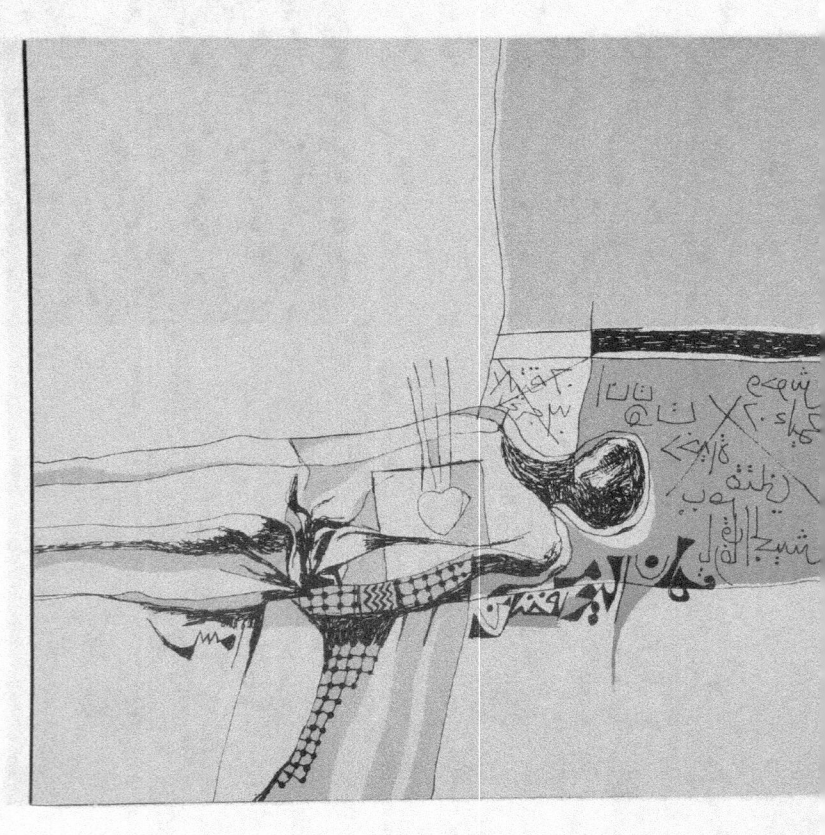

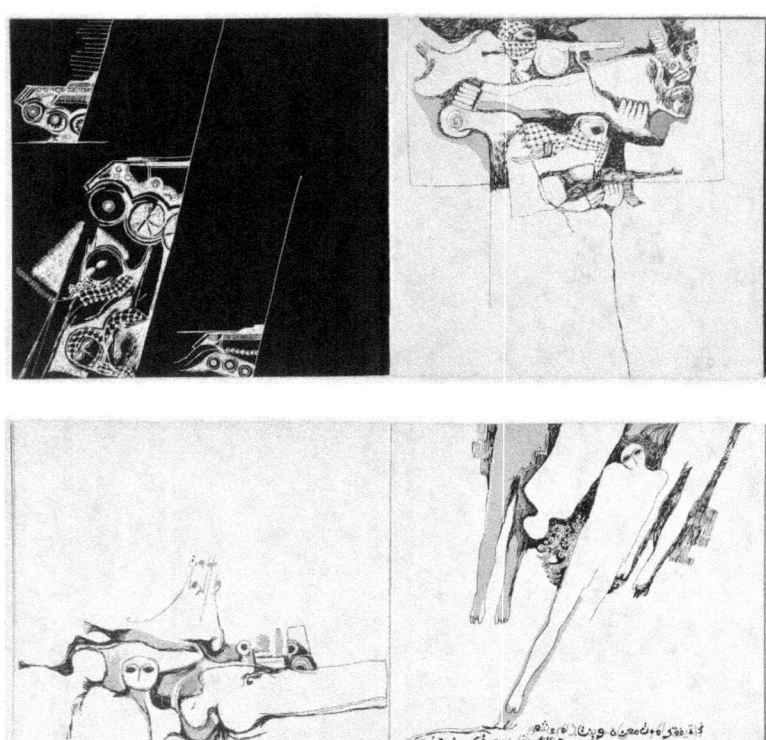

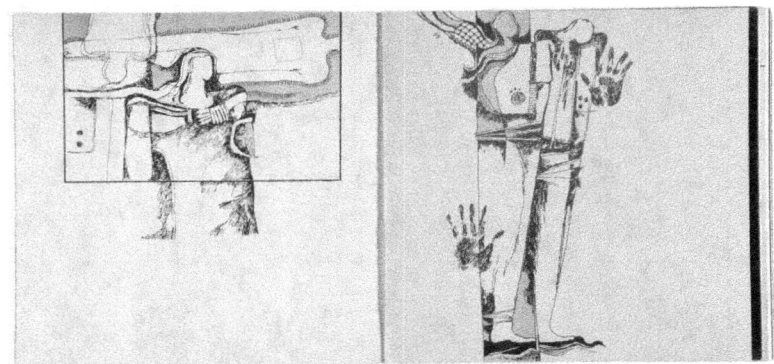

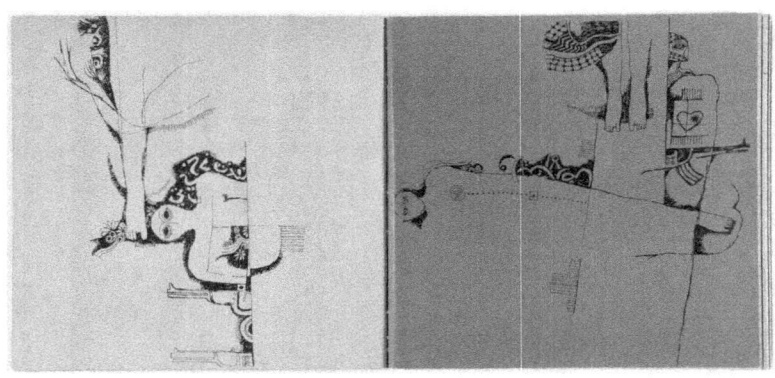
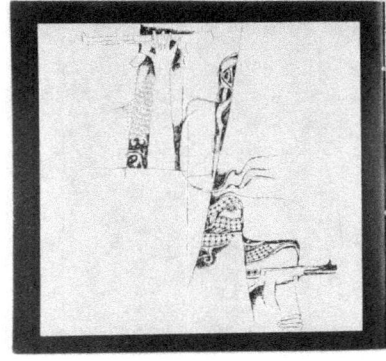

15

Greece in the Third World: solidarity through metonymy in a refugee magazine from the GDR

Mary Ikoniadou

Introduction

Soon after the Cuban Missile Crisis in 1962, the Greek author and translator Thomas Nicolaou met with Cuban revolutionary Miguel Marticorena at the International Students House on Lumumba Street in Leipzig, German Democratic Republic (GDR). His account of the meeting was published in *Pyrsos*, an illustrated magazine published by Greek political refugees in East Germany:

> The Americans interfere in Cuba because they fear the light of the Cuban revolution. But the socialist camp will always be on Cuba's side. Still, a war might break out … With these thoughts, I arrived at the International Students House on Lumumba Street … where I met 26-year-old Miguel. Miguel was very young when he joined the revolution and fought alongside Fidel Castro in Sierra Maestra. He was heavily injured, and he now receives medical treatment in the German Democratic Republic. … Goodbye, Miguel, our people understand the consequence of war, that's why we will always be by your side.[1]

In the text, 'our people' refers to the Greeks and, more specifically, the Greek political refugees in the GDR, who 'understood' the Cubans and what they had gone through, namely, the violent impact of US imperialism. Similar articles appeared regularly in *Pyrsos* magazine, often interweaving the lives and achievements of the Greek political refugees with reports from life in Greece and the Greek diaspora in the West, reports on international struggles and declarations of solidarity with the 'people who have liberated themselves' as well as with those who were 'fighting for their freedom,

Figure 15.1 *Pyrsos* magazine, front covers 1961–68.

for democracy and national independence, for peace'.² As *Pyrsos* characteristically writes in 1964:

> The history of the Greek peoples' liberation struggles is filled with hardship, tyranny, foreign plots, struggles and blood. In our time, it is edifying to see people around the world going through the same struggles, making similar sacrifices against the same tyrants, to abolish the shackles of foreign colonial domination.³

Pyrsos (translated in English as *Torch*) was a Greek-language illustrated magazine initiated by the exiled Communist Party of Greece and published bimonthly from 1961 to 1968 in the GDR. The magazine's high-quality production was supported by the GDR's Department of International Relations, 'in the spirit of solidarity'.⁴ *Pyrsos* was distributed to Greek political refugees in the Soviet Union and the Peoples' Democratic Republics in Eastern and Central Europe (with the exception of Yugoslavia), as well as to individuals and organisations of Greek economic migrants and students in the West (including most of Western Europe as well as Canada and Australia).⁵ The magazine's distribution across both sides of the Cold War does not only differentiate it from other Greek refugee publications but also discloses its editorial strategy and political aims: ultimately, to construct a collective national cultural subjectivity for its diverse readership of Greek émigrés in the 1960s.

This chapter examines *Pyrsos* illustrated magazine as a case study of the aesthetic and political articulations of solidarity with the so-called Third World in the 1960s.⁶ It draws on the specific cultural histories, an analysis of the magazine's corpus, alongside that of comparable periodicals, as well as unpublished archival material and interviews.⁷ The visual analysis pays particular attention to the relationship of images and texts in the design of the magazine and investigates the discourses produced out of their juxtaposition. As such, it involves what is stated, and that which is left unsaid. To this end, Bertolt Brecht's renderings of Marxist dialectics, his aesthetic theories and writings on the restructuring of juxtapositions as dissonances will constitute a central hermeneutic approach.⁸ It is in the productive relationship of the juxtaposition – in the magazine, that of text and images – that I determine the specific ways it constructs solidarity for its readership through metonymy. Such analysis of *Pyrsos* can speak to the distinctions between state and grassroots solidarity against the silenced and largely ignored history of socialist solidarity in the Eastern Bloc in the 1960s. In addition, *Pyrsos*' conditions of production by Greek political refugees and its circulation across Cold War borders unearths hidden histories from the margins. It highlights unusual affective and political connections during the Cold War and contributes to the de-centring of established, primarily Western, paradigms of solidarity in the 1960s.

In what follows, I initially examine the term Third World as a project in the 1960s. I then turn to the specific events that marked the political strategy of the Greek Left since the 1940s and, subsequently, the editorial and visual strategy of the magazine. Having established the concept of solidarity in *Pyrsos* and in state socialism, I focus on its manifestations in the GDR and address political publishing as a layer on top of the state's official solidarity discourse. The discussion of *Pyrsos*' complex editorial strategy leads to an analysis of spreads from the magazine that depict the Vietnam War. I conclude by suggesting that the magazine's articulations of solidarity through identification with Third World struggles derived from a desire for the restitution of the Greek Left and the democratisation of the country in the 1960s.

Third World solidarity

Political geographer David Featherstone defines solidarity as a relation produced through political struggle seeking to challenge forms of oppression.[9] Yet, forms of oppression are never alike or equal. Shared political spaces, connections and alliances are formed through multiple processes of exchange in the articulation and challenge of inequalities and injustices. Solidarity can also be construed and expressed through identification processes and by drawing parallels between politically, historically and aesthetically diverse struggles. As I argue, the political plea for the national liberation, sovereignty and democratisation of Greece in *Pyrsos* magazine drew parallels with the plea for the liberation and self-determination of the anticolonial, anti-imperialist and national liberation struggles in the so-called Third World.

Following Vijay Prashad, I do not construe the notion of the Third World as a place, but as a project; a project that in the 1960s comprised of hopes, dreams and desires for political equality on the world stage.[10] Moreover, as Cynthia Young convincingly argues, the term Third World stood 'as a placeholder, a contradictory edifice of ideas and concepts that expressed ... an "imagined relation"'.[11] Indeed, the term provided national minorities and oppressed people worldwide, such as the Greek political refugees, as well as the violently suppressed Left in Greece – in Young's words, those who 'were not juridically colonised' – with a language and a motivation to 'challenge their own forms of oppression'.[12] Young's study of the US Left's cultural, material and ideological links to the Third World is especially useful to my analysis since it enables the incorporation of Third World terminology as a model for the various distinctive 1960s struggles. Albeit radically, and primarily racially, different to the experience of the US Third World Left in the 1960s, the Greek political refugees, who had similarly been denied their citizenship rights,[13] perceived the USA's imperial cultural and economic interventions in Greece, as identical to the structures underpinning colonialism.[14] Comparable to Young's subject of study, the Greek Left, in exile and in Greece alike, articulated its affiliation with the Third World, and as such identified with a shared international consciousness and mode of transnational solidarity.[15]

In the wake of post-war decolonisation processes, European social movements became increasingly global in terms of their scope, networks and ideas. Historian Kostis Kornetis claims that the 1960s witnessed the collapse of national identities into international ones whereby various social and political movements of different origins and trajectories 'linked' through cultural transfers and shared common references.[16] The circulation of radical ideas and practices informed by the liberation of the Third World 'provided a revolutionary guide' and, it is significant to note here, the chance to consider anew the use of 'violence as a liberating force'.[17]

Print culture and periodicals in particular were very much the medium of the moment in the 1960s, critical in the dissemination of cultural and political ideas across transnational channels. The circulation of political publishing was further reinforced by the increased mobility of young people who were looking to work or study abroad, or both, and who acted 'as transmitters of local stimuli' carrying with them ideas and materials back to their home countries.[18] Yet, the role of political publishing in this period has been largely unexplored in the scholarship, especially with regard to the ways that illustrated magazines (re)produced particular effects on their readers. As my analysis of *Pyrsos* in this chapter demonstrates, articulations of solidarity between movements and struggles were also expressed through aesthetics, rendered visible in the visuality and intertextuality of magazines.

Greeks between the First and the Second Worlds

By the time *Pyrsos* magazine launched its first issue in 1961, the Greek political refugees had been living in what was meant to be a temporary exile for twelve years. Following the defeat of the communist-led Democratic Army of Greece in the Civil War (1946–49), the refugees were granted 'temporary' political asylum in the USSR and the peoples' republics until the political conditions would allow for their return to Greece. When the refugees fled the country, the Greek government issued a series of resolutions, confiscated their properties and stripped them of their citizenship rights, effectively depriving them of the prospect of repatriation, officially until 1982.[19]

Greece emerged from the Civil War completely transformed in every aspect of social and political life. Since the end of the Civil War, and until the dictatorship of the Colonels in 1967, the country experienced a long succession of right-wing, anti-communist governments that operated according to the doctrine of *ethnikofrosyni* (national-mindedness). *Ethnikofrosyni* was the official state doctrine of the victors of the Civil War, which, under the motto 'homeland – religion – and family', had infiltrated all aspects of social and political culture in Greece. The Greek state incorporated Western values, and market capitalism promoted a nationalist ideology and constructed an enemy that was both internal and external – along the lines of the United States' anti-communist Cold War ideology.[20] Additionally, it accused the Greek Left of the disastrous consequences of the Civil War and denied its participation in the 1940s resistance against the Axis occupation of Greece (1941–44).[21] The Greek state closely monitored the beliefs of all its citizens, excluded the Left from the ranks of public administration to keep it 'permanently out of the circle of power'.[22] The objective was to gradually shift the ideological conviction of the population away from the democratic ideas and revolutionary practices of the 1940s.[23] The Greek state continued to persecute its 'enemies', keeping many of them in prisons and exile islands until after the fall of the dictatorship of the Colonels.[24]

By the beginning of the 1960s, Greek public opinion was equating the USA's continuous involvement in the country's domestic politics to the Nazi occupation. In a similar manner, it was perceiving US foreign policy as that of a coloniser.[25] This was primarily a consequence of the United States' interference in the Cyprus issue against the country's right to self-determination. Hostility towards the US intensified when NATO military bases were installed on Greek soil at the beginning of the 1960s.[26]

The US administration's involvement in Greece had begun during the Greek Civil War following the withdrawal of British troops and the subsequent transfer of power.[27] In March of 1947, the implementation of the Truman Doctrine in Greece marked the country's position as a terrain where a conflict of powerful international interests played out. This was the first time that the United States interfered in the domestic politics of a foreign country in the context of the Cold War.[28] The result of the Greek Civil War was determined by US intelligence, military and financial aid to the Greek National Army, which ultimately overpowered the communist-led Democratic Army of Greece – a partisan army that, to a large extent, consisted of former resistance fighters.[29] The defeat of the Democratic Army in 1949 was secured by the US-supplied napalm bombs, the first ever use of napalm in warfare.[30]

The 1960s witnessed an increase of European human rights campaigns that demanded amnesty for the political prisoners and exiles in Greece, often going hand in hand with contemporaneous anti-American, anti-imperialist and nuclear disarmament movements. Historian Kim Christiaens claims that the published materials used by Western European campaigners that 'stimulated' an 'anticolonial reading' of the situation in Greece, were provided by groups of Greek political refugees, in addition to promoting the demands for amnesty and pledges for their repatriation.[31] Such campaigns drew parallels between Greece and the Third World in terms of 'backwardness and underdevelopment' and 'spoke of colonisation in Greece by referring to the involvement of the US government and [its] multinationals'.[32] The 1960s humanist, anticolonial and anti-imperialist rhetoric presented the Greek Left with the opportunity to align its cause with international movements. More importantly, it offered the possibility to rehabilitate its marginalised position in Greece and attempt to de-legitimise the Greek state's ideology.

The decision to publish *Pyrsos* magazine was inspired by the broader 1960s climate; it was in response to the political conditions in Greece and was encouraged by the resilience of the Left in the country, despite its violent repression by the state. Besides, it was in accordance with Khrushchev's de-Stalinisation and 'peaceful coexistence' rhetoric. At the end of the 1950s, the exiled Communist Party of Greece had radically shifted its political and cultural strategy from 'guns at the ready' to a collaboration with the Greek parliamentary Left (EDA) under a common strategy that aimed for: the legitimisation and legalisation of the Left in Greece; the recognition of its 1940s 'National Resistance'; amnesty to political prisoners; and the repatriation of the political refugees.[33]

Solidarity in *Pyrsos* and in state socialism

Pyrsos' rhetoric on solidarity with the people whose lives and struggles were dedicated to 'freedom, democracy, national independence and peace' aligned to its expressions in state socialism, and, more specifically, to its particular version in the GDR. Since the 1940s, the concept of solidarity in state socialism had evolved into an established official policy. Solidarity was orchestrated and supported by the regimes rather than led 'from below', as was usually the case with grassroots activists in the West.[34] Although the implementation of solidarity varied in each socialist state, its manifestations were 'inseparable' from the 'political, ideological, material and financial interests' of the state.[35]

Broadly speaking, histories of socialist solidarity have been at best ignored and largely erased. Recent scholarship, however, such as the work of ethnographer and postcolonial gender studies scholar Kristen Ghodsee and anthropologist Christina Schwenkel, demonstrates that socialist solidarity was not empty of meaningful political content.[36] For one, as Ghodsee demonstrates, solidarity between the Second and the Third Worlds provided the citizens of the Global South with strategic alliances that allowed them to amplify their collective voices on the international stage.[37]

The experiences of thousands of Eastern Europeans who engaged in transnational solidarity work were not merely distanced, sympathetic identifications but actually helped them to form deeply political, optimistic and future-oriented affective attachments.[38] Solidarity provided a process of politicisation by providing a progressive political space; a language of critique, which at times was employed to articulate their own domestic frustrations.[39] Expressions of solidarity often resonated as a requirement in the formation of links between citizens in the Eastern Bloc and countries in the Global South to resist what was perceived as American warmongering and imperialism.[40] Solidarity carried educational value, regularly targeted at youth, as well as directed westwards, asserting 'the moral higher ground of socialism' over 'capitalist, imperialist countries' that could not claim a similar commitment 'to peace and humanity'.[41] This was of particular importance in the GDR following the Hallstein doctrine and towards the state's efforts to achieve international recognition.[42]

In the GDR, international solidarity with those opposing imperialism was clearly articulated in the constitution and, as such, it was ingrained in the state's foreign policy and integral to its 'political identity and self-understanding'.[43] In his analysis of the GDR's manifestations of solidarity with the South West Africa People's Organisation (SWAPO), Toni Weis argues that solidarity put forward a clear identity in the state's anticolonial imaginary; it constituted a way to oppose the West's concept of 'development' and its 'neo-colonial' perspective; it helped promote a positive image at home and abroad, and to distinguish that image from the Federal Republic of Germany.[44]

GDR citizens engaged with the concept of solidarity in different ways. For the older generation of German communist resistance fighters who had fought national socialism, lived in exile, served in the Spanish Civil War, or often a combination of the above, solidarity was a meaningful concept.[45] Such a conception of solidarity was not only encouraged and promoted by the state but was also shared with a large number of state functionaries with similar experiences.

Likewise, for the older generation of Greek political refugees who had fought in the Second World War and the Greek Civil War in the 1940s, practices of everyday solidarity drew on memory and lived experience. Children and youth in the GDR, however, were educated into actively participating in the political life of the country. As such, especially for those who belonged to political organisations, support for solidarity movements was a requirement that regularly manifested 'through fund-raising campaigns and youth projects [that intended] to provide aid for Third World countries'.[46]

Solidarity initiatives generated high levels of enthusiasm in the GDR while solidarity events and bazaars were attended by tens of thousands.[47] Committees and associations were centralist structures with more-often-than-not underlying agendas, some of which I discussed above, such as: seeking diplomatic recognition; advocating state socialism; demonstrating 'socialist friendship'; and in some instances, promoting trade, since solidarity work also aimed to expand further the GDR's cultural, political and economic influence in the Global South. Cultural work that encompassed solidarity and anti-imperialism was manifested through committees and friendship associations based in the GDR as well as in Western, Non-Aligned and so-called Third World countries. Since the early 1950s, such organisations were set up in 'friendship' with/for the people of Asia, Africa and Latin America and expanded beyond, from the 1960s onwards. For instance, the Afro-Asian Solidarity Committee (AASK) had developed over the years as an anti-imperialist solidarity organisation while the fundamental task of the German-Latin American Society established in the 1960s was to expand the GDR's relations with movements in the continent, outside, or 'underneath', the level of government.[48] Besides, these associations were also expected to contribute to the state's efforts towards diplomatic recognition.

The case of the Greek refugees was distinctive in the GDR's official solidarity discourse. To begin with, the committee for the support of the Greek refugees was founded as early as 1948, a year before the establishment of the GDR. Some scholars claim that this policy was directly linked to the efforts of building a new nation-state and, as such, a new socio-political foundation within a unique cultural and national social frame.[49] By 1949, the East German state had received refugees – primarily unaccompanied children – under the responsibility of the People's Solidarity organisation and the Committee for a 'Free Greece'.⁵⁰ German scholar Stefan Troebst writes that the Greek Civil War was highly publicised in the Soviet-controlled German media and, for that reason, had gained considerable support from the East German public.⁵¹ Moreover, it is worth mentioning that the series of successful campaigns organised had not only mobilised acclaimed political and cultural personalities, such as the painter Willi Sitte, but also raised a considerable amount of money for the provision of houses, education and sustenance for Greek refugee children in the GDR.⁵²

Political publishing as a layer in the discourse of state solidarity in the GDR

Pyrsos was produced at the *Verlag Zeit im Bild* publishing house that specialised in the publication of foreign-language magazines and propaganda, intended for distribution abroad.⁵³ The *Verlag Zeit im Bild* was part of the GDR's foreign relations efforts and, as such, beyond promoting the state's agenda towards diplomatic recognition, it also advocated the export of East German goods and services to newly-founded nations and their developing market economies. By 1958, the publisher produced 'foreign magazines to reinforce the strong bonds of friendship and solidarity with the African and Arab nations struggling for their justified social liberation, also in terms of foreign propaganda, and to provide them with the valuable experiences of our progress'.⁵⁴ By 1965, the *Verlag Zeit im Bild*, in collaboration with the GDR's main organisation of International Friendship (LIGA), had produced four million copies of foreign-language titles that circulated in fifteen languages and were distributed to ninety-eight countries.⁵⁵ However, unlike the production of other foreign-language publications, *Pyrsos* was the only magazine edited by non-German staff. I argue that the magazine's distinctive visual language, modernist approach to design and progressive cultural politics were the outcomes of a series of factors and, most importantly, *Pyrsos*' editorial board which was comprised exclusively of Greek intellectuals.

The German technical staff and editors at the *Verlag Zeit im Bild* were not only ideologically supportive 'in the spirit of internationalist solidarity'; they encouraged the production of the magazine and had enabled its 'unhindered publication' by stepping in to cover rent and running costs when, because of its expenses, it was threatened with closure.[56] *Pyrsos*' high production values, large format, good-quality paper with several pages printed in full-colour (including glossy full-colour covers), and an eight-page full-colour supplement dedicated to children, were exceptional among the refugees' publications and when compared with similar East German illustrated magazines in the 1960s.

Images and texts: *Pyrsos*' editorial strategy as a political project

Pyrsos was a political project with multiple aims and a multifaceted, often ambivalent, editorial strategy. Over its pages, past and contemporary depictions of struggles in Greece were juxtaposed with the accomplishments of the young Greek political refugees, the technological advancements of socialism, the 1960s political mobilisation of youth and, as I examine here, anticolonial and liberation struggles in the Global South.[57] As I argue elsewhere, *Pyrsos* propagated the Greek Left's political plea for the sovereignty and democratisation of Greece and endeavoured to (re)imagine the nation, (re)claim its history and (re)position its role in the national narrative from which it had been violently excluded.[58] The magazine, as a political project, strove to construct a collective cultural subjectivity and communicate its aims through its editorial strategy.

Pyrsos' editorial strategy, and consequently its expression of solidarity, was constituted out of the juxtaposition of images and texts and from the complex relationship between form and content. More specifically, *Pyrsos*' layout employed the double-page spread as the primary unit for its design. In its design, visual and textual elements were not merely placed but carefully and consciously assembled to form productive relationships: for example, different types of images, processes and genres, visual and textual fragments, depictions of different temporalities alongside divergent geopolitical or historical contexts, were juxtaposed to conceptually complement and/or antagonise each other. Each image or text needed to be read independently, yet their placement on the page and their juxtaposition across a double-page spread invited particular readings.

Figure 15.2 Cover compositions by artist and *Pyrsos*' art director Nikos Manoussis.

Pyrsos' producers expected the magazine's readership to closely examine the textual, visual, conceptual and material elements to recognise the different voices and layers of signification and, in so doing, to decipher their often-metonymical substitutions in order to produce meaning. Inspired by the demands that Bertolt Brecht's aesthetics expected from audiences, *Pyrsos*' editorial strategy utilised the productive and often dissonant character of juxtaposition in order to evoke particular impressions from readers and to produce specific ideological effects. In a similar manner, the magazine's Greek émigré readership was encouraged to actively participate in the production of meaning by learning to synthesise the 'images of history' and the images of solidarity it was presented with, across the pages of the magazine.[59] Art historian Jérôme Bazin eloquently argues that distance and proximity, 'imagining someone as close or distant, altering the element of "foreign-ness" in what we see,' is both at the core of visuality and the feeling of solidarity.[60] To return to the GDR in the 1960s, Brechtian aesthetics had 'laid the foundations of the shift to a more subjectivist and expressionist forms', particularly influential amongst intellectuals and artists such as *Pyrsos*' editors and, namely, the magazine's art director, Nikos Manousis.[61] Manousis was an established and widely exhibited artist in the GDR prior to his art director post in *Pyrsos*.[62] A student of the acclaimed Weimar artist Lea Grundig at the Hochschule der Bildenden Künste in Dresden, he represented the GDR in the 1957 *All-Union Art Exhibition* in Moscow.[63] Notably, Manousis' most profound engagement with publishing models was his co-editorship of the *Junge Kunst* magazine, alongside prominent GDR intellectuals such as the painter Walter Womacka and the author, playwright and director Heiner Müller.[64] *Junge Kunst*'s design had been likened to that of the *AIZ* magazine because of its affective-laden ideological layout.[65]

I will now turn to analyse examples from *Pyrsos* in its coverage of the war in Vietnam that demonstrate its particular editorial strategy. As I will argue, these offer substantive models of solidarity through metonymy in the magazine, that inform understanding of complex visual articulations of solidarity.

A Greek Third Worldist struggle in Vietnam

Vietnam was a symbol for all anticolonial, anti-imperialist and youth movements around the world. Vietnam inspired and mobilised political and youth groups, independent of the positions they supported. In Greece, demands for democratisation, amnesty for political prisoners and opposition to the Cyprus issue 'paved the way' for further identification with Vietnam.[66] Needless to say, solidarity with the struggles of the Vietnamese was widespread across the Eastern Bloc. As James Mark et al. demonstrate, solidarity with Vietnam helped legitimise official political projects at the same time as generated dissent cultures and forms of political expressions, especially amongst the youth who were nonetheless reminded by authorities to express 'a tempered solidarity'.[67] For *Pyrsos*' readers, a deep-rooted affective connection with the Vietnamese augmented the sense of a shared experience against the same oppressor. I suggest that the violent conflict in Vietnam brought the disastrous and traumatic defeat of the Greek Civil War to the forefront, and as a consequence managed to problematise the Greek Left's official political strategy of 'peaceful coexistence'.

Pyrsos' 1965 double-page spread (Figure 15.3) features a translated article written by well-known US columnist Art Hoppe, originally published in the *San Francisco Chronicle*. In a satirical tone, the article calls for a humane and 'compassionate' extermination of the Vietnamese by the US army, arguing that the use of chemical weapons and poisonous gases are far more Christian ways of extermination than nuclear bombs.[68] Yet, the captions that furnish the black-and-white documentary photographs in the layout do not try to anchor or offer a position that defines the inherent malleability of the images. Instead, I would argue that the captions unfold their own narratives that make them stand as meaning-producing devices in their own right. I am suggesting that the juxtaposition of pictures, texts and captions on the spread, and broadly in *Pyrsos*, is by no means arbitrary. From this perspective, the use of captions echoes Walter Benjamin's call to 'rescue' the photographs from the ravages of modishness and confer upon [them] a revolutionary use-value.[69] In *Pyrsos*, their role is to 'rescue' the images by bestowing additional layers of signification and in so doing propose a complex reading.

324   *Greece in the Third World*

Figure 15.3 Vietnam, The 'Humanists' Chemical War, *Pyrsos* #3, 1965, pp. 6–7. Captions (anti-clockwise from the left): 'Two worlds in the same country. The People's Army of Vietnam helping a villager to transport his hut'; 'Resting before the struggle for the freedom of the country'; 'The foreign invader inspects his lethal weapons'; 'The 'humanist' interrogates'.

In another spread from 1966 (Figure 15.4), the magazine's regular column 'for you women' is dedicated to Vietnamese female guerillas. It is juxtaposed with a portrait of Din, a female Viet Cong combatant, pictured carrying an AK-47. As the title indicates, for *Din and her guerrillas* the use of arms is a legitimate means to oppose the United States' chemical warfare in Vietnam. Although there is not sufficient space here for any expansive engagement on the interchangeable uses of the terms 'guerrilla' and 'partisan', it is important to note that the original in Greek, 'αντάρτες', is a leftist term that specifically stands for the Nazi resistance partisans and the Democratic Army of Greece fighters in the Greek Civil War in the 1940s. In this context, it is not overstated to suggest that *Pyrsos*' use of the term did not only demonstrate 'a shared international consciousness and mode of transnational solidarity', but also drew direct parallels between the Vietnam War and the Greek Left's 1940s resistance; in some ways it inserted the Greek case within a Third Worldist struggle.[70]

Mary Ikoniadou 325

Figure 15.4 Din and her guerrillas, from the column 'For you Women', *Pyrsos* #1, 1966, pp. 36–37.

As indicated previously, since Khrushchev's 1956 speech on 'peaceful coexistence', the exiled Communist Left had abandoned its earlier rhetoric of an armed return to Greece and instead pursued a political strategy-cum-political identity that steered towards parliamentary representation. In this context, direct references to the Greek Civil War, its violence, or the trauma of defeat, were mostly withdrawn from the official discourse of the Communist Left. Instead, the focus was directed to the 1940s resistance and, as such, to a heroic past that provided a positive model of struggle that could inspire and unite. The silence around the Greek Civil War was a painful reality that was difficult to reconcile, especially for the older generation of the Greek political refugees who had fought in that war.[71]

In light of the above, the analysis of *Pyrsos*' spreads that depict the war in Vietnam represent a particular discourse on solidarity beyond the era's anti-American sentiments. In the first instance, *Pyrsos*' representations amplify a sense of struggle against a common enemy: US imperialism. Yet, a close reading of *Pyrsos*' aesthetic articulation of solidarity with the Vietnamese Communists' armed resistance is infused with metonymy, revealing a more complex picture. Eelco Runia puts it aptly when he defines metonymy as a ' "presence in absence", not just in the sense that it presents something that *is* there, the thing that isn't there, is still present'.[72] *Pyrsos*' visual manifestation of solidarity with the struggle of the Vietnamese Communists, who fought a guerrilla war against a powerful enemy equipped with chemical weapons, is (re)presented to the magazine's readers as an affective bond of cross identification.

Pyrsos' layouts propose that it is the same enemy, US imperialism, in a similar manner, employing the same weapons that justifies an armed resistance in Vietnam; in the same way it was experienced by *Pyrsos*' older readers when napalm bombs were dropped in north-western Greece effectively sealing the Democratic Army's defeat in the Civil War.[73] It alludes to the fact that it is the same enemy which has since the 1940s treated Greece as its private estate, as an 'internal colony'.[74] This was not far from the truth since the US administration had viewed Greece as a model for action in Vietnam – a widespread view in US politics, shared by presidents Kennedy and Johnson who characteristically assured American citizens that they would win the war against communist aggression in Southeast Asia as they had won the war in Greece.[75] In the specific layouts discussed here, typical of the magazine's editorial and political discourse manifested across several examples, Vietnam becomes a plane on which to break the silence and articulate the trauma while striving for resilience and, potentially, unity. By inserting the Greek Left's political struggles in the 1960s within a Third Worldist struggle for liberation, *Pyrsos*' solidarity discourse offers a positive model and hope for the future.

Conclusion

Political solidarities can be imagined, symbolic or affective; transnational or international. Shared political spaces, connections and alliances are formed through multiple exchange processes in the articulation and challenge of inequalities and injustices. Solidarity can also be articulated through identification processes and by drawing parallels that at times converge with politically, historically and culturally diverse struggles.

Through its editorial strategy, *Pyrsos* magazine constructed a complex articulation of solidarity that endeavoured to transcend its position beyond the expectations of state socialism and party politics in the 1960s and, as such, created a space from which to perform solidarity through metonymy for its readership. The magazine's solidarity discourse was produced out of the juxtaposition of images and texts, rendered visible through a close reading across the pages of the magazine. Solidarity with Vietnam, Cuba and the African liberation movements in *Pyrsos* speaks to the desire to deal with the past of the Greek Civil War by identifying with Third Worldist revolutionary anti-imperialism. To that end, what is rendered visible as presence in absence – what is not there in the discourse on solidarity with the Third World, is a way to deal with the trauma of defeat and exile; the uncertainties of life in exile and the desire for repatriation; the violence against the Greek Left in the post-Civil War climate in Greece and the struggle for democratisation. As such, the magazine's design constructs a specific approach to history and a restorative access to truth for its readers.

Notes

1 *Pyrsos* #1, 1963 pp. 28–9. Unless stated otherwise, all translations from Greek and German and possible inaccuracies, are the responsibility of the author.
2 *Pyrsos* #1, 1961, p. 1.
3 *Pyrsos* #1, 1964, p. 4.
4 The Socialist Unity Party of Germany [Sozialistische Einheitspartei Deutschlands, SED]. Besides the income from its sales and subscriptions, *Pyrsos* received funding that amounted to 25 per cent of its production costs. The department of Internationale Verbindungen [International Relations] was part of Ministry of Foreign Affairs in the GDR. *Pyrsos*: four-year report, 12 Feb 1965, in ASKI (B291 F13/53/90); N. Akritidis to KE, 8 Dec 1961, in ASKI (B254, F13/16/74).
5 See A. Matthaiou and P. Polemi, *I Ekdotiki Peripeteia ton Ellinon Kommouniston, apo to Vouno stin Yperoria 1947–1968* [The Publishing Adventure of the Greek Communists, from the Mountains to Overtime 1947–1968] (Athens: Vivliorama-ASKI, 2003); also see Contemporary Social History Archives, ASKI, Athens, Greece (B279; F13/41/21: 6).

6 B. Gillham, *Case Study Research Methods* (London & New York: Continuum, 2000).
7 My study of archival material ranged from information on the magazine's production and circulation, to readers' letters and documents of Communist Party meetings amongst many others. I have visited archives and studied a plethora of comparable magazines as well as collected oral histories and conducted interviews in Greece, Germany and Hungary.
8 K. Imbrigotta, 'History and the Challenge of Photography in Bertolt Brecht's Kriegsfibel', *Radical History Review*, 2010:106 (2010), 27–45, p. 33. Also see, W. Benjamin, *Understanding Brecht* (London: Verso, 2003); J. Fredric, *Brecht and Method* (London & New York: Verso, 2000), pp. 79–80; S. E. James, *Common Ground: German Photographic Cultures Across the Iron Curtain* (Yale: Yale University Press, 2013); R. Gillett and G. Weiss-Sussex, (eds), *'Verwisch Die Spuren!': Bertolt Brecht's Work and Legacy: A Reassessment* (Amsterdam & New York: BRILL, 2008).
9 D. Featherstone, *Solidarity: Hidden Histories and Geographies of Internationalism* (London: Zed Books, 2012), p. 5.
10 V. Prashad, *The Darker Nations: A People's History of the Third World* (New York: The New Press, 2007).
11 Young here draws on Althusser (2001), see C. A. Young, *Soul Power: Culture, Radicalism and the Making of a U.S. Third World Left* (Durham, NC: Duke University Press, 2006), p. 15.
12 Young, *Soul Power*, p. 150.
13 Ibid., p. 14.
14 Ibid., p. 150.
15 Ibid.
16 K. Kornetis, '"Everything Links"? Temporality, Territoriality and Cultural Transfer in the '68 Protest Movements', *HISTOREIN*, 9 (2012), 34–45, pp. 42, 39.
17 Ibid., p. 38.
18 Ibid., p. 41.
19 For more on the Greek political refugees see, T. Dritsios, *Apo ton Grammo stin Politiki Prosfygia [From Grammos to Political Refuge]* (Athens: Dorikos, 1983); M. Ikoniadou, ' "We Are and We Remain Greeks". The Radically Patriotic Discourse in *Pyrsos* Magazine, GDR, 1961–1968', in L. Karakatsanis and N. Papadogiannis (eds), *The Politics of Culture in Turkey, Greece & Cyprus: Performing The Left Since The 1960s* (London & New York: Routledge, 2017), pp. 184–207; K. Karpozilos, 'The Defeated of the Greek Civil War: From Fighters to Political Refugees in the Cold War', *Journal of Cold War Studies*, 16 (2014), 62–87; K. Tsekou, *Ellines Politikoi Prosfyges stin Anatoliki Evropi, 1945–1989 [Greek Political Refugees in Eastern Europe, 1945–1989]* (Athens: Alexandreia, 2013).

20 K. Kornetis, *Children of the Dictatorship: Student Resistance, Cultural Politics, and the 'long 1960s' in Greece* (New York: Berghahn Books, 2013), p. 10; Z. Lialiouti, 'Contesting the Anti-Totalitarian Consensus: The Concept of National Independence, the Memory of the Second World War and the Ideological Cleavages in Post-War Greece', *National Identities* (2015), 105–23; I. D. Stefanidis, *Stirring the Greek Nation: Political Culture, Irredentism and Anti-Americanism in Post-War Greece* (Aldershot: Ashgate, 2007).

21 D. Papadimitriou, *Apo ton Lao ton Nomimofronon sto Ethnos ton Ethnikofronon. I Syntiritiki Skepsi stin Ellada, 1922–1967* [From the Law-Abiding People to the Nationalists' Nation. Conservative Thinking in Greece, 1922–1967] (Athens: Savvalas, 2006).

22 N. Papadogiannis, *Militant Around the Clock? Left-Wing Youth Politics, Leisure, and Sexuality in Post-Dictatorship Greece, 1974–1981* (New York & Oxford: Berghahn Books, 2015), p. 32.

23 N. Christofis, 'Collective and Counter Memory: The "Invention of Resistance" in the Rhetoric of the Greek and Turkish Left, 1951–1971', in L. Karakatsanis and N. Papadogiannis (eds), *The Politics of Culture in Turkey, Greece & Cyprus: Performing the Left Since The 1960s* (London & New York: Routledge, 2017).

24 By the end of the Civil War, the Greek government held 18,000 political prisoners and 31,000 detainees in concentration camps, while an estimated 8,000 leftists had been sentenced to death and executed. Until 1963, people needed to obtain so-called 'certificates of loyalty' to enter universities, work in the civil sector or be issued passports. For more on the subject see, M. Mazower, *After the War Was Over: Reconstructing the Family, Nation, and State in Greece, 1943–1960* (Princeton & Oxford: Princeton University Press, 2000); I. Nikolakopoulos, A. Rígos and G. Psallídas (eds), *O Emfylios Polemos: apo ti Varkiza sto Grammo* [The Civil War: From Varkiza to Grammos](Athens: Themelio, 2002); N. Panourgia *Dangerous Citizens the Greek Left and the Terror of the State* (New York: Fordham University Press, 2009); P. Voglis, *Becoming a Subject: Political Prisoners During the Greek Civil War* (New York: Berghahn Books, 2002).

25 See Z. Lialiouti, 'Contesting the Anti-Totalitarian Consensus: The Concept of National Independence, the Memory of the Second World War and the Ideological Cleavages in Post-War Greece', *National Identities*, 18:2 (2016), 105–23; Z. Lialiouti, 'Greek Cold War Anti-Americanism in Perspective, 1947–1989', *Journal of Transatlantic Studies*, 13 (2015), 40–55; D. H. Close, *Greece Since 1945: Politics, Economy and Society: A History* (London: Pearson Education, 2002).

26 K. Christiaens, '"Communists Are No Beasts": European Solidarity Campaigns on Behalf of Democracy and Human Rights in Greece

and East-West Détente in the 1960s and Early 1970s', *Contemporary European History*, 26 (2017), 621–46, p. 628.
27 The British troops had to withdraw primarily because of economic restraints and to deal with the anticolonial conflicts that had emerged across the British Empire.
28 During the Civil War thousands of people were displaced, imprisoned or exiled to Greek islands by the US-supported Greek National Army. See M. Mazower, *Inside Hitler's Greece: The Experience of Occupation, 1941–44* (New Haven: Yale University Press, 1993).
29 See, P. Olkhovsky, 'The Greek Civil War: An Examination of America's First Cold War Victory', *Comparative Strategy*, 10:3 (1991), 287–96; H. Jones, 'Mistaken Prelude to Vietnam: The Truman Doctrine and a "New Kind of War" in Greece', *Journal of Modern Greek Studies*, 10:1 (May 1992), 121–43.
30 Ibid.
31 Christiaens, 'Communists Are No Beasts'.
32 Ibid., 629.
33 See, Ikoniadou, 'We Are and We Remain Greeks'; M. Ikoniadou, 'Re–Claiming Greek National History in the 1960s. The Case of Pyrsos Illustrated Magazine in the GDR.', in M. Hillemann and M. Pechlivanos (eds), *Deutsch-griechische Beziehungen im ostdeutschen Staatssozialismus (1949–1989). Politische Migration, Realpolitik und interkulturelle Begegnung* (Berlin: Edition Romiosini/CeMoG, Freie Universität Berlin, 2017), pp. 123–33.
34 J. Mark P. Apor, R. Vučetić and P. Osęka, '"We are with you, Vietnam": Transnational Solidarities in Socialist Hungary, Poland and Yugoslavia', *Journal of Contemporary History*, 50:3 (2015), 439–64, p. 440.
35 See Mark et al., 'Vietnam'; J. Bazin, 'Seeing Near, Seeing Far: What Do Images Tell Us About Solidarity in Popular Democracies?', in K. Khouri and R. Salti (eds), *Past Disquiet: Artists, International Solidarity and Museums in Exile* (Warsaw: Museum of Modern Art in Warsaw, 2018), pp. 221–36, 222, 228.
36 See, K. Ghodsee, *Second World, Second Sex: Socialist Women's Activism and Global Solidarity During the Cold War* (Durham, NC: Duke University Press, 2019).
37 Ibid., p. 4.
38 Mark et al., 'Vietnam'.
39 Ibid., 457.
40 Ghodsee, *Second World, Second Sex*, p. 157.
41 Mark et al., 'Vietnam', 447.

42 The Hallstein Doctrine, which was named after the general secretary of the Foreign Ministry of the Federal Republic of Germany Walter Hallstein, lasted from 1955 to 1970. According to the doctrine, West Germany claimed to be the only legitimate German state threatening to cut off diplomatic relations with any Western government that recognised the GDR.
43 A. Saunders, *Honecker's Children Youth and Patriotism in East(ern) Germany, 1979–2002* (Manchester: Manchester University Press, 2007), p. 7; P. G. Poutrus and J. C. Behrends, 'Xenophobia in the Former GDR – Explorations and Explanation from a Historical Perspective', in W. Burszta and S. Wojciechowski (eds), *Nationalisms Across the Globe: An Overview of Nationalisms in State-Endowed and Stateless Nations* (Poznań: Wyższa Szkoła Nauk Humanistycznych i Dziennikarstwa, 2005), pp. 155–70 (p. 162). See also P. G. Poutrus, 'Asylum in Postwar Germany: Refugee Admission Policies and Their Practical Implementation in the Federal Republic and the GDR Between the Late 1940s and the Mid-1970s', *Journal of Contemporary History Journal of Contemporary History*, 49:1 (2014), 115–33.
44 T. Weis, 'The Politics Machine: On the Concept of "Solidarity" in East German Support for SWAPO', *Journal of Southern African Studies* 37 (2011), 351–67, p. 357.
45 Toni Weis frames a similar argument in 'The Politics Machine', 357. My hypothesis draws on archival research and the testimonies of Weimar resistance fighters who returned to the GDR following long periods of exile.
46 Saunders, *Honecker's Children*, p. 11.
47 Bazin, 'Seeing Near, Seeing Far', 227.
48 M. Minholz and U. Stirnberg, *Der Allgemeine Deutsche Nachrichtendienst (ADN): Gute Nachrichten Für Die Sed* (Berlin: De Gruyter, 1995), p. 10.
49 See, A. Stergiou, 'Anatoliki Germania [East Germany]', in E. Ampazi and I. O. Katsiardi-Hering, K. Hasiotis (eds), *Oi Ellines stin Diaspora 15os–21os Aionas [Greeks in Diaspora 15th Century–21st Century]* (Rethymno: University of Crete, 2006), p. 147. It must be remembered that in its founding, the GDR was already experiencing a high influx of ethnic displaced Germans of the Second World War.
50 *Komitee 'Freies Griechenland'*.
51 S. Troebst, 'Evacuation to a Cold Country: Child Refugees from the Greek Civil War in the German Democratic Republic, 1949–1989*', *Nationalities Papers Nationalities Papers*, 32 (2004), 675–91, p. 676.
52 SED in collaboration with the Greek-run EVOP, Committee for Child Support, See ASKI, B365, F20/14/61–90. Also see, Hilfskomitee fur

das demokratische Griechenland [German Support Committee for Democratic Greece]. See Troebst, 'Evacuation', 676.
53 N. Abraham, *Die Politische Auslandsarbeit Der DDR in Schweden: Zur Public Diplomacy Der DDR Gegenüber Schweden Nach Der Diplomatischen Anerkennung (1972–1989)* (Berlin: Lit, 2007).
54 *Verlag Zeit im Bild*, The development of the publishing house Zeit im Bild Dresden, Timeline (draft), Document of the personal archive of Professor Siegfried Lokatis, 2012, Leipzig.
55 Rofouzou, *Oi Politistikes*, 129, 130.
56 ASKI, B254, F3/16/21.
57 The magazine's breadth of content included articles and extracts of literature and poetry, essays on history and culture as well as cartoons, architecture, interiors, fashion and food recipes amongst others, reports on politics and travelogues from Greece, the socialist states, and the West.
58 Ikoniadou, 'We Are and We Remain', 187; Ikoniadou, 'Re-Claiming', 126.
59 K. Imbrigotta, 'History and the Challenge of Photography in Bertolt Brecht's Kriegsfibel', *Radical History Review*, 2010:106 (2010), 27–45, p. 33.
60 Bazin, 'Seeing Near, Seeing Far', 235.
61 J. Aulich and M. Sylvestrová, *Political Posters in Central and Eastern Europe, 1945–1995: Signs of the Times* (Manchester: Manchester University Press, 2000), p. 26.
62 Nikos Manousis was credited as *Pyrsos*' art director until the fourth issue of 1967, the first following the establishment of the dictatorship of the Colonels in Greece. There were only three issues released after that, but it is unclear if Manousis was still working for the magazine until it ceased publication in February 1968. He appears as Nikolaus Manoussis in the German archives and printed publications.
63 University of Fine Arts in Dresden, Archives of the Akademie der Künste, AdK, Berlin, Germany (AdK-O 0144; AdK-O 4016; AdK-O 0151; AdK-O 0171; VBK-Fotos 7749).
64 *Junge Kunst*'s affective-laden ideological layout was likened to the *German* illustrated magazine *Arbeiter-Illustrierte-Zeitung, AIZ [The Workers Pictorial Newspaper]*, famous for John Heartfield's montages, published between 1924 and March 1933 in Berlin. See Ikoniadou, 'Re-Claiming', 127.
65 Arbeiter-Illustrierte-Zeitung or *AIZ* [The Workers Pictorial Newspaper] German illustrated magazine published between 1924 and March 1933 in Berlin notably included it published the radical photomontages of John Heartfield. For Junge Kunst see P. Sabine, '*Irgendwie Rochen*

Alle, Dass Da Frische Luft Ist' – *Das Kurze Leben Der Zeitschrift 'junge Kunst'* (Berlin: Zeitschrift des Forschungsverbundes SED-Staat, Freie Universität Berlin, 2009), pp. 70–92.

66 A. Makris, 'The Greek Peace Movement and the Vietnam War, 1964–1967', *Journal of Modern Greek Studies*, 38 (2020), 159–83, p. 166. In Pyrsos magazine, Cyprus was the subject of two special editions (1964–63; 1966–65) that featured articles on the country's sociopolitical, cultural and everyday life.

67 On the role of the socialist states' solidarity with Vietnam see Mark et al., 'Vietnam', 439–64, p. 451.

68 *Pyrsos* #3, 1965, 6–7.

69 W. Benjamin, *Understanding Brecht* (London: Verso, 2003), p. 95.

70 Young, *Soul Power*.

71 This discourse was not accepted without opposition amongst Stalin supporters, a fact that resulted in violent clashes amongst Communist Party members in Tashkent, Uzbekistan. The events led to the purge of KKE's leader, Nikos Zahariadis, and his sentence to a Siberian gulag. Other Stalinists and Zahariadis' followers were also expelled and, or, silenced.

72 Italics in the original. E. Runia, 'Presence', *History and Theory* 45:1 (2006), 1–29.

73 P. Olkhovsky, 'The Greek Civil War: An Examination of America's First Cold War Victory', *Comparative Strategy*, 10:3 (1991), 287–96; H. Jones, 'Mistaken Prelude to Vietnam: The Truman Doctrine and a "New Kind of War" in Greece', *Journal of Modern Greek Studies*, 10:1 (May 1992), 121–43.

74 The concept of the internal colony merits further research that is beyond the scope of this chapter.

75 H. Jones, 'Mistaken Prelude to Vietnam: The Truman Doctrine and a "New Kind of War" in Greece', *Journal of Modern Greek Studies*, 10:1 (May 1992), 121–43.

16

Solidarity as an absence: the productive limits of Adorno's thought

Patricia McManus

Introduction

The work of Theodor Adorno, and more widely of the first generation of the Frankfurt School, has long been a resource for postcolonial theorists but has, more recently, been subject to forms of radical rethinking as part of the project of decolonising critical theory. This scholarship has opened up lines of possibility for the future of an internationalist, anticolonial critical theory, one which adequately 'provincialises' the Frankfurt School – subjecting that work to a critique which is clear-eyed about its Eurocentric limits – while not hesitating to raid that body of work for any resources it can offer the project of emancipation.[1]

This chapter aims to contribute to that work. It uses Adorno's conceptualisation of solidarity to identify the limits placed on solidarity by the phenomenon Enzo Traverso terms 'the colonial unconscious of classical critical theory'.[2] The chapter goes on, however, to make a case for the repurposing of Adorno's concept of solidarity as providing a potential route to an understanding of solidarity not bound to the supposedly decaying consciousness of the white working classes of Europe and North America. That Adorno could not find a political place for solidarity in the 1960s is well known. I wish to use that incapacity here to both illustrate the hold the epistemic horizon of colonial power had on Adorno's thought, and also to push through the limits of that thought by using solidarity's relationship with aesthetic work to refigure what a radical imagination of solidarity can do.

For Traverso, the stubborn absence of the history and constitutive work of colonialism in Adorno's pursuit of the myriad mechanisms through which enlightenment was domination is a consequence of the inability of the scholars of the Frankfurt School to 'break the epistemic horizon of Marx'.[3] The critical theory of the School – formed in the wake of World War I, amidst the collapse of the Weimar Republic and the surge of fascism in Europe – opened up to analysis relations between capitalism and philosophies of 'progress' as the unfolding of the cancellation of the promise of freedom in the lived experience of universal domination.

> After the catastrophes that have happened, and in view of the catastrophes to come, it would be cynical to say that a plan for a better world is manifested in history and unites it. Not to be denied for that reason, however, is the unity that cements the discontinuous, chaotically splintered moments and phases of history – the unity of the control of nature, progressing to rule over men, and finally to that over men's inner nature.[4]

The historical and spatial horizon of the death-dealing 'civilisation' of modernity remained the industrial regions of Europe and North America, however. This was an epistemic fixity which for Adorno survived World War II and seemed only to harden in his understanding of the Cold War in the 1950s and 1960s.

For Traverso, the anti-fascism of the first generation of Frankfurt School thinkers 'rejected biological racism, whose most radical expression was anti-Semitism, but remained silent on colonialism'.[5] Reading that silence as symptomatic not of Marxism *per se* but of what would later be termed 'Western Marxism' – one of the triangle of anti-Stalinist Marxist currents grappling with history in the 1930s and 1940s, alongside 'classical Marxism' and 'Black Marxism' – Traverso is right, I think, to suggest that the Holocaust cemented the 'Eurocentrism' of Adorno's understanding of contemporary history and politics. Entering the historical consciousness of the West even as a wave of anticolonial movements struggled to disentangle themselves from that West, the lethal consequences of fascism and the seemingly bottomless capacity of Europe to forget, absorbed the world and shrank the horizon of Adorno's intellectual work and political understanding.

If construed narrowly as a political theorist, Adorno has clearly no relevance at all to accounts of the transnational solidarity of the 1960s. Utterly unable to see events and actors in the anticolonial struggles and postcolonial movements of the Global South in the

1940s, 1950s and 1960s, or able to see them only through a Cold War lens within which they appeared as proxies for the 'Great Powers', Adorno is eloquent only of the Marxism which failed to grasp the constitutive reciprocity of imperialism and capitalism. I want therefore to make a case for the value of exploring Adorno's concept of solidarity in spite of and not because of the way Adorno used it. This seems to me to be useful work as any account of the 1960s, and more so of the political value knowledge of that decade might hold for us in our own predicament now, needs to grapple with the coexistence of the failure of solidarity – or solidarity's absence – alongside the many-layered and rich histories of transnational solidarity that long decade generated.

The question of what blocks solidarity is as important to any understanding of solidarity as an appreciation of its existence as a concept, a value and a set of practices in the world. Solidarity has to be imagined even as it is enacted; its imagination is not a matter of crossing physical distances but of crossing differences. They 'who are not you' need to be twisted in thought to come around and rest in some third space, neither subject nor object, whose imaginative existence alters also the thinker as she comes to rest in that third space too. This third space, part of the grammar of collectivity, is not constituted by the recognition of a shared oppression or even by oppression itself but by the standing together against it. This 'we' or 'us', the remade collective position of solidarity, has been constructed out of its moment, a limited moment but a powerful one. The subject of solidarity can and even must be transnational, but it needs also to be inter-generational, approaching the past as itself a field of differences which must be negotiated to find or remember the seeds of solidarity that past contains.

Solidarity: breaking the compulsions of self-preservation

In one of the entries from 1944 in *Minima Moralia* (1951) 'Cat out of the Bag', 'solidarity' is positioned as socialism's 'most honourable mode of conduct' and as 'ill':

> Even solidarity, the most honourable mode of conduct of socialism, is sick. Solidarity was once intended to make the talk of brotherhood real, by lifting it out of generality, where it was an ideology, and

reserving it for the particular, the Party, as the sole representative in an antagonistic world of generality. It was manifested by groups of people who together put their lives at stake, counting their own concerns as less important in face of a tangible possibility, so that, without being possessed by an abstract idea, but also without individual hope, they were ready to sacrifice themselves for each other.[6]

The brief passages in 'Cat out of the Bag' touch on two moments in the dialectic of solidarity's history. The first is the coming into stasis of solidarity as, with liberty and equality, one of the epilogues of European enlightenment. This is the moment which results in solidarity being elevated to a formal potency – as 'mankind' – a state-centred potency or 'ideology' which stems from and secures its divorce from revolutionary praxis. Adorno's understanding of Europe's attempt at enlightenment routes the reification of 'humane' values or of the constituent values of a universal humanity, through a 'dominant *ratio* … and the world which corresponds to its image'.[7] Such reason, the instrumental rationality of universal domination, brings Europe to fascism: '[n]ot merely the ideal but the practical tendency to self-destruction has always been characteristic of rationalism, and not only in the stage in which it appears disguised'. We can relate the 'stage' in which the tendency to self-destruction 'appears disguised' to the mode of appearance of this model of rationality and its frozen avatars – equality, liberty, fraternity – in the colonial project. According to Nelson Maldonado-Torres, Frantz Fanon's and C. L. R. James articulated a concept of reason which could power decolonisation. This conceptual work required a wrestle with the violent imprint of enlightenment rationality outside Europe. Maldonado-Torres elaborates: 'monological violent colonial rationality cannot expect to reason with those whom it oppresses and silences, no matter how praiseworthy, advantageous and close to "objective validation" its ideas might be'.[8]

The second conceptual step or stage in 'Cat out of the Bag' is Adorno's tracing of the return of solidarity to praxis with the making of the parties of socialism. The nineteenth-century movement of 'groups of people who together put their lives at stake' did so for a possibility whose tangibility was enhanced even in their coming together. The idea of solidarity is here not abstract but a mode of existence, or of 'conduct', a collective mode centred on a collectivised hope. That this mode of conduct is now 'ill' is – for

Adorno – due to the segueing of that second moment into a new and antithetical one: the calcification of solidarity in the apparatus of a Party which has substituted itself for the class whose expression it was to be.

The Party demands solidarity and in doing so destroys the capacity of solidarity to be a mode of conduct which can open a breach in the compulsions of self-preservation. A demanded solidarity, that is, is no solidarity at all but furthers the closure and blindness of self-preservation by installing fear or duty as solidarity's cause. The 'prerequisites' for the waiving of self-preservation realised by the step into solidarity were (and are) 'knowledge and freedom of decision: if they are lacking, blind particular interest immediately reasserts itself'.[9] That 'knowledge and freedom of decision' are here prerequisites for the breach in self-preservation contained in solidarity does not mean that the subject of solidarity is posited as self-defining or autonomous. That autonomy at the level of the individual or as the realisation of individuality is, on the one hand, impossible or possible only in the antinomies of idealism – the figure of the *autonome ratio* – or, on the other hand, where the subject is posited by the machinery of the social world as in possession of knowledge and freedom of decision – freely choosing, freely exchanging – her autonomy is real but self-cancelling.[10]

To survive, she must move monad-like through a world composed of other monad-figures, each isolated and blocked from the other except as they can form reciprocally instrumental relations in the process of which autonomy only stretches so far as to enable the objectification of she who has it.

We must stress here how valuable solidarity is as that which enables a breach in that logic of self-preservation which would otherwise wholly capture the subject. The self-preservation of the ego is one of the expressions of the entanglement of reason with domination traced in *Dialectic of Enlightenment* (1944). Freed from the threat of a ravaging or fearsome nature by recourse to a form of thought which objectifies and secularises that now unified world of an objectified nature, a world distinct from the self who thus thinks it, the rational individual is yet not free as he has internalised the domination which had to be wreaked on nature to 'tame' it, and turned it against what was once nature or the natural in himself.[11]

The ego both conceals and mediates the drive to domination and in doing so ensures that the self is not free to do anything else. The conversion of nature into 'manipulable material' is mirrored in the conversion of the self into its own disciplinary object: reason is realised in domination not only of others but also of the self. Compelled by its own constitution to blindness to what that constitution conceals and denies, subjectivity is equally compelled to relate to the world around it as a means towards the end of its own preservation:

> The self ... once sublimated into the transcendental or logical subject, would form the reference point of reason, of the determinative instance of action. Whoever resigns himself to life without any rational reference to self-preservation would according to the Enlightenment – and Protestantism – regress to prehistory.[12]

The logic of self-preservation is the logic of domination: in Adorno's terms it is the logic of class society and its lethal irrationalities. It is inescapable in individual terms and generative of both individual and social self-destructiveness or 'regression'.[13] That this logic governs also the colonising projects of European modernity is an argument made by several scholars who have traced the reciprocities of colonial modes of domination as a way of incorporating the layered historicity of imperialism into critiques of a universal history or of 'progress'.[14] Much of the work done by contemporary scholars builds on analyses which were contemporary with Adorno's, as illustrated by Enzo Traverso's narrative of C. L. R. James' understanding of fascism as the return transfer into Europe of the systemic destruction and oppression it had experimented with in the colonial world.[15] In 'Césaire with Adorno', Fadi A Bardawil positions Aimé Césaire's *Discourse on Colonialism* (1950) in proximity with the concept of the 'personality' Adorno and his colleagues used to sketch a historical schema for fascism's pull in *The Authoritarian Personality* (1950). For Césaire, the coloniser

> who in order to ease his conscience gets into the habit of seeing the other man as an *animal*, accustoms himself to treating him like an animal, and tends objectively to transform *himself* into an animal ... No human contact, but relations of domination and submission which turn colonizing man into a classroom monitor, an army sergeant, a prison guard, a slave driver, and the indigenous man into an instrument of production. ... [C]olonization = 'thingification'.[16]

There is no easy or smooth passage to be traced between the work of anticolonial thinkers and Adorno. Nonetheless the resemblance in the understanding of enlightenment as a form of domination - which compels the casting of the world into that which dominates and that which is to be dominated - is clear in a way which makes Adorno's blindness to the colonial project sharply prominent. That much work must be done to reconfigure Adorno's own thought to make it porous to the different modes of being in modernity – all the way from the existence of classic imperialism as an unacknowledged source and mode of domination, to the existence of forms of resistance and their modes of thought which transcend the Cold War borders of Adorno's thought – is clear. That it is work worth doing, I hope this chapter will at the very least suggest.

For Adorno, domination over nature promised freedom but exacted, as the cost of what remained only a promise of freedom, the self's immurement in itself, and a socially divided world which demanded that the self daily reproduce its own immurement. The

> social work of every individual in bourgeois society is mediated through the principle of self; for one, labour will bring an increased return on capital; for others, the energy for extra labour. But the more the process of self-preservation is effected by the bourgeois division of labour, the more it requires the self-alienation of the individuals who must model their body and soul according to the technical apparatus.[17]

Solidarity brings together these wounded or self-alienated individuals, generating an interest in practice which is antagonistic yet not particular. Solidarity thus assumes and exercises the possibility of *a non-formal but social mode of universality which could shed self-preservation while securing the self*. That such a possibility was organised politically in the idea of, and the various local activities of, the parties of socialism is not itself what sickened solidarity. Rather it is the official or state socialism of the USSR which had captured solidarity, frozen it into a demanded loyalty and thus destroyed the prerequisites for the 'waiving of self-preservation ... knowledge and freedom of decision'.[18]

Bertolt Brecht's line that 'the Party has a thousand eyes' is true in so far as it suggests something of the uniform that solidarity had to put on to stay 'swimming with the tide of history'. She who expresses or practices solidarity because the Party demands it from her destroys what solidarity could do: '[a]ny temporary security gained in this way is paid for by permanent fear, by toadying, manoeuvring and ventriloquism: the strength that might have been used to test the enemy's weakness is wasted in anticipating the whims of one's own leaders'.[19] Outside the grip of official or Party socialism, solidarity fares no better. Here it is individuals who demand solidarity but do not reciprocate. The 'orthodox, but also the deviationists all too like them', approach the individual expecting solidarity:

> But the moment he looks for the slightest proof of the same solidarity from them, or mere sympathy for his own share of the social product of suffering, they give him the cold shoulder ... These organisation men want the honest intellectual to expose himself for them, but as soon as they only remotely fear having to expose themselves, they see him as the capitalist and the same honesty on which they were speculating, as ridiculous sentimentality and stupidity.[20]

The slippage from individual to intellectual at the close of this passage is both typical and telling. All are failed individualities in the late modernity of Adorno's Europe: the dreamt-of individuality of liberal humanism is the wound which constitutes the modern self, and it is the reminder of the wreckage of liberal humanism. In the twentieth century, the Stalinised Communist Party holds out the promise of a false reconciliation of the damaged individual with the world; or the Culture Industry does so in countries where the total administration of liberal domination marks the limits of the totality. In either scenario, individual consciousness – itself the sign or symptom of damaged social being – is threatened. The only subjectivity capable of identifying and evading the temptations of false reconciliation is she who holds back from the temptations of reconciliation, which include false solidarities. The ideal type capable of such holding back is the critical thinker who holds to her duty to thought, and the artist who insists on remaining immune to commitment. The only collective mode of such autonomy is critical theory, and art itself. The conceptual and historical legs of solidarity have thus disappeared.

The path thus open to solidarity seems to be a rigorous and pained intellectual isolation: '[f]or intellectuals, unswerving isolation is the only form in which they can vouchsafe a measure of solidarity'.[21]

Unswerving isolation is not an easeful or restful position: it is not one taken lightly or worn superficially: it takes constant or ceaseless energy and wariness. Isolation must be made anew and anew: 'All collaboration, all the human worth of social mixing and participation, merely masks a tacit acceptance of inhumanity. It is the sufferings of men that should be shared: the smallest step towards their pleasures is one towards the hardening of their pains.'[22] Over twenty years after he wrote these passages on solidarity, in the midst of the tumult of 1968 in Frankfurt, Adorno, along with Günter Grass, Jürgen Habermas, Ludwig von Friedeburg and others of those whom his biographer, Stefan Müller-Doohm, terms 'prominent left-wing intellectuals', took part in a talk in late September with the leading figures of the student movement on the topic, 'Authority and Revolution'. One anecdote must suffice here to serve up the terms the debate took then and that it seems to have taken ever since: Hans-Jürgen Krahl, Adorno's PhD student and a theoretician of the student resistance in the Socialist Student Alliance (the SDS) and the Extra-Parliamentary Opposition (ApO), spoke thus:

> Six months ago ... when we were besieging the council of Frankfurt University, the only professor who came to the students' sit-in was Professor Adorno. He was overwhelmed with ovations. He made straight for the microphone, and just as he reached it, he ducked past and shot into the philosophy seminar. In short, once again, on the threshold of practice, he retreated into theory.[23]

Günter Grass later wrote to Adorno about this meeting and suggested that Adorno was being opportunistic and was perhaps lacking in the courage needed to act in solidarity. Adorno's response involves words which will become important here: he was firmly resolved he wrote, to not let himself

> be browbeaten into what for years now I have called the principle of unilateral solidarity ... I increasingly see it as my task simply to say what I think without taking anyone else into consideration. This goes together with a mounting aversion to practical politics of whatever kind, an aversion in which my natural disposition and the objective futility of practical action at this moment of history coincide.[24]

Two phrases there – the principle of unilateral solidarity, something you might be browbeaten into; and the objective futility of practical action at this moment of history – are important here and

I will return to them. For now, however, it may be worth pulling back the focus a bit. I have no interest here in rehearsing the debates between those who would champion Adorno's resistance to what then becomes the dogmatism of praxis at any costs, or those (fewer) voices which would castigate Adorno's refusal to more richly and openly support the students' work, a refusal which resulted on one occasion in Adorno's calling the police to protect Institute property. It is the *absence* of solidarity I am interested in, the absence of solidarity as an object of enquiry in Adorno's thought at this moment, and the failure of the events of 1968 to push him to rethink the closures or assimilation of a late-capitalist social order. For, regardless of the actual political analysis underlying Adorno's disagreement with the efficacy of praxis in 1968, would he not have looked out onto a world in which forms of solidarity were everywhere being practised: from Algeria to Cuba, from Uruguay to New Orleans. As has been documented in much work on the dynamic of anti-imperialism which impelled political movements across Europe, the US and the Global South to identify imperialism as alien to neither Stalinism or the 'free world', 1968 was a decade in the making. In that making, it is the figure of the worker and of the colonial militant, much more so than the figure of the student, who centres solidarity both as the basis of praxis and as one of its goals. Kristin Ross points out that in the context of France's 1968, the 'international dimension' not only played a role in catalysing the threads of the French uprisings internally but 'united those uprisings to the insurrections occurring in Germany, Japan, the United States, Italy and elsewhere – namely the critique of American imperialism and that nation's war against Vietnam'.[25] In his reworking of the complex realities of the West German student movements of the 1960s, Quinn Slobodian likewise brings back to the surface the role played by internationalism in the practice of solidarity. Slobodian is at pains to point out that it was not only news of, or even political links with, events in the Global South but the presence in West German universities of student activists from Asia, South America and Africa which gave weight and purpose to the meanings of internationalism. These were meanings which were imbricated with the experience of decolonisation and with the 'subsequent emergence of the Third world as a political category'.[26] This new understanding and practice of internationalism helped split the West German left in the 1960s. The students and intellectuals of a self-described New Left rejected the Old Left of labour and social democracy for its abandonment of the language of class struggle, its rigid Cold War mentality, and its refusal to criticize overseas U.S. overseas military interventions ... They asked penetrating questions. Why should a self-described democracy outlaw the opposition as the West German government had with the ban on the Communist Party in 1956? Why was the Soviet invasion of Hungary an outrage but the violent suppression of independence movements in Algeria and Angola by 'free world' allies was not?[27]

It is normal for scholarship on Adorno to point to the dead hand of the Stalinised Communist Parties as part of the matrix of his narrow and negative understanding of the political movements of 1968. And it is the case that internationalist 'solidarity' was indeed instrumentalised by those Parties in a vast and elaborate network of initiatives, political and cultural, institutional and 'spontaneous', to dramatise the decay and corruption of the 'free world'.[28] Anti-imperialist political movements could find ways to bend, and in Yugoslavia to violently bend, the bounds of the rhetoric of those nationally-specific versions of official solidarity, turning the terms of that rhetoric into modes of conduct directed against the stifling of political life 'at home', twisting Party imperatives to support national liberation movements into 'a language of anti-imperialism that could be directed against "oppressors" closer to home'.[29]

Art's autonomy as solidarity?

I want to step back for a moment to consider two things: first, the model of social order which underpinned Adorno's argument that praxis for the foreseeable future was postponed; and second, why the international movements of the 1960s did not alter his model.

The model of social order which underpinned Adorno's analysis of both the events of 1968, and the position of theory in relation to them, is that of a totally administered society. This model builds on the trajectory of domination Adorno developed with Horkheimer in the early 1940s, positing that the historical process has been largely driven by instrumental reason. In the decades after Auschwitz, Adorno elaborated the situation of the administered world as one in which instrumental reason triumphs in the guise of exchange value as 'the spell cast over mankind by the system has been strengthened by the process of integration'.[30] In the development of technological and organisational standardisation, and in the spread of the mode of commodity production to every aspect of human relations, an image of the world which is illusory yet everywhere commands adaptation rules.

In *The Dialectic of Enlightenment* the position or dilemma of humankind was sketched out: written against and to understand the emergence into full force and into legitimacy of fascism, that text begins the articulation of history-nature-freedom as a negative dialectic, one in which every move towards freedom is a move which enriches and entrenches domination. More attention is paid to the state than to capitalism as it is the state which occupies a newly dynamic and enabling role since the moment of capitalism analysed by Marx. Later, it is the state of a corporate capitalism in America or Western Europe, or the centralised state of Stalinist regimes, which occupy the horizons of Adorno's sociology.[31]

Adorno's own arguments for this position can be found in *Negative Dialectics* but also in both the early essay, 'Reflections on Class Theory' (written in 1942 but not published till 1972), or the late essay, 'Late Capitalism or Industrial Society?' (1969). These essays articulate an understanding of late-capitalist societies modelled along the lines of total absorption, total administration, but they also contain insights which do not rest there but which push the argument along the lines of potential openings, potential breaches. Typically, indeed, these are abstract, not drawn from sociological descriptions and rarely have a purchase on the latter, but they do alter the nature of the argument. For me in particular, the moments which push at openness are meaningful in relation to how Adorno saw what literature, and more widely art, could do.

It should be noted here that while I wish to argue the importance of Adorno's understanding of the fight a cultural object conducts so as to be autonomous, and further to position that autonomy as art's own protection of solidarity, this argument is not one which can seal over or forget the flaws in Adorno's wider model of the relations between politics and social movements. It is not necessary, however, to adopt Adorno's model of late modernity *in toto* when using his dialectical conceptualisation of the situation of literature in the world. The postcolonial scholar Neil Lazarus, in one powerful example, uses Adorno's model of modernism as offering us an understanding of how to interpret a type of 'writing in extremity'. Through this model, Lazarus reads examples of white South African literature to generate an interpretation of how that work can be 'oppositional' regardless of an author's intention: it is 'not this factor of self-consciousness that renders their work oppositional, but rather the manner in which this work enters into history – or more precisely, refuses to be encoded seamlessly into history'.[32]

Lazarus' critique of Adorno's theory of modernity centres precisely on what our exploration of solidarity here has thrown up: Adorno's insight into the potential power of solidarity is negated by his use of a model of social order which forbids solidarity any route into practice. Suggesting that the 'insufficiency of Adorno's conception of modernity is categorical, not historical', Lazarus argues that Adorno conflates instances of reification and rationalisation, thus rendering 'the potential efficacy of resistive practices in modern society unimaginable in advance: to him nothing that does not – at least co-optively – serve to confirm the implacable hegemony of total administration can find air to breathe in the modern era'.[33] For Lazarus, who writing in 1986 was 'neither quite ready nor willing to admit the impracticality of what in South Africa is called "meaningful change"', it was essential to rethink the lines of Adorno's model so as to develop from it: 'an alternative conception of modernity, one more capable of grappling with the exigencies of modern social formations as contradictory – hence potentially alterable – structures-in-dominance'.[34] It is arguably just as important now for a Marxist theory of culture's relationship with the imagination of solidarity to insist on a historical materialist attention to form within the conceptual openings of such a grasp of late capitalism as contradictory. For any such theory, Adorno is a necessary yet difficult antidote to the opposing lures of what Keya Ganguly calls 'the rock-kicking realism of positivistic thought', or the magic of a textualism for which the literary text promises everything so long as it is only a promise.[35] The importance rests on culture's capacity to shape or share the possibilities of solidarity. For many authors and activists of Adorno's generation, and since, a 'committed' artistic practice is the only valid mode of solidarity in or for culture. Adorno held, against such valorisations of 'committed' cultural practices, that only art which secured its own autonomy was capable of reproducing the breach in self-preservation which is also the capacity of solidarity. His deep argument with Sartre's version of a 'committed' literature, for example, turns on his argument not for a 'pure' or isolated aesthetic realm but for the political potency of an aesthetic which sticks to its job:

> The type of literature that, in accordance with the tenets of commitment but also with the demands of philistine moralism, exists for many, betrays him by traducing that which could help him, if only it did not strike a pose of helping him.
>
> But any literature which therefore concludes that it can be a law unto itself, and exist only for itself, degenerates into ideology no less.[36]

For any rethinking of the relationship between cultures and solidarity, or the conditions of solidarity's imagination, Adorno's insistence on an autonomy – that which is not granted but fought for – seems an urgent and timely reminder of the contradictory hold of history on form, and of form on meaning. The most valuable element Adorno's aesthetics can offer us in such a moment is a warning about the embeddedness of literary and cultural forms in histories not of their own making. This is arguably not an insight confined either to Adorno's thin model of modernism or to the richer understanding of modernisms outside those canonised as such.[37]

It is his insistence on thinking the totality, however, which makes Adorno an indispensable thinker for the project of conceptualising the political force or dynamics culture is capable of. This includes the possibility not of cultures of solidarity but of cultural practices which could do justice to how the social world is capable of solidarity, a capability which is at once a terrible and yet a beautiful thing just as solidarity itself has its existence simultaneously in suffering and the yearning or will to end that suffering. In terms of Adorno's own thought, solidarity was in trouble: it was cut off from practice in the Soviet states by a state apparatus which made a mockery of it; and it was cut off from practice in the 'West' by objective conditions which would not yield to it. In an intellectual situation which had only this polarised, Cold War conceptualisation of the world and its potential, the only route open to thought or to critical theory was to insist on its own autonomy, a pained and hurt autonomy yet the only mode of a thinking which would 'find an exit':

> [p]eople locked in desperately want to get out. In such situations one doesn't think anymore, or does so only under fictive premises. Within absolutized praxis only reaction is possible and therefore false. Only thinking could find an exit ... If the doors are barricaded, then thought more than ever should not stop short. It should analyse the reasons and subsequently draw the conclusions. It is up to thought not to accept the situation as final.[38]

This is a model which seems to render solidarity off bounds to all but culture and, further, to make it possible for culture only at the expense of a rejection of any form of intervention. The demands made by autonomy mean that cultural forms cannot exist as vehicles for political meanings or political responses. A narrative form, for example, cannot accommodate anger or rage, or be used for the taking of sides, without those meanings being subject to a transformation in the work itself which would deform both the meanings and the work. The autonomous work of art is political, however, and is so in an oppositional manner, where it exists *in and as itself*. What it holds out for its 'beholder' is the existence, the possibility itself, of formed life, of life which can be formed other than it is: the

> uncalculating autonomy of works which avoid popularisation and adaptation to the market, involuntarily becomes an attack on them. The attack is not abstract, not a fixed attitude of all works of art to the world which will not forgive them for not bending totally to it. The distance these works maintain from empirical reality is in itself partly mediated by that reality.[39]

The minimal yet powerful promise of happiness which Kafka's or Beckett's work contains, a promise of happiness 'which refuses to be traded for comfort, cannot be had for a price less than total dislocation, to the point of worldlessness. Here every commitment to the world must be abandoned to satisfy the ideal of the committed work of art.'[40] The paradox – that the most autonomous work of art is the most committed – is only a seeming one: 'Kafka's prose and Beckett's plays, or the truly monstrous novel, *The Unnameable*, have an effect by comparison with which officially committed works look like pantomimes ... The inescapability of their work compels the change of attitude which committed works merely demand.'[41]

In contact with the autonomous work of art, the reader will be compelled to change her attitude where she might resist a command to do so. In the work's mode of addressing her, she is prohibited from finding consolation that she and the work know the world is bad. What is she left with once she has changed her attitude, our speculative reader? There is no comfort, consequently there is no chance of false reconciliation: there is only 'total dislocation, to the point of wordlessness'. It is this dislocation which provides a negative glimpse of utopia: the world can be seen as it is and in seeing it as such, there is a form of knowledge as well as pleasure. Autonomous works 'are knowledge as non-conceptual objects. This is the source of their nobility. It is not something of which they have to persuade men, because it has been given into their hands.'[42] This relationship, one which begins as being between the reader and her text but which alters in the process so that the reader is changed by what she reads, is a mimetic approximation of solidarity as Adorno outlined it in *Minima Moralia*. The work of art is encountered in itself as the other is encountered as their self in solidarity. The work of art, when autonomous, does not wish to persuade or rebuke or inform the reader, it has no 'message' to be delivered but is merely itself. In so doing it opens a precious and powerful relationship.

The autonomous work of art is thus capable of enacting that 'polemical alienation which Brecht as a theorist invented, and as an artist practised less and less as he committed himself more firmly to the role of a friend of mankind'.[43] In this way, it opens a world for the reader. The price is that the reader and the work cannot open their moment of solidarity to anyone else, cannot spread it to any other moment or space. It is an approximation, it is not solidarity. But that is something: to see or to feel or to recognise your own alienation, and in that recognition to recognise the alienation of the world. By paying such close attention to the moments in modern life where a subject chooses to think, and is addressed as a thinking subject, Adorno offers us the possibility of a critical theory of cultural work, one which neither floats free from politics nor is instrumentalised by politics.

In the letters exchanged by Adorno and Marcuse in the early months of 1969, we can trace both the potency of Adorno's conception of solidarity, and the limits of his understanding of the social situation which forbade him from practising that conception.

By the spring term, Adorno's relations with the students in Frankfurt had deteriorated badly. He had been part of the staff group which had called the police in late January 1969 when the series of protests, which had included boycotts of lessons, entered into a phase of occupation. Marcuse wrote to Adorno of his consternation at hearing what had happened: to put it brutally, he wrote, 'if the alternative is the police or left-wing students, then I am with the students':

> You know me well enough to know that I reject the unmediated translation of theory into praxis just as emphatically as you do. But I do believe that there are situations, moments, in which theory is pushed on further by praxis – situations and moments in which theory that is kept separate from praxis becomes untrue to itself ... We know (and they know) that the situation is not a revolutionary one, not even a pre-revolutionary one. But this same situation is so terrible, so suffocating and demeaning, that rebellion against it forces a biological, physiological reaction: one can bear it no longer, one is suffocating and one has to let some air in.[44]

The key thing, when reading Adorno's response, is to remember that for Adorno, there was no objective moment or outlet for praxis in the current situation. As he wrote to Marcuse in a later letter in 1969,

> [y]ou think that praxis – in its emphatic sense – is not blocked today; I think differently. I would have to deny everything that I think and know about the objective tendency if I wanted to believe that the student protest movement in Germany had even the tiniest prospect of effecting a social intervention.[45]

Just a month before the words quoted above, Adorno wrote:

> The strongest point you make is the idea that the situation could be so terrible that one would have to attempt to break out of it, even if one recognises the objective impossibility. I take that argument seriously. But I think that it is mistaken ... To put it bluntly: I think that you are deluding yourself in being unable to go on without participating in the student stunts, because of what is occurring in Vietnam or Biafra. If that really is your reaction, then you should not only protest against the horror of napalm bombs but also against the unspeakable Chinese-style tortures that the Vietcong carry out permanently. If you do not take that on board too, then the protest against the Americans takes on an ideological character.[46]

And there we have it, the moment for solidarity – theory of and practise of – is the absent moment. In all of Adorno's published reflections on this dilemma – the resurgence of resistance movements, the taking of sides, the development of new vocabularies of resistance to enrich the older critiques of capitalism and of the authoritarianism it harbours, there is no use made of solidarity. It had no presence in Adorno's thought except the negative present of an 'ill' value or mode of conduct commandeered by the official communist parties to blackmail or browbeat their subjects into loyalty.

When Adorno used the phrase 'unilateral solidarity' in 1968, to describe the position he would not be beaten into, he departed from the model of solidarity he had outlined in *Minima Moralia* over two decades before, a model which he had continued to adhere to in his understanding of what an autonomous art could do. The artwork for Adorno acts in solidarity, it gives unilaterally what it has to give. This pulls the artwork into the history of solidarity. For what is solidarity if not a unilateral giving, a recognition of suffering and a standing with the person or people so suffering, standing on their side as it were so as to bring about the end or if not that, then to signal the intolerability of that suffering? Solidarity cannot be reciprocal without first being that unilateral giving, a giving which must be done without an expectation of return. It is unforgiveable, however, to register the potential for solidarity in art – the necessity for an understanding of how art can work for solidarity – and yet to bar that solidarity a route into practice. A solidarity denied access to the world of praxis makes of the autonomous work of art an ornament, its own promise of solidarity an unwitting parody of what might be. Nevertheless, the richness of both Adorno's conceptualisation of solidarity, and his understanding of aesthetic autonomy as potently political, remain open for a rethinking of an anti-imperial and transnational culture of solidarity.

Notes

1 The term 'provincialise' is taken from Dipesh Chakrabarty's *Provincialising Europe: Postcolonial Thought and Historical Difference* (Princeton: Princeton University Press, 2nd ed., 2008). A sample of the type of scholarship involved in decolonising critical theory would include Amy Allen's *The End of Progress: Decolonising the Normative*

Foundations of Critical Theory (New York: Columbia University Press, 2016); Antonio Y. Vazquez-Arroyo 'Universal History Disavowed: on Critical Theory and Postcolonialism', *Postcolonial Studies*, 11:4 (2008), 451–73; Namita Goswami 'The (M)other of all Posts: Postcolonial Melancholia in the Age of Global Warming', *Critical Philosophy of Race*, 1:1, 104–20; Walter D. Mignolo, *The Darker Side of Modernity: Global Futures, Decolonial Options* (Durham, NC: Duke University Press, 2011); Walter D. Mignolo, 'Epistemic Disobedience and the Decolonial Option: A Manifesto', *Transmodernity*, 1:1 (2011), 44–66.

2 Enzo Traverso (2016) *Left-Wing Melancholia: Marxism, History and Memory* (New York: Columbia University Press, 2016), p. 174.

3 Ibid., pp. 174–5.

4 Theodor Adorno, *Negative Dialectics* (1966), trans. E. B. Ashton (London & New York: Routledge, 2004), p. 320.

5 Traverso notes the exception to this situation provided by the later work of Herbert Marcuse. Traverso, *Left-Wing Melancholia*, p. 175. Adorno's *Negative Dialectics* provides the richest account of the entanglement of fascism's dynamic with the patterns of an instrumentalising reason though it examines this at the level of theory's predicament. 'The Meaning of Working through the Past' (1960) provides a more socially inflected exploration of the conditions of possibility of fascism, and the dangers of its forgetting. This essay is included in Rolf Tiedemann (ed.) *Theodor Adorno: Can One Live after Auschwitz? A Philosophical Reader* (Stanford: Stanford University Press, 2003).

6 Theodor Adorno, *Minima Moralia: Reflections from Damaged Life*, trans. E. F. N. Jephcott (London: Verso, 2005), p. 51.

7 Theodor W. Adorno and Max Horkheimer, 'Preface' (1944) *Dialectic of Enlightenment* (1947). Trans. John Cummings (London: Verso, 1997), p. xvii.

8 Nelson Maldonado-Torres (2005) 'Frantz Fanon and C. L. R. James on Intellectualism and Rationality', *Caribbean Studies*, 33:2), 155. The term 'objective validation' in the quotation above refers back to Fanon's point that '[t]he truth objectively expressed is constantly vitiated by the lie of the colonial condition'. (Fanon (1965) *A Dying Colonialism*, p. 128. Cited Maldonado-Torres, 155.)

9 Adorno and Horkheimer, *Dialectic of Enlightenment*, p. 51.

10 On the limited and negative truth of idealist models of the subject, see Adorno, 'Subject and Object' (1969), in Brian O'Connor (ed.) *The Adorno Reader* (Oxford: Blackwell, 2000), pp. 137–51. For Adorno's own understanding of the use late capitalism made of the subject, see Susan Buck-Morss, *The Origin of Negative Dialectics: Theodor W. Adorno, Walter Benjamin, and the Frankfurt Institute* (New York: Macmillan, 1977), pp. 82–94.

11 I switch to the use of 'he' and 'his' as pronouns here as there is no purpose in any de-gendering of Adorno and Horkheimer's use of the bourgeois male subject as the content of the formal subject of reason.
12 Adorno and Horkheimer, *Dialectic of Enlightenment*, p. 29.
13 Already in *Dialectic of Enlightenment*, the subject of 'liberal' capitalism is being described as being subsumed in what Adorno will later term the mechanisms of 'late capitalism' – for example: 'in the end the transcendental subject of cognition is apparently abandoned as the last reminiscence of subjectivity and replaced by the much smoother work of automatic control mechanisms' (*Dialectic*, p. 30). See also Peter Dews on Adorno's understanding of 'post-liberal capitalism' as 'characterized by a progressive liquidation of the distinction between the ego and the unconscious in a narcissistic personality type ... The predominant social character becomes a "subjectless subject"', in Dews, *Logics of Disintegration: Post-Structuralist Thought and the Claims of Critical Theory* (London: Verso 1987/2007), p. 174.
14 See, for example, Allen, *The End of Progress*; Goswami, 'The (M)other of All Posts'; Mignolo, *The Darker Side of Western Modernity*.
15 Traverso, *Left-Wing Melancholia*, pp. 166–77.
16 Aimé Césaire (1950/1972) *Discourse on Colonialism*, trans. Joan Pinkham (New York: Monthly Review Press), p. 42. See also Fadi A. Bardawil, 'Cesaire with Adorno: Critical Theory and the Colonial Problem', in *The South Atlantic Quarterly* 117:4 (2018), 773–89.
17 Adorno and Horkheimer, *Dialectic of Enlightenment*, pp. 29–30.
18 Adorno, *Minima Moralia*, p. 51.
19 Ibid. See Susan Buck-Morss' Chapter 5: 'A Logic of Disintegration' for the supposed parallels between Brecht's one-thousand-eyed Party, and the Nazi slogan 'The Individual is nothing, the people everything', Buck-Morss (1977) p. 82. See also Adorno in *Negative Dialectics*. On Brecht's line, Adorno wrote that it was 'as false as any bromide ever. A dissenter's exact imagination can see more than a thousand eyes peering through the same pink spectacles, confusing what they see with universal truth, and regressing. Against this stands the individuation of knowledge.' Adorno, *Negative Dialectics*, pp. 46–7.
20 Adorno, *Minima Moralia*, p. 52.
21 Ibid., p. 5.
22 Ibid.
23 Stefan Müller-Doohm, *Adorno: A Biography*, trans. Rodney Livingstone (Cambridge: Polity, 2005), p. 461.
24 Ibid., p. 461.
25 Kristin Ross, *May '68 and its Afterlives* (Chicago: University of Chicago Press, 2002), p. 10.

26 Quinn Slobodian, *Foreign Front: Third World Politics in Sixties West Germany* (Durham, NC: Duke University Press, 2012), p. 12.
27 Ibid., p. 12.
28 See, for example, the examples in James Mark, Péter Apor, Radina Vučetić and Piotr Osęka, ' "We are with You, Vietnam": Transnational Solidarities in Socialist Hungary, Poland and Yugoslavia', *Journal of Contemporary History* 50:3 (2015), 445.
29 Ibid., 458–9.
30 Adorno, 'Late Capitalism or Industrial Society?' (1969), in Tiedemann (ed.) *Theodor Adorno: Can One Live after Auschwitz?* p. 118.
31 Peter Uwe Hohendahl, *Prismatic Thought: Theodor W. Adorno* (Lincoln & London: University of Nebraska Press, 1995), pp. 66–7.
32 Neil Lazarus, 'Modernism and Modernity: T. W. Adorno and Contemporary White South African Literature', in *Cultural Critique*, 5 (Winter, 1986–87), 134. The writers whose work is explored in this paper include Nadine Gordimer, J. M. Coetzee, Breyten Breytenbach and Andre Brink.
33 Ibid., p. 135.
34 Ibid.
35 Keya Ganguly, 'Adorno, Authenticity, Critique', in Crystal Bartolovich and Neil Lazarus (eds) *Marxism, Modernity and Postcolonial Studies* (Cambridge: Cambridge University Press, 2002), p. 243.
36 Adorno, 'Commitment' (1962), in *Theodor Adorno, Walter Benjamin, Ernst Bloch, Bertolt Brecht and George Lukács: Aesthetics and Politics* (London: Verso 2006), p. 193.
37 On the latter, see Neil Lazarus' *The Postcolonial Unconscious* (Cambridge: Cambridge University Press, 2011). Chapter 2, 'The Politics of Postcolonial Modernism' provides a critique of both the narrowly canonical *and* the postcolonial models of modernism.
38 Adorno, 'Resignation' (1969), in Theodor W. Adorno, *Critical Models: Interventions and Catchwords*, trans. Henry W. Pickford (New York: Columbia University Press, 1998/2005), p. 291. See also Adorno's essay (unpublished in his lifetime) 'Marginalia to Theory and Praxis,' in the same volume.
39 Adorno, 'Commitment', p. 190.
40 Ibid., p. 189.
41 Ibid., p. 191.
42 Ibid., p. 193.
43 Ibid., p. 187.
44 Marcuse to Adorno (5 April 1969), in *New Left Review* (Jan–Feb. 1999) 1/233, p. 125.
45 Adorno to Marcuse (June 1969), ibid., p. 129.
46 Ibid. (5 May 1969), p. 127.

Index

Page numbers in **bold** refer to figures.

Abou-El-Fadl, Reem 7, 290
absence, solidarity as 334–51
Ação Libertadora Nacional (ALN) 121
accountability 35
Adorno, Theodor 21
  and autonomy 344–51
  and the compulsions of self-preservation 336–44
  conceptualisation of solidarity 334–51
  Dialectic of Enlightenment 338–9, 345, 353n13
  Eurocentrism 335
  'Late Capitalism or Industrial Society?' 345
  Minima Moralia 336–8, 349, 351
  model of social order 344–7
  Negative Dialectics 345, 352n5
  'Reflections on Class Theory' 345
  relevance 335–6
  theory of modernity 345–7
advocacy networks 283, 294, 296n16
African diaspora 9
African National Congress 202
African Party for the Independence of Guinea and Cabo Verde xx–xxi
Afro-Asian Peoples' Solidarity Organization 135, 184
Afro-Asian Solidarity Committee 317
agency 17–18
Ahmed, Fayyaz 259
Ahmed, Talat 20
Aillaud, Gilles 83, 100n24
Al-Assifa (film) 266
Alexander, M. Jacqui 182, 198
Algeria 39, 123
Algerian War of Independence 3, 57, 114
al-Ghazali, Zeinab 191
Algiers 11, 13
Ali, Tariq 211, 233, 237, 249–50, 251, 252, 285–6
alienation 38, 39, 49
Alliance for Progress project 113–14
Althusser, Louis 49
Al-Zayyat, Latifa 189, 191, 192, 192–3

American Committee of Africa
19, 154–68
  Emergency Relief to Angola
    (ERA) programme 154–68,
    158–68
  organisational strategy 155–6
  origins and growth 155–8
  strategies and methods 160
Americans for South African
  Resistance 155
Amin, Qasim 190
Angola 19, 131, 133, 137, 139,
  145, 146, 172–3n57, 202
  ACOA support 154–68
  armed struggle 157, 162
  ERA suspension 164–7
  factional struggles 165–6
  medical relief programme 162
  reality
  refugees 157–8, 162, 166
Anti-Apartheid Movement 210–14,
  217, 218–19
anticolonial solidarity 6–13
anticolonial violence 81
anti-imperialism 89, 115
anti-racist feminism 19
Anwar, Raja 240
Apartheid, sporting boycott
  movement 19–20, 202–20
  Anti-Apartheid
    Movement 210–14
  Campaign Against Race
    Discrimination in Sports
    204, 204–8, 209–10
  Movement for Colonial
    Freedom 204
  Shimlas tour, 1968 214–16
  South African cricket tour,
    1960 208–10
  South African cricket tour,
    1965 210–14
  South African cricket tour,
    1970 218–20

  Stop the Seventy Tour Committee
    203–4, 217, 218–20
  West Indian Campaign Against
    Apartheid in Cricket 204, 218
Appadurai, Arjun 12
Arab feminism 183
Arab-Israeli June War 3
Arafat, Yasser 64
Argentina 92–3, 93–4, 123
Arroyo, Eduardo 83, 100n24
art, autonomy of 344–51
artist militancy 12–13, 25–6n46,
  78–96, **86, 87, 95, 103,
  104**, 105–8
  bearing witness 300–1, **300,
    302–7**, 308
  importance 88–93
  *International Exhibition
    of Solidarity with
    Palestine* 99n20
  political effectiveness 93–4
  Salon de la Jeune Peinture 83
  Salón de Mayo exhibition 82–8,
    86, 87, 89
  symbolic power 94
  The Third World (El tercer
    mundo) exhibition 90
  Tricontinental echoes 80–2
Asdar Ali, Kamran 274–5
Association for Islamic Arts and
  Culture (HSBI) 288
Australia 16
autonomy 58–9, 338, 341, 344–51
Ayub Khan 232–4, 234–7, 239–8,
  251, 263
al-Azzawi, Dia, drawings 300–1,
  300, 302–7, 308

Badran, Margot 182–3, 183
Baldwin, James 15
Bandung conferences 3, 184, 287–90
Bardawil, Fadi A 339
Baron, Beth 195

Barros, Víctor 19
Baxter, Joe 118
Bazin, Jérôme 322
bearing witness 81–2, 87, 300–1, 300, 302–7, 308
Ben Ali, Djilali 69–70, 77n37
Ben Barka, Mehdi 123
Bengochea, Ángel 'Vasco' 117–18, 120, 124
Berger, Peter 282
Bhambra, Gurminder K. 284
Bhashani, Maulana Abdul Hamid Khan 242, 244
Bhutto, Zulfikar Ali 240–1
Bier, Laura 184, 191
Birchall, Ian 211–12
Black Dwarf (newspaper) 249
Black Lives Matter movement 9
Black Panthers 6
Black September 55, 63–6, 300–1, 300, 302–7, 308
blood and soil 16
Bloody Sunday, Northern Ireland 33
Bolivia xxiii, 84, 116
Bosgra, Sietse 133, 138
Bosquet, Michel 42
Bouchariou, Said, death of 72
Bouhired, Djamila 269–70
Boumediene, Houari 66–7
Brazil xxii, 110, 114, 120–1, 124
Brecht, Bertolt 311, 322, 340–1
Bristol 2
British Empire 8, 35
Brizola, Leonel 120
Brutus, Dennis 206, 208, 218
Buenos Aires 92–3
Bustos, Ciro 116–17, 122–3

Cabo Verde 146
Cabral, Amílcar xx–xxi, 9, 141, 142, 143, 144, **177–9**
Cahora Bassa colonial project 140–1

Campaign Against Race Discrimination in Sports 204, 204–8, 209
capitalism 180–1, 187–8, 197, 353n13
Cardozo, Marina 19, 21
Carmichael, Stokely 87
Carter, Sean 271
Castells, Manuel 42
Castro, Fidel xviii–xx, xxiii, 81, 83, 86, 133
Central Intelligence Agency xviii, 286
Césaire, Aimé 9, 339
CFDT *see Confédération française démocratique du travail*
CGT *see Confédération générale du travail*
Charquero, Gutemberg 123
Chifflet, Guillermo 119, 122
Chisaan, Choirotun 287–8, 289
Christiaens, Hans 315
Christiansen, Samantha 3
cinema 255–9, **260**, 261–76, **262, 264, 268**
civil rights movements 2, 20, 29–35
Cleaver, Kathleen 9
Cold War 21, 80, 96, 109, 111, 133, 161, 312, 335, 347–8
collective experience 32
collectivisation 88
Collings, Elizabeth Fuller 291
colonising projects, logic of 339
comités Palestine 19, 55–74, 59
  activists 56–7
  attack on the Jordanian embassy 67–8
  and Black September 63–6
  creation 60, 63–4
  dissolution 69–73
  divisions 68, 69
  and the GP 58–63

comités Palestine (*continued*)
  mobilisation 66–9
  objective 60–1
  political platform 73–4
  political space 56–8
  proletarianisation 66
  repression 65, 66–7, 68–9
  student committees 65–6
Confédération française démocratique du travail 60, 71
Confédération générale du travail 58, 60
connectedness 17
Constantine, Sir Learie 215
context 16
Continental Congress of Solidarity with Cuba 122
Cooke, John William 118
critical theory 334, 335
Cuba xviii–xix, xxi, 19, 99n22, 117, 121, 123, 133
  Salón de Mayo exhibition 82, 82–8, **86**, **87**, 89
  The Third World (El tercer mundo) exhibition 90
  see also Havana Cultural Congress, 1968
Cuba Colectiva mural 87–8, **87**
Cuban Missile Crisis 309
Cuban Revolution xviii–xix, 3, 81, 112, 115, 118, 120, 121, 122, 133
Cueco, Henri 83
cultural autonomy 59
cultural colonization 89
cultural encounters 19
cultural guerrilla manifesto 13, 78–96, 105–8
  goals 85–6
  importance 88–93
  origins 78–9
  Tricontinental echoes 80–2

Culture Industry 341
Cycle of Experimental Art 92–3
Cyprus 315

Dabashi, Hamid 275
Dacca National Awami Party 241–2
Darul Islam 290–2, 293
Davidson, Basil 172n51
Davis, Angela 17, 19, 184–98, 200–1n40, 201n43
  encounters with peasant women 194–6
  on gender relations 187–91
  and race 194
  self-reflexivity 193–4
  on shared experiences 184–7
  Women, Culture, and Politics 180
de Broglio, Chris 208
de Certeau, Michel 37, 44, 49
de Keyser, Ethel 212–13
Debray, Régis 12, 92–3, 116, 119
debt crisis xxiii
decolonisation 313
dehumanisation 49
Demir, Ipek 284
Democratic Students Federation 247–8
Derichs, Claudia 20–1
Devlin McAliskey, Bernadette 6, 14, 20, 28–35
difference, role of 181
diplomacy 6, 157
distant others, connection with 167, 271
Djerdi, Sadok 72
Dodds, Klaus 271
D'Oliveira, Basil 216–17
dos Santos, Marcelino 141, 142, 143–4
Douglas, Emory 13
Dubost, Nicolas 47–8

Duff, Peggy 226–7
Durham University 214, 214–16

East Germany, Greek political refugees 21, 309, **310**, 311–20, **321**, 322–7, **324**, **325**
Eguren, Alicia 118
Egypt 180–98
  feminist movement 181, 181–4, 196–8
  gender relations 187–91, 191–6
  gender solidarity 196–8
  Muslim Brotherhood 281, 292, 294n1
  peasants 194–6
  and race 194
  shared experiences 184–7
  state feminism 188–9, 196
Ejército Guerrillero del Pueblo (EGP) 116–17, 118
el Saadawi, Nawal 185
Elbaz, Shehida 189, 192, 193
El-Nadi, Bahgat 61
El-Sebai, Youssef 136
Emergency Relief to Angola (ERA) programme 154–68
  fundraising 159–64
  impact 167–8
  origins and aims 158–9
  suspension 164–7
Época (newspaper) 121–2
ethics, of solidarity 15
ethnocentrism 161
Eurocentrism 8, 112, 335, 337
exploitation 43–4

factional struggles 165–6
Fanon, Frantz xix, 9, 81, 337
Fatah 265, 266, 277n4
Favario, Eduardo 93–4
Featherstone, David 7, 26n55, 204, 312
fida'iyeen 62–3, 64
Feltrinelli, Giangiacomo 123–4

feminism 16–17, 19, 28, 180–98
  and gender relations 187–91
  gender solidarity 196–8
  and race 194
  shared experiences 184–7
  solidarity 186
  transnational 181–4
  transnational solidarity 180
First, Ruth 213
First Solidarity Conference of the Peoples of Africa, Asia and Latin America xviii–xix
FLN 39, 57, 69–70
Floyd, George, murder of 1–2
FNLA 159, 161, 163, 165–7
France xix–xx, 8, 137, 143–4, 343
  anti-Arab hate campaign 66–7
  Circulaires Marcellin-Fontanet 58
  class struggle 62
  comités Palestine 19, 21, 55–74
  far-left groups 39–40
  general strike, May–June 1968 41–2
  immigrant workers 18–19, 37–51, 50, 55–74
  May '68 3, 37, 79
  New Left 19, 38
  O.S. (*Ouvrier Spécialisé*) 38–40, 40–3, 49–50
  political space 56–8
  student unrest 10, 41
Frankfurt School 334, 335
Franqui, Carlos 83
freedom 8, 338, 340
French Communist Party 58
Fuerzas Armadas de la Revolución Nacional (FARN) 118
fundraising 159, 159–64

Ganguly, Keya 346
Garoeb, Moses 220
Garreiro, Elsa 123

Gauche Prolétarienne (GP) 39, 40, 43–6, 46–7, 56, 58, 58–63
Geismar, Alain 61
gender 16–17, 230
gender relations 180, 181, 182, 187–91, 191–6
gender solidarity 196–8
General Union of Palestinian Students (GUPS) 63, 64
geographic connections 7
German-Latin American Society 318
Ghodsee, Kristen 316–17
Gilchrist, F. Ian 160–4, 164–7, 172–3n57, 172n52
Gilchrist, William Sidney 171–2n48
Gilman, C. 81–2
Gilroy, Paul 16
global approach 4
Global North, the 7
global revolution 50–1
Global South, the 3, 7, 9, 17, 197, 269
Gopal, Priyamvada 8, 203
Gorz, André 42–3
Goulart, Joao 120
Grass, Günter 342
grassroots activists 6–7
Greece and the Greek Civil War 314–16, 318, 319, 320, 323, 324, 325–6, 327, 329n24, 330n28
guerrilla warfare 79, 81, 94, 96
Guevara, Che xix, 9, 12, 81, 84, 92–3, 94, 133
Guillén, Abraham 118, 118–20, 124
Guinea-Bissau 19, 139, 145, 146
Gulf Committee 225–7, 228, 229–31
Guridi, Javier 116
Gurney, Christabel 210–11

Habash, George 61
Haider, Sabah 20–1
Hain, Peter 203–4, 217, 220
Hajjat, Abdellali 18–19
Hall, Stuart 219
Halliday, Fred 227, 229
Hamchari, Mahmoud 56, 61, 64
Harman, Chris 250
Hatem, Mervat 189–90
Havana Cultural Congress, 1968 13, 78–96
    agenda 78–9
    manifesto 88–9, 105–8
    Tricontinental echoes 80–2
Høgsbjerg, Christian 19–20
Holocaust, the 335
Houser, George 154, 156–7, 158, 160–1, 168n3
housing 30–1, 71, 188
Huddleston, Trevor 204–5
Huidobro, Fernández 120
Hume, John 31
Hussein, King of Jordan 67, 68
hybrid war xix

identity 17, 30, 197–8, 267
identity politics 231
identity-based movements 231
Ikoniadou, Mary 21
immigrant workers, France 18–19, 37–51
    citizenship rights 39
    double absence 49–50
    établis 46–8
    and French solidarity with Palestine 55–74
    French workforce 40–3
    language diversity 46, 47
    national groups 40–1

O.S. (*Ouvrier Specialisé*) 38–40,
    40–3, 49–50
  political engagement 57
  revolutionary potential 41–2
  voice 43–51, 50
imperialism xviii–xxiii, 141, 143,
    197, 198
independence, inalienable right
    to xx
Indian Workers Association 249
Indonesia xxii, 20–1, 294
  Bandung conferences 287–90
  genocide, October 1965 284–7,
    289–90, 290, 298n52
  Islamist activism 280–1, 283–4,
    284–93
  political Islam 290–3
Indonesian Council for Islamic
    Propagation (DDII) 290–2
insurgent collective voice 37,
    43–51, 50
International Association for
    Women (IAW) Congress,
    1939 183, 187
International Confederation
    for Disarmament and
    Peace 226–7
*International Exhibition
    of Solidarity with
    Palestine* 99n20
international institutions 140
International Mobilization
    Committee 136–7
International Olympics
    Committee 206
internationalisation 132, 134
internationalism 343–4
internet, the 230–1
Iranian revolution xxii, 281, 282–3
Islamic Jihad 289
Islamist activism 280–94
  Indonesia 280–1, 283–4, 284–93
  political Islam 281, 290–3

social movement theory 281–4
Islamist extremism 252
Islamist resurgence
    movements 20–1
isolation 341–2
Israel 225–6

Jabra, Jabra Ibrahim 300
Jacoby, Roberto 94–6, 95
Jad, Islah 191
Jalib, Habib 259
James, C.L.R. 337, 339
Jameson, Fredric 8
Japan 285
Japanese Red Army 283, 289
Jayasinghe, Stanley 213
Jelin, Elizabeth 112
Jordan 63
Jouffroy, Alain 81
Jouhl, Avtar Singh 249
journalists 243–4
Julião, Francisco 121, 122
July, Serge 44

Kabir, Alamgir 267–9
Kalak, Azzedine 56, 63, 76n18
Kashmir 266–7
Kasrils, Ronnie 202
Katjasungkana, Nursyahbani 287
Khalili, Laleh 17
Khan, Roedad 247
Khartoum Conference 131, 132–3,
    133–7, 145
King, Martin Luther, Jr. xxii
Kolisi, Siya 220
Kornetis, Kostis 313
Krahl, Hans-Jürgen 342

Lackner, Helen 20, 225–7,
    228, 229–31
Lam, Wifredo 83, 88, 99n19
language 46, 47
Latin America 19, 109–24

Latin American Solidarity
    Organization 83–4
Lazarus, Neil 346
Le Parc, Julio 78, 79, 80,
    82, 97–8n3
leadership 138
left politics 9
Lévy, Léo 61
Lewin, Hugh 220
liberation 8, 8–9
liberation theology 111
Ligue Communiste
    Révolutionnaire 60
Linhart, Robert 43–4, 46–7,
    48–9, 51
Linhart, Virginie 48–9
London 20, 237–9
long sixties, the 3, 8–9, 11, 14,
    16, 17, 96, 111, 133, 145,
    156, 280–94
Lopes, Rui 137
López, Paula Barreiro 13, 19
Lorde, Audre 181–2
Lumumba, Patrice, assassination
    xxi, 164
Luzzatto, Lucio 140

Maasri, Zeina 271
McGlew, Jackie 210
McManus, Patricia 21
Maldonado-Torres, Nelson 337
Mamadou, S. E. Keita 144
Mandela, Nelson 211
Manousis, Nikos 322, 332n63
Mansour, Jihad 5
Maoism 44, 59–60, 63, 79
Marcha (newspaper) 121, 129n49
Marching, Soe Tjen 286
Marcum, John 158, 170n28
Marcuse, Herbert 349–50, 352n5
Marighella, Carlos 121
Mark, James 323

Martí, José 111
Marticorena, Miguel 309
Martínez, José 124
Marx, Karl xxiii
Maspero, François 100n30, 124
Massey, Doreen 16
Matta, Roberto 78, 79, 80, 82, 92,
    97n2, 98n8
Maudling, Reginald 33, 36n5
May '68 3, 37, 79
Mendoza, Breny 196
metonymy 325–6, 327
Middlemas, Keith 140
migration 18–19, 247–51
Milani, Ada 141
Milice ouvrière multinationale 62
modernisation 10
modernity 251–2, 335, 339,
    341, 345–7
Mohanty, Chandra Talpade 15–16,
    182, 197
Mohiuddin, Makhdoom xxii
Montagu, Ivor 204
Montevideo 11–12, 19, 109–24
    the Coordinador 112–15,
    115–17, 119–20, 123, 124
    newspapers 121–2
    transnational
        connections 115–22
Morocco 57
Mouvement des travailleurs arabes
    55, 58, 73
mouvement du 22 mars xx
Movement for Colonial
    Freedom 204
Movimiento Nacionalista
    Revolucionario Tacuara
    (MNRT) 116, 117
Mozambique 19, 131–2,
    133, 137, 139, 140, 145,
    146, 202
museums-in-exile 13

Index

Muslim Brotherhood 281, 291, 292, 294, 294n1, 295n15
Muslim identity 20
Myers, Matt 18–19

Nabarawi, Saiza 182, 183, 186
Nasser, Gamal Abdel 63, 188
National Front for the Liberation of Angola 154
National Mobilization Committee to End the War in Vietnam xx
National Support Committee for the Liberation Struggle in Portuguese Colonies 137
National Union of Mineworkers 210, 212–13
NATO 141, 143, 315
Natsir, Mohammad 290–1
nature, domination over 339–40
Navillat, Mario 119
Nazi Germany 207
neoliberalism 197, 198
Netherlands Meeting 131, 133, 138–40, 145
Neto, Agostinho 141, 144
New International Economic Order xxi
New Left, the 2, 4, 10, 19, 38, 109–24, 286
New Radical Left, the 133
new social movements 38
Newcastle University 214
newspapers 121, 121–2
Nicaragua xxii, 81
Nicolaou, Thomas 309
NIEO *see* New International Economic Order
Nihash, Sarfaraz Fareed 261, 264–5, 269–70, 271
nodal cities 11–12, 83–4
Non-Aligned Movement 133, 287
Northern Ireland 6
  Bloody Sunday 33, 36n4
  borders 28
  civil rights movement 20, 29–35
  Good Friday Agreement 36n2
  parliamentary system 36n3
  peace process 29, 34, 36n2
  reform movement 30–1
  Troubles 20, 28–35
  unemployment 31
  unionist population 31
Nouvelle résistance populaire 62

Oman 226, 227, 229
oral history 111
Organization of Solidarity with the People of Africa, Asia and Latin America 13
orientalist tropes 272–3
OSPAAAL *see* Organization of Solidarity with the People of Africa, Asia and Latin America
Oxford University Press 245

PAIGC *see* African Party for the Independence of Guinea and Cabo Verde
Painters and Guerrillas exhibition 86–7, **86**
Pakistan xxii, 20, 283
  Democratic Action Committee 245
  migratory transnational solidarity 247–51
  uprising, 1968–69 232–52
  Zerqa (film) 255–9, **260**, 261–76, **262**, **264**, **268**
Pakistan Federal Union of Journalists 243–4
Pakistan People's Party 240–1
Pakistani Workers Association 249
Palabra Obrera 118

Palestine 5, 32, 185
  Black September 300–1, **300**, 302–7, 308
  French solidarity with 19, 55–74
  through Pakistani cinema 255–9, 260, 261–76, **262**, **264**, **268**
Palestine Liberation Organisation 21, 56, 61, 225–6, 255, 257, 267, 269, 301
Paris xx, 56–8, 66–9, 71, 90–2, 124
Partisans (journal) 100n30
past, the, legacy of 35
paternalism 8, 161
Paton, Alan 208
Paul VI, Pope 141
Pendry, Tom 212
Petiwala, Ada 261–2, 278n18
Pitti, Laure 38
place, sense of 28–9
political Islam 281, 290–3
political publishing, *Pyrsos* (magazine) **310**, 311–20, **321**, 322–7, **324**, **325**
political solidarity 26n55
political theatre 244
Popular Front for the Liberation of Oman and the Arabian Gulf 227, **228**, 229, 231
Popular Front for the Liberation of Palestine 61, 267, 283
Portuguese African colonies 131–46, **177–9**
  ACOA support 154–68
  armed struggle 133
  flow of information 162
  Khartoum Conference 131, 132–3, 133–7, 137, 145
  Netherlands Meeting 131, 133, 138–40, 145
  Rome Solidarity Conference 131, 133, 138, 144, 145
  solidarity 142–4

postmodernism 197
Potere Operaio 39
poverty 188
Powell, Enoch 220
power dynamics 195–6
Prashad, Vijay 6, 313
presentism 251–2
Presthold, Jeremy 12
propaganda 112–13, 139
public mobilisation 32
public opinion, global 135
Pyrsos (magazine) 21, 309, **310**, 311–20, **321**, 322–7
  distribution 311
  editorial strategy 320, 322, 327, 332n57
  funding 327n4
  political background 314–16
  solidarity in 316–19, 327
  Third World solidarity 312–14
  Vietnam War coverage 323–6, **324**, **325**

Quebec 32
Qutb, Sayyid 291, 299n56

race and racism 9, 194, 239
radical 1960s, the xxi–xxiii
Rahim, J. A. 237
Rama, Germán 128n23
Rancière, Jacques 7, 14–15
refugees 157–8, 162, 166, 290–3
Reid, Donald 45
religion 280–94
respectability strategy 203
Ribeiro, Darcy 124
Rifaat, Adel 61
Riss, Christian 67
Roa, Raúl 83
Roberto, Holden 157, 164, 165–7
Rodríguez, Ruben 118
Rolin, Olivier 40, 61, 62

Rome Solidarity Conference 131, 133, 140–1, 144, 145
Ross, Kristin 3, 8, 37, 95–6, 343
Rostgaard, Alfredo 91
Rule Britannia 34–5, 36n6
Runia, Eelco 326
Russo, Vincenzo 141

Sadat, Anwar el 189, 196–8
Salem, Sara 17, 19
Salon de la Jeune Peinture 83, 88–9
Salón de Mayo exhibition 82, 82–8, **86, 87,** 89
sameness 274–5
Sandino, Augusto César 81
Santos, Aurora Almada e 19
Sarkar, Bhaskar 270
Sartre, Jean-Paul 42, 44–5, 46, 61, 347
Saudi Arabia 281, 291, 292–3
Savimbi, Jonas 165, 166, 175n81
Sayad, Abdelmalek 49–50
Scarlett, Zachary 3
Schwenkel, Christina 316–17
secularization paradigm and thesis 280, 281–2
Seguí, Antonio 92
self-determination 6, 8
self-preservation, compulsions of 336–44
Sendic, Raúl 114–15, 116, 118, 122, 123
separatism 29
sexual violence 187
Shahid, Riaz 265, 269
Shaikh, Ahmed 233
Sharpeville massacre 202–3, 209
Sheikh, Khalid 265
Singh, Nikhil Pal 17
Sitte, Willi 318
sixties, decentring the 2–4

Slobodian, Quinn 343
Smith, Barbara 13–14, 15
SOAS *see* University of London School of Oriental and African Studies
SOBRE 94
social justice 30
social media 230–1
social movement theory 281–4
Socialist Party (PSU) of Uruguay 114–15
solidarity 4, 10, 15–16, 30, 38, 80, 226
  as absence 334–51
  anticolonial 142–4
  border crossing 1–2, 10–12, 13–18
  building 19–20
  Cabral statement on **177–9**
  and the compulsions of self-preservation 336–44
  definition 312
  false 341
  performance 154–68
  in state socialism 316–19
  Third World 312–14
solidarity meetings
  Khartoum Conference 131, 132–3, 133–7, 137, 145
  Netherlands Meeting 131, 133, 138–40, 145
  Rome Solidarity Conference 131, 133, 138, 144, 145
South Africa 202 *see also* Apartheid, sporting boycott movement
South Africa Non-Racial Olympics Committee 208–9, 218
South African cricket tour, 1960 208–10
South African cricket tour, 1965 210–14

South African cricket tour, 1970 218–20
South African Sports Association 208
South East Asia Treaty Organisation 248
South Lebanon 20
South West Africa People's Organisation 317
South-South interlocutions 111
South-South solidarity 20–1
sovereignty xxi
speech, power of 47–8
sporting boycott movement 19–20, 202–20
　Anti-Apartheid Movement 210–14
　Campaign Against Race Discrimination in Sports 204, 204–8, 209–10
　direct action 214–17
　Movement for Colonial Freedom 204
　the Olympic principle 206–7
　respectability strategy 203
　Shimlas tour, 1968 214–16
　South African cricket tour, 1960 208–10
　South African cricket tour, 1965 210–14
　South African cricket tour, 1970 218–20
　Stop the Seventy Tour Committee 203–4, 217, 218–20
　West Indian Campaign Against Apartheid in Cricket 204, 218
Stacey, Nicholas 206
state socialism 316–19, 340–1
state-building 166
statue toppling 2

Steel, Anthony 205, 206
Stein, E. 283–4
Stop the Seventy Tour Committee 203–4, 217, 218–20
student unrest xix–xx, 10, 41, 65–6
　Pakistan uprising, 1968–69 237–52
　United Kingdom 20, 225–7, 228, 229–31
Supreme Council for Sport in Africa 208–9
symbolic power 94

Tacchi, José Luis Nell Tacchi 118, 123
Taylor, Ian 214
Tchernia, Gil 146
The Third World (El tercer mundo) exhibition 90
Third World internationalism 10, 12
Third World Left 9
Third World movements 17
Third World, the 3, 7, 14, 312, 312–14
Third Worldist summits 10
Third-Worldism 44, 79
Thompson, E.P. 43
Tilly, Charles 159–60
Torres, Jorge 119–20
Touraine, Alain 38
Traboulsi, Fawwaz 227
trade unions 45, 60, 249
translocal visuality 271–2
transnational feminism 181–4
Traverso, Enzo 334–5, 339, 352n5
Trías, Vivián 114
Tricontinental (magazine) 123–4
Tricontinental Conference xviii–xix, xx–xxi, xxii, 3, 78, 80–1, 89, 143

Tricontinental effect, the 96
Troebst, Stefan 319
Tunisia 57
Tupamaros 11–12, 19, 109–24
 the Coordinador 112–15, 115–17, 119–20, 123, 124
 initial militancy 109–10
 origin of term 124–5n1
 propaganda operations 112–13
 transnational connections 115–22

unemployment 31
UNHCR *see* United Nations High Commissioner for Refugees
Unión de Trabajadores Azucareros de Artigas 115
Union of the Peoples of Angola 156–7, 159
United Kingdom 20, 31, 32, 218
 migratory transnational solidarity 247–51
 and Pakistan uprising, 1968–69 232–4
 Pakistani community 238–9
 Shimlas tour, 1968 214–16
 South African cricket tour, 1960 208–10
 South African cricket tour, 1965 210–14
 South African cricket tour, 1970 218–20
 sporting boycott movement 19–20, 202–20
 student unrest 20, 225–7, **228**, 229–31
 war crimes 35
 Windrush generation 249
 see also Northern Ireland
United Nations xxi, 163
United Nations High Commissioner for Refugees 162

United States of America 6, 248
 Alliance for Progress project 113–14
 civil rights movement 9, 29, 156, 160
 and Cuba xviii–xix
 cultural colonization 89
 imperialism xxii
 interventions in Uruguay 113–14
 involvement in Greece 315, 316, 326, 330n28
 Operation Cyclone xxii
 student unrest xx
 Third World Left 313
 see also American Committee of Africa
University of London School of Oriental and African Studies 20, 225–6, 227
University of St Andrews 214
Uruguay 19, 109–24
 the Coordinador 112–15, 115–17, 119–20, 123, 124
 newspapers 121–2, 129n49
 transnational connections 115–22
 US interventions 113–14

van Bruinessen, Martin 285, 291, 293, 299n58
Venezuela xxiii
Vietnam Solidarity Campaign 204
Vietnam War xix, xx, 3, 115, 133, 156, 285, 323–6, **324**, **325**, 343
Vigna, Xavier 38
violence xix
voice 37, 43–51, **50**
 power of 47–8
Volpi, F. 283–4
voting rights 30, 39

war crimes 35
Weis, Toni 317, 331n45
West Germany 137, 143–4
West Indian Campaign Against Apartheid in Cricket 204, 218
Wieringa, Saskia 287
Windrush generation 249
women
   African American 13–14
   dualistic representation 187
   emancipation 190–1
   peasant 194–6
   racialisation 194
   and sex 185
   sexualising 191–3
   shared experiences 180, 184–7, 198
   transnational solidarity 180
   treatment 28
women's movement 230, 231
Woods, Donald 210
workerism 66
World Muslim League/ Islamic World League 281
World Peace Conference 242
World Peace Council 135
Worrell, Frank 208

Yaffé, Jaime 113
Young, Cynthia 9, 313
youth movement 28

Zaghloul, Safiyyah 199n10
Zerqa (film) 20, 255–9, 261–76, **262**
   cast 256
   as a cultural text 275–6
   Eh Falasteen! 255–6
   impact 267–70
   message and ideological goal 264–5, 272–3
   narrative 257–8, 272
   political context 263–7
   relatability 271–5
   release 256–7
   soundtrack 258–9, 261–2
Zionism 61
Zolov, Eric 111
Zuhri, S. 289

EU authorised representative for GPSR:
Easy Access System Europe, Mustamäe tee 50,
10621 Tallinn, Estonia
gpsr.requests@easproject.com

www.ingramcontent.com/pod-product-compliance
Lightning Source LLC
Chambersburg PA
CBHW051555230426
43668CB00013B/1858